Power Transformer Diagnostics, Monitoring and Design Features

Power Transformer Diagnostics, Monitoring and Design Features

Special Issue Editor

Issouf Fofana

MDPI • Basel • Beijing • Wuhan • Barcelona • Belgrade

MDPI

Special Issue Editor
Issouf Fofana
Université du Québec à Chicoutimi (UQAC)
Canada

Editorial Office
MDPI
St. Alban-Anlage 66
4052 Basel, Switzerland

This is a reprint of articles from the Special Issue published online in the open access journal *Energies* (ISSN 1996-1073) from 2015 to 2018 (available at: https://www.mdpi.com/journal/energies/special_issues/power-transformer)

For citation purposes, cite each article independently as indicated on the article page online and as indicated below:

LastName, A.A.; LastName, B.B.; LastName, C.C. Article Title. *Journal Name* **Year**, *Article Number, Page Range.*

ISBN 978-3-03897-441-3 (Pbk)
ISBN 978-3-03897-442-0 (PDF)

Contents

About the Special Issue Editor

Issouf Fofana, Professor, IET Fellow, held the Canada Research Chair on insulating liquids and mixed dielectrics for electrotechnology (ISOLIME) from 2005 to 2015. At his university, he is the Director of the international research Centre on Atmospheric Icing and Power Network Engineering (CENGIVRE) and holds the research chair on the Ageing of Power Network Infrastructure (ViAHT). Dr. Fofana is/was a member of technical/scientific committees of international conferences (e.g., IEEE ICDL, IEEE CEIDP, IEEE ICHVE, CATCON, ISH, etc.), IEEE DEIS, and CEIDP AdComs. He also serves on the scientific committee as associate editor for IET GTD, IEEE TDEI, a Guest Editor of Energies, and chair of the IEEE DEIS Technical Committee on Dielectric Liquids. He is also a member of several working groups (i.e., CIGRE and ASTM). Dr. Fofana's research in the area of HV engineering has emphases on insulation systems relevant to power equipment. His lifetime publication record is more than 270 scientific publications and 3 patents.

energies

MDPI

Editorial

Power Transformer Diagnostics, Monitoring and Design Features

Issouf Fofana [1,*] and **Yazid Hadjadj** [2]

[1] Aging of Power Network Infrastructure (ViAHT), Université du Québec à Chicoutimi,
    Chicoutimi, QC G7H 2B1, Canada
[2] Measurement Science and Standards, National Research Council (NRC),
    Ottawa, ON K1A 0R6, Canada; yazid.hadjadj@nrc-cnrc.gc.ca
[*] Correspondence: ifofana@uqac.ca; Tel.: +1-418-545-5011

Received: 12 October 2018; Accepted: 13 November 2018; Published: 22 November 2018

1. Introduction

The reliability of the power grid system directly contributes to the economic well-being and the quality of life of citizens in any country. In the electric power distribution and transmission systems, it is essential that key equipment such as transformers function properly for many years. In these important equipment, the Achilles' heel is the insulation system, i.e., (a) insulation between the high voltage (HV) winding and the tank; (b) insulation between the HV and the low voltage (LV) windings; and (c) inter-phase insulation. Over the past decade, various types of insulating materials have been introduced in these machines. Assessment methods have allowed monitoring their conditions with the aim of providing the basic information required for power grid operators and maintenance planners to understand the issues related to aging. Also, aging indicator indices have been the aim of a large number of investigations.

Many transformers around the world are now approaching the end of their theoretical design life. In this context, managing the aging population of power transformers has become one of the most critical issues today's maintenance planners and engineers have to face. With increasing age, there are potential risks of extremely high monetary losses due to unexpected failures and outages. A simple solution would be to replace all aging and risky transformers at once with new ones. Such an approach is obviously not a fiscally realistic solution. The main objectives are: to extend their service life and optimize their performance through increased availability. For these reasons, transformer life management in the past few decades has gained an ever-increasing interest due to economic and technical reasons. The greatest challenges are related to the need for methods to assess the condition and life expectancy along with the improvement of transformer efficiency by noble designs and/or application of new materials.

The special issue was focused on theoretical and practical developments with a special emphasis on new research and development (R&D) trends in transformer designs/diagnostics and maintenance. Additionally, today, "sustainable development" has become a world-wide concept for the scientific community. The focus is now on harvesting renewable resources instead of fossil fuels, and using environmentally friendly materials. In this context, new materials are emerging for the design of electrotechnical insulation systems including biodegradable insulating materials, with properties that are at least equal to conventional materials. Esters with excellent high temperature performance, enhanced fire safety, increased environmental protection and increased moisture tolerance are gaining importance. Some aspects regarding the application of biodegradable fluids in these important machines were therefore also of particular interest. Listed hereafter, among others, were some of the topics of interest considered:

- New or emerging diagnostic/monitoring technologies;

- Mineral oils of improved characteristics, additives;
- Nanofluids and synthetic/vegetable dielectric liquids;
- New materials for transformers;
- Transformer life management.

2. An Outlook of the Special Issue

This special issue from *Energies*, has been successfully organized with the support extended by the editorial team of the journal and the MDPI publishing team. The average processing time of the articles was noted to be 75.67 days. The guest editor is very much grateful to all reviewers for reviewing and revising the manuscripts. Devoting their valuable time to reviewing papers is essential for upholding the voluntary peer review process and is highly commendable. Their constructive comments and suggestions to the authors and confidential reports to the editors ensured that the high standard of this journal is maintained.

Response to our call was excellent, with the following statistics:

- Submissions: (21);
- Publications: (12);
- Rejections: (9);
- Article types: review articles (3); research articles (9);
- Authors' geographical distribution (published papers):

  ✓ China (6);
  ✓ Poland (2);
  ✓ Australia (1);
  ✓ Canada (1);
  ✓ Cote D'Ivoire (1);
  ✓ UK (1).

The summary of the articles published in this issue is discussed in the subsequent sections of this editorial.

3. A Review of the Special Issue

A number of articles involve several subjects about power transformer diagnostics, insulation characterization, and new materials for transformers have been published in this issue.

Sun et al. [1] proposed a new decision-making model for transformer condition assessment. The new model integrates the merits of fuzzy set theory, game theory and modified evidence combination extended by D numbers. It was shown that compared to the evidential reasoning-based method, the final evaluation result of the presented method could clearly show the health condition of the transformer.

Li et al. [2] introduced a new intelligent sensor for ultra-high-frequency (UHF) partial discharge (PD) online monitoring in power transformers. The statistical characteristic quantities of UHF PD signals were acquired by means of a new method, namely the level scanning method which is the base of the intelligent sensor. The experimental results of the proposed sensor under laboratory conditions showed that the intelligent sensor could accurately acquire statistical characteristic quantities of the UHF PD signal, which indicated that the proposed intelligent sensor was qualified for UHF PD online monitoring.

In recent years, a lot of research has been directed towards environmentally friendly insulating liquids, as an alternative to mineral oils. However, as the chemical compositions of these fluids are very different than those for mineral oils, new specification standards for non-mineral oils have been produced. In this Issue a comparison study of streamer propagation and breakdown between Ester liquids and mineral oil was conducted by Rozga [3].

The work was focused on the comparison of light waveforms registered using the photomultiplier technique. The results indicated that both esters demonstrated a lower resistance against the appearance of fast energetic streamers than mineral oil.

Xiang et al. [4] also presented a comparison study of the formation of dissolved gases in mineral- and vegetable- insulating oils. The authors used four interpretation dissolved gas analysis (DGA) methods and they confirmed that the diagnosis methods developed for mineral oil were not suitable for the diagnosis of electrical and thermal faults in vegetable-insulating oils and needed some modification. Thus, the proposed modified Duval Triangle method based on Duval Triangle 3 is used to diagnose the thermal and electrical fault of FR3 oil and camellia oil through redefining zone boundaries of Duval Triangle 1 and obtains more accurate diagnostic results. Furthermore, the generation mechanisms of gases in vegetable oils have been interpreted by means of unimolecular pyrolysis simulation and the reaction enthalpies calculation. Bandara et al. [5] investigated the performance of natural ester (NE) in moisture-rich environments. They have compared the aging behaviour of NE and mineral oil impregnated pressboard (PB) insulation. While NE insulating oil possesses resistance to the aging of PB insulation, it was noted that the acidity and the color of NE oils could increase rapidly due to the pronounced hydrolytic degradation in a moisture rich environment. On the other hand, dielectric dissipation factor (DDF), viscosity, and the dielectric breakdown voltage, were suitable for the assessment of the overall condition of NE insulation oils.

Wang et al. [6] have introduced a new aspect for overload capability assessment of power transformers. In their article they estimated the running time of a power transformer under overload conditions by means of the hot-spot temperature. The overloading probability was then fitted by the Weibull distribution, in which the desired parameters were computed according to a new proposed objective function.

Wang et al. [7] investigated the influence of initial moisture contents in oil impregnated paper of the condenser bushing. The results of their experience indicated that the initial moisture content has appreciable impact on the degradation of the insulation paper during the initial aging period. They found that it was possible to evaluate the aging degree and moisture of solid insulation of bushing by doing some analysis of the DDF.

As discussed earlier, this Special Issue also reported on three comprehensive surveys [8–10]. A snapshot look at some significant developments and applications over the last decades were addressed and future research hotspots and notable research topics were also discussed for the benefit of researchers. Two reviews about physicochemical and electrical-based diagnostic techniques for insulation condition assessment were presented by Fofana et al. [8,9] considering 149 and 137 references, respectively. In the article written by N'cho et al. [8], in addition to traditional diagnostic techniques, some modern physicochemical diagnostic techniques such as Fourier transform infrared spectroscopy (FTIR), UV/visible spectroscopy, turbidity analysis were introduced. The benefits of using alternative insulating materials has also been discussed. In [9], Fofana and Hadjadj reported detailed descriptions and interpretations of traditional and advanced electrical diagnostic techniques. Online condition monitoring of power transformers were also discussed. Finally, the authors presented some suggestions/recommendations related to the nature of the defect or fault in the power transformer's main component. The third review article by Tang et al. [10], reported on the space charge behavior in an oil-paper insulation system. Research progress during the last two decades was critically reviewed considering 62 references. The influences of applied voltage, temperature, moisture content and aging on the space charge evolution in the oil-paper insulation has been demonstrated. This review ends with future work on space charge measurement of oil-paper insulation materials.

Sikorski et al. [11] reported on important aspects regarding PDs monitoring on power transformers. They reported that PDs activity under thermal runaway should be associated with moisture changes in the insulating system.

Zou et al. [12] proposed a new way for assessing the aging condition of oil-paper insulation based on confocal laser Raman spectroscopy (CLRS) in conjunction with principal component analysis (PCA) and multi-classification support vector machine (SVM). The investigations were performed in laboratory conditions using 160 oil-paper insulation samples and the approach validated with 105 oil-paper insulation samples. The results reported demonstrated the feasibility of using CLRS in conjunction with the PCA-SVM technique for aging stage assessment of oil-paper insulation.

4. Closing Remarks

The contributions in this Special Issue discussed a wide range of subjects relevant to power transformer monitoring and applications. Power transformers are amongst the costliest equipment in the power grid. Maintaining these important machines in a pristine condition is therefore very important for power grid reliability. Even though the articles reported very interesting applications and monitoring techniques developed thus far, there are still many gaps to close to improve service reliability.

Combined with the ever-increasing global demand for energy, it has become essential to find new solutions, based on the ability to properly diagnose the condition of transformers and to delay/slow down the aging process. According to Victor Hugo "what to foresee is the unforeseen". An important strategy consists in reducing the risk of failures through remote monitoring and optimized maintenance. However, to be cost-effective, this requires an accurate assessment of the condition of the transformers. The general trend towards smart-grids, digital systems and the continued reduction in the cost of these technologies, combined with the existence of a communications infrastructure in a growing number of facilities, will facilitate the implementation of monitoring technologies.

In today's grids, power transformers must withstand not only transients due to lightning, and switching operations with load changes or fault occurrences but also the increase penetration of renewable energy sources/plug-in vehicles. These machines have a common denominator; they consist mainly of a large core of magnetic sheets around which are wound insulated conductors immersed in oil. However, their design philosophy and manufacture (based on years of R&D and experience) require a considerable number of calculations, verifications and precautions. However, in a world where everything is changing rapidly, the key strategy must be based on continuous improvement of every aspect of the manufacturing elements. Innovative strategies/concepts that can improve the quality of these important machines are therefore required.

Author Contributions: The authors contributed equally to this work.

Funding: This research received no external funding.

Acknowledgments: Issouf Fofana is grateful to the MDPI Publisher for the invitation to act as the guest editor of this special issue and is indebted to the editorial staff of "*Energies*" for their kind cooperation, patience and committed engagement. The guest editor would also like to thank the authors for submitting their excellent contributions to this special issue. Thanks is also extended to the reviewers for evaluating the manuscripts and providing helpful suggestions.

Conflicts of Interest: The authors declare no conflicts of interest.

References

1. Sun, L.; Liu, Y.; Zhang, B.; Shang, Y.; Yuan, H.; Ma, Z. An Integrated Decision-Making Model for Transformer Condition Assessment Using Game Theory and Modified Evidence Combination Extended by D Numbers. *Energies* **2016**, *9*, 697. [CrossRef]
2. Li, J.; Li, X.; Du, L.; Cao, M.; Qian, G. An Intelligent Sensor for the Ultra-High-Frequency Partial Discharge Online Monitoring of Power Transformers. *Energies* **2016**, *9*, 383. [CrossRef]
3. Rozga, P. Streamer Propagation and Breakdown in a Very Small Point-Insulating Plate Gap in Mineral Oil and Ester Liquids at Positive Lightning Impulse Voltage. *Energies* **2016**, *9*, 467. [CrossRef]
4. Xiang, C.; Zhou, Q.; Li, J.; Huang, Q.; Song, H.; Zhang, Z. Comparison of Dissolved Gases in Mineral and Vegetable Insulating Oils under Typical Electrical and Thermal Faults. *Energies* **2016**, *9*, 312. [CrossRef]

5. Bandara, K.; Ekanayake, C.; Saha, T.; Ma, H. Performance of Natural Ester as a Transformer Oil in Moisture-Rich Environments. *Energies* **2016**, *9*, 258. [CrossRef]

6. Wang, C.; Wu, J.; Wang, J.; Zhao, W. Reliability Analysis and Overload Capability Assessment of Oil-Immersed Power Transformers. *Energies* **2016**, *9*, 43. [CrossRef]

7. Wang, Y.; Xiao, K.; Chen, B.; Li, Y. Study of the Impact of Initial Moisture Content in Oil Impregnated Insulation Paper on Thermal Aging Rate of Condenser Bushing. *Energies* **2015**, *8*, 14298–14310. [CrossRef]

8. N'cho, J.S.; Fofana, I.; Hadjadj, Y.; Beroual, A. Review of Physicochemical-Based Diagnostic Techniques for Assessing Insulation Condition in Aged Transformers. *Energies* **2016**, *9*, 367. [CrossRef]

9. Fofana, I.; Hadjadj, Y. Electrical-Based Diagnostic Techniques for Assessing Insulation Condition in Aged Transformers. *Energies* **2016**, *9*, 679. [CrossRef]

10. Tang, C.; Huang, B.; Hao, M.; Xu, Z.; Hao, J.; Chen, G. Progress of Space Charge Research on Oil-Paper Insulation Using Pulsed Electroacoustic Techniques. *Energies* **2016**, *9*, 53. [CrossRef]

11. Sikorski, W.; Walczak, K.; Przybylek, P. Moisture Migration in an Oil-Paper Insulation System in Relation to Online Partial Discharge Monitoring of Power Transformers. *Energies* **2016**, *9*, 1082. [CrossRef]

12. Zou, J.; Chen, W.; Wan, F.; Fan, Z.; Du, L. Raman Spectral Characteristics of Oil-Paper Insulation and Its Application to Ageing Stage Assessment of Oil-Immersed Transformers. *Energies* **2016**, *9*, 946. [CrossRef]

Review

Review of Physicochemical-Based Diagnostic Techniques for Assessing Insulation Condition in Aged Transformers

Janvier Sylvestre N'cho [1], Issouf Fofana [2,*], Yazid Hadjadj [2] and Abderrahmane Beroual [3]

[1] Département Génie Électrique et Électronique, Institut National Polytechnique Houphouët Boigny (INP-HB), BP 1093 Yamoussoukro, Ivory Coast; nchosylvestre@yahoo.fr
[2] Research Chair on the Aging of Power Network Infrastructure (ViAHT), Université du Québec à Chicoutimi, 555 Boulevard de l'Université, Chicoutimi, QC G7H 2B1, Canada; yazid.hadjadj@uqac.ca
[3] Ecole Centrale de Lyon, Université de Lyon, Ampère CNRS UMR 5005, 36 Avenue Guy de Collongue, 69134 Ecully, France; Abderrahmane.Beroual@ec-lyon.fr
* Correspondence: ifofana@uqac.ca; Tel.: +1-418-545-5011; Fax: +1-418-545-5012

Academic Editor: Enrico Sciubba
Received: 23 March 2016; Accepted: 3 May 2016; Published: 13 May 2016

Abstract: A power transformer outage has a dramatic financial consequence not only for electric power systems utilities but also for interconnected customers. The service reliability of this important asset largely depends upon the condition of the oil-paper insulation. Therefore, by keeping the qualities of oil-paper insulation system in pristine condition, the maintenance planners can reduce the decline rate of internal faults. Accurate diagnostic methods for analyzing the condition of transformers are therefore essential. Currently, there are various electrical and physicochemical diagnostic techniques available for insulation condition monitoring of power transformers. This paper is aimed at the description, analysis and interpretation of modern physicochemical diagnostics techniques for assessing insulation condition in aged transformers. Since fields and laboratory experiences have shown that transformer oil contains about 70% of diagnostic information, the physicochemical analyses of oil samples can therefore be extremely useful in monitoring the condition of power transformers.

Keywords: power transformers; insulating oil/paper; diagnostics; color/visual examination; particle count; inhibitor content; moisture; DGA; acidity; interfacial tension; viscosity; DP; furan; HPLC; gas chromatography-mass spectrometry coupling; FTIR spectroscopy; UV/visible spectroscopy; dissolved decay products; turbidity; methanol; free radicals

---

1. Introduction

Today's power transformers constitute a major part of the capital equipment of power utilities all over the world. It is therefore important they function reliably. They are indispensable equipment for power generation plants, transmission systems and large industrial plants. Outage of power transformers while in service usually lead to significant revenue loss to the utility, potential environmental damage, explosion and fire hazards and expensive repairing or replacement costs. The cost of replacing the transformers varies from a few hundred dollars to several million dollars [1]. Early detection of problems can reduce repair costs by 75 percent and loss of revenue by 60 percent, and that annual cost savings equal to two percent of the price of a new transformer—*i.e.*, approximately 40,000 to 80,000 US dollars (USD)—can be achieved [2]. Hence, it is desirable that the transformers should be utilized to the maximum extent consistent with adequate service life [3]. In order to reach such a device management, diagnostic techniques and condition monitoring are becoming increasingly important in assessing the condition of transformers and prevent incipient electrical failures. Any improved preventive maintenance procedures should help extending their life.

In these important machines, the Achilles heel is the insulation system, *i.e.,*: (a) insulation between the high voltage (HV) winding and the tank; (b) insulation between the HV and the low voltage (LV) windings; and (c) inter-phase insulation. These parts are the most sensitive to the insulation deterioration as they usually have the smallest margins in the dielectric strength. The life of the transformer is actually the life of the internal insulation system. Analysis of the insulating system, consisting of oil and paper provides information not only on the quality of the latter, but also can detect the warning signs of failure. The monitoring of the solid and liquid insulation in these machines is therefore of utmost importance [3]. By monitoring accurately the condition of the insulation, it is possible to detect on time incipient defects and avoid potential failures. Consequently, an effective approach to maintenance can be adopted and the optimum intervals determined for replacement. Common diagnostic techniques for transformers rely on testing based on physical, chemical, and electrical parameters. Physical measurements, in general, involve measurement of temperature, vibration, acoustic emission, *etc.* However, the diagnostic methods that give useful information on transformation insulation condition are chemical and electrical tests [3]. The term "diagnostics" indicates incorporation of advanced analysis that are capable of performing reliable assessment of equipment condition and suggesting actions to be taken. As each diagnosis method is developed and applied in real-life situations, it is always weighed up against other methods [3]. Methods that have been established over the years satisfy important criteria, among which [4]: sensitivity to important parameters of transformer condition, reproducibility of results over time and for different testing personnel, compensation of raw data for significant environmental effects like temperature, good correlation with other established methods availability of valuable information for the time and expense involved. The purposes of diagnostic testing are threefold: (a) to identify increased aging aspects; (b) to identify the cause of aging; and (c) to identify, if possible, the most appropriate corrective actions.

The life of the transformer being connected with that of its insulation, the evaluation of the insulation system condition is essential to assess the condition of the transformer when new and after several years of use. This evaluation necessarily involves both electrical and physicochemical techniques/diagnostic methods. The currently used techniques include modern methods and improved conventional techniques, allowing providing additional information on the condition of insulation. Figure 1 adapted from [5], sketches the functional based classification of oil properties. This review encompasses physicochemical-based diagnostic techniques for assessing insulation condition in aged transformers, while electrical-based diagnostic techniques are for concern in a companion paper submitted in this journal [6]. In addition to electrical methods, the physicochemical diagnostic methods are very important for the condition monitoring or for studying the degradation of electrical insulation in power transformer. This review is subdivided into traditional and modern diagnostic methods.

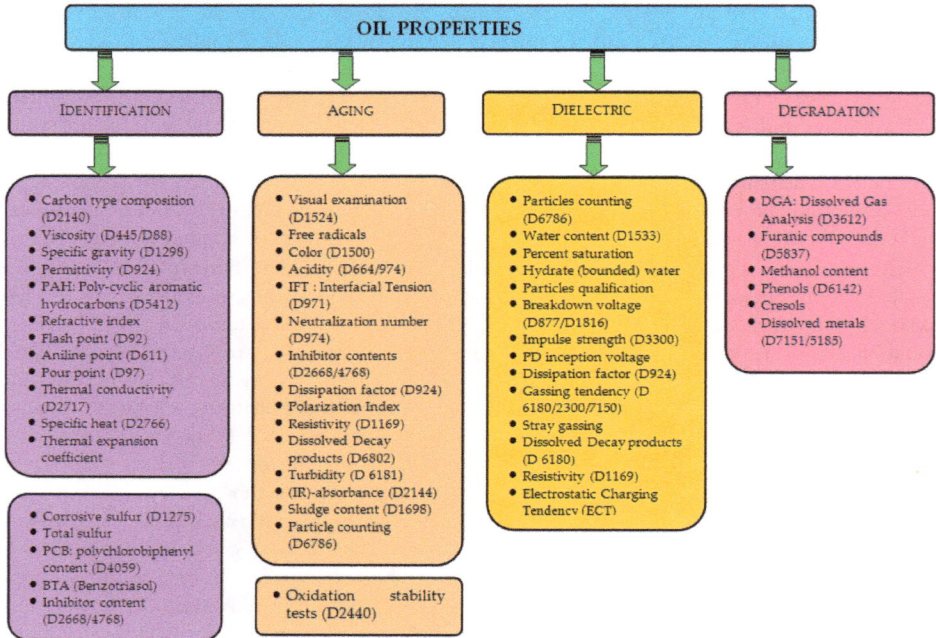

Figure 1. Functional based classification of oil properties adapted from [5]. Specifications in brackets are ASTM (American Society for Testing and Materials) standards.

2. Traditional Diagnostics Techniques

2.1. Color/Visual Examination

Color [7] is often used as a qualitative method. The technique is based on the comparison of oil color to a standard colored and numbered disc [8]. An oil's color comes from the light transmitting through it. Different colors are formed depending on the concentration and type of light-absorbing groups dissolved species in oil. Color of new oil is generally accepted as an index of the degree of refinement. For oils in service, an increasing or high color number is an indication of contamination, deterioration, or both. Oxidation is a common cause of an over-all darkening to occur. Comparisons between oil condition and color are reported in Table 1.

Table 1. Oil condition based on color comparisons [9].

Color Comparator Number	Color	Oil Condition
<7	Pale yellow	Good oil
7–10	Yellow	Proposition A oil
10–11	Bright yellow	Service-aged oil
11–14	Amber	Marginal condition
14–15	Brown	Bad condition
16–18	Dark brown	Severe condition (reclaimed oil)
>18	Black	Extreme condition (scrap oil)

The visual examination [10] is applicable to electrical insulating liquids that have been used in transformers, oil circuit breakers, or other electrical apparatus as insulating or cooling media, or both. An oil sample is visually examined by passing a beam of light through it to determine transparency and identify foreign matters. Poor transparency, cloudiness, or the observation of particles indicates contamination such as moisture, sludge, or other foreign matter.

2.2. Particle Count

It is recognized that particles have a harmful effect on the dielectric strength of insulating liquids [11]. Large amount of particle contaminations can lead to transformer failure. It was reported that moisture in combination with particles reduces significantly the breakdown voltage of the oil and increases the risk of static electrification, partial discharge activity and tracking [12]. Particle size, type and shape are also contributing factors. The most detrimental particles are the conductive ones (metal, carbon, wet fiber, *etc.*). Particle identification and counting is an important procedure for condition monitoring [11,13].

Miners [14] reported the effect of particles and moisture on the breakdown voltage of insulating transformer oil using Verband der Elektrotechnik, Elektronik, Informationstechnik (VDE) electrodes. This author has considered different sizes and concentrations of iron, copper and cellulose fibers. He noticed very low breakdown strength for the combined effects of moisture and particles type, size and concentration. In a recent work presented at a The Council on Large Electric Systems (CIGRE) session [15], a comparison between the performance of ester liquids and mineral oil have shown that the breakdown voltages of both ester liquids and mineral oil decreased with the increase in cellulose particle-based content. However, it was found that the breakdown voltage of mineral oil is more sensitive to the particle contamination than ester liquids. This might be due to the higher viscosity of ester which slower the motion of metallic particles and therefore reduces breakdown occurrence [16]. Sarathi and Archana [17] investigated the role played by conducting particle in partial discharge activity under alternative current (AC) voltages by using an ultra-high frequency (UHF) technique. They have observed a partial discharge current pulse formation and frequency signal radiation due to particle movement, and when the applied voltage increased, the UHF signal magnitude formed due to particle movement increased.

A multiple sources of particles contamination have been reported by CIGRE Working Group 12.18 [13].

In new equipment, the insulating liquid may contain cellulose fibers, iron, aluminum, copper and other particles from the manufacturing process. In used transformer, sludge particles forms slowly during utilization at normal and overload temperatures. Carbon particles due to the localized overheating may also produce and migrate by leakage or other accident errors from the on load tap changer (OLTC) diverter to the bulk liquid compartment and contaminate the active parts. Pump bearing wear is considered as a typical source of metallic particles [13].

Actually, there are many methods for counting and determining the size and shape of particles. Such methods are based on the light extinction, light scattering, coulter principle or direct imaging. However, the automatic particle counters using light extinction are the most widespread for counting in hydrocarbons and lubricants. For transformer insulating liquids, the measurements are performed using standards such as American Society for Testing and Materials (ASTM) D6786 or International Electrotechnical Commission (IEC) 60970. These standards are based on the International Organization for Standardization (ISO) 11171 calibration. IEC 60422 [18] and CIGRE brochure 157 [11] provide some guidelines to judge the condition of oil based on the level of contamination. In 1983, Oommen published an interesting study on particle levels in 200 samples taken from field and factory units [19]. Atomic absorption spectroscopy was used to determine the content of iron, copper and others.

2.3. Inhibitor Content

Although insulating oils are carefully refined, the impact of mechanical, electrical, thermal and chemical stresses, produces a variety of degradation products. Most of new brand insulating oil contain small amount of unstable hydrocarbons. The electronegative character of oxygen makes it very effective to attack vulnerable hydrocarbons [20]. The oxidation rate is accelerated by temperature, oxygen and catalysts such as copper. The results to such reactions are the formation of hydro-peroxides which brown the oil. Insoluble molecules which may be adsorbed at the surface of cellulose fibers are formed. These impurities reduce life expectancy and reliability of in-service transformers. To reduce the impact of oxygen and enhance the oxidation stability, synthetic oxidation inhibitors are usually incorporated in the oil. Therefore, as long as the inhibitors are present, the oil will be protected against oxidation and therefore increase the expected lifetime of the insulation. The antioxidants perform better in these cleaner oils since they do not have to counteract the negative aspects of contaminants. However, as the service life proceed, the inhibitor will be consumed and when is gone the oxidation rate become higher. Since the anti-oxidant is a consumable material, the initial chemical stability of new insulating oil gradually decreases. Their amount has to be monitored and must be replenished if necessary. Thus, the determination of the inhibitor content is an important factor in maintaining long service life of insulating oil. Actually, phenolic inhibitors are often used in transformers. The commonly used inhibitors are 2,6-di-*tert*-butyl-paracresol (DBPC) and 2,6-di-*tert*-butyl-phenol (DBP) [12]. In recent study, Mehanna *et al*. [21] examined the characteristics of several inhibitors dissolved in mineral insulating oils including 2,6-di-*tert*-butyl-p-cresol (DBPC), 2,6-di-*tert*-butyl-phenol (DBP), dibenzyl disulfide (DBDS), 2-*tert*-butyl-p-cresol (2-*t*-BPC), N-phenyl-1-naphthylamine, 1,2,3-benzotriazol (BTA) and methylated-BTA. The obtained results confirmed that the DBPC and DBP are the most suitable to be used as inhibitors in transformer mineral oils. ASTM D3487 defines two types of mineral oils according to the inhibitors content (0.08% for type I and 0.3% for type II). Detection and measurements of the inhibitor content shall be done according to IEC 60666 Standard [22]. Three used analytical methods are presented in this standard, related to infrared spectrophotometry (IR), high performance liquid chromatography (HPLC) and gas chromatography-mass spectrometry (GC-MS).

2.4. Moisture in Oil Determination

Moisture is considered enemy number one of transformer insulation. Each time the moisture is doubled in the solid insulation of a transformer, the life of the insulation is cut by one-half [23]. The presence of moisture in the solid and liquid insulation is known to play a critical role on transformer life [24,25]. The moisture in transformer is generated from several sources [12]: remaining moisture in insulation during manufacturing, humid air from outside during transportation and/or assembling in substation, humid air from outside through the breather (non-sealed), moisture ingress through gaskets, chemical decomposition of cellulose, moisture absorption from outside during some maintenance operations such as on site control of active part or bushing replacement, topping-up of oil level made with humid oil (non-dried). An accurate method of measuring very small amount of moisture in oil is the Karl Fischer Titration technique. This technique can indicate moisture content as low as 1–2 ppm [26,27]. As oils become very oxidized with increasing amounts of polar aging byproducts, their water solubility characteristics also increases. At elevated temperatures, some amount of hydrated compounds may transfer into dissolved water. Bonded water cannot be revealed by Karl Fischer (KF) titration. The KF method can therefore overestimate water content because iodine can react with peroxides, acids, and other impurities that may be present as a result of oil degradation [24,28]. The KF titration is therefore not very accurate for aged oils where active contaminants are accumulated capable of forming hydrates with bonded water [13].

The moisture content of oil can change quickly within an operational transformer. For on-site measurements, the water migration being commonly running, the transformer is in a non-equilibrium state. Direct measurement of moisture content in paper insulation (cellulose) is complex; moisture partitioning curves (Figure 2) between oil/ester and paper under equilibrium conditions have been reported by several authors [29–31].

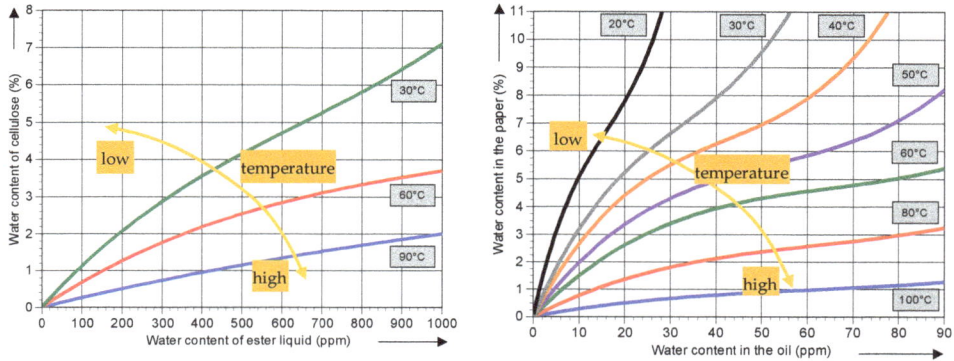

Figure 2. Equilibrium curves for moisture partition between oil and paper (ppm *vs.* water content of paper) [31].

These curves were used to estimate the moisture of paper by measuring moisture in oil at different temperatures. However, complications may arise due to fast dynamic diffusion processes. Another problem with the partitioning diagrams is that they are based on new oil/ester and do not take into account the effects of aging by-products found in aged transformers [32]. In a study conducted at Monash University under an Electric Power Research Institute (EPRI), USA sponsored project, a new method of moisture assessment in operating transformers was developed, based on a water-in-paper activity concept. The parameter of water-in-paper activity is used to access moisture conditions in both new and in service-aged transformer insulation systems. Another term, "active water content of paper (WCPA)", was also introduced [33].

In the last decades, capacitive probes are in use for determining the relative moisture to saturation. Advantages of capacitive probes are follows: very convenient for onsite and online applications, possibility of continuous measurement, no error due to oil sampling, transportation and the type of oil and oil condition do not affect the measurement [26]. With continuous monitoring, diffusion time can be taken into account and significant improvement in the estimation of moisture content can be achieved [26].

Over the last decades, dielectric spectroscopic techniques have been used to assess moisture content inside the solid insulation. However, it must be emphasized that moisture and aging separation still constitute a challenging point in this domain [6,34,35].

2.5. Dissolved Gas Analysis (DGA)

During its use, power transformers insulation systems degrades under the effects of various stresses, leading to the generation of dissolved gases in oil. The identification of these gases can be very useful for determining defects in transformers and avoid unforeseen interruptions. According to ASTM Designation D 3612-02 [36], Section 1.2, indicates that the individual component gases that may be identified and determined include: hydrogen—H_2, oxygen—O_2, nitrogen—N_2, carbon monoxide—CO, carbon dioxide—CO_2, methane—CH_4, ethane—C_2H_6, ethylene—C_2H_4, acetylene—C_2H_2, propane—C_3H_8 and propylene—C_3H_6. Except O_2 and N_2, all mentioned gases must have an unpaired electron when the breakdown occurs; this means that these gases are in fact the results of secondary chemical reaction. Actually, gas generation are caused by the breaking of hydrocarbon molecules due to electrical and/or thermal stresses. These gases are referred to as key gases. Among the used methods to detect and identify the generated gases, DGA is considered as the most informative method. Over the decades, Dissolved Gas Analysis (DGA) monitoring has become a very useful diagnostic tool and is being universally applied by the utilities or manufacturers for condition assessment of power transformer and in more recent years load tap-changers and bulk oil circuit. However, some drawbacks of the dissolved gas analysis have been underscored by The Institute of Electrical and Electronics Engineers (IEEE) Std. C57.104 [37] as follows: "Many techniques for the detection and the measurement of gases have been established. However, it must be recognized that analysis of these gases and interpretation of their significance is at this time not a science, but an art subject to variability". Further, "The result of various ASTM testing round robins indicates that the analytical procedures for gas analysis are difficult, have poor precision, and can be wildly inaccurate, especially between laboratories". Finally, "However, operators must be cautioned that, although the physical reasons for gas formation have a firm technical basis, interpretation of that data in term of the specific cause or causes is not an exact science, but is the result of empirical evidence from which rules for interpretation have been derived".

Generally, dissolved key gases are always presented in transformer oils at some level [38]. The quantity of generated gases depends upon the type of fault. Some of key gases and their related faults are listed in Table 2.

Table 2. Categories of key gases and general fault conditions [39].

Key Gases	Potential Fault Type
Methane, ethane, ethylene and small amounts of acetylene	Thermal condition involving the oil
Hydrogen, methane and small amounts of acetylene and ethane	Partial discharge
Hydrogen, acetylene and ethylene	Sustained arcing
Carbon monoxide and carbon dioxide	Thermal condition involving the paper

When an increase in key gases concentration exceeds certain limits, additional gas analyses are recommended for determining defects type within the transformer. Several DGA interpretation methods are used in practice [3,37,40–42]. These interpretation methods are based on key gases, key ratios and graphical representations analysis. To date, about twenty empirical DGA interpretation methods have been developed:

- Incipient Fault Types, Frank M. Clark, 1933–1962 [43]
- Dörnenburg Ratios, E. Dörnenburg, 1967, 1970 [40]
- Potthoff's Scheme, K. Potthoff, 1969 [44]
- Absolute limits, various sources, early 1970 [45]
- Shank's Visual Curve method, 1970s [46]
- Trilinear Plot Method, 1970 [43]
- Key Gas Method, David Pugh, 1974 [47]
- Duval's Triangle, Michel Duval, 1974 [42]
- Rogers Ratios, R.R. Rogers, 1975 [41]
- Glass Criterion, R.M Glass, 1977 [43]
- Trend Analysis, various sources, early 1980s [45]

    - total volume per day
    - ppm per day

- Church Logarithmic Nomograph, J.O. Church, 1980 [48]
- Expert System Analysis, Richard Lowe, 1985 [49]
- Expert System Monitor Program, Karen Barrett, 1989 [43]
- IEEE C57.104, Limits, rates and total dissolved combustible gas (TDCG), 1978–1991 [37]
- Artificial Neural Networks (ANNs) and Fuzzy Logic

- X. Ding, E. Yao, Y. Liu and Paul Griffin, 1996 [50]
- Vladimiro Miranda and Adriana Garcez Castro, 2004 [51]
- Donald Lamontagne, 2006 [52]

- IEC 60599 Ratios, Limits and gassing rates, 1999 [53]
- Data mining and Log Transformation, Tony McGrail, 2000 [54]
- Vector Algorithm, Nick Dominelli, Mike Lau and David Pugh, 2004 [43]
- Duval's Pentagon, Michel Duval, 2014 [55]

Among these methods, the most used are IEC, Rogers, Duval' Triangle and the Key Gas method [43,56]. The ratio methods have the advantages that they are independent on the transformer oil volume. However, they are vulnerable to misinterpretation. For that reason, they should be always used in parallel with other methods such us the key gas methods. In addition, some DGA results using ration methods may fall outside ratio codes and no diagnosis can be achieved. The last problem of the ration methods is resolved by the Triangle method as it is a closed system rather than an open system. However, the Duval triangle method uses only the value of three gases, CH_4, C_2H_4 and C_2H_2. In a recent work, Duval has proposed pentagon-based method to interpret the detected gas [55]. This method uses five combustible gases instead of three, CH_4, C_2H_4, C_2H_2, C_2H_6 and H_2. Therefore, a complementary Duval's pentagon has been developed [57].

All of these methods still show a certain percentage of incorrect diagnoses. This is probably due to the fact that all of these techniques are based on heuristic in nature and not on scientific formulation. Some pitfalls of DGA testing were emphasized [43]:

- Gases produced not as a result of incipient fault condition;
- Leaking between tap changers and main tank;
- Welding producing acetylene and other gases ;
- Out-gassing of paints and gaskets (which are usually CO and CO_2);
- Galvanic reactions (*i.e.*, steel + water + O_2 = hydrogen production);
- Lower voltage transformers having higher CO and CO_2 values as a result of non-vacuum treatment, oxygen + heat;
- Stray gassing characteristics;
- Contaminants produce gases;
- Decomposition of additives such as passivators can produce gases as well (H_2 and CO_2).

In recent works, the theoretical premise that some of contaminants in the oil may contribute to gassing was experimentally verified under laboratory conditions [39]. The results of these works have shown that oil born decay products may affect the diagnostics by DGA.

Another difficulty of DGA is that the absorption of any given gas in oil depends on the pressure and temperature of the oil, on the type of gas involved and the nature of the oil itself (whether antioxidants are present) [58].

Nowadays, several types of alternative liquids, mainly used in distribution transformers, are available. Due to their high degree of sustainability, there is a strong demand to use them in power transformers. A number of articles on the impact of alternative liquids on the dissolved gas analysis have been published [59,60]. CIGRE working group WG D1.32 has developed a new Duval triangle with modified diagnosis boundaries for DGA of alternative liquids [61].

The advantages and disadvantages [58] of DGA analysis for determining the gas content and the make-up of the gases are follows: no need to header space, extracts of gases from oil, require sophisticated equipment to extract the gases from the oil, applicable to all fluid containing components where it is possible to access the oil.

Even though DGA techniques are actually widely used, still some improvements are needed for accurate diagnostics. Since all the available methods are based on heuristic in nature and not based on scientific formulation, intelligent agent-based DGA diagnostic was proposed to reduce the risk of mistaken diagnostics and enhance accuracy [56]. Artificial intelligence (AI) is also being proposed to overcome the inconsistent interpretations of DGA results [62].

2.6. Acidity and Interfacial Tension (IFT) Analyses

The acid number (AN) of oil, measured in mg KOH/g, is a quantitative measure of the amount of acidic materials present in oil. It is determined by the amount of potassium hydroxide (KOH) in milligrams (mg) required to neutralize the acid in one gram of transformer oil. The AN measures both weak and strong organic and inorganic acids within the oil. As the oxidation level of in service oil increases, polar compounds, particularly organic acids form in the oil, therefore increasing the acid number. New transformer oils are practically free of acids. Used oil having a high acid number indicates that the oil is either oxidized or contaminated with materials such as varnish, paint, or other foreign matter. The AN is generally viewed as an indicator of nitration, oxidation and contamination, hence a tool of diagnostic. It is recommended that the oil be reclaimed when the acid number reaches 0.20 mg KOH/g [63].

The interfacial tension (IFT) of transformer oil is another effective diagnostic index that can be used to identify the degradation rate of insulating oil. It is expressed in dynes per centimeter required to rupture a small wire ring upward a distance of one centimeter through the oil-water interface [64]. When certain contaminants such as soaps, paints, varnishes, and oxidation products are present in the oil, the film strength of the oil is weakened, thus requiring less force to rupture. For oils in service, a decreasing value indicates the accumulation of contaminants, oxidation products, or both. The IFT is a precursor of objectionable oxidation products which may attack the insulation and interfere with the cooling of transformer windings. Good clean oil will make a very distinct line on the top of water and gives an IFT number of 40 to 50 dynes per centimeter. It is recommended to reclaim the oil when the IFT decreases down to 25 dynes per centimeter. At this level, the oil is very contaminated and must be reclaimed to prevent sludging, which begins at around 22 dynes per centimeter [65]. If oil is not reclaimed, sludge will settle on windings, insulation, cooling surfaces, *etc.*, and cause loading and cooling problems. There is a definite relationship between the acid number and the IFT. Any increase in the AN is normally related to a drop in the IFT. Although lower values of IFT and AN is an unusual situation, it does occur because of contamination such as solid insulation materials, compounds from leaky pot heads or bushings, or from a source outside the transformer [66]. Field experiences have also revealed both aging indexes may failed in diagnosing incipient failures [67]. The 500-kV generator step-up units of Salto Grande were sealed and a periodic oil analyses procedure implemented. Measuring the interfacial tension and the organic acidity of oil, confirmed the lack of oxidation products while the analysis of the relative content of dissolved decay products (DDPs) in the oil by UV-vis spectrophotometry [68] has shown a higher content of dissolved oxidation decay products in the units with punctured rubber by bladders.

2.7. Paper Degradation Assessment

In transformer, one of the key maintenance "musts" is to ensure that the electrical system remains isolated through effective insulation. This is achieved through the use of insulating paper. It is critical to monitor the paper state by direct measurements to ensure that the paper continues to provide effective insulation for the transformer. However, direct analysis of the paper insulation is an invasive procedure that requires the transformer to be taken out of service.

Insulation paper is made from wood pulp by Kraft process and contains 90% cellulose, 6%–7% hemicellulose and 3%–4% lignin. Cellulose is a linear polymer comprising anydro D-glucopyranose units held together at the first and fourth carbon atoms through a glycosidic-linkage [69]. The monomer units are combined in long straight chains within the paper insulation and the number of monomer units in a polymer is known as degree of polymerization (DP) [3]. This parameter is mechanical strength of paper. The degree of polymerization, measured by viscometric method (*DPv*), represents the average number of glucose units per cellulose chain) [69,70].

This technique is accurate in evaluating the condition of paper. The measurement of DPv is used as a diagnostic tool for determining the condition of the solid insulation within a transformer. The *DPv* (average number of glucose units per cellulose chain) of insulation paper after manufacturing varies between 1000 and 1300 [71,72]. The mechanical strength of the paper is considered roughly constant between 1000 and 500. Below 500, the *DPv* drops linearly with the mechanical strength [73,74]. When correctly perform, the reproducibility of DP measurements are very good. The advantages and disadvantages of DP measurement are described in Table 3.

Table 3. Advantages and disadvantages of degree of polymerization (DP) measurement [3].

Advantages	Disadvantages
Easy to make DP measurements	Direct analysis of the paper insulation is an invasive procedure that requires the transformer to be taken out of service
The mechanical strength of paper is related to the average DP	The type of paper and its final chemical treatment significantly influence the rate of degradation

To overcome the problems related to direct measurement, many studies were conducted to develop indirect techniques for assessing the state of insulating paper. These techniques are based on the analysis of chemical indicators or markers present in oil due to the degradation of insulating paper. Most of the indirect methods investigated up to now were based on the analysis of the dissolved CO + CO_2 in oil [75] and on the furanic compounds as an indicator of paper aging [76]. The ratio of CO and CO_2 concentration is normally used as an indicator of thermal decomposition of cellulose [37,77]. The ratio of CO and CO_2 is normally more about seven, while the respective values of CO_2 and CO should be greater than 5000 ppm and 500 ppm in order to improve the certainty factor. However, the disadvantage of diagnosing paper insulation condition using CO/CO_2 is that this method is not reliable since carbon oxides may be generated from the long-term oxidation of oil components or could present as a result of atmospheric leak [73,78].

Another alternative method of assessing paper degradation is the determination of furans compounds present in oil. The major furanic compounds that are released into the oil are as follows: 2-furfuraldehyde (2FAL), 5-hydroxy-methyl 2-furfuraldehyde (5H2F), 2-acetylfuran (2ACF), 5-methyl 2-furfuraldehyde (5M2F), and 2-furfuryl-alcohol (2FOL). These compounds result of paper oxidation and hydrolysis processes characterize the thermal decomposition of insulation paper [71]. Among the furan compounds, it was found that 2-furfuraldehyde (2FAL) is the most abundant; its concentration within the oil is related directly to the degree of polymerization value (*DP_v*) and therefore to the mechanical strength of the solid insulation. However, as CO/CO_2 analysis, some drawbacks have been observed for the Furan analysis. The major limitation is that the concentration of 2FAL is affected by oil replacement or by oil reconditioning processes [79]. Other sources influencing the concentration of 2FAL are linked to its thermal instability, the effect of moisture on the rate of production [73,78,80]. Some disadvantages of 2-FAL are its low sensitivity in the aging of thermally upgraded (TU) paper (more often used by new transformers), along with its exponential behavior [74]. The 2-FAL concentration in oil shows a noticeable increase only when paper is extremely aged (*DPv* ⩽ 400) [81]. To overcome this drawback, several alternative chemical markers are being investigated an indirect detection of the insulation paper degradation. Among all the studied markers (acetone, acetaldehyde, butanol, 2-butanone and carbon disulfide...), Methanol (CH_3OH) has shown the highest stability at different temperatures [82]. Consequently, methanol was of particular interest for monitoring paper depolymerization [83]. The use of methanol (CH_3OH) has been reported for the first time in the literature by Jalbert *et al.* [83]. As reported by [81] the main advantage of this molecule over 2-FAL is its ability to be generated in the presence of thermally upgraded paper regardless of the temperature and the moisture present in the insulation. It could readily be used to sort out the problematic units of a given family and technology. In addition, contrary to carbon oxides, because of its high affinity for paper, methanol will tend to re-equilibrate in the oil after the latter has been regenerated. Annelore Schaut *et al.* reported that a linear correlation exists between DP_v and formation of Methanol even at early stages of its formation [84]. Arroyo *et al.* [74] reported the relationship between the generation of methanol and the number of scissions. It was proved that methanol is a robust indirect method for describing the condition of insulating paper. Another correlation between the methanol content within the fluid and the tensile index has been observed by the same authors. This method opens the door to a methodology for assessing the real condition of the paper in power transformers. Studies are still going on worldwide, the objective being the improvement of this finding that is fully mature.

Furanic concentration in oil can be quantified by using high performance liquid chromatography (HPLC) or gas chromatography-mass spectrometry (GC-MS).

High-performance liquid chromatograph (HPLC) is now one of the most powerful tools in analytical chemistry. They have the ability to separate and quantify the compounds that are present in any sample that can be dissolved in a liquid with detection levels approaching 0.01 trillionths of a gram (10^{-14} of a gram) [85]. The amount of furans present in oil could be a good indicator of the condition of cellulose insulation [3]. The measurement method of furan concentrations in oil has been described in [86,87].

The measurement is achieved in two phases [3]: solid stationary phase and mobile phase. In the solid stationary phase, 1–5 mL of oil is diluted with 5 mL of hexane and injected in a steel tube packed with particle of solid material. The commonly used solid in the stationary phase is octadecyl groups bonded to silica particles. It is then washed with 10 mL of hexane to remove the oil. Nitrogen is applied for 5 min to evaporate the hexane. The furans are then eluted with 1.5 mL acetonitrile. About 20 µL of the elute solution is then injected into the HPLC column. A solvent called the mobile phase is then pumped through the column. The solvent is a mixture of methanol and water. The flow of the mobile phase separates the furan components. The different extent to which the different furan components interact with the solid stationary phase and the mobile phase determines the extent of separation of furan components. The detector senses the components as they are eluted from the column. The results are usually reported in terms of parts per billion (ppb). Table 4 highlights the advantages and limitations of HPLC.

Table 4. Advantages and limitations of high performance liquid chromatography (HPLC) [88].

Advantages	Limitations
• Rapid and precise quantitative analysis • Automated operation • High-sensitive detection • Quantitative sample recovery • Amenable to diverse samples	• No universal detector • Less separation efficiency than capillary gas chromatography (GC) • More difficult for novices

Determination of furan by HPLC with DP gives an indication of the remaining structural strength of the paper insulation and is an indication of the remaining life of the paper and the transformer itself. Lütke *et al.* [89] have shown that it is not possible to predict the remaining life of a transformer only based on the content of furanic compounds and that it is not possible to derive an exact DP value correlation from the furanic content. According to these authors, only one mosaic stone and only the sum of different procedures (DGA, humidity in oil and paper, *etc.*) with fingerprinting and trend analysis will enable the life assessment.

Alternative assessments based on FTIR spectroscopy, molecular weight measurement by gel permeation chromatography (GPC) and thermogravimetry analysis of cellulose paper insulation has also been reported [90,91]. However, their practical use is hampered by the difficulty in taking paper samples from an operating transformer.

2.8. Heat Transfer Properties

Key properties regarding heat transfer properties or heat transfer coefficient of the oil include pour point, viscosity profile, specific heat, relative density and thermal conductivity [92]. These properties determine the efficiency with which the fluid may cool the transformer windings. To evaluate the heat transfer coefficient, thermal conductivity, specific heat capacity kinematic viscosity and density, need to be measured at different temperatures.

High thermal conductivity (measured in watts per meter kelvin (W/(m· K))) is a primary limitation in the development of energy-efficient heat transfer fluids required in many industrial and commercial applications including power transformers. Thermal conductivity is essentially "the measure of the ability of a material to conduct heat" [93] or, more simply, the heat transfer rate. The higher the thermal conductivity is, the higher the fluid capability to transfer heat quickly from the transformer windings to the outside air is [94].

The specific heat (in Joule per Kelvin: J/K) also known as heat capacity is a thermodynamic property that is a measure of the amount of energy required to produce a given temperature change within a unit quantity of a given substance. It is used in engineering calculations that relate to the manner in which a given system may react to thermal stresses [95].

Viscosity is another important thermodynamic parameter in design calculations for heat transfer by either natural convection in smaller self-cooled transformers or forced convection in larger units with pumps and the impregnation process [96]. It is the resistance of oil to flow under the force of gravity. The SI unit is the meter squared per second also known as the Stoke (m^2s^{-1} or St). The more common term is the centistoke (cSt), which is a millimeter squared per second. The measurement at 40 °C is useful for early detection of oxidation, polymerization and thermal failure of the oil. Measurement at 100 °C has advantages in the detection of viscosity index improver shear down and its best suited for components that operate at high temperatures. Both temperatures may be employed where the calculation or change of the viscosity index is important and where multiples objectives need to be achieved [97].

Pour point (in °C), which represents the lowest temperature at which the oil can still flow [98], is another important parameter to consider in cold climates. This means that this temperature, oil flows and can transport heat away from windings and core.

The relative Density (or Specific gravity) is the ratio of weights of equal volumes of oil and water at a given temperature [99]. In natural convection cooled oil filled transformers, when the fluid temperature increases, its density reduces. The fluid rises upwards and transfers its heat to outside air through tank and radiators.

The heat transfer properties of oil used as a coolant influences heat transfer rates and consequently the temperature rise of an apparatus. The heat transfer properties of oil also influences the speed of moving parts in tap changers and circuit breakers. Oils of high viscosity oils are less desirable, especially in cold climates. The heat transfer properties of oil can be affected by polymerization, oxidation, formation of carbon and oxide insoluble [97]. Contaminants such as water, air, soot and oil admixtures can also worsens the heat transfer properties. Decay products deposit themselves on solid insulations and other parts, blocking ducts and concomitant overheating of the oil and windings. A fluid with low viscosity and density, higher thermal conductivity and specific heat capacity are important parameters for higher heat transfer coefficient.

2.9. Corrosive Sulfur

Scientifically, corrosive sulfur is defined as elemental sulfur and thermally unstable compounds in electrical insulating oil that can cause corrosion of certain metals such as copper and silver [100]. Sulfur is commonly found in crude oil. There are five basic groups of sulfur and sulfur compounds in crude oil [101]: elemental sulfur (S), mercaptans (R–SH), sulfides (R–S–R'), disulfides (R–S_S–R) and thiophenes. The aftereffects of the corrosive sulfur into transformers are disastrous. Corrosive sulfur affects not only adversely the conductor material and other metal surfaces but may have also drastic effects on paper insulation. Copper sulfide reduces electrical strength of conductor insulation. Copper sulfide deposits produce a low resistance path across and through the cellulose insulation and can lead to internal discharges and flashover. Recent work [102] showed that the amount of Cu_2S deposition on insulation paper and copper wire surface increase with the aging time; sulfur corrosion of copper wires can reduce the permittivity of oil-paper insulation. The electrical breakdown strength of oil-paper insulation with copper sulfide depositions declines greatly, and this would lead to internal insulation failure of transformers. One of the main preventive measures used to address this problem is the addition of organic copper surface passivators to transformer oil. These passivators bind to copper surfaces and create an impermeable boundary between the bulk of the metal and the surrounding insulating cellulose and oil [103]. Passivators can be described as a chemical varnish of the windings that protects the copper from the oil and the oil from the copper. The most widely used is the Irgamet 39, a molecule currently recommended for use in transformers for preventing the copper dissolution. This molecule is made significantly less hydrophilic by amino-methylation and fully miscible with oils [103].

3. Modern Physicochemical Diagnostics Techniques

3.1. Fourier Transform Infrared Spectroscopy (FTIR)-Based Determinations

Fourier Transform Infrared (FTIR) spectroscopy is considered as a very powerful tool for monitoring the condition of lubricants and oils, since it can identifies compound and sample composition. Because each bond type has a unique wave-number fingerprint, it can be readily identified. This sensitivity to oil constituents can be used to trace almost all aging by-products. The concept is different from UV-vis spectroscopy techniques. UV-vis or UV/vis spectroscopy or ultraviolet-visible spectrophotometry refers to absorption spectroscopy or reflectance spectroscopy in the ultraviolet-visible spectral region. This principle consists in using light in the visible and adjacent (near-UV and near-infrared (NIR)) ranges. The absorption or reflectance in the visible range directly affects the perceived color of the chemical substance under investigation.

Infrared (IR) spectroscopy uses an electrically heated glow-bar as infrared radiation source; this radiation is passed through the sample to the detector. The chemical constituents of the sample absorb some of the infrared at reproducible and specific wavenumbers. The technique FTIR or Fourier Transform infrared uses something called the Michelson interferometer. This nifty device utilizes a moving mirror, whose speed is monitored by a laser, which also acts as a wavelength reference. The detector then measures the summation of all the frequencies over time resulting in a time dependent interference pattern called an interferogram. A computer algorithm called a Fast Fourier Transform is then used to convert this signal to an absorbance or transmission spectrum.

FTIR identify unknown materials; determine the quality or consistency of a sample and the amount of components in a mixture. Insulation oil used in power transformers consists of saturated hydrocarbons as paraffin and naphtene and can neither conduct current nor solute water. Oil conductivity depends on oil type and increases with aging by-products. Contaminants such as residues from refinery, pollution and particularly aging/oxidation products enable the oil to conduct ionic current. Oil oxidation/degradation by-products is subdivided into soluble (dissolved) and insoluble (suspended) products [104]:

- the dissolved impurity particles are peroxide (R–OOR), alcohol (ROH), aldehyde (ROHO), ketone (RCO–R), organic acid (R–COOH), acid anhydride ($(RC(O))_2O$) organic peroxide (ROOH), ester (R–COO–R′), metallic soap ((RCOO)nM) (M means metal atoms), *etc.*
- the suspended impurity particles include asphaltic sludge, soap sludge, carbon sludge, *etc.*

Oxidation by-products (peroxide gas, water soluble acids, low molecular weight acids, fatty acids, water, alcohols, metallic soap, aldehydes, ketones, lacquers, sludges of asphaltene) change the chemical make-up of the oil to allow more water to be dissolved. FTIR determines the level of oxidation by a general response in the carbonyl (C=O) region of between 1800 to 1670 cm^{-1}. In this region, infrared energy is absorbed due to the carbon oxygen bonds in the oxidized oil. Sulfur compounds are typically found in crude oils and may also be used as additives in lubricating oils to achieve certain desired properties. Sulfate by-products such as SO_2 and SO_3 are formed by the oxidation of these Sulfur containing compounds. Sulfates are measured by FTIR in the same way as oxidation and nitration, by monitoring the increase in their infrared absorbance characteristics, *i.e.*, between 1180 and 1120 cm^{-1} [105].

The usefulness of FTIR in determining oxidation is dependent on the base oil used to formulate the fluid. Synthetic fluids often contain ester compounds which have a significant peak in the infrared spectra area where the oxidation level for mineral oils is measured. For this reason, it is important not to use FTIR results alone for diagnostics but instead to trend these results and view them in conjunction with other oil-related parameters like viscosity and AN [106]. More recently, some researchers developed FTIR detectors that allow detecting most of the gases of interest and quantify their amounts. These methods are capable of providing a greater understanding of the load, temperature, and time dependencies of generated gases [3]. Fourier transform infrared spectroscopy is preferred over dispersive or filter methods of infrared spectral analysis for several reasons:

- It is a non-destructive technique;
- It provides an accurate measurement method which requires no external calibration;
- It can increase speed, collecting a scan every second;
- It can increase sensitivity—one second scans can be co-added together to ratio out random noise;
- It has greater optical throughput; and
- It is mechanically simple with only one moving part.

Recently, alternative of determining moisture content in un-aged and aged mineral insulating oil samples by FTIR spectroscopy was proposed [107]. Accuracy, repeatability, and reproducibility of the FTIR method were assessed by analyzing a variety of oil samples, including new, thermally aged oils and oils taken from in-service transformers relative to their moisture content determined by KF. The key benefit from this approach would be that an FTIR equipped with an auto-sampler could provide a means of automating moisture analysis in a manner analogous to what has been done in the lubricant sector [108].

3.2. Combined Gas Chromatograph-Mass Spectrometry (GC-MS)-Based Testings

Gas chromatography/mass spectrometry (GC-MS) is an instrumental technique, consisting of a gas chromatograph (GC) coupled to a mass spectrometer (MS), by which complex mixtures of chemicals may be separated, identified and quantified. GC-MS analysis requires highly trained analysts and expensive equipment [109]. This makes it ideal for the analysis of the hundreds of relatively low molecular weight compounds found in environmental materials. The GC works on the principle that a mixture will separate into individual substances when heated [110,111]. The heated gases are carried through a column with an inert gas (such as helium). As the separated substances emerge from the column opening, they flow into the MS. Mass spectrometry identifies compounds by the mass of the analyzed molecule. A library of known mass spectra, covering several thousand compounds, is stored on a computer. Each compound has a unique or near unique mass spectrum that can be compared with a mass spectral database and thus identified [110,111]. Mass spectrometry is considered the only definitive analytical detector. To analyze a given compound by GC-MS, it must be sufficiently volatile and thermally stable. In addition, functionalized compounds may require chemical modification (derivatization) prior to analysis to eliminate undesirable adsorption effects that would otherwise affect the quality of the obtained data.

3.3. UV/Visible Spectroscopy-Based Testings

UV-visible spectroscopy is a technique that readily allows one to determine the concentrations of substances or the quantitative analysis of all molecules that absorb ultraviolet and visible electromagnetic radiation [112]. UV-visible spectrometers can be used to measure the absorbance of ultra violet or visible light by a sample, either at a single wavelength or perform a scan over a range in the spectrum. The UV region ranges from 190 to 400 nm and the visible region from 400 to 800 nm. The light source (a combination of tungsten/halogen and deuterium lamps) provides the visible and near ultraviolet radiation covering the 200–800 nm. The output from the light source is focused onto the diffraction grating which splits the incoming light into its component colors of different wavelengths, like a prism but more efficiently. For liquids the sample is held in an optically flat, transparent container called a cell or cuvette. The reference cell or cuvette contains the solvent in which the sample is dissolved and this is commonly referred to as the blank. The technique can be used both quantitatively and qualitatively. For each wavelength, the intensity of light passing through both a reference cell (I_0) and the sample cell (I) is measured. The Bouguer-Lambert-Beer law forms the mathematical-physical basis of light-absorption measurements on gases and solutions in the UV-vis and IR region [113]:

$$\log\left(\frac{I_0}{I}\right) = \log\left(\frac{100}{T\,(\%)}\right) \equiv A = \varepsilon.c.d \qquad (1)$$

where $A = \log\left(\frac{I_0}{I}\right)$ is the absorbance (absorbance does not have any units), $T\,(\%) = \frac{I_0}{I}.100$ is the transmittance, ε is the molar dedicated extinction coefficient, I_0 is the intensity of the monochromatic light entering the sample and I is the intensity of this light emerging from the sample; c is the concentration of the light-absorbing substance and d is the path-length of the sample in cm. The ASTM D 6802 [68] is used in transformer insulating oils. This method is based upon the observation that in the range of visible spectrum all brands of new insulating liquids are almost completely transparent to a monochromatic beam of light. On the contrary, when the fluid contains decay products, the absorbance curve, as determined by a scanning spectrophotometer, significantly shifts to longer wavelengths. The numerical integration of the area below these absorbance curves permits the relative content of dissolved oxidation decay products in the fluid samples. Under normal operating conditions, transformer oil deteriorates as a result of various stresses, electrical, chemical and thermal. This results in dissolved decay products which are the result of aging of the oil in service. The content of dissolved decay products in the insulating oil consists of a variety of compounds, such as peroxides, aldehydes, ketones, and organic acids each of which is partially adsorbed onto the large surface of the of the insulation paper leading to premature aging of transformers. This process occurs long before other less sensitive analytical methods may indicate. Therefore, the relative evaluation of the formation of by-products can be used as insulation aging indicator of oil/paper complex, as well as changes in the dielectric properties of the windings. Table 5 highlights the guidelines for DDP values, expressed in arbitrary unit (a.u.).

Table 5. Guidelines for dissolved decay products (DDPs) [114].

Oil Condition	DDP (a.u.)
Good oils	0–10
Proposition A oils	10–25
Marginal oils	4–10
Bad oils	25–50
Very bad oils	50–300
Extremely bad oils	>550

UV/vis spectroscopy was used to monitor decay products in reclaimed oils [115]. An example of the results from UV-vis spectroscopy is given in Figure 3 [115]. It shows the progress of service-aged oil reclamation process with two different types of Fuller's earth.

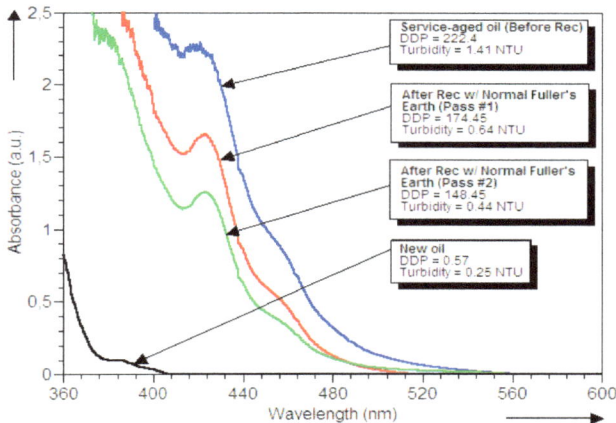

Figure 3. Comparison between new oil and service-aged oil reclaimed with two different types of Fuller's earth [115]. DDP, dissolved decay product; NTU, nephelometric turbidity unit; Rec, reclamation; Rec w/ Normal Fuller's Earth, reclaimed with Normal Fuller's Earth.

Ultraviolet (UV) and visible spectrometers have been used the last 35 years and they became the most important analytical instrument in the modern day laboratory. In many applications, other techniques could be employed but none rival UV-visible spectrometry for its simplicity, versatility, speed, accuracy and cost-effectiveness. UV-visible spectrometers are available as single beam or double beam. The advantage of the double beam spectrophotometers is that they make it possible to differentiate measurements between the sample and the analytical blank. They are preferable to single beam model if the solutions are turbid. The bandwidth of the best devices can go down to 0.01 nm [116].

IFT measurements require trained person and some precautions as mentioned in the ASTM D971 to perform the measurements. To overcome this, a novel method based on using UV-vis spectroscopy combined with artificial intelligence models have been recently proposed to estimate the IFT of transformer oil [117]. It seems that this method gives good results. However, a greater number of samples are necessary to validate this method.

Recently, new approach based on spectroscopic analysis to estimate furan compounds has been proposed [118]. This method is based on UV-vis spectral response and artificial intelligence [119,120]. The results reported shows good correlation between furan concentrations in transformer oil and its spectral response parameters.

Another important UV-vis spectroscopy based technique is the free radicals determination. Free radicals play a major role in a wide variety of aging processes. The detection of these reactive species in oil may, in principle, provide useful information for monitoring oil degradation. The paramount importance of free radicals in the physical organic chemistry of mineral insulating oils has been underscored by John Tanaka at the Nineteenth Symposium on Electrical Insulation [121]. These by-products are deleterious to the transformer and catalyze further oxidation of the oil. Free radicals are very reactive and can adversely affect the chemical, physical, and dielectric properties of the insulating liquid [122,123]. The reactive free radical reagent, 2,2-diphenyl-1-picrylhydrazyl (DPPH), is added to a solution, the free radical concentration of which is to be determined [124]. The presence of free radicals in solution will increase the rate at which DPPH disappears from the background solution; the higher the free radical concentration in the test specimen, the faster DPPH disappears. The relative free radical concentration of an insulating oil test specimen is determined as follows [124]: initially, the absorbance of the background solution of known concentration is recorded. Subsequently the decreasing absorbance of the oil specimen added to the background solution is plotted. Finally the subtraction of the oil specimen absorbance from the background solution results in a display curve of the reaction. The absorbance at 240 s/4 min from the beginning of the reaction is reported [122]. This method is applicable to new, reclaimed, or used oils as well as naturally or artificially oxidized oil (the cause of aging can be chemical, physical, or electrical).

3.4. Turbidity Analysis

Turbidity is the cloudiness or haziness of a liquid caused by suspended solids that are usually invisible to the naked-eye. Usually, a liquid contains suspended solids that consist of many different particles of varying sizes. Some of the particles are large and heavy enough to eventually settle to the bottom of a container if a sample is left standing (these are the settle-able solids). The smaller particles will only settle slowly, if at all (these are the colloidal solids). It is these particles that cause the liquid to look turbid. The turbidity of a liquid uses the principle of the interaction between an incident light wave and a particle in suspension mainly generating phenomena of diffusion, reflection, absorption and refraction. This claimed particle size, kind, shape, refractive index and its intensity causes a dispersion of the incident light in all directions. Turbidity working principle is based on nephelometry. This latter is measured by photometry concentration of particles in a liquid by diffusion at 90°. When used in correlation with nephelometry and other angles, attenuation-angled photodetectors can assist in improving turbidity meter accuracy. This is often referred to as a ratio design. Ratio or ratiometric turbidity meters are still categorized under nephelometric technology as a 90° angle is used as the primary detector. With multiple photodetector angles, algorithms may be used to compensate for optical interferences and increase instrument sensitivity. The Standard Methods ratiometric method uses the following algorithm [125,126]:

$$T = \frac{I_{90}}{d_0.I_t + d_1.I_{fs} + d_2.I_{bs} + d_3.I_{90}} \tag{2}$$

where T = turbidity in NTU (0–10,000); d_0, d_1, d_2, d_3 = calibration coefficients; I_{90} = 90 degree detector current; I_t = transmitted detector current; I_{fs} = forward scatter detector current; and I_{bs} = back scatter detector current.

The ASTM Designation 6181 [127] method is an accurate optical laboratory technique developed to quantitatively determine the amount of microscopic solid suspension that may exist in both new and in-service fluids. Increasing turbidity signifies increasing fluid contamination. Other turbidity sources, such as water droplets or gas bubbles, are eliminated [127]. Under normal operating conditions, oil insulation/paper power transformers undergoes slow degradation process. The electrical, heat, aggressive behavior of dissolved oxygen and the catalytic effect of copper combine to accelerate this deterioration. Resulting degradation products are gradually changing the physical, chemical and dielectric properties of the insulating oil. Some are soluble in the dielectric fluid. However, secondary chemical reactions can generate insoluble solid particles, invisible and microscopic dimensions, known under the generic name "sludge". These invisible suspensions are able to clog the pores of the paper insulation, which inhibits the ability of the oil to dissipate the thermal energy generated by the coils. It is therefore extremely important to detect these suspensions before the oil breakdown voltage is decreased. Measuring the amount of insoluble suspensions therefore appears to be very important, since these by-products clearly contribute to the insulation electrical and thermal degradation. Some guidelines for turbidity values are given in Table 6.

Table 6. Guidelines suggested for turbidity [114].

Oil Condition	Turbidity (NTU)
Good oils	0–1
Proposition A oils	1–4
Marginal oils	4–10
Bad oils	10–30
Very bad oils	30–150
Extremely bad oils	>150

Different types of electronic turbidimeter are available. The use of multiple detectors can improve accuracy and decrease the interference from dissolved colored materials and stray light [128]. Their advantages and limitations are listed in Table 7.

Table 7. Advantages and limitations of turbidimeter.

Advantages	Limitations
• Very accurate • Useful for measuring very low turbidity (less than 5 NTU)	• High cost • Need power supply • Easily damaged

4. Alternative Insulating Materials

The philosophy of power transformer design is founded on many years of research and development. However, in a world where everything evolves and changes rapidly, the key strategy must be based on the continuous improvement to each material involved in the design. Facing the paramount role played by temperature in the transformer degradation process, thermally-upgraded insulation was introduced more than 40 years ago to improve the stability of these critically important equipment in the transmission and distribution of electric energy. The effects of thermally-upgraded paper on the diagnostic techniques, such as furan analysis and chemical markers (alcohols) in the oil, are being investigated [74,89,129].

Even though thermally upgraded offers a 15° C higher temperature rating than normal Kraft paper, still the same basic limitations exist with cellulose (combination of high moisture absorption, auto-accelerating hydrolysis degradation in the presence of moisture, and relatively poor thermal stability) [130,131]. Another approach used aramid-based materials by Dupont, but high costs limit their use in most liquid-filled transformer applications. The Aramid paper (known by its trade name: Nomex) is mainly used as insulator for high temperatures applications such as traction transformers. To optimize cost and performance, hybrid insulation materials combining meta-aramid and cellulose have been proposed to provide incremental improvements in thermal stability. Several studies have been conducted to evaluate the performance of Aramid paper which has very good thermal properties [132–134]. To optimize costs and performance, hybrid insulation materials combining aramid and cellulose have been proposed to provide incremental improvements in thermal stability. The results of some works performed on hybrid insulation have shown that this type of insulation not only allows to increase the operating temperature [135], but also retard the degradation of insulating oil [136]. Recently, ASTM has developed a new standard test method for tensile testing of Aramid-based paper published as D7812, to be used for quality control [137].

A clear opportunity emerged to develop a flexible insulation material by 3M made by a wet-laid paper process (an organic binder, short cut fibers, and inorganic filler). Compared to Kraft paper, this flexible insulation provides [138]:

- Low moisture absorption
- Stable electrical properties in the presence of moisture
- Increased thermal conductivity
- Higher rated IEEE thermal class of 155 °C, which is a 50 °C improvement over Kraft—and a 35 °C improvement over thermally upgraded (TU) Kraft
- Resistance to hydrolysis
- Acceptable levels of mechanical and dielectric strength

In the last decades, environmental concerns are being considered as important factor to consider in the choice of insulation liquids. The impacts on the environment (toxicity) in terms of accidental release together with treatment at the end of life of insulation systems (recycling, reuse, disposal, incineration, landfilling...) are essential factors to consider. Many researches are therefore being directed towards environmentally friendly insulating liquids, as alternative to mineral oils [139]. Faced with the growing interest focused to "green insulating liquids", many synthetic or vegetable based fluids are being investigated for application in power transformers. Even though Siemens delivered in 2014 the world's first vegetable oil transformer in the 420 kV capacity range, research in this field is still at its earlier stage.

Throughout this article, the techniques described referred to mineral oil as this is something we are all familiar with. The properties of the alternatives fluids cannot be correlated directly to that of a mineral oil as their chemistries are very different [140]. They are so different, in fact, that ASTM has produced a new specification just for non-mineral oils [141,142]. IEC has also produced related specifications [142–145]. A Work Item (ASTM WK46195) by ASTM D27.02 subcommittee is developing a standard entitled: "New Specification for Synthetic Ester Fluids Used in Electrical Apparatus". Related IEEE standards are also available [146–148].

Applicability of a number of electrical and physicochemical parameters, including acidity value, dielectric dissipation factor (DDF), viscosity and color for assessing the quality of these alternative fluids is possible (Table 8). For the most part, the same tests used to evaluate mineral oil are used to evaluate silicone, natural/synthetic esters [31,149]. It should be emphasized that results and the meaning of the tests are differently interpreted.

Table 8. Fluid testing methods adapted from [31]. Most commonly used IEC methods are in blue; most commonly used ASTM methods in red while standard not quoted but generally used are in black.

Properties	Mineral Oil	Synthetic Ester	Natural Ester	Silicone Fluid
Acidity	IEC 62021 1/IEC 62021 2 ASTM D974	IEC 62021 1/IEC 62021 2 ASTM D974	ASTM D974	IEC 62021 1 ASTM D974
Appearance	ISO 2049/ASTM D1524	ISO 2049/ASTM D1524	ASTM D1524	ISO 2049 ASTM D1524
Breakdown voltage	IEC 60156/ASTM D1816	IEC 60156/ASTM D877/D1816	ASTM D877/D1816	IEC 60156 ASTM D877/D1816
Colour	ISO2049/ISO 2211/ASTM D1500	ISO 2211/ASTM D1500	ASTM D1500	ISO 2211 ASTM D1500
Corrosive sulphur	IEC 62535/ASTM D1275	-	ASTM D1275	-
Dielectric dissipation factor	IEC 60247/IEC 61620/ASTM D924	IEC 60247/ASTM D924	ASTM D924	IEC 60247/ASTM D924
Density	ISO 3675/ISO 12185/ASTM D1298	ISO 3675/ASTM D1298	ASTM D1298	ISO 3675 ASTM D1298
DGA analysis	IEC 60567/ASTM D3612	CIGRE brochure 443	ASTM D2945/ASTM D3284/ASTM D3612	CIGRE brochure 443
Fire point	ISO 2592/ASTM D92	ISO 2592 ASTM D92	ASTM D92	ISO 2592 ASTM D92
Flash point	ISO 2719/ISO 2592/ASTM D92	ISO 2719 ISO 2592 ASTM D92	ASTM D92	ISO 2719 ISO 2592 ASTM D92
Furanic compounds	IEC 61198/ASTM D5837	ASTM D5837	ASTM D5837	ASTM D5837
Gassing tendency	IEC 60628/ASTM D2300/ASTM D6180	IEC 60628/ASTM D2300/ASTM D6180	ASTM D2300/ASTM D6180	IEC 60628/ASTM D2300/ASTM D6180
Interfacial tension	ISO 6295/ASTM D971	ASTM D971	ASTM D971	ASTM D971
Kinematic viscosity	ISO 3104/ASTM D445	ISO 3104	ASTM D445	ISO 3104
Kinematic viscosity at low temperature	IEC 61868	-	-	-
Lightning impulse breakdown	IEC 60897/ASTM D3300	-	ASTM D3300	-
Oxidation stability	IEC 61125 IEC 62036/ASTM D2112/ASTM D2440	IEC 61125	-	-
PCB content	IEC 61619/ASTM D4059	-	ASTM D4059	-
Permittivity	IEC 60247/ASTM D924	IEC 60247/ASTM D924	ASTM D924	IEC 60247/ASTM D924
Pour point	ISO 3016/ASTM D97	ISO 3016	ASTM D97	ISO 3016
Refractive index	ISO 5661	ISO 5661	-	ISO 5661
Resistivity	IEC 60247/ASTM D1169	IEC 60247/ASTM D97	ASTM D1169	IEC 60247/ASTM D97
Specific heat	ASTM D2766	-	ASTM D2766	-
Stray gassing	CIGRE brochure 296	-	-	-
Thermal conductivity	ASTM D2717	-	ASTM D2717	-
Thermal Expansion coefficient	ASTM D1903	-	ASTM D1903	-
Visual examination	ASTM D1524	-	ASTM D1524	-
Water content	IEC 60814/ASTM D1533	IEC 60814/ASTM D1533	ASTM D1533	IEC 60814 ASTM D1533

ASTM, American Society for Testing and Materials; CIGRE, Council on Large Electric Systems; DGA, dissolved gas analysis; IEC, International Electrotechnical Commission; ISO, International Organization for Standardization; PCB, polychlorinated biphenyl.

5. Conclusions

This review summarizes the main physicochemical diagnostics techniques and demonstrates their usefulness in transformers. The critical nature of transformers and the recognition that they need continuous maintenance and a thorough understanding of multiple potential failure processes has raised the importance of dielectric fluid analysis to the forefront. This has been driven by the need to obtain better and faster analyses and a better methodology of defining the health of the asset. These techniques can be summarized as follows:

- HPLC is effective in the separation, detection and quantification of the furaldehydes produced as degradation by-products of paper.
- GC-MS, the gas chromatography stage separates the various gaseous species, by preferential attraction to a feed column, prior to them being injected into a mass spectrometer for identification and quantification.
- FTIR, this technique makes uses of the resonant vibrational frequencies of molecules to identify the structural groupings within a material. Its potential for characterizing the degree of degradation of oil/paper insulation is also emphasized.
- The dissolved decay products uses a spectrophotometer to evaluate the absorbance curve of insulating fluids in the visible spectrum. The numerical integration of the area below the absorbance curves permits the relative content of dissolved oxidation decay products.
- The Turbidity utilizes a ratio turbidimeter to evaluate the degree of contamination by solid particles in suspension produced either from external sources such as varnish and metallic particles from the materials used in transformers or internal chemical reactions such as oxidation. The IFT is affected by certain contaminants such as soaps, paints, varnishes, and oxidation products present in the oil. While IFT measurements require trained person and some precautions as mentioned in the ASTM D971 to perform, the measurements turbidity is very simple and quick.
- Methanol is a promising chemical marker for early-stage paper degradation of in-service transformer. This marker could permit an easier estimation of the end-of-life of the transformer.
- Free radicals measurement is possible by using reactive free radical reagent, 2,2-diphenyl-1-picrylhydrazyl (DPPH) added in oil.

The diagnostic methods presented in this review are usually applied to the mineral oil and standard insulating paper. However, currently there is considerable effort to establish diagnostic standards for biodegradable oil and thermally upgraded paper. As part of an overall maintenance strategy, these tests might therefore enhance the effectiveness of predictive maintenance procedures. This allows maintenance planners to make the best use of maintenance and replacement budgets, allocating funds to high-risk units.

Author Contributions: All authors contributed equally to the reported research and writing of the paper.

Conflicts of Interest: The authors declare no conflict of interest.

Abbreviations

The following abbreviations are used in this manuscript:

CIGRE	International Council of Large Electric Systems
ISO	International Organization for Standardization
ASTM	American Society for Testing and Materials
ASTM D	American Society for Testing and Materials Designation
IEC	International Electrotechnical Commission
IFT	Interfacial tension
AN	Acid number
LV	Low voltage
HV	high voltage
2FAL	2-furfuraldehyde

DP	Degree of polymerization
DP*v*	Degree of polymerization value
TDCG	Total dissolved combustible gas
TU	Thermal upgraded
DDP	Dissolved decay products
DDPH	2,2-Diphenyl-1-picrylhydrazyl
a.u.	Arbitrary unit
NTU	Nephelometric turbidity unit
VDE	Verband der Elektrotechnik, Elektronik, Informationstechnik
HPLC	High performance liquid chromatograph
FTIR	Fourier transform infrared spectroscopy
DGA	Dissolved gas analysis
NIR	Near infrared
GC-MS	Gas chromatography-mass spectrometry
GPC	Gel permeation chromatography
UMR	Unité Mixte de Recherche
CNRS	Centre National de la Recherche Scientifique
ViAHT	VIeillissement de l'Appareillage à Haute Tension
KF	Karl Fisher
DBPC	2,6-Di-*tert*-butyl-paracresol
DBP	2,6-Di-*tert*-butyl-phenol
OLTC	On load tap changer
UHF	Ultra-high frequency
WCPA	Active water content of paper
UV-vis	Ultraviolet and visible

References

1. The Council on Large Electric Systems (CIGRE). *CIGRE Technical Brochure 248*; Economics of Transformer Management, CIGRE: Paris, France, 2004.
2. Boss, P.; Lorin, P.; Viscardi, A.; Harley, J.W.; Isecke, J. Economical aspects and experiences of power transformer on-line monitoring. In *CIGRE Session 2000*; CIGRE: Paris, France, 2000.
3. Chakravorti, S.; Dey, D.; Chatterjee, B. *Recent Trends in the Condition Monitoring of Transformers: Theory, Implementation and Analysis*; Springer-Verlag: London, UK, 2013.
4. Fetherston, F.; Finlay, B. Power transformer condition assessment-the second century and beyond. In Proceedings of the Australasian Universities Power Engineering Conference (AUPEC), Perth, Australia, 23–26 September 2001.
5. Fofana, I.; Zié, Y.; Farzaneh, M. *Recent Advances in Dielectric Materials: Dielectric Response Methods for Diagnostics of Power Equipment*; Nova Science Publishers Inc.: New York, NY, USA, 2009.
6. Fofana, I.; Hadjadj, Y. Review of Electrical Diagnostic Techniques for Assessing Insulation condition in Aged Transformers. *Energies* **2016**. submitted.
7. The American Society for Testing and Materials (ASTM). *Standard Test Method for ASTM Color of Petroleum Products (ASTM Color Scale)*; ASTM D1500-12; ASTM International: West Conshohocken, PA, USA, 2012.
8. The American Society for Testing and Materials (ASTM). *Standard Test Method for Color of Transparent Liquids (Gardner Color Scale)*; ASTM D1544-04; ASTM International: West Conshohocken, PA, USA, 2010.
9. Hadjadj, Y.; Fofana, I.; Sabau, J.; Briosso, E. Assessing insulating oil degradation by means of turbidity and UV/VIS spectrophotometry measurements. *IEEE Trans. Dielectr. Electr. Insul.* **2015**, *22*, 2653–2660.
10. The American Society for Testing and Materials (ASTM). *Standard Test Method for Visual Examination of Used Electrical Insulating Liquids in the Field*; ASTM D1524-15; ASTM International: West Conshohocken, PA, USA, 2015.
11. CIGRE Technical Brochure 157. In *Effect of Particles on Transformer Dielectric Strength*; Final Report of CIGRE SC 12; WG 17 (Particles in Oil); CIGRE: Paris, France, 2000.
12. CIGRE Working Group A2.34. *Guide for Transformer Maintenance*; CIGRE Report ISBN: 978-2-85873-134-3; CIGRE: Paris, France, 2011.
13. Sokolov, V.; Laport, J.; Harley, J.; Goosen, P.; Guuinin, P. *CIGRE Technical Brochure 227*; Life Management Techniques for Power Transformers, Final Report of CIGRE SC A2 WG 18; CIGRE: Paris, France, 2002.

14. Miners, K. Particles and Moisture Effect on Dielectric Strength of Transformer Oil using VDE Electrodes. *IEEE Trans. Power Appar. Syst.* **1982**, *PAS-101*, 751–756. [CrossRef]

15. Wang, Z.D.; Liu, Q.; Wang, X.; Yi, X.; Jarman, P.; Wilson, G.; Dyer, P. *Ester Insulating Liquids for Power Transformers*; CIGRE session A2-209; CIGRE: Paris, France, 2012.

16. Wang, X.; Wang, Z.D.; Noakhes, J. Motion of conductive particles and the effect on AC breakdown strengths of esters. In Proceedings of the 2011 IEEE International Conference on Dielectric Liquids (ICDL), Trondheim, Norway, 26–30 June 2011; pp. 1–4.

17. Sarathi, R.; Archana, M. Investigation of partial discharge activity by a conducting particle in transformer oil under harmonic AC voltages adopting UHF technique. *IEEE Trans. Dielectr. Electr. Insul.* **2012**, *19*, 1514–1520. [CrossRef]

18. International Electrotechnical Commission (IEC). *Mineral Insulating Oils in Electrical Equipment—Supervision and Maintenance Guidance (Annex B)*; IEC 60422:2005; IEC: Geneva, Switzerland, 2005.

19. Oommen, T.V.; Petrie, E.M. Particle Contamination Levels in Oil-Filled Large Power Transformers. *IEEE Trans. Power Appar. Syst.* **1983**, *PAS-102*, 1459–1465. [CrossRef]

20. Ferguson, R.; Lobeiras, A.; Sabau, J. Suspended particles in the liquid insulation of aging power transformers. *IEEE Electr. Insul. Mag.* **2002**, *18*, 17–23. [CrossRef]

21. Mehanna, N.; Jaber, A.; Oweimreen, G.; Abulkibash, A. Assessment of dibenzyl disulfide and other oxidation inhibitors in transformer mineral oils. *IEEE Trans. Dielectr. Electr. Insul.* **2014**, *21*, 1095–1099. [CrossRef]

22. IEC. *Detection and Determination of Specified Anti-Oxidant Additives in Insulating Oils*IEC 60666:2010, 2nd ed.; IEC: Geneva, Switzerland, 2010.

23. Facilities Instructions, Standards and Techniques (FIST) Volume 3–31, Transformer Diagnostics. June 2003. Available online: https://www.usbr.gov/power/data/fist/fist3_31/fist3-31.pdf (accessed on 3 February 2016).

24. Arakelian, V.G.; Fofana, I. Water in Oil Filled High Voltage Equipment. Part I: States, Solubility and Equilibrium in Insulating Materials. *IEEE Electr. Insul. Mag.* **2007**, *23*, 15–27. [CrossRef]

25. Webb, M. Water in oils. In Proceedings of IEE Colloquium on an Engineering Review of Liquid Insulation, London, UK, 7 January 1997; pp. 2/1–2/6.

26. CIGRE Working Group A2.30. *Moisture Equilibrium and Moisture Migration within Transformer Insulation Systems*; CIGRE Report ISBN:978-2-85873-036-0; CIGRE: Paris, France, 2008.

27. IEC 60814. In *Insulating Liquids Oil-Impregnated Paper and Pressboard: Determination of Water by Automatic Coulometric Karl Fischer Titration*; IEC: Geneva, Switzerland, 1997.

28. Arakelian, V.G.; Fofana, I. Water in Oil Filled High Voltage Equipment. Part II: Water Content as Physico-chemical Tools for Insulation Condition Diagnosis. *IEEE Electr. Insul. Mag.* **2007**, *23*, 15–24. [CrossRef]

29. Du, Y.; Zahn, M.; Lesieutre, B.C.; Mamishev, A.V. Moisture equilibrium in transformer paper-oil systems. *IEEE Electr. Insul. Mag.* **1999**, *15*, 11–20. [CrossRef]

30. Oommen, T.V. Moisture equilibrium charts for transformer insulation drying practice. *IEEE Trans. Power App. Syst.* **1984**, *PAS-103*, 3063–3067. [CrossRef]

31. CIGRE Brochure 436. In *Experiences in Service with New Insulating Liquids*; CIGRE WG A2-35; CIGRE: Paris, France, 2010.

32. Fofana, I. 50 Years in the Development of Insulating Liquids. *IEEE Electr. Insul. Mag.* **2013**, *29*, 13–25. [CrossRef]

33. Davydov, V.G.; Roizman, O. Moisture assessment in power transformers: Lessons learned. Available online: http://www.vaisala.com/Vaisala%20Documents/Vaisala%20News%20Articles/VN160/VN160_AllPages.pdf (accessed on 3 February 2016).

34. Betie, A.; Meghnefi, F.; Fofana, I.; Yeo, Z.; Ezzaidi, H. On the feasibility of aging and moisture of oil impregnated paper insulation discrimination from dielectric response measurements. *IEEE Trans. Dielectr. Electr. Insul.* **2015**, *22*, 2176–2184. [CrossRef]

35. Saha, T.K.; Purkait, P. Understanding the impacts of moisture and thermal aging on transformer's insulation by dielectric response and molecular weight measurements. *IEEE Trans. Dielectr. Electr. Insul.* **2008**, *15*, 568–582. [CrossRef]

36. The American Society for Testing and Materials (ASTM). *Standard Test Method for Analysis of Gases Dissolved in Electrical Insulating Oil by Gas Chromatography*; ASTM D3612-02; ASTM International: West Conshohocken, PA, USA, 2009.

37. The Institute of Electrical and Electronics Engineers (IEEE) Standard. *IEEE Guide for the Interpretation of Gases Generated in Oil-Immersed Transformers—Section 1.2 Limitations*; C57.104; IEEE: Piscataway, NJ, USA, 1991.

38. *IEEE Guide for the Detection and Determination of Generated Gases in Oil-Immersed Transformers and Their Relation to the Serviceability of the Equipment*; ANSI/IEEE Std. C57.104-1978; IEEE: Piscataway, NJ, USA, 1978.

39. Ghalkhani, M.; Fofana, I.; Bouaicha, A.; Hemmatjou, H. Influence of aging byproducts on the gassing tendency of transformer oils. In Proceedings of the 2012 Annual Report Conference on Electrical Insulation and Dielectric Phenomena (CEIDP), Montreal, QC, Canada, 14–17 October 2012; pp. 870–873.

40. Dornenburg, E.; Strittmatter, W. Monitoring oil cooled transformers by gas analysis. *Brown Boveri Rev.* **1974**, *61*, 238–247.

41. Rogers, R.R. IEEE and IEC codes to interpret incipient faults in transformers, using gas in oil analysis. *IEEE Trans. Electr. Insul.* **1978**, *13*, 349–354. [CrossRef]

42. Duval, M. Fault gases formed in oil-filled breathing EHV power transformers: The interpretation of gas analysis data. IEEE Paper No. C74 476-8. In Proceedings of IEEE Summer Meeting, Anaheim, CA, USA, 14–19 July 1974.

43. Lewand, L. Techniques for Interpretation of Data for DGA from Transformers. In Proceedings of IEEE/PES Transformers Committee Meeting, Montreal, QC, Canada, 26 October 2006.

44. Muller, R.; Potthoff, K.; Soldner, K. The analysis of gases dissolved in the oil as a means of monitoring transformers and detecting incipient faults. Paper 12-02. In Proceedings of CIGRE 1970 Session, Paris, France, 24 August–2 September 1970.

45. Carbonara, J.; Lynch, M.; Hunt, M.; Brazil, J. The transformer gas analyzer—A practical expert system for the diagnosis of operational faults in electrical transformers. In Proceedings of the American Power Conference, Chicago, IL, USA, 26 April 1994; Part I. Volume 56, pp. 342–347.

46. Barraclough, B.; Bayley, E.; Davies, I.; Robinson, K.; Rogers, R.R.; Shanks, E. CEGB experience of the analysis of dissolved gas in transformer oil for the detection of incipient faults. In Proceedings of the IEE Conference on Diagnostic Testing of High Voltage Power Apparatus in Service, London, UK, 6–8 March 1973.

47. Pugh, D.R. Advances in fault diagnosis by combustible gas analysis. In Proceedings of the Minutes of 41st International Conference of Doble Clients, Boston, MA, USA, 3–8 April 1974; pp. 10:1201–10:1208.

48. Church, J.O.; Haupert, T.J.; Jacob, F. Analyze incipient faults with dissolved gas Nomograph. *Electrical World* **1987**, *201*, 40–44.

49. Riese, C.E.; Stuart, J.D. A knowledge-engineering facility for building scientific expert systems. In *Artificial Intelligence Applications in Chemistry*; American Chemical Society: Washington, DC, USA, 1986; Volume 306, pp. 18–36.

50. Ding, X.; Yao, E.; Liu, Y.; Griffin, P.J. ANN based transformer fault diagnosis using gas-in-oil analysis. In Proceedings of the 57th American Power Conference, Chicago, IL, USA, 18–20 April 1995.

51. Miranda, V.; Castro, A.R.G. Improving the IEC table for transformer failure diagnosis with knowledge extraction from neural networks. *IEEE Trans. Power Deliv.* **2005**, *20*, 2509–2516. [CrossRef]

52. Lamontagne, D.R. An artifical neural network approach to transformer dissolved gas analysis and problem notification at Arizona public service. In Proceedings of the EPRI Substation Equipment Diagnostics Conference XIV, San Diego, CA, USA, 16–19 July 2006.

53. International Electrotechnical Commission. *Mineral oil-filled electrical equipment in service—Guidance on the interpretation of dissolved and free gases analysis, IEC 60599*; IEC: Geneva, Switzerland, 2015.

54. McGrail, A.J.; Gulski, E.; Allan, D.; Birtwhistle, D.; Blackburn, T.R.; Groot, E.R.S. Data mining techniques to assess the condition of high voltage electrical plant. In Proceedings of International Conference on Large High Voltage Electric Systems, CIGRE Session No. 39, paper 12-02, Paris, France, 25–30 August 2002.

55. Mansour, D.E.A. A new graphical technique for the interpretation of dissolved gas analysis in power transformers. In Proceedings of the 2012 Annual Report Conference on Electrical Insulation and Dielectric Phenomena (CEIDP), Montreal, QC, Canada, 14–17 October 2012; pp. 195–198.

56. Akbari, A.; Setayeshmehr, A.; Borsi, H.; Gockenbach, E.; Fofana, I. Intelligent Agent-based System using Dissolved Gas Analysis to Detect Incipient Faults in Power Transformers. *IEEE Electr. Insul. Mag.* **2010**, *26*, 28–41. [CrossRef]

57. Duval, M.; Lamarre, L. The Duval pentagon—A new complementary tool for the interpretation of dissolved gas analysis in transformers. *IEEE Electr. Insul. Mag.* **2014**, *30*, 9–12.

58. Hepburn, D.M.; Shields, A.J.; Kemp, I.J. High voltage plant monitoring through oil/paper analysis. In Proceedings of the Eighth International Conference on Dielectric Materials, Measurements and Applications, Edinburgh, UK, 17–21 September 2000; pp. 218–223.

59. Imad, U.K.; Wang, Z.; Cotton, I.; Northcote, S. Dissolved gas analysis of alternative fluids for power transformers. *IEEE Electr. Insul. Mag.* **2007**, *23*, 5–14. [CrossRef]

60. Jovalekic, M.; Vukovic, D.; Tenbohlen, S. Dissolved gas analysis of alternative dielectric fluids under thermal and electrical stress. In Proceedings of the 2011 IEEE International Conference on Dielectric Liquids (ICDL), Trondheim, Norway, 26–30 June 2011; pp. 1–4.

61. CIGRE. CIGRE Brochure 443. In *DGA in Non-Mineral Oils and Load Tap Changers and Improved DGA Diagnosis Criteria, WG D1.32*; CIGRE: Paris, France, 2010.

62. Sharma, N.K.; Tiwari, P.K.; Sood, Y.R. Review of Artificial Intelligence Techniques Application to Dissolved Gas Analysis on Power Transformer. *Int. J. Comput. Electr. Eng.* **2011**, *3*, 577–582. [CrossRef]

63. Myers, S.D.; Kelly, J.J.; Parrish, R.H. *Transformer Maintenance Guide*; Transformer Maintenance Institute: Akron, OH, USA, 1991.

64. American Society for Testing and Materials (ASTM). *Standard Test Method for Interfacial Tension of Oil against Water by the Ring Method*. D 971. Available online: http://www.biolinscientific.com/zafepress.php?url=%2Fpdf%2FAttension%2FApplication%20Notes%2FAT_AN_10_astm.pdf (accessed on 12 February 2016).

65. FIST Volume 3–5, Maintenance of Liquid Insulation: Mineral Oils and Askarels, 1992. Available online: http://www.worldcat.org/title/maintenance-of-liquid-insulation-mineral-oils-and-askarels/oclc/45032750 (accessed on 10 January 2016).

66. Gray, I.A.R. A Guide to Transformer Oil Analysis. Available online: http://www.satcs.co.za/Transformer_Oil_Analysis.pdf (accessed on 10 November 2014).

67. Industry news. Punctured Rubber Bladders Detected by New ASTM Oil Test. *IEEE Electr. Insul. Mag.* **2006**, *22*, 55. Available online: http://www.insoil.ca/video/Industry%20News(3).pdf?SID=f5c2662d5f5da6a739a858eab7ab92ac (accessed on 10 January 2016).

68. The American Society for Testing and Materials (ASTM). *Test Method for Determination of the Relative Content Of Dissolved Decay Products in Mineral Insulating Oils by Spectrophotometry*; ASTM D6802-02; ASTM International: West Conshohocken, PA, USA, 2010.

69. Shroff, D.H.; Stannett, A.W. A review of paper aging in power transformers. *IEEE Proc. C* **1985**, *132*, 312–319. [CrossRef]

70. Emsley, A.M.; Stevens, G.C. Review of chemical indicators of degradation of cellulosic electrical paper insulation in oil-filled transformers. *IEE Proc. Sci. Meas. Technol.* **1994**, *141*, 324–334. [CrossRef]

71. The American Society for Testing and Materials (ASTM). *Standard Test Method for Measurement of Average Viscometric Degree of Polymerization of New and Aged Electrical Papers and Boards*; ASTM D4243-99; ASTM International: West Conshohocken, PA, USA, 2009.

72. *Measurement of the Average Viscometric Degree of Polymerization of New and Aged Cellulosic Electrically Insulating Materials*; IEC 60450; IEC: Geneva, Switzerland, 2007.

73. Gilbert, R.; Jalbert, J.; Duchesne, S.; Tétreault, P.; Morin, B.; Denos, Y. Kinetics of the production of chain-end groups and methanol from the depolymerization of cellulose during the aging of paper/oil systems. Part 2: Thermally-upgraded insulating papers. *Cellulose* **2010**, *17*, 253–269. [CrossRef]

74. Arroyo-Fernandez, O.H.; Fofana, I.; Jalbert, J.; Ryadi, M. Relationships between methanol marker and mechanical performance of electrical insulation papers for power transformers under accelerated thermal aging. *IEEE Trans. Dielectr. Electr. Insul.* **2015**, *22*, 3625–3632. [CrossRef]

75. Tamura, R.; Anetai, H.; Ishii, T.; Kawamura, T. Diagnostic of aging deterioration of insulating paper. *JIEE Proc. Pub. A* **1981**, *101*, 30.

76. Burton, P.J.; Graham, J.; Hall, A.C.; Laver, J.A.; Oliver, A.J. Recent developments by CEGB to improve the prediction and monitoring of transformer performance. In Proceedings of International Conference on Large High Voltage Electric Systems, CIGRE, paper 12-09, Paris, France, 29 August–6 September 1984.

77. De Pablo, A. Furfural and aging: How are they related. In Proceedings of the IEE Colloquium on Insulating Liquids (Ref. No. 1999/119), Leatherhead, UK, 27 May 1999; pp. 5/1–5/4.

78. Norazhar, A.B.; Abu-Siada, A.; Islam, S. A review on chemical diagnosis techniques for transformer paper insulation degradation. In Proceedings of The Australasian Universities Power Engineering Conference, Hobart, Australia, 29 September–3 October 2013.

79. Lewand, L.R. Practical experience gained from furanic compound analysis. In Proceedings of the 73rd Annual International Doble Client Conference, Boston, MA, USA, 8–14 April 2006.

80. Jalbert, J.; Gilbert, R.; Denos, Y.; Gervais, P. Chemical markers for the determination of power transformer insulating life, a step forward. Paper IM-3. In Proceeding of the 76th Annual International Doble Client Conference, Boston, MA, USA, 29 April–3 May 2009.

81. Jalbert, J.; Gilbert, R.; Denos, Y.; Gervais, P. Methanol: A Novel Approach to Power Transformer Asset Management. *IEEE Trans. Power Deliv.* **2012**, *27*, 514–520. [CrossRef]

82. Schaut, A.; Eeckhoudt, S. Identification of early stage paper degradation by methanol. Paper A2-107. In Proceedings of CIGRE 2012, Paris, France, 26–31 August 2012.

83. Jalbert, J.; Gilbert, R.; Tétreault, P.; Morin, B.; Lessard-Déziel, D. Identification of a chemical indicator of the rupture of 1,4-β-glycosidic bonds of cellulose in an oil-impregnated insulating paper system. *Cellulose* **2007**, *14*, 295–309. [CrossRef]

84. Schaut, A.; Autru, S.; Eeckhoudt, S. Applicability of methanol as new marker for paper degradation in power transformers. *IEEE Trans. Dielectr. Electr. Insul.* **2011**, *18*, 533–540. [CrossRef]

85. Robinson, N. Liquid chromatography and its application in transformer oil analysis. *Wearcheck Technical Bulletin* **2012**, *54*. Available online: http://www.wearcheck.co.za/blog/item/35-liquid-chromatography-and-its-application-in-transformer-oil-analysis (accessed on 25 March 2016).

86. Emsley, A.M.; Xiao, X.; Heywood, R.J.; Ali, M. Degradation of cellulosic insulation in power transformers. Part 2: Formation of furan products in insulating oil. *IEE Proc. Sci. Meas. Technol.* **2000**, *147*, 110–114. [CrossRef]

87. Burton, P.J.; Carballiera, M.; Duval, M.; Fuller, J.; Graham, C.W.; De Pablo Samat, J.; Spicar, E. Applications of liquid chromatography to the analysis of electrical insulating materials. In Proceedings of the CIGRE International Conference on Large High Voltage Electrical Systems, Paris, France, 28 August–3 September 1998.

88. Dong, M.W. *Modern HPLC for Practicing Scientists*; John Wiley & Sons, Inc.: Hoboken, NJ, USA, 2006.

89. Lütke, H.; Höhlein, I.; Kachler, A.J. Transformer aging research on furanic compounds dissolved in insulating oil. Paper 15-302. In Proceedings of the CIGRE International Conference on Large High Voltage Electrical Systems, Paris, France, 25–30 August 2002.

90. Łojewska, J.; Miśkowiec, P.; Łojewski, T.; Proniewicz, L.M. Cellulose oxidative and hydrolytic degradation: In situ FTIR approach. *J. Polym. Degrad. Stab.* **2005**, *88*, 512–520. [CrossRef]

91. Saha, T.K.; Darveniza, M.; Hill, D.J.T.; Le, T.T. Electrical and chemical diagnostics of transformers insulation. B. Accelerated aged insulation samples. *IEEE Trans. Power Deliv.* **1997**, *12*, 1555–1561. [CrossRef]

92. Krawiec, S.; Leath, S. Improved heat transfer capability using *iso*-paraffins *versus* naphthenics in transformers. August 2011. Available online: http://lubricants.petro-canada.ca/pdf/LUB2403E-ImprovedHeatTransfer.pdf (accessed on 22 February 2016).

93. Paul, G.; Chopkar, M.; Manna, I.; Das, P.K. Techniques for measuring the thermal conductivity of nanofluids: A review. *Renew. Sustain. Energy Rev.* **2010**, *14*, 1913–1924. [CrossRef]

94. American Society for Testing and Materials (ASTM). *Standard Test Method for Thermal Conductivity, Thermal Diffusivity and Volumetric Heat Capacity of Engine Coolants and Related Fluids by Transient Hot Wire Liquid Thermal Conductivity Method*; ASTM D7896-14; ASTM International: West Conshohocken, PA, USA, 2014.

95. American Society for Testing and Materials (ASTM). *Standard Test Method for Specific Heat of Liquids and Solids*; ASTM D2766-95; ASTM International: West Conshohocken, PA, USA, 2009.

96. Loiselle, L.; Fofana, I.; Sabau, J.; Magdaleno-Adame, S.; Olivares-Galvan, J.C. Comparative Studies of the Stability of Various Fluids under Electrical Discharge and Thermal Stresses. *IEEE Trans. Dielectr. Electr. Insul.* **2015**, *22*, 2491–2499.

97. Evans, J.S. The ups and downs of viscosity. *Wearcheck Technical Bulletin* **2007**, *38*. Available online: http://www.wearcheck.co.za/downloads/bulletins/bulletin/tech38.pdf (accessed on 10 February 2016).

98. American Society for Testing and Materials (ASTM). *Standard Test Method for Pour Point of Petroleum Products*; ASTM D97-16; ASTM International: West Conshohocken, PA, USA, 2016.

99. American Society for Testing and Materials (ASTM). *Standard Test Method for Density, Relative Density (Specific Gravity), or API Gravity of Crude Petroleum and Liquid Petroleum Products by Hydrometer Method;* ASTM D1298-99; ASTM International: West Conshohocken, PA, USA, 1999.

100. American Society for Testing and Materials (ASTM). *Standard Terminology Relating to Electrical Insulating Liquids and Gases;* ASTM D2864-10e1; ASTM International: West Conshohocken, PA, USA, 2010.

101. Lewand, L.R. The Corrosive Sulphur in transformers and transformer oil. In Proceedings of the 69th Annual International Doble Client Conference, Boston, MA, USA, 7–12 April 2002.

102. Li, J.; He, Z.; Bao, L.; Yang, L. Influences of Corrosive Sulfur on Copper Wires and Oil-paper Insulation in Transformers. *Energies* **2011**, *4*, 1563–1573. [CrossRef]

103. Wiklund, P.; Levin, M.; Pahlavanpour, B. Copper dissolution and metal passivators in insulating oil. *IEEE Electr. Insul. Mag.* **2007**, *23*, 6–14. [CrossRef]

104. N'cho, J.S.; Fofana, I.; Beroual, A.; Aka-Ngnui, T.; Sabau, J. Aged Oils Reclamation: Facts and Arguments based on Laboratory Studies. *IEEE Trans. Dielectr. Electr. Insul. (TDEI)* **2012**, *19*, 1583–1592. [CrossRef]

105. Robinson, N. Monitoring oil degradation with infrared spectroscopy. *Wearcheck Technical Bulletin* **2000**, (Issue 18). Available online: http://www.wearcheck.com.gh/downloads/bulletins/bulletin/tech18.pdf (accessed on 10 February 2016).

106. Lara-Lee Lumley, S. CH$_4$ can be worth so much more: the role of oil analysis in gas engine reliability (part 2). *Wearcheck Technical Bulletin* **2015**, (Issue 61). Available online: http://www.wearcheck.co.za/shared/Technical%20Bulletin%2061%20LR.pdf (accessed on 10 February 2016).

107. Hadjadj, Y.; Fofana, I.; van der Voort, F.R.; Bussieres, D. Potential of Determining Moisture Content in Mineral Insulating Oil by FTIR Spectroscopy. *IEEE Electr. Insul. Mag.* **2016**, *32*, 34–39. [CrossRef]

108. van de Voort, F.R.; Tavassoli-Kafran, M.H.; Curtis, J.M. Stoichiometric determination of moisture in edible oils by Mid-FTIR Spectroscopy. *Anal. Chim. Acta* **2016**, *918*, 1–7. [CrossRef] [PubMed]

109. Gray, I.A.R. Guide for Polychlorinated Biphenyl (PCB) Management of Insulating oil in South Africa. Available online: http://www.wearcheck.co.za/downloads/PCB%20information%202004.pdf (accessed on 22 February 2016).

110. McMaster, M. *GC/MS: A Practical User's Guide*, 2nd ed.; John Wiley & Sons, Inc.: Hoboken, NJ, USA, 2008.

111. Hübschmann, H.-J. *Handbook of GC/MS: Fundamentals and Applications;* Wiley-VCH Verlag GmbH & Co. KGaA: Weinheim, Germany, 2015.

112. Perkampus, H.H. *UV-vis Spectroscopy and Its Applications;* Springer Verlag: Berlin, Germany; London, UK, 1992.

113. Kortüm, G. *Kolometrie, Photometrie und Spektrometrie, Kap 1.5,4. Aufl;* Springer: Berlin, Germany, 1962.

114. Fofana, I.; Bouaicha, A.; Farzaneh, M.; Sabau, J.; Bussières, D. Decay Products in the Liquid Insulation of Power Transformers. *IET Electr. Power Appl.* **2010**, *4*, 177–184. [CrossRef]

115. N'cho, J.S.; Beroual, A.; Fofana, I.; Aka-Ngnui, T.; Sabau, J. Verification of Oil Reclamation Process by Turbidity and Spectrophotometry Measurements. *J. Energy Power Eng.* **2012**, *6*, 703–712.

116. Rouessac, F.; Rouessac, A.; Cruché, D.; Duverger-Arfuso, C.; Martel, A. *Analyse Chimique: Méthodes et Techniques Instrumentales*, 7th ed.; Dunod: Paris, France, 2009.

117. Bakar, N.A.; Abu-Siada, A. A novel method of measuring transformer oil interfacial tension using UV-Vis spectroscopy. *IEEE Electr. Insul. Mag.* **2016**, *32*, 7–13. [CrossRef]

118. Lai, S.P.; Siada, A.A.; Islam, S.M.; Lenco, G. Correlation between UV-vis spectral response and furan measurement of transformer oil. In Proceedings of the 2008 International Conference on Condition Monitoring and Diagnosis, Beijing, China, 21–24 April 2008.

119. Abu-Siada, A.; Lai, S.P.; Islam, S.M. A Novel Fuzzy-Logic Approach for Furan Estimation in Transformer Oil. *IEEE Trans. Power Deliv.* **2012**, *27*, 469–474. [CrossRef]

120. Sin Pin, L.; Abu-Siada, A.; Islam, S. Furan measurement in transformer oil by UV-vis spectral response using Fuzzy Logic. In Proceedings of the 5th International Conference on Electrical and Computer Engineering ICECE 2008, Dhaka, Bangladesh, 20–22 December 2008.

121. Tanaka, J. Free radicals in electrical insulation. In Proceedings of the 19th Symposium of Electrical Insulating Materials, Osaka, Japan, 13–15 June 1986.

122. Abdolall, K. Feasibility of free radical detection for condition assessment of oil/paper insulation of transformers. In Proceedings of the Conference Record of the 2008 IEEE International Symposium on Electrical Insulation (ISEI), Vancouver, BC, Canada, 9–12 June 2008; pp. 182–186.

123. Pryor, W.A. *Introduction to Free Radical Chemistry*; Prentice Hall: Upper Saddle River, NJ, USA, 1966.

124. Fofana, I.; Sabau, J.; Betie, A. Measurement of the relative Free radical content of Insulating Oils of Petroleum Origin. *Energies* **2015**, *8*, 7690–7702. [CrossRef]

125. Standard Methods. *Standard Methods for the Examination of Water and Wastewater*, 19th ed.; American Public Health Association: Washington, DC, USA, 1995.

126. Franson, M.H.; Eaton, A.D.; Clesceri, L.S.; Greenberg, A.E., Eds.; *American Public Health Association, AWWA, and Water Environment Federation*; Port City Press: Baltimore, MD, USA, 1995.

127. American Society for Testing and Materials (ASTM). *Standard Test Method for Measurement of Turbidity in Mineral Insulating Oil of Petroleum Origin (Withdrawn 2012)*; ASTM D6181-03; ASTM International: West Conshohocken, PA, USA, 2005.

128. Sabau, J.; Sadar, M. Determination of solid suspensions in electrical insulating oils by turbidimetry. In Proceedings of SAIT/CEA Technology Symposium, Calgary, AB, Canada, 11–12 June 1998.

129. Yamagata, N.; Miyagi, K.; Oe, E. Diagnosis of thermal degradation for thermally upgraded paper in mineral oil. In Proceedings of the 2008 International Conference on Condition Monitoring and Diagnosis, Beijing, China, 21–24 April 2008.

130. Moser, H.P.; Dahinden, V. *Transformerboard II: Properties and Application of Transformerboard of Different Fibres*; Scientia Electrica: Zurich, Switzerland, 1987.

131. Miyagi, K.; Oe, E.; Yamagata, N. Evaluation of Aging for Thermally Upgraded Paper in Mineral Oil. *J. Int. Counc. Electr. Eng.* **2011**, *1*, 181–187. [CrossRef]

132. Ul-Haq, S. Influence on moisture on dielectric strength in polyamide (aramid) paper. In Proceedings of the Annual Report Conference on Electrical Insulation and Dielectric Phenomena, Albuquerque, NM, USA, 19–22 October 2003; pp. 325–328.

133. Endoo, K.; Uwano, Y.; Hiraishi, K.; Oonuma, T.; Uemura, R. Improvement of dielectric strength on transformer winding using new aramid paper. *Electr. Eng. Jpn.* **1995**, *115*, 41–51. [CrossRef]

134. Filliben, S.A. New test method to evaluate the thermal aging of aramid materials. In Proceedings of the 30th Electrical Insulation Conference (EIC), Annapolis, MD, USA, 5–8 June 2011; pp. 449–453.

135. Song, I.K.; Lee, B.S. Hybrid insulation enables better transformer design. In *Transmission and Distribution World*; Korea Electric Power Research Institute: Changwon, Korea, 2005; Volume 57, pp. 71–77.

136. Kassi, K.S.; Fofana, I.; Meghnefi, F.; Yeo, Z. Impact of local overheating on conventional and hybrid insulations for power transformers. *IEEE Trans. Dielectr. Electr. Insul.* **2015**, *22*, 2543–2553.

137. *ASTM D7812-16, Standard Test Method for Tensile Testing of Aramid Paper*; ASTM International: West Conshohocken, PA, USA, 2016.

138. 3M™. Properties and Benefits of 3M™ Liquid-Filled Transformer Insulation. Available online: http://multimedia.3m.com/mws/media/1098968O/3m-liquid-filled-transformer-insulation-white-paper.pdf (accessed on 21 April 2016).

139. Bandara, K.; Ekanayake, C.; Saha, T.; Ma, H. Performance of Natural Ester as a Transformer Oil in Moisture-Rich Environments. *Energies* **2016**, *9*, 258. [CrossRef]

140. Lewand, L. Laboratory Testing of Natural Ester Dielectric Liquids. Available online: http://www.netaworld.org/sites/default/files/public/neta-journals/ChemPerWtr04.pdf (accessed on 5 March 2016).

141. American Society for Testing and Materials (ASTM). *Standard Specification for Natural (Vegetable Oil) Ester Fluids Used in Electrical Apparatus*; ASTM D6871-03; ASTM International: West Conshohocken, PA, USA, 2008.

142. American Society for Testing and Materials (ASTM). *Standard Specifications for Silicone Fluid Used for Electrical Insulation*; ASTM D4652-05; ASTM International: West Conshohocken, PA, USA, 2012.

143. IEC 61099. In *Insulating Liquids—Specifications for Unused Synthetic Organic Esters for Electrical Purposes*, 2nd ed.; IEC: Geneva, Switzerland, 2010; p. 28.

144. IEC 62770. In *Fluids for Electrotechnical Applications—Unused Natural Esters for Transformers and Similar Electrical Equipment*, 1st ed.; IEC: Geneva, Switzerland, 2013; p. 34.

145. IEC 60836. In *Specifications for Unused Silicone Insulating Liquids for Electrotechnical Purposes*, 3rd ed.; IEC: Geneva, Switzerland, 2015; p. 21.

146. IEEE C57.147-2008. In *Guide for Acceptance and Maintenance of Natural Ester Fluids in Transformers*; IEEE: Piscataway, NJ, USA, 2008.

147. IEEE C57.111-1989. In *Guide for Acceptance of Silicone Insulating Fluid and Its Maintenance in Transformers*; IEEE: Piscataway, NJ, USA, 1989.

148. IEEE C57.155-2014. In *Guide for Interpretation of Gases Generated in Natural Ester and Synthetic Ester Immersed Transformers*; IEEE: Piscataway, NJ, USA, 2014.
149. Muhamad, N.A.; Phung, B.T.; Blackburn, T.R. Application of common transformers faults diagnosis methods on biodegradable oil-filled transformers. *Electr. Eng.* **2012**, *94*, 207–216. [CrossRef]

Review

Electrical-Based Diagnostic Techniques for Assessing Insulation Condition in Aged Transformers

Issouf Fofana * and Yazid Hadjadj

Research Chair on the Aging of Power Network Infrastructure (ViAHT), Université du Québec à Chicoutimi, 555 Boulevard de l'université, Chicoutimi, QC G7H 2B1, Canada; yazid.hadjadj@uqac.ca
* Correspondence: ifofana@uqac.ca; Tel.: +1-418-545-5011

Academic Editor: Chunhua Liu
Received: 20 March 2016; Accepted: 8 August 2016; Published: 26 August 2016

Abstract: The condition of the internal cellulosic paper and oil insulation are of concern for the performance of power transformers. Over the years, a number of methods have been developed to diagnose and monitor the degradation/aging of the transformer internal insulation system. Some of this degradation/aging can be assessed from electrical responses. Currently there are a variety of electrical-based diagnostic techniques available for insulation condition monitoring of power transformers. In most cases, the electrical signals being monitored are due to mechanical or electric changes caused by physical changes in resistivity, inductance or capacitance, moisture, contamination or aging by-products in the insulation. This paper presents a description of commonly used and modern electrical-based diagnostic techniques along with their interpretation schemes.

Keywords: power transformers; diagnostic techniques; insulation condition; transformer aging; partial discharge (PD); return voltage (RV); dielectric response; dielectric dissipation factor (DDF); dielectric response analysis; mechanical or electrical integrity of the core and windings

---

1. Introduction

Power transformers, are indispensable components of power generation plants, transmission systems and large industrial plants. Composite oil/paper insulation systems have being used in these important machines for more than a century. Despite great strides in electrical equipment design in recent years, the Achilles heel in the equipment performance is still the insulation system. During service, the electrical insulation of transformer is subjected to several types of stresses (electrical, mechanical, thermal and environmental), some of them inter-related, occurring in different parts of the structure which degrade the insulation. As power transformers age, their internal insulation degrades, increasing the risk of failure. Insulation degradation/aging is recognized to be one of the major causes of transformer breakdown [1,2]. The weakest part the insulation system is the vulnerability to moisture content, oxygen, to excessive heat and mechanical stresses. When these elements are combined, the aging process is accelerated. When electrical equipment fails, more often than not, the fault can be traced back to defective insulation.

Since most installed power transformers are approaching the end of their design life, it is important to know, by means of suitable diagnostic tests, the condition of their insulation. Increasing requirements for appropriate tools allowing diagnosing power transformers non-destructively and reliably in the field have promoted the development of modern diagnostic techniques complementary to the classical insulation resistance (IR), power frequency dissipation factor (DF) and polarisation index measurements. During the last three decades, the understanding of oil-paper insulation degradation has significantly improved because of the development of several non-destructive techniques.

The life of the transformer being connected with that of its insulation, the evaluation of the transformer insulation is essential to assess the condition of the unit when new and after several years of in-use service. This evaluation necessarily involves both electrical and physicochemical techniques and diagnostic methods. It should be emphasized that it is very difficult to cover all those techniques in one paper. This review encompasses electrical-based diagnostic techniques for assessing insulation condition in aged transformers, while physicochemical-based diagnostic techniques are the concern of a companion paper published in this special issue [3]. Together with the physicochemical methods, the electrical-based diagnostic methods are very important for the condition monitoring or for studying the degradation of the insulation in power transformer.

In recent years, many research works have been undertaken to develop or improve the electrical-based diagnostic methods while the basic concept has stayed almost the same. Figure 1 summarizes the typical problems that may be detected with electrical-based test methods [2].

Type of Problem

	Diagnostic Technique	Magnetic Circuit Integrity	Magnetic Circuit Insulation	Winding Geometry	Winding/Bushing/OLTC Continuity	Winding/Bushing Insulation	Winding Turn to Turn Insulation
Basic Electrical	Winding ratio	●					
	Winding Resistance		●				
	Magnetisation current	●					●
	Capacitance and DF/PF			●	●	●	●
	Leakage Reactance				●		
	Insulation Resistance			●		●	
	Core Ground Test					●	
Advanced Electrical	Frequency Response of Stray Losses		●	●			
	Frequency Response Analysis	●			●	●	●
	Polarisation/ Depolarisation			●			
	Frequency Domain Spectroscopy			●			
	Recovery Voltage Method			●			
	Electrical Detection of PD	●	●				
	Acoustical Detection of PD	●	●				
	UHF Detection of PD	●	●				

Figure 1. Electrical Tests Diagnostic Matrix, based on the one proposed in [2]. OLTC: on load tap changer; DF: dissipation factor, PF: power factor; PD: partial discharge; UHF: ultra high frequency.

2. Traditional Electrical Diagnostic Techniques

The dielectric dissipation factor (DDF) at power frequency and breakdown strengths at both power frequency and lightning impulse, have been the most often controlled parameter describing the oil-paper's function as an insulant. When the oil-paper insulation ages in a transformer, these parameters do not change drastically. Very little systematic research had therefore been undertaken for condition monitoring or for studying the degradation of electrical insulation in power transformers until 1990 [2].

2.1. Breakdown Strength

The Alternative Current (AC) electric strength, also known as breakdown voltage at power frequency, is one of the most controlled parameters describing the liquid's function as an insulant. This parameter is strongly sensitive to the following factors [4]:

- Chemical makeup of the fluid;
- Temperature;
- Amount of contamination (impurities, moisture, etc.);
- Sampling and preparation conditions;

The AC electric strength, therefore, serves primarily to indicate the presence of contaminants such as water or particles [2]. New, dry and clean insulating fluids exhibit breakdown voltages higher than 70 kV for mineral oils, esters and 50 kV for silicone fluids [5,6], which can be reduced dramatically when solid particles and free and/or dissolved water are present [7]. Most of the breakdown voltage specifications for in-service transformers require a minimum of 30 kV with a 2.5 mm gap [8], when measured with disc electrodes. However, it should be emphasized that a high value does not necessarily indicate that the fluid is free of contaminants [4].

2.2. Static Electrification and Flow Electrification

Problems due to static electrification in power transformers have been reported by many utilities around the world since the 1970s [9,10]. The physicochemical process appearing at the oil-pressboard interface leads to an electrical double layer (EDL). This phenomenon is due to the formation of a EDL at the oil-pressboard interface [11].

Static electricity generation occurs in forced oil cooled power transformers due to the flows of oil through the surface of the pressboard. The flow of oil leads to charge separation at the oil-paper interfaces. During its motion, the oil acquires a positive or negative charge depending on the surface over which it travels [12,13]. If relaxation does not eliminate oil charges, and the charge accumulation at the insulating surfaces is high, static electrical fields can be produced, which may end in a static electrical discharge [12,14]. The combination of this static charge with impulse and switching surges may produce localized stresses of sufficient magnitude that they can initiate a catastrophic transformer failure [10]. The static charge is referred as static electrification but also known as flow or streaming electrification [9]. Many papers on flow electrification in transformers have been published to identify the various factors that influence this phenomenon. The most important ones are temperature, moisture, the oil flow rate, aging of oil, oil electrical charging tendency, and surface condition [10,15–18]. Some experimental measurements have reported that the overall flow electrification increases with temperature to a certain limit situated between 40 °C and 60 °C before decreasing [19]. Mas et al. [14], have shown that the temperature gradient influences the magnitude of the charge accumulated in the pressboard, but not the depth of the charge penetration. Oommen and Petrie [20], have reported that the electrostatic charge tendency of oil increases when the moisture content of the oil decreases. Studies have shown that the electrostatic charging tendency (ECT) increases as the oil flow increases [15]. It was reported also that the flow conditions—laminar or turbulent—also have a strong impact on the streaming current [21,22]. A direct relationship between ECT and aging was observed [23–25]. Sulfoxide compounds and hydrogen ions are identified as the prime compounds that increase ECT of mineral insulating oil [23]. In recent work, it was found that the dissolved decay products content and suspended particles are also contributing factors [26]. It was also demonstrated that the electrification current is affected by the quantity of free radicals present [27].

The influence of these parameters and the quantification of the charging tendency of insulating oil have been carried out by employing different experimental methodologies, developed in laboratories. One of the most commonly applied measurements is the mini static tester (MST) developed by Westinghouse Electric Corporation [28]. However, the MST protocol does not take into account a number of factors that can influence the ECT, such as the air and rate of injection [29]. This is why some modifications have been made by different authors to improve the accuracy of the protocol and ensure the reproducibility of measurements [30]. Other devices have been developed using a Couette charging apparatus where the fluid fills the Couette device consisting of rotating coaxial cylinders. The metal cylinder walls can be covered with insulating paper [16,31]. Kedzia [32] introduced an alternative method for testing the electrification of transformer oil based on a spinning disk in the liquid. Due to the simple construction and the small volume of oil needed, this method was recommended in a modified form by CIGRE [33]. Other than mineral oil, studies of ester behavior versus electrostatic hazard due to flow electrification have shown that even if ester oils increase the charge generation in comparison with mineral oil, the charge accumulation on the solid surface is not excessive [34]. To prevent static electrification, certain countermeasures have been worked out. The insulator edges are rounded and duct structures are designed so as to suppress turbulence and direct blow up of oil flow into the coils. In addition, flow speeds are limited [35]. In Japan, a method of suppressing charging tendency by using benzotriazole (BTA) as an insulating oil additive was developed [36,37]. It was confirmed that BTA suppresses not only flow electrification, but also copper sulphide generation [38].

Actually, the measurement of the ECT in power transformers is still as important as fifteen years ago, when research on the problems of static electrification started. Since ECT affects volume resistivities, partial discharges (PDs) and dielectric losses, a capacitive sensor was recently proposed to assess power transformer behaviour towards flow electrification and electrostatic hazard. This capacitive sensor is intended for online monitoring of the flow electrification hazards in transformers [39].

2.3. Capacitance and Dielectric Dissipation Factor (or Power Factor)

This test method, and its result, may be variously referred to by many terms such as loss factor, loss angle, dielectric loss angle (DLA), tanδ or tangent delta, δ, DDF, DF, power factor (PF), cosφ or cosθ. PF measurements relate mainly to the bushings of transformers. The DDF indicates the dielectric loss or the leakage current associated with watts loss of oil; thus the dielectric heating. Transformers aging by-products are mostly polar in nature and will affect conductivity as well as permittivity and capacitance. Any decrease in the resistivity results in an increase in the DDF/PF. The DDF/PF and capacitance are useful as a means of quality control, and as an indication of changes in quality resulting from contamination, aging and deterioration in service (damaged or short-circuited foil) or as a result of handling. The capacitance tends to increase with insulation degradation, poor impregnation methods and change of the geometry between windings. Higher capacitance implies higher permittivity, and hence worse condition of the insulation. The capacitance and DDF are the most common techniques for assessing the bushing condition. This test is normally performed at 10 kV for bushing on-site measurements. Bushings' capacitance and PF can also be monitored by measuring the leakage current through capacitance tap (where capacitance taps are available) [40,41].

The capacitance and DDF of a dielectric is a complex function of at least two variables—frequency and temperature, although moisture and pressure may be other physical variables. The test voltage characteristics and temperature must therefore be recorded. The DDF test results are to be compared to nameplate values or previous tests. An increase or decrease from reference values is an indication of the presence of [2]:

- contamination products such as moisture, carbon or other conducting matter, metal soaps caused by acids attacking transformer metals and oxidation byproducts; or
- deterioration of the insulation system.

Acceptable limits depend largely upon the type of equipment. For in-service oils, the limit is less than 0.5% at 25 °C [42]. If the PF is greater than 0.5% and less than 1.0%, further investigations are required; the oil may require treatment through three different processes (filtration, reclamation, reconditioning or re-refining [43]. If the PF is greater than 1.0% at 25 °C, the oil may cause failure of the transformer and immediate replacement or reclamation of the oil is required [44]. Above 2%, the oil should be removed from service and replaced because equipment failure is imminent. This oil can no longer be reclaimed.

2.4. Ratio and Winding Resistance Measurements

These tests are part of the tests applicable to liquid-immersed distribution, power, and regulating transformers mentioned in the standard IEEE Std C57.12.90-2010 [45]. The ratio test determines the ratio of the number of turns in the high voltage (HV) winding to that in the low voltage (LV) winding [46]. This test is useful to verify whether or not there are any shorted turns or open winding circuits. The measured ratio is 0.5% of the ratio of the rated voltage between windings, as specified on the transformer nameplate [45–48]. There are three accepted methods for performing the ratio test: the voltmeter method, the comparison method, and the ratio bridge [46].

Transformer winding resistance measurements are of fundamental importance as they address the calculation of the winding conductor I^2R losses, where I is the rated current of the winding in amperes, and R is the measured of Direct Current (DC) resistance of the winding [45]. This measurements is used also to determine the average winding temperatures at the end of a temperature rise test [45]. Because winding resistance varies with conductor temperature, from the change in resistance, the change in temperature can be deduced [49]. The winding resistance measurements are used as type test as well as routine test. It is also employed as base for assessing possible damage, including contact problems on the tap selector, contact problems on the diverter switch, broken conductors, broken parallel strands, shorted winding disks, shorted winding layers, poor bushing connections [2]. For subsequent comparison, the measurement temperature should be recorded and the resistance converted to a reference temperature. A variation of more than 5% may indicate winding damage [47]. The transformer winding resistances can be measured either by the voltmeter-ammeter method or the bridge method [45]. The IEEE Std C57.12.90 standard indicates that the bridge method is to be used in the cases where the rated current of the transformer winding is less than 1 A, while the voltmeter-ammeter one is employed when the rated current of the transformer winding is 1 A or more [48].

2.5. Insulation Resistance, Polarisation Index and Core Ground Tests

IR is one of the traditional methods used to determine the transformer insulation deterioration, dryness or failures in the windings or core earthing. A high DC voltage (typical values are 1 kV up to 5 kV) is applied to the winding under test. The leakage current is measured and the IR calculated and indicated by the instrument. A guard ring electrode is recommended in IR measurements to avoid influence of unwanted leakages.

In a dry/less contaminated transformer, the resistive leakage current is small and constant. In poor insulation, the resistive leakage current which consists of four different components (conductance, capacitance, absorption and surface leakage, each of which adds up to a composite response) may be quite large and may increase with time. IR profiles of healthy insulation systems appear as an inverse exponential function in form because of the four primary components of the current, two of them decrease exponentially. The measurements are performed at 1, 2, 5, 50 and 100 min. If two successive measurements give the same results, the test may be stopped, and the values used to calculate the IR. Otherwise, the IR is reported as function of the electrification time. IR values have to be compared with values from previous measurements on the same unit or a sister unit in order to evaluate the actual condition of the insulation. Otherwise, bushing surfaces must be well cleaned before commencing the measurements. IR is a temperature-dependent test and not reliable enough in identifying partially wet insulation [2]. Unlike conductors where the resistance increases with temperature, IR is inversely proportional to temperature so IR decreases with temperature.

Another way of applying this testing is to use the polarization index (PI), a variation of the IR test by measuring the current after 1 and 10 min of voltage application. The PI index is the ratio of the IR measured after voltage has been applied for 10 min (R10), to the IR measured after just one minute (R1). This index, independent from temperature, was introduced to detect contaminated or wet rotating machines winding insulation. The IR and PI have been used by the electricity utilities for a long time to ascertain the transformer moisture condition [2]. In the last decades, field and laboratory investigations have revealed that for the complex oil-cellulose insulation system, the PI results can be misinterpreted [49,50]. Recall that the resistive leakage current is affected in different ways by the presence of moisture, contamination, temperature, and the insulation condition itself [51,52]. Field measurements are generally performed just after de-energising the transformer. Thus at onsite measurements, water migration is commonly occurring, the transformer is in a non-equilibrium state. Under such circumstances, large thermal variations may affect the results, since moisture distribution inside the insulation is not in complete equilibrium condition. Therefore PI is not considered as a good indicator for the state of the oil impregnated insulation condition, but the resistance itself is [50,51]. Dielectric response analyses are preferred for quantitative assessments of moisture in the insulation.

Power transformers are usually supplied with a ground from the core to the tank (earth/ground) to divert high potentials induced into the core safely to ground. The core ground also provides a low-resistance path to ground if there is a short circuit between the winding and the core, allowing protective relaying to detect it [53].

The core ground test is performed by disconnecting the core grounding outside the tank and the IR of the core to ground measured. This test is performed as a routine maintenance task to detect if the core has shifted, making contact with its tank, but usually performed when a transformer is first installed, moved or if a problem is indicated by dissolved gas analysis (DGA) with an increase in the combustible gases [2,54]. These gases are created by heat within the core produced by circulating currents. Typical values are in the order of 10 MΩ or higher. Values lower than 100 kΩ can indicate core grounding problems [2]. In some cases resistances (normally in the order of several kΩ) are used to ground separated core lamination packets.

Measurements of the core ground current in service show values in the order of some mA for a well-insulated core; if the core has grounding faults, the current is several amps or even higher [2].

2.6. Leakage Reactance and Magnetising Current

The leakage reactance of transformer is the consequence of the leakage flux in transformer. This self-reactance associated with resistance is the impedance of transformer which may induce voltage drops in both primary and secondary transformer windings. This test is performed to detect windings deformation following current faults, high inrush currents, Buchholz relay tripping, and protective relay tripping [2].

An AC source (preferable with variable frequency) connected to each phase of the HV winding with the corresponding LV winding short circuited, is required for measuring the leakage reactance. The leakage impedance is then determined from the measured current and the voltage across the HV winding. The measured value should be within ±2% compared to the factory test report. This is because the difference between phases is usually less than 2% [2]. Any changes higher than 1% should be further investigated with other tests such as frequency response analysis (FRA). Care is recommended when comparing three phase and one phase test measurements.

The magnetising current is the current which flows in the primary winding when an AC source is connected to each phase of the HV windings with the secondary windings unloaded. The voltage across the HV winding and the magnetising current are measured along with the phase angle if possible. The test voltage can be connected to the LV windings, but in this case the values have to be corrected using the square of the winding ratio. This test is performed to detect core faults (shorted laminations), shorted turns or winding parts.

Some test equipment may allow winding ratio to be measured concurrently. In this condition, the magnetising current measurement should be performed before winding resistance tests since, the residual flux could impact the measurement.

The measured value at rated voltage should be within 0.1%–0.3% of rated current. Normally, the outer phases have similar values within 5%. The current on the middle phase can be up to 30% lower [2]. Since this is a voltage-dependent test, the same test voltage and tap position should be used for comparison.

3. Advanced Electrical Diagnostic Techniques

To meet the pressing needs of the power industry advanced maintenance technologies/tools are necessary. In recent years new diagnostic methods complementary to the classical IR, power frequency DF and polarisation index measurements have been promoted. Some of these modern diagnostic methods include PDs detection, dielectric spectroscopic techniques, sweep frequency response analysis (SFRA), etc. Contrary to the basic electrical techniques (IR, PI, DDF, etc.), dielectric response measurements provide sufficient information about the condition of insulation, which is necessary for a reliable condition assessment. These methods are now available as user-friendly methods, and can be used to monitor, diagnose and check new insulating materials, qualification of insulating systems during/after production of power transformer non-destructively.

3.1. Partial Discharge Detection Techniques

PD is an electrical phenomenon that occurs inside a transformer and the magnitude of such discharges can cause progressive deterioration and sometime may lead to insulation failure. There are vast numbers of papers available on PD processes, PD patterns and fault mechanisms and are beyond the scope of this paper. A number of researchers have worked on the measurement of dielectric strength of pressboard and paper with different wave shapes power frequency or lightning impulse or switching impulse or combinations of these.

A PD is defined as a localized dielectric breakdown of a small portion of the electrical insulation, without completely bridging the conductors [55]. PD can be initiated by voids, cracks or inclusions within solid dielectric, at interfaces within solid or liquid dielectrics, in bubbles within liquid dielectrics or along boundaries between different insulation materials. PD deteriorate progressively the insulation and can lead to electrical breakdown which ultimately leads to equipment damage and can cause a considerable economic losses [56]. The affected component needs to be closely analysed to make sure the PD will not lead to further damage or even complete destruction. Therefore, the integrity of the insulation of HV equipment should be confirmed using PD analysis during its manufacturing, its commissioning and during its lifetime. In transformers, some PD sources include gas bubbles in the oil, voids in solid insulation material or floating metallic particles. The long term effect of PD on insulating systems is destructive, leading to the insulation deterioration or breakdown of power transformers [47,57]. PD activity in power transformers is often measured during factory acceptance testing using the conventional measurement according to IEC 60270 [55]. Depending on the voltage and the size of the transformer, the acceptable limits of PD for new transformers are in the range < 100 pC to < 500 pC [46]. Early detection and localization of PD is of utmost importance, it facilitates preventive repairs to avoid unforeseen breakdowns [56–58].

According to [59], PD can occur at difference locations within power transformer: core and coils assemlby, bushings, on load tap changer (OLTC), oil-barrier-paper structure and oil, etc. PD can be associated with operating voltage, voltage induced by main magnetic flux, voltage induced by stray flux. The source of PD can also be associated with switching processes, to reversible changes of insulation condition and to irreversible degradation of insulating materials.

An analysis of the root causes of transformer bushing failures following five incidents occurred at Jaalan Bani Bu (JBB) Ali Grid station on 2011, has been conducted by Feilat et al. [60]. Based on visual inspection of the failed bushings, comprehensive power quality measurements, frequency scan, and OLTC daily operations, they concluded that the failure could be attributed to internal localized insulation breakdown as indicated by the burn-through marks on the condenser paper and two melted spots on the HV central conductor.

PD occurrence is usually followed by many electrical and chemical phenomena, such as current pulses characterised by short duration in the range of nanoseconds, electromagnetic radiations, ultrasonic waves, light, heat and gas pressure [55,61,62]. Based on the types of signals generated by PD, various sensing methods including electrical, acoustic, optical, electromagnetic and chemical methods have been proposed for detection and localization of PD in power transformers [61,63].

3.1.1. Electrical Detection of PDs

The electrical methods used for detection of PD are based on the electrical phenomena accompanying the discharge such as electromagnetic radiation and electric current pulses. Therefore, two electrical-based detection methods can be distinguished: conventional PD measurement and the ultra-high frequency (UHF) methods [56]. The conventional electrical method consists in coupling sensors and a data acquisition system. In transformers, capacitive and inductive coupling sensors are generally used. The bushing tap of the transformer is used as a capacitive coupling sensor, while the current is measured by mean of high frequency current transformer (HFCT) which is an inductive coupling sensor [56,61,63–66]. The electrical measurements are very accurate and can provide information about the PD intensity, and possible determination of the defect type. However, as the power transformer environment contain high levels of electrical noise, in online electrical PD system, it is very hard to distinguish between noise and PD [67]. In such cases, offline measurements can be performed in order to eliminate some of noise, but this can lead to lost revenue for the power company. The conventional measurements, according to IEC 60270 is an approved PD measurements and is often used in power transformers during factory acceptance testing. The conventional method uses apparent charge, measured in pC, which represents the integrated current pulse caused by a PD.

The PD pulse current has a short rise time, and radiates magnetic waves with frequencies up to the ultra-high range, therefore, the electromagnetic wave generated by PD has a frequency component in the UHF band. As the PD pulses propagate through the winding of transformer, they undergo a significant distortion and attenuation. To achieve an appropriate sensitivity in analyzing at what portion of the transformer the PD can be detected, an appropriate bandwidth can be used [65].

UHF sensors are able to detect the electromagnetic waves generated by PD, generally in the bandwidth range from 300 MHz to 3 GHz [56,61]. In this frequency range and due to the shielding characteristic of the transformer tank, this method is less sensitive to the external interference compared to the electrical method [67–72]. However, the geometry inside the transformer acts as a waveguide in the UHF range and highly affects reflections and standing of UHF signals. It is therefore necessary to recalibrate UHF sensors for each transformer design [67]. Another issue is that, there is no standardized sensitivity check procedure for UHF sensors used for power transformers. The only methods established is based on the CIGRE recommendation transfer function (TF) 15/33.03.05 [68] for gas-insulated switchgear (GIS). The CIGRE method for GIS links the conventional PD measurements according to IEC 60270 in pC to UHF measurements. However, no correlation between the conventional PD measuring method (pC) and the UHF signals (mV) for power transformers has yet been established [73].

The phenomenon of UHF signal attenuation within power transformers, due to the influence of the internal structure (windings, cores, field deflections etc.) on the propagation of UHF signals has been investigated [73,74]. For a reliable measurement several UHF antenna are used around the transformer tank using oil valves [75]. The PD location is usually detected using acoustic probes. However, the propagation times measured in the UHF range have been investigated for geometrical location of PD [76,77]. According to Coenen and Tenbohlen [76], the accuracy seems to be adequate to determine the phase limb where the PD is located, but additional acoustic measurement are always needed.

3.1.2. Acoustical and Optical Detection of PDs

Acoustic signals that occur during the PD event, can be captured using acoustic sensors such as piezoelectric transducers as well as fiber optic acoustic sensors, accelerometers, condenser microphones and sound-resonance sensors [61]. This acoustic signal is created by the explosion of mechanical energy caused by vaporisation of material around the hot streamer within the void. This energy propagates through the transformer tank in the form of a pressure field [78–81]. The benefit of acoustic methods is the ability to localize PD sources using multiple sensors in different positions on the transformer tank [79,81–84]. One of the common methods used to localize the PD is the so called arrival time analysis [83]. Acoustic waves are actually strongly influenced by the geometry of transformer as well as by the insulation medium [85]. This leads to a change in the sound propagation, resulting in damping, absorption and scattering effects on the measurable acoustic compression. PD localization can help plant technicians locate faults in insulation for repair purposes. Consequently, many researchers have proposed different algorithms allowing precisely localization of the PD locations in transformers [82,84,86,87]. Potential for the on-line detection of PDs of a new generation of piezoelectric sensors (high temperature ultrasonic transducers, (HTUTs)) is reported by Danouj et al. [88]. An advantage of acoustic methods is their immunity to electromagnetic interference which makes them suitable for online real-time applications [56,61]. However, acoustic sensors also have some limitations, as they are less sensitive compared to electrical signal methods, due to the attenuation mechanisms inside the transformer [78].

Fiber-optic acoustic sensors have been developed to increase the sensitivity of acoustic signals detection [89–92]. Actually, the fiber sensor uses an optical signal to measure acoustic signals. Unlike the acoustic sensors that are placed on the tank of the transformer, the optical fiber sensor can be placed inside the transformer. The main advantages of this method are the immunity from electromagnetic interferences, high sensitivity, the ability to with stand high temperatures, large bandwidth and resistance to chemical corrosion. However, their major disadvantage are the high cost and end-user unfamiliarity [93]. The detection process of this method is based on the change of the optical fiber length and refraction index caused by acoustic waves [64]. The acoustic wave in the transformer oil can be detected using an optical fibre acoustic sensor. This sensor is made up by bonding silica tubing and silica diaphragm together to form a sealed fibre optic extrinsic Fabry–Perot interferometer. The acoustic wave induces a dynamic pressure on the diaphragm which lead to the vibration of the diaphragm. Therefore, it is very important to design the sensor head to ensure high enough frequency response and sensitivity to achieve optimum detection of PDs [92].

3.1.3. Chemical Detection of PDs

DGA using gas chromatography is one of the most sensitive and reliable techniques used for assessing the condition of oil-filled transformers. Under electrical and thermal stresses, small quantities of gases may be liberated due to decomposition of oil and cellulose insulation. The quantity and composition of the liberated gases depends on the type of fault [94]. The distribution of these gases can help identifying different types of PD using standard interpretation methods [95,96].

The other method which is used for PD detection is the high performance liquid chromatography (HPLC) method. The HPLC test measures the glucose by-product produced due to the cellulose insulation breakdown [61]. The disadvantages of chemical detection is that both methods take too much time between the collection of sufficient quantities of gases or by-products and the initiation of PD source to be detected. This mean that chemical methods cannot be used for real-time and online monitoring [61]. Furthermore, chemical methods are not able to provide information about the position of the PD source or the extent of insulation damage. Unfortunately, there is no calibration standard between chemical methods and apparent charge. As a consequence the chemical methods are used to verify the presence of errors [85]. One of the most important phenomena that can lead to initiation of PD is the accumulation of the electrostatic charge. It is very important to study and understand how this can occur to avoid catastrophic failures.

3.2. Frequency Response Analysis

FRA is a powerful tool in advanced power transformer assessments to evaluate the mechanical or electrical integrity of the core and windings by measuring the electrical transfer functions over a wide frequency range. The results can be compared to the outcomes of traditional tests such as transformer turn ratio (TTR), winding resistance or leakage reactance. International standardization and research entities have approved two standards and two guides on SFRA testing [97–100].

This technique is sensitive to changes in the configuration of transformer windings, because any changes in the winding geometry affect the internal winding inductance and capacitance, and consequently the relevant characteristic frequencies. This test is performed to detect windings deformation/displacement, shorted turns, core faults, faulty core grounding, faulty screen connections, and damage during transportation, etc.

FRA is a comparative method, that evaluates the transformer condition by comparing the obtained set of results to reference results on the same, or a similar unit [101–103]. Two testing procedures are available [2]:

(1) SFRA consisting in connecting a sinusoidal AC voltage with variable frequency (several Hz to several MHz) to each phase of the HV and the LV windings with all other windings unloaded. The input voltage (U_{in}) and the output voltage (U_{out}) are measured at different frequencies.
(2) Impulse frequency response analysis (IFRA) consisting in injecting an impulse to each phase of the HV and the LV windings with all other windings unloaded. The input and output impulse curves of the windings are recorded. The time domain results are transformed into the frequency domain by using fast Fourier transform (FFT) algorithms. The U_{in} and the U_{out} are calculated for different frequencies.

For both methods, the ratio "20 log (U_{out}/U_{in})" (in dB) is calculated for each frequency and the results are plotted on a trace. Both methods give satisfactory results, but the IFRA does not give results in the low frequency range (below 1 kHz) [2]. The measurements can record a unique "fingerprint" of a transformer which can be compared to a previous measurement. The differences between them indicate that mechanical and electrical changes that have occurred inside the transformer. For each fault, the transfer impedance or TF is measured and compared to the original frequency response without defects. However, interpretations of frequency responses remain very vague and do not precisely locate emerging faults.

Care should be taken when interpreting FRA spectra. The total capacitance variations due to the temperature and moisture changes in the test objects can lead to misinterpretation. Statistical indices in FRA evaluation were proposed to explore their capability in FRA spectrum interpretation once the moisture content of paper insulation is changed [104].

Another important fundamental shortcoming related to this technique is the fault discrimination and location. Using rational function based on vector fitting (VF) approaches, index, and synthesized zeros/poles are introduced to specify the type, level and location of the fault in the winding [105–107]. Results presented demonstrate the feasibility of the approaches.

The FRA test is valuable when the result is compared to a baseline measurement performed under similar conditions to guarantee repeatability of the results; however, as per the inherent characteristics of the FRA test, repeatability can be easily compromised [98–100].

One of the main concerns with SFRA is its limitation to offline testing since the method requires injection of a test signal into the transformer windings through the high-voltage bushings. Behjat et al. [108] investigated the feasibility for online transfer function monitoring of the power transformers windings through a quite simple, economic, and noninvasive capacitive sensor installed on the surface of the transformer bushing is presented.

3.3. Dielectric Response Analysis

The fundamental theories behind dielectric measurements were first developed by Jonscher [109] but was never used as a diagnostic tool. Only recently [110], that is to say, during the last two decades, extensive research was centered to this diagnostic technology. The insulation system of power transformers consists of oil and cellulose, whose dielectric properties are strongly influenced by moisture, temperature and aging. Their condition can therefore, be evaluated using dielectric response measurements. Indeed, the dielectric response, which is a unique characteristic of the particular insulation system, can provide indication into aging and moisture content of the transformer insulation [111]. There are three methods referred to dielectric response analysis (DRA) [51,110–134]:

(1) Recovery voltage measurement (RVM), sometimes also called return voltage (RV) measurement;
(2) Polarization and depolarisation current (PDC);
(3) Frequency domain spectroscopy (FDS).

All these methods reflect the same fundamental polarization and conduction phenomena [113], they are available as portable user-friendly methods, and can be used to monitor, diagnose and check new insulating materials, qualification of insulating systems during/after production of power equipment non-destructively. Material properties and geometry must also be taken into account when moisture in the solid insulation is to be derived from any of these three methods. These techniques are global methods, i.e., each test object is regarded as a "black box" accessible only by its electric terminals. Therefore, only global changes of the insulation can be identified but not localized defects [113]. Sophisticated analysis methods [51,110–115] can determine the water content of cellulose (paper/pressboard).

3.3.1. Polarization and Depolarization Current

The measurement of PDC following a DC voltage step allows investigating slow polarization processes [110]. Before PDC measurements, the dielectric memory of the test object must be cleared. A ripple- and noise-free DC voltage source is required to record the small polarization current with sufficient accuracy. The procedure consists in applying a DC charging voltage to the test object for a long time. During this time, the polarization current through the test object arising from the activation of the polarization process with different time constants corresponding to different insulation materials and to the conductivity of the object, which has been previously carefully discharged is measured. The voltage is then removed and the object short-circuited, enabling the measurement of the depolarization current (or discharging, or desorption) in the opposite direction, without contribution of the conductivity. In both cases (polarization and depolarisation), a long charging time is required (generally 10,000 s) in order to assess the interfacial polarization and paper condition [51,110–115].

The prevailing method of representation consists in plotting the relaxation measurement results in a log/log scale with charging and discharging current of $t = 10^4$ s (Figure 2). The interpretation scheme allows a separation between influences of moisture in solid insulation and other influences (e.g., oil conductivity). According to this common interpretation scheme, the first 1–100 s are influenced by oil conductivity. The end value of polarisation current is determined by the pressboard resistance and therefore by moisture. Initial values of the polarization current are related to the oil conductivity while the transient current variation is determined by geometry and oil properties.

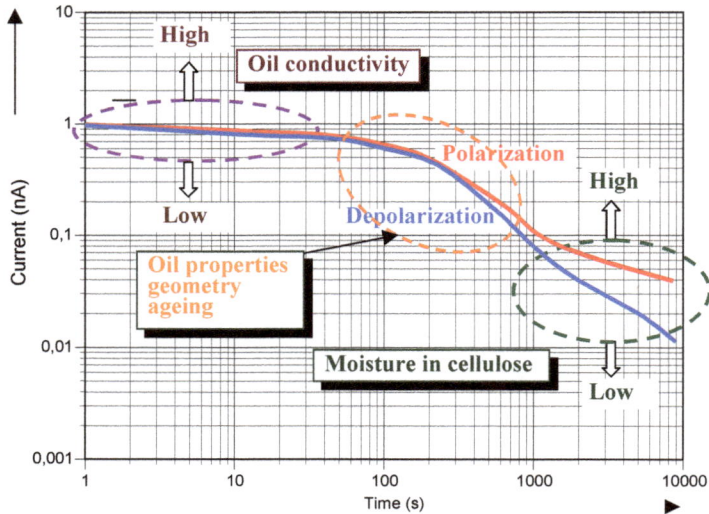

Figure 2. Interpretation of PDC measurement data.

3.3.2. Recovery Voltage Method

The recovery voltage method is another method in the time domain to investigate slow polarisation processes. This technique for the on-site measurement of the bulk dielectric properties for power transformers appeared about three decades ago [111]. The insulation condition can be physically monitored by various parameters of RV measurement, including the maximum peak voltage, central time constant and the initial slope of the RV curve [2,111].

This offline non-destructive diagnostic technique consists in applying a DC voltage U_c over the electrodes of a completely discharged test object. Typically, a DC voltage between 0.5 and 2 kV is applied to the test object. During the charging period T_d, the polarisation current $I_{pol}(t)$ flows through the test object. Following this period, the test object is short-circuited (grounded) and the depolarisation current $I_{depol}(t)$ flows. Both currents are, however, not measured. After a defined discharging period T_d, a recovery voltage, $U_R(t)$ is measured while the DC source is disconnected. After the short-circuiting (grounding) period is finished, the charge bounded by the polarization will turn into free charges i.e., a voltage will build up between the electrodes on the dielectric [121]. The RV is measured under opened circuit conditions (Figure 3). The sequence of RVM is repeated sequentially for charging time T_c for values varying from 1 s to 1200 s. The used ratio of charging and discharging time (T_c/T_d) is 2. The polarization spectrum is obtained by plotting the peak value of recovery voltage (U_{max}) as a function of the charging time T_c.

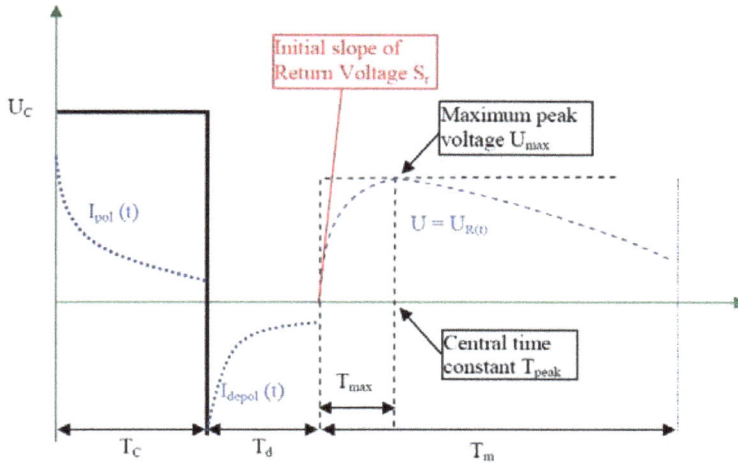

Figure 3. Schematic diagram of the recovery voltage measurement (RVM) process.

Interpretation of RVM results is usually based on the magnitude and the position of global maximum of the recovery voltage curve. As aging duration increases, the maximum of recovery voltage increases too. The resulting curve, U_{max} as a function of T_c, is called the polarisation spectrum. The initial derivative, $Sr = dU_R/dt$ of the recovery voltage is also found and can be plotted as a function of T_c.

The interpretation scheme must allow separating between the influences of moisture in the cellulose and other influences (e.g., oil conductivity), which is possible with the common scheme for the PDC and FDS methods but not for the RVM. CIGRE Task Force 15.01.09 reported the interaction of different effects on the "polarisation spectrum", which is used to evaluate RV measurements. The "polarisation spectrum" and its "central time constant" is mainly a mirror of interfacial polarisation. It is believed that the RV and peak time spectra are more dependent on the moisture content of the insulation than the aging [112]. However, it has been reported by several researchers that RVM is a complex convolution of the individual effects of oil and paper and their moisture and aging conditions [116]. The moisture content of the solid insulation influences this "spectrum" too, but it can't be separated from oil conductivity [111]. The RVM curves therefore do not depict unambiguously the separation of aging and moisture impacts on oil impregnated paper insulation condition [2,111].

Consequently, an alternative interpretation was proposed, to resolve previous anomalous moisture determinations. The moisture content in the solid insulation is instead, estimated from the polarisation spectrum which is examined for evidence of any subsidiary maxima away from the dominant time constant. The so called "Guuinic signature" has been found a useful aid in this process, in particular for confirming that the dominant time constant corresponds to the oil peak (narrow "nose") and assessing if there is any sign of polarisation activity above the dominant time constant [111]. In the "Guuinic signature" plot (Figure 4), the initial slope S_r is plotted against the maximum recovery voltage U_{max} [121]. The moisture content is then estimated from this corresponding time constant using the published calibration curves [121].

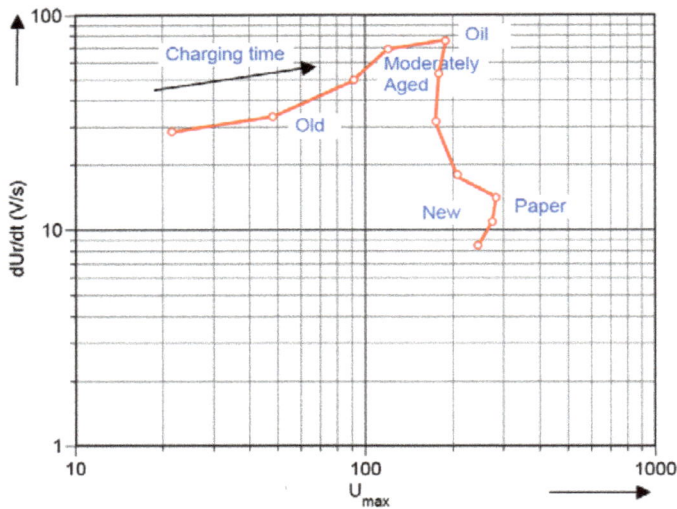

Figure 4. Guuinic representation [121].

According to this representation, while charging time T_C increases S_r increases with U_{max}. New paper depicts low Sr values for large values of U_{max}, while aged insulation paper depict lower S_r values at lower U_{max}. Moderately aged paper exibits higher values of S_r at moderate U_{max}.

3.3.3. Frequency Domain Spectroscopy

The measurement principle is the same as capacitance and DDF/PF described previously but differs by being applied at different frequencies, typically from 0.001 Hz to 1000 Hz.

The frequency response of the dielectric materials is being widely used as a diagnostic tool for insulation systems [51,110–119]. The monitoring of the complex permittivity and the DF of transformer insulation, as function of frequency provides inside information concerning the state of insulation within the components.

The relative complex permittivity (ε_r) is a dimensionless quantity, which compares the complex permittivity of a material (ε) to the permittivity of the free space ($\varepsilon_0 = 8.854 \times 10^{-12}$ F/m). It describes the interaction of a material with the electric field and consists of a real part $\varepsilon'(\omega)$, which represents the storage, while the imaginary part of the complex relative permittivity, $\varepsilon''(\omega)$, (loss part) contains both the resistive (conduction) losses and the dielectric (polarisation) losses.

The behaviour of the complex relative permittivity when the resistive losses are dominant is that its imaginary part, $\varepsilon''(\omega)$, has a slope of ω^{-1} and the real part $\varepsilon'(\omega)$ is constant [2]. It is therefore possible to determine the conductivity of the test object from the measured imaginary part of the complex relative permittivity.

The DDF (also known as tanδ, the ratio between the imaginary and real part of the complex relative permittivity) is a property of an electrical insulation system; low values of it are usually regarded as proof of good quality of the insulation. One practical advantage of the DDF is that it is independent of the test object geometry. The progressive increase of the DDF is closely related to the chemical degradation which accompanies aging/moistening of the insulation system.

When a sinusoidal voltage is applied across an insulation system, polarization processes start inside the insulation material resulting in a flow of current through it [109]. In the FDS techniques, the sample under test is subjected to sinusoidal voltage over a wide frequency range and the amplitude and phase of the response current flowing through the insulation are recorded from which, DF and complex capacitance are determined.

When the test object geometry is known, $\varepsilon'(\omega)$ and $\varepsilon''(\omega)$, provide separately more information (conductivity σ_{dc}, high-frequency component of the relative permittivity $\varepsilon\infty$, and dielectric susceptibility $\chi(\omega)$).

The moisture prediction is based on a model formulation which varies all insulation parameters (consisting of spacer, barrier and oil duct) to simulate every possible geometrical design. To make a precise moisture estimation of the oil-paper insulation in a transformer a library containing data on dielectric properties $\varepsilon\infty$, σ_{dc} and the dielectric function $f(t)$, of well characterised materials (oils and impregnated pressboard) at different humidity content is needed [111]. This information is needed for calculating the dielectric response of the composite duct insulation and for comparison with the results of the measurements. The software creates master curves and compares them to the measured DDF curve until the best possible match is reached. The Arrhenius equation is also applied to compensate for temperature dependence in the material. The final results are presented as a percent of moisture in paper and a separate value for oil conductivity.

The FDS measurement is carried out as a frequency sweep from 1 kHz down till 0.1 mHz, thus causing unavoidable large measuring time due to the very low frequency oscillations. The prevailing method of representation consists in plotting the C-tanδ frequency scans in a log/log scale as depicted in Figure 5.

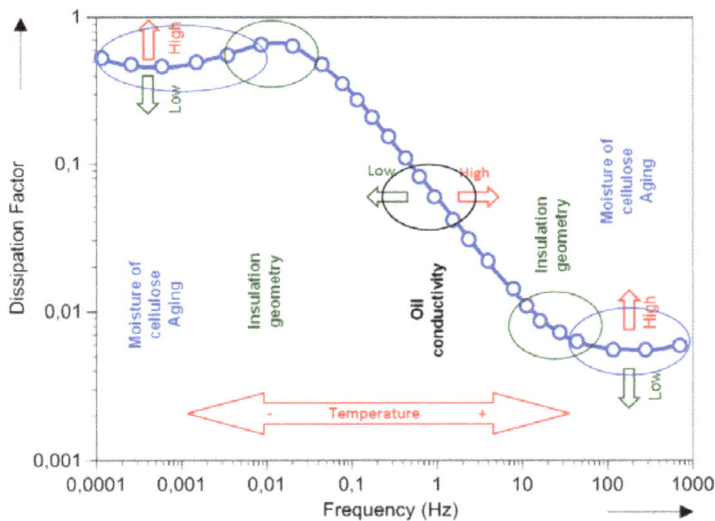

Figure 5. Separate impacts of oil conductivity and moisture in cellulose on frequency domain spectroscopy (FDS).

Different parts of the response, in frequency axis, are separately sensitive to properties of oil and solid parts of the insulation, as illustrated in Figure 5. At the very low frequency range ($<10^{-2}$ Hz) the response is mainly influenced by the condition of the cellulose. The same is true for the higher frequency range (>10 Hz). The central part of the response is, on the other hand, influenced by the properties of the oil, mainly by its conductivity [51,110–119].

A large number of papers have been published in this last decade to close some gaps in our understanding. Theoretical and experimental results have been reported in many contributions to demonstrate the effects of temperature, electric field, ageing and moisture content of paper and oil on the FDS results (e.g., [51,110–119]). It is now well accepted that FDS measurement techniques can provide indication onto aging and moisture content of the transformer insulation. However, Saha et al. [118] revealed that moisture content has a dominant influence on nearly all electrical based diagnostic techniques for assessing the condition of insulation, and indeed, masks their capability to determine the presence and extent of aging by-products of the insulation [121]. However, it must be emphasize that moisture and aging separation still constitute a challenging point in this domain.

Transformation of the results from time domain into the frequency domain has been an alternative that allowed reducing measurement duration (e.g., [29,30]). The time of measurement can be reduced to less than three hours in the lower frequency ranges. More recently, some authors [125,126] have proposed an alternative testing techniques to reduce the measuring time by measuring multiple sinusoidal oscillations simultaneously. Digital Fourier transformation (DFT) is used to separate the individual oscillations in the frequency domain. The proposed alternative techniques allow reducing the measuring time by up to 73%.

Another important aspect, reported by many researchers is the influence of several factors, including temperature, rain and electromagnetic disturbances together with transformer's volume/geometry on the FDS measurements [9,19,51,114–130]. Producing a FDS measure for insulation which does not require volume/geometry might therefore be very helpful. Hadjadj et al. [131] reported the feasibility of using poles to get rid of/encompass equipment volume effect. Attempts to separate moisture and aging have been reported in the last decades [131–134].

3.3.4. PDC, RVM or FDS?

Analysis of the PDC measurements can provide reliable information about the condition of transformer insulation. With sophisticated analysis methods, the PDC measurement can predict the moisture content in the solid insulation along the conductivities of the oil and paper. Other diagnostic quantities like tanδ, PI and polarization spectra can be calculated from PDC measurements directly.

Dielectric FDS enables measurements of the composite insulation capacitance, permittivity, conductivity (and resistivity) and loss factor in dependency of frequency. The real and imaginary part of the capacitance and permittivity can be separated. This non-destructive technique also provides the moisture content in the solid insulation material and C-ratio diagnostic quantity. The RVM technique has been criticised on various grounds [122,123]:

- moisture determinations, as derived by the evaluation method used, were often much higher than values obtained by other methods such as Karl Fisher titration;
- the recommended interpretation scheme is too simplistic;
- the technique does not take into account dependencies on geometry and oil properties.

It is also sometimes argued that it is easier to interpret data in the frequency domain than data in the time domain since the frequency data sometimes show nice features, like peaks [111]. A further comparison with PDC makes it clear, that while RVM is less noise-sensitive and simpler to set up on-site, the measuring results are sensitive to leakage currents due to the input impedance of the measuring instrument, polluted terminations, length and electrical characteristics of the connecting cable [128]. Furthermore the test duration is often longer and the RVM response depends critically on the charging and grounding duration [129]. Also the transformation of the RV measured data to the frequency domain is more difficult than those measured from PDC.

A brief comparison between Time Domain Method (TDM) and FDS techniques reveals that FDS has better noise performance and separates the behaviour of polarizability ($\chi''(\omega)$) and losses ($\chi'(\omega)$) of a dielectric medium, while the dielectric response of an insulating system can be measured with the PDC method in shorter times and with a good accuracy [127]. All these methods appear to have their own strengths and weaknesses. As a result CIGRE Working Group Task Force 15.01.094 reviewed these polarisation techniques and concluded that although such techniques showed promise, more work are required to validate them and improve the interpretation of results [111]. Fields and laboratory investigations have revealed that moisture content has a dominant influence on nearly all electrical based diagnostic techniques for assessing the condition of insulation, and indeed, masks their capability to determine the presence and extent of aging by-products of the insulation [132]. According to Saha et al. [132], there are two main reasons why electrical techniques mostly do not provide good measures of the aging of insulation:

- the dominant effect of moisture on most electrical properties;
- the electrical properties of the oil impregnated paper and pressboard are probably more a complex function of oil and cellulose.

Therefore, electrical techniques may be not very sensitive to measure the extent of aging of paper/pressboard insulation. The interpretation of the DRA test results still remains a difficult task as it is believed to be influenced by various parameters including insulation ageing condition, moisture content, and insulation geometry/volume together with environmental condition such as temperature.

4. Online Condition Monitoring and Diagnosis for Power Transformers

Online condition monitoring of transformers is an essential element that helps to ensure the continuity and reliability of their operation. This therefore allows one to reduce costs and economic losses associated with their unavailability. Many tools to continuously monitor transformers are increasingly being used [135]. This is achieved by collecting data provided by a sensor setup [136]. A multitude of different measurable variables can be collected for on-line monitoring. For data acquisition, the sensors are connected to a monitoring module installed at the transformer, where the analogue signals are digitised before sending them to the monitoring server [136]. By means of advanced computational intelligence techniques, data are converted into useful information to correctly interpret various fault phenomena and accurately detect incipient faults [135]. Online monitoring systems show the capability to detect oncoming failures within active parts, bushings, on-load tap changers and cooling units [136]. However, active parts are considered the main aspects of transformer condition monitoring and assessment, including oil temperature and oil level, temperature of the ambient air and of the cooling medium, service voltage and current, over-voltages, dissolved gas, PD as far as measurable, tap changer position, torque movement of the OLTC motor drive, winding deformation and oil humidity which should be monitored closely in order to determine power transformer conditions, etc. [135,136]. Besides monitoring of the abovementioned quantities those sensors allow further monitoring functionalities with regard to the different components of a transformer as active parts, bushings, cooling units, etc. The Smart Grid concept represents an unprecedented opportunity to move the energy industry into a new era of reliability, where online monitoring is going to affect the future of power transformer diagnostics.

5. Testing Suggestions/Recommendations

To monitor transformer conditions, various test are required as addressed in this manuscript. The selection of some testing method depends on the nature of the defect or fault and the concerned component. CIGRE WG 12.18 have reported guidelines for recommendations and evaluations of tests and groups of tests for specific defects and faults. Table 1 summarises the corresponding tests in matrix format. Detailed recommendations can be found in the CIGRE WG 12.18 norms [137].

Table 1. Graphical suggestions/recommendations related to the nature of the defect or fault in power transformer's main component, adapted from [137]. Non-electrical-based techniques are in red. IR: insulation resistance; DDF: dielectric dissipation factor; DGA: dissolved gas analysis; IFT: Interfacial Tension; DRA: dielectric response analysis.

Components	Nature of the Defect or Fault			
	Thermal (T)	Dielectric (D)	Mechanical (M)	Contamination or aging (C)
Bushing (B)	- DDF/PF - DGA - Infrared thermal image tests	- DDF/PF - IR - PD	- Infrared (if external) - DGA (if internal) - Winding resistance	- DDF/PF - PD - IR - DGA - Visual - Water content - Oil tests
Core (C)	- Magnetizing current - IR - DDF/PF - Furans (furfuraldehyde) analysis (FFA) - DGA - Loss measurement	-	- IR - PD - DGA	-
Driver, Tap changer (D)	- Temperature monitoring, - Infrared thermal image tests, - Contact resistance measurement - DGA	-	- Visual - On-line monitor: motor amps at 2 kHz, relay timing	- Winding resistance - Turns ratio - DGA - Visual (internal after de-energization)
Oil (O)	- DGA - On-line oil temperature measurement	- Resistivity - DDF/PF - Electric or acoustic PD - DGA - IFT - Neutralization number - Polar compounds - Moisture in oil - Particle count - Breakdown voltage - Pump bearing monitor	-	- Resistivity - DDF/PF - Electric or acoustic PD - DGA - IFT - Neutralization number - Polar compounds - Moisture in oil - Particle count - Breakdown voltage - Pump bearing monitor

Table 1. Cont.

Components	Nature of the Defect or Fault			
	Thermal (T)	Dielectric (D)	Mechanical (M)	Contamination or aging (C)
Selector (S)	- DC resistance - Electric or acoustic PD - On-line temperature differential	-	- Visual - On-line monitor: motor amps at 2 kHz, relay timing	- Winding resistance - Turns ratio - DGA
Tank and accessories (T)	- DGA - Infrared scan of tank	-	- Acoustic PD - DGA	- Visual - DGA - Neutralization number - Dissolved metals
Winding, major insulation and leads (W)	- DC resistance - Electric or acoustic PD - DGA (combustible gases and CO$_2$) - DGA (consumption of oxygen) - Visual - Measure oil temperature - Furans (furfuraldehyde) analysis (FFA)	- Electric or acoustic PD - Turns ratio - Magnetizing current - Winding resistance - FRA - DC resistance - DGA	- Leakage reactance - Capacitance change - FRA/transfer function analysis - Vibration - DGA - Sound level measurement - visual	- DDF/PF - RVM - Electric or acoustic PD - IR - IFT - Acid - Neutralization number - Oxidation stability - Sludge precipitation - Furans (furfuraldehyde) analysis (FFA) - Methanol content - DP - Moisture in oil - Water heat run - Moisture in paper (DRA) - DGA - Particle count - Breakdown voltage - Dissolved metals

6. Conclusions

This paper was authored by focusing on recent developments in electrical-based diagnostic techniques and to shed light on the opportunities provided for the diagnosis of faults in power transformers. A systematic review attempt determined that there are a variety of electrical-based diagnostic techniques available for monitoring power transformers, and many of them are moisture, temperature and aging dependant.

First, traditional methods have been discussed with currently available interpretation schemes. A number of modern diagnostic techniques were also presented in this paper and their usefulness and critical points highlighted. Some of them are standardised. None of the proposed method can be considered as the best diagnostic method. Since moisture content has a dominant influence on nearly all electrical-based diagnostic techniques for assessing the condition of insulation, combinations with physicochemical ones are sometimes essential for an accurate diagnosis.

Frequency domain spectroscopy measurements are preferred for quantitative assessments of the moisture in the insulation. However, despite being a promising area for research, the moisture and aging separation still constitute a challenging point. A number of attempts have been made by many authors in the last decade to solve this problem and this research is still ongoing.

Author Contributions: Both authors contributed equally to the reported research and writing of the paper.

Conflicts of Interest: The authors declare no conflict of interest.

Abbreviations

The following abbreviations are used in this manuscript:

CIGRE	International Council of Large Electric Systems
EDL	Electrical double layer
ECT	Electrostatic charging tendency
MST	Mini static tester
BTA	Benzotriazole
DLA	Dielectric loss angle
DDF	Dielectric dissipation factor
RVM	Recovery voltage measurement
RV	Recovery voltage
PDC	Polarization and depolarisation current
FDS	Frequency domain spectroscopy
DF	Dissipation factor
DFT	Digital Fourier transformation
PF	Power factor
IEEE	Institute of Electrical and Electronic Engineers
HV	High voltage
LV	Low voltage
IR	Insulation resistance
PI	Polarization index
FB	Frequency band
FRA	Frequency response analysis
FFA	Furfuraldehyde
SFRA	Sweep frequency response analysis
IFRA	Impulse frequency response analysis
TF	Transfer function
VF	Vector fitting
OLTC	On load tap changer

PD	Partial discharge
PRPD	Phase resolved partial discharge pattern
UHF	Ultra-high frequency
IEC	International Electrotechnical Commission
FFT	Fast Fourier transform
HFCT	High frequency current transformer
TTR	Transformer turn ratio

References

1. Fofana, I.; Sabau, J. Application of Petroleum-Based Oil in Power Transformer. In *Natural Gas Research Progress*; David, N., Michel, T., Eds.; Nova Science Publishers, Inc.: Hauppauge, NY, USA, 2008; pp. 229–251.
2. *Guide for Transformer Maintenance*; CIGRE WG A2.34; CIGRE: Paris, France, 2011; Volume 445, pp. 51–61.
3. N'Cho, J.S.; Fofana, I.; Hadjadj, Y.; Beroual, A. Review of the Physicochemical-Based Diagnostic Techniques for Assessing Insulation Condition in Aged Transformers. *Energies* **2016**, *9*, 367. [CrossRef]
4. Sierota, A.; Rungis, J. Electrical Insulating Oils, Part 1 Characterization and Pre-Treatment of New Transformer Oils. *IEEE Electr. Insul. Mag.* **1995**, *11*, 8–20. [CrossRef]
5. *Standard for Insulating Liquids—Determination of the Breakdown Voltage at Power Frequency—Test Method*; IEC 60156; International Electrotechnical Commission: Geneva, Switzerland, 1995.
6. *Standard Test Method for Dielectric Breakdown Voltage of Insulating Liquids Using VDE Electrodes*; ASTM D1816-12; ASTM International: West Conshohocken, PA, USA, 2012; Volume 10.3.
7. CIGRE Working Group A2-35. *Experiences in Service with New Insulating Liquids*; Cigré Report 436; CIGRE: Paris, France, 2010.
8. *Standard Test Method for Dielectric Breakdown Voltage of Insulating Liquids Using Disk Electrodes*; ASTM D877/D877M-13; ASTM International: West Conshohocken, PA, USA, 2013.
9. Crofts, D.W. The electrification phenomena in power transformers. *IEEE Trans. Electr. Insul.* **1988**, *23*, 137–146. [CrossRef]
10. Johnson, D.L. Insulating Oil Qualification and Acceptance Tests from a User's Perspective. In *Electrical Insulating Oils*; STP998; ASTM International: West Conshohocken, PA, USA, 1988.
11. Zhang, J.; Cao, L.J. The study on flow electrification of oil-cellulose insulating system in large power transformer. In Proceedings of the 1995 International Conference on Energy Management and Power Delivery, Singapore, 21–23 November 1995; Volume 1, pp. 416–427.
12. Mitchinson, P.M.; Lewin, P.L.; Strawbridge, B.D.; Jarman, P. Tracking and surface discharge at the oil—Pressboard interface. *IEEE Electr. Insul. Mag.* **2010**, *26*, 35–41. [CrossRef]
13. Metwally, I.A. Influence of solid insulating phase on streaming electrification of transformer oil. *IEEE Trans. Dielectr. Electr. Insul.* **1997**, *4*, 327–340. [CrossRef]
14. Mas, P.; Paillat, T.; Moreau, O.; Touchard, G. Flow electrification in power transformers: Temperature influence on space charge distribution and charge accumulation in pressboard. *J. Electrost.* **2001**, *51–52*, 488–493. [CrossRef]
15. Poovamma, P.K.; Jagadish, R.; Dwarakanath, K. Investigation on static electrification characteristics of transformer oil. *J. Electrost.* **1994**, *33*, 1–14. [CrossRef]
16. Lyon, D.J.; Melcher, J.R.; Zahn, M. Couette charger for measurement of equilibrium and energization flow electrification parameters: Application to transformer insulation. *IEEE Trans. Electr. Insul.* **1988**, *23*, 159–176. [CrossRef]
17. Radwan, R.M.; El-Dewieny, R.M.; Aish, T.D.; Metwally, I.A.H. Factors affecting transformer oil flow electrification in electric power apparatus. In Proceedings of the Annual Report Conference on Electrical Insulation and Dielectric Phenomena, Pocono Manor, PA, USA, 28–31 October 1990; pp. 642–647.
18. Bouslimi, Y.; Fofana, I.; Hemmatjou, H.; Volat, C. Static electrification assessment of transformer oils in the spinning disc system. In Proceedings of the 2010 International Conference on High Voltage Engineering and Application (ICHVE), New Orleans, LA, USA, 11–14 October 2010; pp. 337–340.
19. Shimizu, S.; Murata, H.; Honda, M. Electrostatics in Power Transformers. *IEEE Trans. Power Appar. Syst.* **1979**, *PAS-98*, 1244–1250. [CrossRef]
20. Oommen, T.V.; Petrie, E.M. Eelectrostatic Charging Tendency of Transformer Oils. *IEEE Trans. Power Appar. Syst.* **1984**, *PAS-103*, 1923–1931. [CrossRef]

21. Tanaka, T.; Yamada, N.; Yasojima, Y. Characteristics of streaming electrification in pressboard pipe and the influence of an external electric field. *J. Electrost.* **1985**, *17*, 215–234. [CrossRef]
22. Higaki, M.; Kako, Y.; Moriyama, M.; Hirano, M.; Hiraishi, K.; Kurita, K. Static Electrification and Partial Discharges Caused by Oil Flow in Forced Oil Cooled Core Type Transformers. *IEEE Trans. Power Appar. Syst.* **1979**, *PAS-98*, 1259–1267. [CrossRef]
23. Okabe, S.; Kohtoh, M.; Amimoto, T. Investigation of electrostatic charging mechanism in aged oil-immersed transformers. *IEEE Trans. Dielectr. Electr. Insul.* **2010**, *17*, 287–293. [CrossRef]
24. Okabe, S.; Kohtoh, M.; Amimoto, T. Diagnosis on increase in electrostatic charging tendency of mineral insulating oil for power transformers due to aging. *IEEE Trans. Dielectr. Electr. Insul.* **2010**, *17*, 953–963. [CrossRef]
25. Kanno, M.; Oota, N.; Suzuki, T.; Ishii, T. Changes in ECT and dielectric dissipation factor of insulating oils due to aging in oxygen. *IEEE Trans. Dielectr. Electr. Insul.* **2001**, *8*, 1048–1053. [CrossRef]
26. Fofana, I.; Bouslimi, Y.; Hemmatjou, H.; Volat, C.; Tahiri, K. Relationship between static electrification of transformer oils with turbidity and spectrophotometry measurements. *Int. J. Electr. Power Energy Syst.* **2014**, *54*, 38–44. [CrossRef]
27. Talhi, M.; Fofana, I.; Flazi, S. Impact of various stresses on the streaming electrification of transformer oil. *J. Electrost.* **2016**, *79*, 25–32. [CrossRef]
28. Oommen, T.V. Static electrification properties of transformer oil. *IEEE Trans. Electr. Insul.* **1988**, *23*, 123–128. [CrossRef]
29. Bourgeois, A. Study of Flow Electrification Phenomena on High Power Transformers Pressboards. Ph.D. Thesis, Institut National Polytechnique de Grenoble—INPG, Grenoble, France, 2007.
30. Isaka, S.; Miyao, H.; Tsuchie, M.; Kobayashi, S.; Kobayashi, T.; Ono, T.; Ikeda, M.; Okubo, H. Investigation for standardization of electrostatic charging tendency measurement of transformer oil in Japan. In Proceedings of the 1999 IEEE 13th International Conference on Dielectric Liquids (ICDL '99), Nara, Japan, 20–25 July 1999; pp. 495–498.
31. Washabaugh, A.P.; Zahn, M. Flow electrification measurements of transformer insulation using a Couette flow facility. *IEEE Trans. Dielectr. Electr. Insul.* **1996**, *3*, 161–181. [CrossRef]
32. Kedzia, J. Investigation of transformer oil electrification in a spinning disk system. *IEEE Trans. Dielectr. Electr. Insul.* **1989**, *24*, 59–65. [CrossRef]
33. *Static Electrification in Power Transformers*; Gernaral Session, paper CE/SC 15/12-03; CIGRE: Paris, France, 1992.
34. Zelu, Y.; Paillat, T.; Morin, G.; Perrier, C.; Saravolac, M. Study on flow electrification hazards with ester oils. In Proceedings of the 2011 IEEE International Conference on Dielectric Liquids (ICDL), Trondheim, Norway, 26–30 June 2011; pp. 1–4.
35. Kobayashi, T.; Yajima, K.; Yamada, S.; Amimoto, T.; Hosokawa, N. Increase of static electrification in an aged oil-immersed transformer. *Electr. Eng. Jpn.* **2009**, *167*, 10–19. [CrossRef]
36. Ieda, M.; Okugo, H.; Tsukioka, H.; Goto, K.; Miyamoto, T.; Kohno, Y. Suppression of static electrification of insulating oil for large power transformers. *IEEE Trans. Dielectr. Electr. Insul.* **1988**, *23*, 153–157. [CrossRef]
37. Okabe, S.; Kohtoh, M.; Amimoto, T. Suppression of increase in electrostatic charging tendency of insulating oil by aging used for power transformer insulation. *IEEE Trans. Dielectr. Electr. Insul.* **2010**, *17*, 294–301. [CrossRef]
38. Kawamura, T.K.T.; Amimoto, T.; Murakami, H.; Shirasaka, Y.; Ebisawa, Y. *Failure Modes of Oil-Immersed Transformers Due to Static Electrification and Copper Sulphide Generation, and Suppressive Effect of BTA*; CIGRE A2-206; CIGRE: Paris, France, 2008.
39. Paillat, T.; Touchard, G.; Bertrand, Y. "Capacitive Sensor" to Measure Flow Electrification and Prevent Electrostatic Hazards. *Sensors* **2012**, *12*, 14315–14326. [CrossRef] [PubMed]
40. Setayeshmehr, A.; Akbari, A.; Borsi, H.; Gockenbach, E. On-line monitoring and diagnoses of power transformer bushings. *IEEE Trans. Dielectr. Electr. Insul.* **2006**, *13*, 608–615. [CrossRef]
41. Riendeau, S.; Picher, P.; Léonard, F.; Gauvin, M.; Bertrand, H. On-line monitoring of transformer bushings using a new decentralized measurement system. In Proceedings of the Conference Record of the 2010 IEEE International Symposium on Electrical Insulation (ISEI), San Diego, CA, USA, 6–9 June 2010; pp. 1–5.
42. *Reference Book on Insulating Liquids and Gases (RBILG) 391*; Doble Engineering Company: Boston, MA, USA, 1993.

43. *IEEE Guide for the Reclamation of Insulating Oil and Criteria for Its Use*; IEEE Std C57.637-2015 (Revision of IEEE Std 637-1985); IEEE Standards Association: Piscataway, NJ, USA, 1985.

44. Transformer Diagnostics. In *Facilities Instructions, Standards, and Techniques (FIST)*; Volume 3-31; United States Department of the Interior, Bureau of Reclamation: Washington, DC, USA, 2003; pp. 1–63.

45. *IEEE Standard Test Code for Liquid-Immersed Distribution, Power, and Regulating Transformers*; IEEE Std C57.12.90-2010 (Revision of IEEE Std C57.12.90-2006); IEEE Standards Association: Piscataway, NJ, USA, 2010; pp. 1–100.

46. Winders, J. *Power Transformers: Principles and Applications*; CRC press: Boca Raton, FL, USA, 2002.

47. Wang, M.; Vandermaar, A.J.; Srivastava, K.D. Review of condition assessment of power transformers in service. *IEEE Electr. Insul. Mag.* **2002**, *18*, 12–25. [CrossRef]

48. *IEEE Standard Test Code for Liquid-Immersed Distribution, Power, and Regulating Transformers and IEEE Guide for Short-Circuit Testing of Distribution and Power Transformers*; ANSI/IEEE Std C57.12.90-1987; IEEE Standards Association: Piscataway, NJ, USA, 1988; p. 0_1.

49. Harlow, J.H. *Electric Power Transformer Engineering*, 3rd ed.; CRC Press: Boca Raton, FL, USA, 2012.

50. Supatra, A.B. The latest on-site non-destructive technique for insulation analysis of electrical power apparatus. In Proceedings of the the 2004 Weidmann-ACTI Annual Technical Conference, Sacramento, CA, USA, 8–10 November 2004.

51. Fofana, I.; Hemmatjou, H.; Farzaneh, M. Low Temperature and Moisture Effects on Polarization and Depolarization Currents of Oil-Paper Insulation. *Electr. Power Syst. Res.* **2010**, *80*, 91–97. [CrossRef]

52. *Recommended Practice for Insulation Testing (2300 V and Above) with High Direct Voltage*; IEEE Std 95-2002; IEEE Standards Association: Piscataway, NJ, USA, 2002.

53. *Methods of Test for Volume Resistivity and Surface Resistivity of Solid Electrical Insulating Materials*; IEC 60093; International Electrotechnical Commission: Geneva, Switzerland, 1980.

54. White, J. Transformers core—A different path to maintaining insulation systems. *Electr. Today* **2013**, *26*, 42–44.

55. IEC 60270. *High-Voltage Test Techniques—Partial Discharge Measurements*, 3rd ed.; International Electrotechnical Commission: Geneva, Switzerland, 2000.

56. Wu, M.; Cao, H.; Cao, J.; Nguyen, H.-L.; Gomes, J.B.; Krishnaswamy, S.P. An overview of state-of-the-art partial discharge analysis techniques for condition monitoring. *Electr. Insul. Mag. IEEE* **2015**, *31*, 22–35. [CrossRef]

57. Fuhr, J. Procedure for identification and localization of dangerous PD sources in power transformers. *IEEE Trans. Dielectr. Electr. Insul.* **2005**, *12*, 1005–1014. [CrossRef]

58. Raymond, W.J.K.; Illias, H.A.; Bakar, A.H.A.; Mokhlis, H. Partial discharge classifications: Review of recent progress. *Measurement* **2015**, *68*, 164–181. [CrossRef]

59. Sokolov, V.; Mayakov, V.; Kuchinsky, G.; Golubev, A. On-Site Partial Discharge Measurement of Transformers. Available online: http://es.eaton.com/InsulGardSalesTool/Documentation/PD%20Transformer.pdf (accessed on 23 August 2016).

60. Feilat, E.A.; Metwally, I.A.; Al-Matri, S.; Al-Abri, A.S. Analysis of the Root Causes of Transformer Bushing Failures. *Int. J. Comput. Electr. Autom. Control Inf. Eng.* **2013**, *7*, 791–796.

61. Yaacob, M.; Alsaedi, M.; Rashed, J.; Dakhil, A.; Atyah, S. Review on partial discharge detection techniques related to high voltage power equipment using different sensors. *Photonic Sens.* **2014**, *4*, 325–337. [CrossRef]

62. Morshuis, P.H.F. Degradation of solid dielectrics due to internal partial discharge: Some thoughts on progress made and where to go now. *IEEE Trans. Dielectr. Electr. Insul.* **2005**, *12*, 905–913. [CrossRef]

63. Stone, G.C. Partial discharge diagnostics and electrical equipment insulation condition assessment. *IEEE Trans. Dielectr. Electr. Insul.* **2005**, *12*, 891–904. [CrossRef]

64. Niasar, M.G. Partial Discharge Signatures of Defects in Insulation Systems Consisting of Oil and Oil-impregnated Paper. Licentiate Thesis, KTH School of Electrical Engineering, Stockholm, Sweden, 2012.

65. Álvarez, F.; Garnacho, F.; Ortego, J.; Sánchez-Urán, M. Application of HFCT and UHF Sensors in On-Line Partial Discharge Measurements for Insulation Diagnosis of High Voltage Equipment. *Sensors* **2015**, *15*, 7360–7387. [CrossRef] [PubMed]

66. Schwarz, R.; Judendorfer, T.; Muhr, M. Review of Partial Discharge Monitoring techniques used in High Voltage Equipment. In Proceedings of the 2008 Annual Report Conference on Electrical Insulation and Dielectric Phenomena (CEIDP 2008), Quebec, QC, Canada, 26–29 October 2008; pp. 400–403.

67. Gautschi, D.; Weiers, T.; Buchs, G.; Wyss, S. *Ultra High Frequency (UHF) Partial Discharge Detection for Power Transformers: Sensitivity Check on 800 MVA Power Transformers and First Field Experience*; CIGRE A2-115; CIGRE: Paris, France, 2012.

68. *Partial Discharge Detection System for GIS: Sensitivity Verification for the UHF Method and the Acoustic Method*; CIGRE Task Force 15/33.03.05; ÉLECTRA No. 183; CIGRE: Paris, France; pp. 74–87.

69. Stone, G.C. Partial discharge. VII. Practical techniques for measuring PD in operating equipment. *IEEE Electr. Insul. Mag.* **1991**, *7*, 9–19. [CrossRef]

70. Judd, M.D.; Li, Y.; Hunter, I.B.B. Partial discharge monitoring for power transformer using UHF sensors. Part 2: Field experience. *IEEE Electr. Insul. Mag.* **2005**, *21*, 5–13. [CrossRef]

71. Judd, M.D.; Li, Y.; Hunter, I.B.B. Partial discharge monitoring of power transformers using UHF sensors. Part I: Sensors and signal interpretation. *IEEE Electr. Insul. Mag.* **2005**, *21*, 5–14. [CrossRef]

72. Tenbohlen, S.; Denissov, D.; Hoek, S.M.; Markalous, S.M. Partial discharge measurement in the ultra high frequency (UHF) range. *IEEE Trans. Dielectr. Electr. Insul.* **2008**, *15*, 1544–1552. [CrossRef]

73. Coenen, S.; Tenbohlen, S.; Markalous, S.M.; Strehl, T. Sensitivity of UHF PD measurements in power transformers. *IEEE Trans. Dielectr. Electr. Insul.* **2008**, *15*, 1553–1558. [CrossRef]

74. Coenen, S.; Tenbohlen, S.; Markalous, S.M.; Strehl, T. Attenuation of UHF signals regarding the sensitivity verification for UHF PD measurements on power transformers. In Proceedings of the International Conference on Condition Monitoring and Diagnosis (CMD 2008), Beijing, China, 21–24 April 2008; pp. 1036–1039.

75. Su, C.Q. *Electromagnetic Transients in Transformer and Rotating Machine Windings*; IGI Global: Hershey, PA, USA, 2012.

76. Coenen, S.; Tenbohlen, S. Location of PD sources in power transformers by UHF and acoustic measurements. *IEEE Trans. Dielectr. Electr. Insul.* **2012**, *19*, 1934–1940. [CrossRef]

77. Judd, M.D. Experience with UHF partial discharge detection and location in power transformers. In Proceedings of the Electrical Insulation Conference (EIC), Annapolis, MD, USA, 5–8 June 2011; pp. 201–205.

78. Lazarevich, A.K. Partial Discharge Detection and Localization in High Voltage Transformers Using an Optical Acoustic Sensor. Master's Thesis, Faculty of the Virginia Polytechnic Institute and State University Blacksburg, VA, USA, 2003.

79. Lundgaard, L.E. Partial discharge. XIII. Acoustic partial discharge detection-fundamental considerations. *IEEE Electr. Insul. Mag.* **1992**, *8*, 25–31. [CrossRef]

80. Harrold, R.T. Acoustical Technology Applications in Electrical Insulation and Dielectrics. *IEEE Trans. Electr. Insul.* **1985**, *EI-20*, 3–19. [CrossRef]

81. Harrold, R.T. Acoustic Waveguides for Sensing and Locating Electrical Discharges in High Voltage Power Transformers and Other Apparatus. *IEEE Trans. Power Appar. Syst.* **1979**, *PAS-98*, 449–457. [CrossRef]

82. Liu, H.-L. Acoustic partial discharge localization methodology in power transformers employing the quantum genetic algorithm. *Appl. Acoust.* **2016**, *102*, 71–78. [CrossRef]

83. Markalous, S.; Tenbohlen, S.; Feser, K. Detection and location of partial discharges in power transformers using acoustic and electromagnetic signals. *IEEE Trans. Dielectr. Electr. Insul.* **2008**, *15*, 1576–1583. [CrossRef]

84. Veloso, G.F.C.; da Silva, L.E.B.; Lambert-Torres, G.; Pinto, J.O.P. Localization of Partial Discharges in Transformers by the Analysis of the Acoustic Emission. In Proceedings of the 2006 IEEE International Symposium on Industrial Electronics, Montreal, QC, Canada, 9–13 June 2006; pp. 537–541.

85. Muhr, M.; Strehl, T.; Gulski, E.; Feser, K.; Gockenbach, E.; Hauschild, W.; Lemke, E. *Sensors and Sensing Used for Non-Conventional PD Detection*; CIGRE Working Group: Paris, France, 2006; Volume D1-102.

86. Hekmati, A. A novel acoustic method of partial discharge allocation considering structure-borne waves. *Int. J. Electr. Power Energy Syst.* **2016**, *77*, 250–255. [CrossRef]

87. Hekmati, A. Proposed method of partial discharge allocation with acoustic emission sensors within power transformers. *Appl. Acoust.* **2015**, *100*, 26–33. [CrossRef]

88. Danouj, B.; Tahan, A.A.; David, E. Using a new generation of piezoelectric sensors for partial discharge detection. *Measurement* **2013**, *46*, 660–666. [CrossRef]

89. Posada-Roman, J.; Garcia-Souto, J.A.; Rubio-Serrano, J. Fiber Optic Sensor for Acoustic Detection of Partial Discharges in Oil-Paper Insulated Electrical Systems. *Sensors* **2012**, *12*, 4793–4802. [CrossRef] [PubMed]

90. Wang, X.; Li, B.; Roman, H.T.; Russo, O.L.; Chin, K.; Farmer, K.R. Acousto-optical PD detection for transformers. *IEEE Trans. Power Deliv.* **2006**, *21*, 1068–1073. [CrossRef]

91. MacAlpine, M.; Zhao, Z.; Demokan, M.S. Development of a fibre-optic sensor for partial discharges in oil-filled power transformers. *Electr. Power Syst. Res.* **2002**, *63*, 27–36. [CrossRef]
92. Deng, J.; Xiao, H.; Huo, W.; Luo, M.; May, R.; Wang, A.; Liu, Y. Optical fiber sensor-based detection of partial discharges in power transformers. *Optics Laser Technol.* **2001**, *33*, 305–311. [CrossRef]
93. Yin, S.; Ruffin, P.B.; Yu, F.T.S. *Fiber Optic Sensors*, 2nd ed.; CRC Press: Boca Raton, FL, USA, 2008.
94. Chakravorti, S.; Dey, D.; Chatterjee, B. *Recent Trends in the Condition Monitoring of Transformers: Theory, Implementation and Analysis*; Springer: London, UK, 2013.
95. Bakar, N.A.; Abu-Siada, A.; Islam, S. A review of dissolved gas analysis measurement and interpretation techniques. *IEEE Electr. Insul. Mag.* **2014**, *30*, 39–49. [CrossRef]
96. Duval, M.; de Pabla, A. Interpretation of gas-in-oil analysis using new IEC publication 60599 and IEC TC 10 databases. *IEEE Electr. Insul. Mag.* **2001**, *17*, 31–41. [CrossRef]
97. *Frequency Response Analysis on Winding Deformation of Power Transformers*; DL/T 911-2004; National Development and Reform Commission of the People's Republic of China: Beijing, China, 2005.
98. Cigré WG A2/26. *Mechanical condition assessment of transformer windings using Frequency Response Analysis (FRA)*; CIGRE: Paris, France, 2008.
99. *Power Transformers -Part 18: Measurement of Frequency Response*; IEC 60076-18; International Electrotechnical Commission: Geneva, Switzerland, 2012.
100. *IEEE Guide for the Application and Interpretation of Frequency Response Analysis for Oil-Immersed Transformers*; IEEE Std C57.149; IEEE Standards Association: Piscataway, NJ, USA, 2012.
101. *The Short-Circuit Performance of Power Transformers*; CIGRE WG 12.19; CIGRE Technical Brochure 209; CIGRE: Paris, France, 2002.
102. Sweetser, C.; McGrail, T. *Sweep Frequency Response Analysis Transformer Applications*; Doble Engineering Company: Watertown, MA, USA, 2003.
103. *Mechanical-Condition Assessment of Transformer Windings Using Frequency Response Analysis (ERA)*; CIGRE WG A2.26.; CIGRE Report 342; CIGRE: Paris, France, 2008.
104. Bagheri, M.; Phung, B.T.; Blackburn, T. Influence of temperature and moisture content on frequency response analysis of transformer winding. *IEEE Trans. Dielectr. Electr. Insul.* **2014**, *21*, 1393–1404. [CrossRef]
105. Karimifard, P.; Gharehpetian, G.B.; Tenhohlen, S. Localization of winding radial deformation and determination of deformation extend using vector fitting-based estimated transfer function. *Eur. Trans. Electr. Power* **2009**, *19*, 749–762. [CrossRef]
106. Mohamed, Y.R.; Meghnefi, F.; Fofana, I. Frequency Response Analyses via Rational Function Fitting. In Proceedings of the 2012 IEEE Annual Conference on Electrical Insulation and Dielectric Phenomena (CEIDP), Montreal, QC, Canada, 14–17 October 2012.
107. Bigdeli, M.; Vakilian, M.; Rahimpour, E. A New Method for Detection and Evaluation of Winding Mechanical Faults in Transformer through Transfer Function Measurements. *Adv. Electr. Comput. Eng.* **2011**, *11*, 23–30. [CrossRef]
108. Behjat, V.; Vahedi, A.; Setayeshmehr, A.; Borsi, H.; Gockenbach, E. Diagnosing Shorted Turns on the Windings of Power Transformers Based Upon Online FRA Using Capacitive and Inductive Couplings. *IEEE Trans. Power Deliv.* **2011**, *26*, 2123–2133. [CrossRef]
109. Jonscher, K. *Dielectric Polarisation/Depolarisation in Solids*; Chelsea Dielectric Press: London, UK, 1984.
110. Zaengl, W.S. Application of Dielectric Spectroscopy in Time and Frequency Domain for HV Power Equipment. *IEEE Electr. Insul. Mag.* **2003**, *19*, 9–22. [CrossRef]
111. CIGRE Task Force 15.01.09. *Dielectric Response Methods for Diagnostics of Power Transformers*; Cigre brochure 254, Electra 202; CIGRE: Paris, France, 2003; pp. 25–36.
112. Saha, T.K. Review of Modern Diagnostic Techniques for Assessing Insulation Condition in Aged Transformers. *IEEE Trans. Dielectr. Electr. Insul.* **2003**, *10*, 903–917. [CrossRef]
113. Zaengl, W.S. Dielectric Spectroscopy in Time and Frequency Domain for HV Power Equipment, Part I: Theoretical Considerations. *IEEE Electr. Insul. Mag.* **2003**, *19*, 5–19. [CrossRef]
114. Seytashmehr, A.; Fofana, I.; Eichler, C.; Akbari, A.; Borsi, H.; Gockenbach, E. Dielectric Spectroscopic Measurements on Transformer Oil-Paper Insulation under Controlled Laboratory Conditions. *IEEE Trans. Dielectr. Electr. Insul.* **2008**, *15*, 1100–1111. [CrossRef]

115. Fofana, I.; Hemmatjou, H.; Meghnefi, F. Effect of Thermal Transient on the Polarization and Depolarization Current Measurements of Oil-Paper Insulation. *IEEE Trans. Dielectr. Electr. Insul.* **2011**, *18*, 513–520. [CrossRef]

116. Liao, R.; Hao, J.; Chen, G.; Yang, L. Quantitative analysis of ageing condition of oil-paper insulation by frequency domain spectroscopy. *IEEE Trans. Dielectr. Electr. Insul.* **2012**, *19*, 821–830. [CrossRef]

117. Suriyah-Jaya, M.; Leibfried, T. Accelerating Dielectric Response Measurements on Power Transformers—Part II: A Regression Approach. *IEEE Trans. Power Deliv.* **2014**, *29*, 2095–2100. [CrossRef]

118. Yousof, M.F.M.; Ekanayake, C.; Saha, T.K. Examining the ageing of transformer insulation using FRA and FDS techniques. *IEEE Trans. Dielectr. Electr. Insul.* **2015**, *22*, 1258–1265. [CrossRef]

119. Blennow, J.; Ekanayake, C.; Walczak, K.; Garcia, B.; Gubanski, S.M. Field experiences with measurements of dielectric response in frequency domain for power transformer diagnostics. *IEEE Trans. Power Deliv.* **2006**, *21*, 681–688. [CrossRef]

120. Pradhan, M.K.; Yew, K.J.H. Experimental investigation of insulation parameters affecting power transformer condition assessment using frequency domain spectroscopy. *IEEE Trans. Dielectr. Electr. Insul.* **2012**, *19*, 1851–1859. [CrossRef]

121. Van Bolhuis, P. *Applicability of Recovery Voltage and on-line Partial Discharge Measurements for Condition Assessment of High Voltage Power Transformers*; Optima Grafische Communicatie: Rotterdam, The Netherlands, 2002; pp. 105–153.

122. Kachler, A.J.; Baehr, R.; Zaengl, W.S.; Breitenbauch, B.; Sundermann, U. Kritische Anmerkungen zur Feuchtigkeitsbestimmung von Transformatoren mit der "Recovery-Voltage-Methode". *Elektrizitätswirtschaft* **1996**, *95*, 1238–1245. (In German)

123. Kachler, A.J. Ageing and Moisture Determination in Power Transformer Insulation Systems. Contradiction of RVM Methodology, Effects of Geometry and Ion Conductivity. In Proceedings of the 2nd International Workshop on Transformers, Lodz, Poland, 24–27 November 1999.

124. Saha, T.K.; Purkait, P. Investigations of temperature effects on the dielectric response measurements of transformer oil-paper insulation system. *IEEE Trans. Power Deliv.* **2008**, *23*, 252–260. [CrossRef]

125. Jaya, M.; Geißler, D.; Leibfried, T. Accelerating dielectric response measurements on power transformers—Part I: A frequency domain approach. *IEEE Trans. Power Deliv.* **2013**, *28*, 1469–1473. [CrossRef]

126. Jaya, M.; Leibfried, T. Accelerating Dielectric Response Measurements on Power Transformers—Part II: A Regression Approach. *IEEE Trans. Power Deliv.* **2014**, *29*, 2095–2100. [CrossRef]

127. Shayegani, A.A.; Gockenbach, E.; Borsi, H.; Mohseni, H. Investigation on the transformation of time domain spectroscopy data to frequency domain data for impregnated pressboard to reduce measurement time. *Electr. Eng.* **2006**, *89*, 11–20. [CrossRef]

128. Farahani, M.; Borsi, H.; Gockenbach, E. Dielectric Response Studies on Insulating System of High Voltage Rotating Machines. *IEEE Trans. Dielectr. Electr. Insul.* **2006**, *13*, 383–393. [CrossRef]

129. Birlasekaran, S.; Yu, X. Relaxation Studies on Power Equipment. *IEEE Trans. Dielectr. Electr. Insul.* **2003**, *10*, 1061–1077. [CrossRef]

130. Dong, M.; Ren, M.; Wen, F.; Zhang, C.; Liu, J.; Sumereder, C.; Muhr, M. Explanation and analysis of oil-paper insulation based on frequency-domain dielectric spectroscopy. *IEEE Trans. Dielectr. Electr. Insul.* **2015**, *22*, 2684–2693.

131. Hadjadj, Y.; Meghnefi, F.; Fofana, I.; Ezzaidi, H. On the Feasibility of Using Poles Computed from Frequency Domain Spectroscopy to Assess Oil Impregnated Paper Insulation Conditions. *Energies* **2013**, *6*, 2204–2220. [CrossRef]

132. Saha, T.K.; Purkait, P. Understanding the impacts of moisture and thermal aging on transformer's insulation by dielectric response and molecular weight measurements. *IEEE Trans. Dielectr. Electr. Insul.* **2008**, *15*, 568–582. [CrossRef]

133. Yao, Z.T.; Saha, T.K. *Separation of Ageing and Moisture Impacts on Transformer Insulation Degradation by Polarisation Measurements*; CIGRE: Paris, France, 2002; pp. 15–304.

134. Betie, A.; Meghnefi, F.; Fofana, I.; Yeo, Z.; Ezzaidi, H. Neural network approach to separate aging and moisture from the dielectric response of oil impregnated paper insulation. *IEEE Trans. Dielectr. Electr. Insul.* **2015**, *22*, 2176–2184. [CrossRef]

135. Tang, W.H.; Wu, Q.H. *Condition Monitoring and Assessment of Power Transformers Using Computational Intelligence*; Springer: London, UK, 2011.

136. Tenbohlen, S.; Stirl, T.; Bastos, G.; Baldauf, J.; Mayer, P.; Stach, M.; Breitenbauch, B.; Huber, R. *Experience-Based Evaluation of Economic Benefits of On-line Monitoring Systems for Power Transformers*; CIGRE Session 2002; Paris, France, 2002; pp. 12–110.

137. CIGRE WG 12.18 Life Management of Transformers. Guidelines for Life Management Techniques for Power Transformers. Draft Final Report Rev. 2, 22 June 2002. Available online: http://www.buenomak.com.br/publicacoes/pdf/TRANSFdePOTEN-2002_life_management_techniques.pdf (accessed on 9 May 2016).

Review

Progress of Space Charge Research on Oil-Paper Insulation Using Pulsed Electroacoustic Techniques

Chao Tang [1,2,*], Bo Huang [2], Miao Hao [2], Zhiqiang Xu [2], Jian Hao [3] and George Chen [2]

[1] College of Engineering and Technology, Southwest University, Beibei, Chongqing 400715, China
[2] School of Electronics and Computer Science, University of Southampton, Highfield Campus, Southampton SO17 1BJ, UK; bh2e13@ecs.soton.ac.uk (B.H.); mh2e10@soton.ac.uk (M.H.); zx4@ecs.soton.ac.uk (Z.X.); gc@ecs.soton.ac.uk (G.C.)
[3] State Grid Chongqing Electric Power Corperation Chongqing Electric Power Research Institute, Chongqing 401123, China; cquhaojian@126.com
* Correspondence: tangchao_1981@163.com; Tel./Fax: +86-23-6825-1265

Academic Editor: Issouf Fofana
Received: 19 November 2015; Accepted: 12 January 2016; Published: 18 January 2016

Abstract: This paper focuses on the space charge behavior in oil-paper insulation systems used in power transformers. It begins with the importance of understanding the space charge behavior in oil-paper insulation systems, followed by the introduction of the pulsed electrostatic technique (PEA). After that, the research progress on the space charge behavior of oil-paper insulation during the recent twenty years is critically reviewed. Some important aspects such as the environmental conditions and the acoustic wave recovery need to be addressed to acquire more accurate space charge measurement results. Some breakthroughs on the space charge behavior of oil-paper insulation materials by the research team at the University of Southampton are presented. Finally, future work on space charge measurement of oil-paper insulation materials is proposed.

Keywords: space charge; insulation oil; insulation paper; pulsed electroacoustic technique (PEA); temperature; moisture content; simulation

---

1. Introduction

High Voltage Direct Current (HVDC) systems have been used for energy transmission since the 1950s. In comparison with the conventional transformers used in HVAC transmission systems, converter transformers have a more complex structure and operate under more severe conditions. These severe conditions include the overvoltage from lightning and switching, the combined AC and DC voltage, and the polarity reversal applied at the DC side windings.

The reliability and the sustainable operation of the converter transformer are of great significance. The reason is that the failure of the converter transformer could lead to the breakdown of the power supply, resulting in large economic losses. The main insulation of the converter transformer normally consists of insulation oil and cellulose paper. The aging of insulation materials cannot be avoided under the complex operation conditions mentioned above. According to reports, half of transformer failures result from the insulation aging phenomenon [1,2]. The space charge density is closely related to the aging status of the insulation material. Therefore, the amount of space charge could be an indicator of the aging status of insulation materials. The space charge formation could lead to the distortion of the electric field distribution and speed up the aging rate. Considering the space charge serves an important role correlated with the conduction and breakdown phenomena, therefore, the topic of space charge is widely studied.

In this paper, firstly, the recent twenty years of research progress have been critically reviewed. Secondly, some aspects have been proposed with special attention on how to achieve more accurate measurements of space charge dynamics in oil-paper insulation materials. Thirdly, recent researches conducted by the University of Southampton on oil-paper insulation materials has been critically analyzed. Finally, future work will be proposed to predict the future research trends of space charge behavior in the oil-paper insulation materials.

2. PEA Technique in Space Charge Test

The pulsed electroacoustic (PEA) technique was developed in the 1980s. It can measure the space charge behavior during the poling process, *i.e.*, under the stress of the electric field, or during depolarization, *i.e.*, after the removal of the electric field. Therefore, it can provide essential information on space charge dynamics within the insulation materials [3]. In comparison to other traditional methods, the PEA method offers a nondestructive way to observe charge behavior in dielectric materials, making it possible to understand the physical processes behind the phenomena and to minimize the risks of partial discharge and electrical breakdown of insulation materials. Therefore, it could serve as a possible method to select better insulation materials with the consideration of surface states.

The details of a PEA system can be found in the literature [4], and the basic set-up and schematic diagram are shown in Figure 1. Generally speaking, after the application of the electric pulse on the insulation materials between two electrodes, acoustic waves are produced at charge locations at both electrodes and inside the test material. The acoustic signals are detected by a piezo-electric sensor at the back side of one electrode. The electric signal obtained in the time domain represents the charge distribution [5]:

$$V_s\left(t\right) = K\left[\sigma_1 + \sigma_2 + v_{sa} \times T \times \rho\left(x = v_{sa} \times t\right)\right] \times e_P \tag{1}$$

where σ_1 and σ_2 are the surface charges at the electrodes, v_{sa} is the sound velocity through the material, T is the pulse width, $\rho\left(x\right)$ is the bulk charge and e_P is the pulse amplitude.

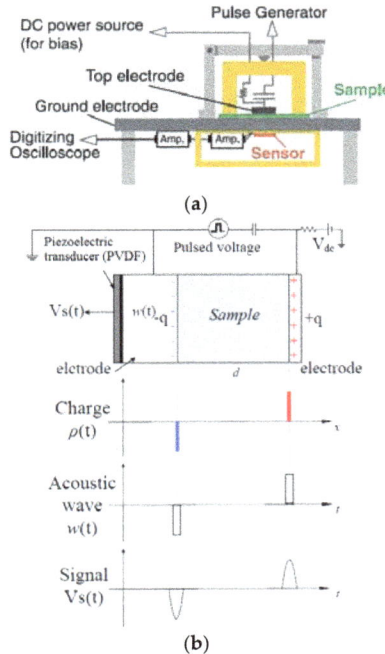

(a)

(b)

Figure 1. Basic set-up (**a**) and schematic diagram (**b**) of PEA method.

3. Research Progress

The earliest studies on space charge in oil-paper insulation were performed by the ABB Corporate Research Center in Sweden in 1994. Experiments were performed by using the pressure wave propagation (PWP) method. However, the research results were not so good because of the limitations of the test equipment available at that time [6–8]. Since 1997, a few studies have been performed on the space charge in oil-paper insulation using the PEA method. Morshuis and Jeroense [9] made some important space charge tests and discussions on oil-impregnated insulation paper. Ciobanu in 2002 suggested that the evolution of PEA derived parameters, such as charge density, apparent trap-controlled mobility and variation of trap depth distribution, can be successfully used for promoting criteria for the best choice of oil-paper insulation technology for DC cable applications [10]. Since 2008, much more research on space charge behaviors in oil-paper insulation has been reported. Therefore, the research progress in recent years has been critically reviewed from the applied voltage, temperature, moisture, aging, interfaces, polarity reversal, and AC electric field perspectives.

3.1. Applied Voltage

In general, at a relatively low temperature (20 °C), the applied DC voltage had a great influence on the amount of charge density as well as the depth of charge injection (Figure 2). With the increase of applied DC voltage, the amount of charge density and charge injection depth increase within the bulk sample.

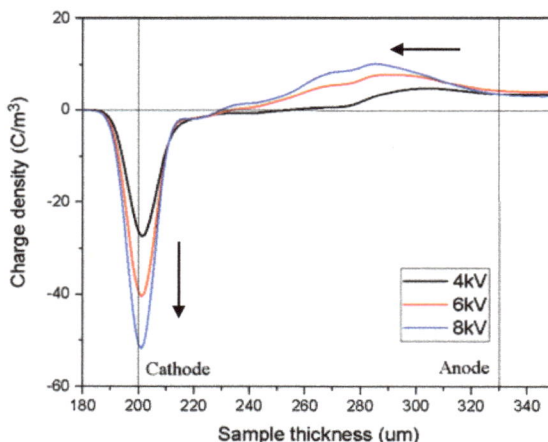

Figure 2. Space charge dynamics at different DC electric fields (volt-on 30 min at 20 °C, three layers, about 130 μm in total sample thickness).

The volt-off tests (instantaneous power off under different applied DC voltages) verified that with the increase of the applied voltage, a large amount of charges at the electrodes were induced by the higher amount of homo-charge injection (Figure 3). Moreover, the real injection charges also had an increasing trend with the increase of the applied voltage.

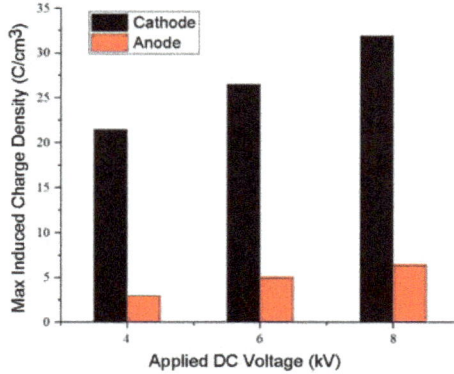

Figure 3. Max induced charge density on the electrodes after instantaneous power off under different DC voltages at 20 °C (volt-off).

3.2. Test Temperature

A series of measurements were carried out where an oil-paper insulation system was subjected to different test temperatures (from 15 °C to 60 °C) [11–14]. The results showed that the temperature had a limited effect on the threshold voltage of the space charge. Under different test temperatures (less than 60 °C), space charges injection took place at nearly the same voltage level. However, the temperature can have a greater influence on the distribution and mobility of space charge within oil-paper samples. The higher temperature could lead to higher space charge injection mobility and injection depth. The space charge decay process also satisfies the previous rule.

Besides, comparing the peak value of charge density at the cathode under different DC voltages and temperatures (Figure 4), it was clear that both the applied voltage and testing temperature have a great effect on charge density at the cathode, which might occur at the anode as well. When the temperature came to 60 °C and the applied DC voltage was 8 kV (about 60 kV/mm), the charge density at the cathode reached the maximum value. This indicated that the combination of a high temperature and a high level of electric stress may result in fatal impacts to the performance of the oil-paper insulation system.

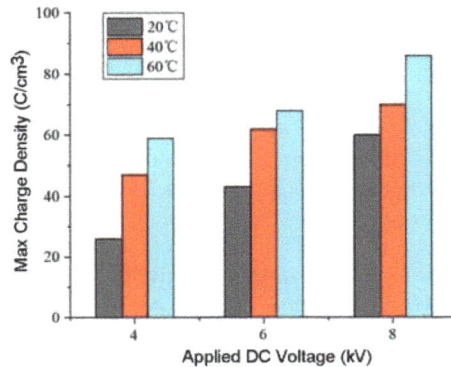

Figure 4. Max charge density on the negative electrode under different DC voltages and temperatures (three layers, about 130 μm in total thickness).

3.3. Moisture Content

Normally, in industrial applications, the moisture content in oil-paper insulation in power transformers should be controlled to quite a low level like less than 0.5% by weight by vacuum drying and preprocessing of the oil and paper. The main reason is that moisture is one of the most important parameters which influences the properties of transformer insulation. It has a detrimental effect on oil-paper insulation life by lowering the electrical breakdown strength and thermal endurance, resulting in an increased risk of dielectric breakdown. Moisture is recognized as "enemy number one" after the temperature [4].

The space charge dynamics varied in three layers of the oil-paper insulation system with three different moisture concentrations (0.28%, 1.32% and 4.96%), which were investigated using the PEA technique under 6 kV (about 28.5 kV/mm) [15]. Within the frequency range from 10^{-2} Hz to 10^2 Hz, the oil conductivity of oil-impregnated paper increased significantly with the increase of moisture content. It has been proved that the moisture has a great effect on the charge distribution in a multi-layer oil-paper insulation system. A higher moisture content of the oil-paper sample could lead to a larger positive and negative charge injection. There are fewer slow moving charges trapped in the sample due to higher conductivity (Figure 5). Besides, the total absolute amount of fast moving charges in the sample also has a close relation with the moisture content.

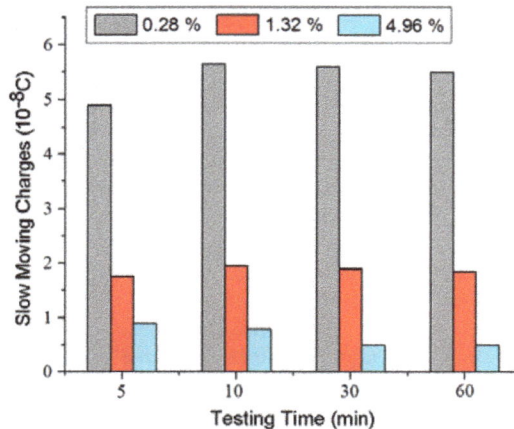

Figure 5. Total absolute amount of slow moving charges in the oil-paper sample with different moisture content under the volt-off condition (6 kV) at 15 °C.

Zhou studied five kinds of oil-paper with moisture concentrations of 1%, 3%, 5%, 7% and 9% at 25 °C (10 kV/mm) [16]. Figure 6 illustrates the space charge distribution profiles of unaged samples with different moisture concentrations at 30 min of polarization. It is suggested that the effect of moisture changes with the variation of contents itself, when the moisture concentration was less than 7%, a higher moisture concentration was helpful for the equilibrium establishment of space charge, while if it were larger than 9%, it would affect results contrarily [16].

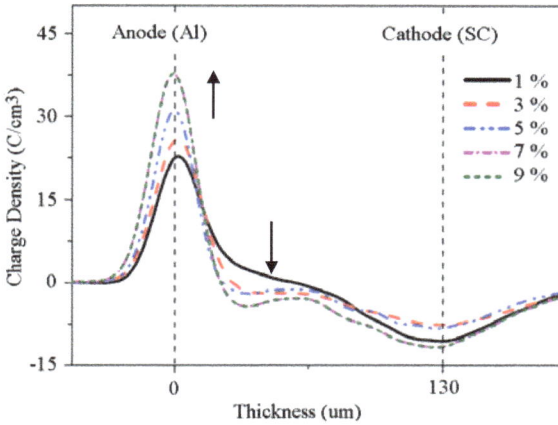

Figure 6. Space charge distribution curves of unaged samples with different moisture concentrations at the end of 30 min polarization [16].

3.4. Ageing

Insulation life is normally determined by measuring the time from the beginning of service to final breakdown. During operation, a deterioration in the chemical, physical and electrical properties of an insulation material is termed as ageing, which reduces the operation life of the insulation material. For years, the single thermal stress ageing (accelerated ageing) test procedures have proved to have been useful and can be performed in the laboratory to deduce the lifespan of liquid and solid insulation systems [17,18]. Thus, based on the ageing experiment, the effects of material ageing on space charge behaviors were investigated.

3.4.1. Aged Paper + New Oil

To investigate the effect of paper ageing on space charge behavior, an accelerated thermal ageing experiment of mineral oil immersed paper at 130 °C was conducted for 18 days (single layer with a thickness of 50 μm) [19]. After that, the paper samples were impregnated with new mineral oil in a sealed oven under vacuum conditions, in preparation for the space charge tests (30 kV/mm). The DP of paper was less than 600 after 10 days' ageing, which represents the mid-term status of the insulation lifespan, and less than 300 after 18 days' ageing, which was close to the end of service life.

The results showed that as the ageing time increased, the polar or conductive byproducts increased, which made space charge injection into the bulk sample easier. With further deterioration of the paper, the larger amount of charge density observed at the anode and in the bulk led to a higher total amount of charges accumulated in the oil-paper sample (Figures 7 and 8). Compared with the unaged oil-paper sample, the maximum value of electrical field strength for seriously aged (18 days) oil-paper samples was more than 70% higher than the average electrical field strength [19].

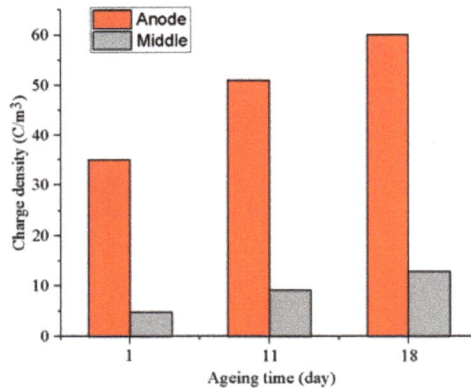

Figure 7. The charge density of the charges accumulated at the anode and in the middle position of the paper [19].

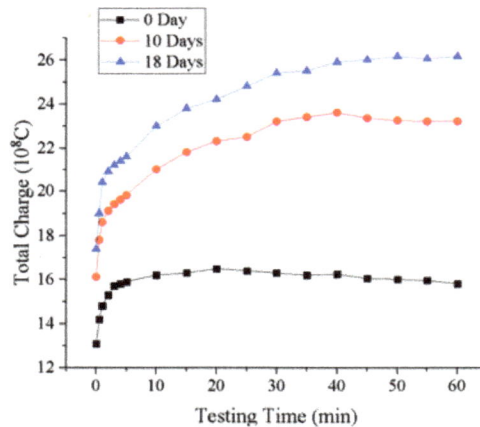

Figure 8. Total amount of charges in the oil-paper insulation with paper aged for different days under the electrical field of 30 kV/mm [19].

3.4.2. Aged Oil + New Paper

Another topic of great significance is to investigate the influence of oil ageing on the space charge characteristics of oil-paper insulation. In Southampton, Gemini X mineral oil was thermally aged at 130 °C for up to 22 days, and then, preprocessed unaged paper samples were impregnated with oil of different ageing status to form a series of oil-paper insulation samples. After that, the space charge dynamics of these oil-paper samples were investigated using the PEA technique under DC 6 kV (three layers, 210 μm in thickness, 30 kV/mm) [20].

The results showed that the oil properties could have a significant effect on the space charge behavior of the oil-paper samples. With the deterioration resulting from oil ageing, the oil acidity increased. The polar/conductive byproducts generated led to easier charge injection and more charge accumulation in the bulk of the sample. The maximum charge density of both negative charges trapped in the vicinity of the cathode and positive charges trapped at the paper-paper interface near the cathode increased with the increase of oil deterioration. Besides, the trap energy density of the paper sample with seriously aged oil was much higher than that with new oil, and the amount of slow moving charges trapped in the paper sample with oil aged for 22 days was more than two times that seen with new oil. Therefore, it resulted in an increase of the total amount of slow moving charges, and a more serious electric field distortion (Figures 9 and 10). The maximum percentage of electric field enhancement during volt-on process under 6 kV is 55% after 14 days' ageing and 25% after 22 days' ageing, respectively.

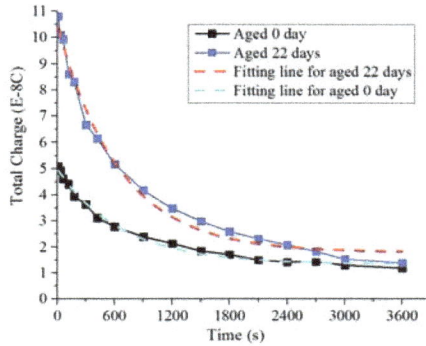

Figure 9. Charge decay in samples with new and 22 days' aged oil under 6 kV [20].

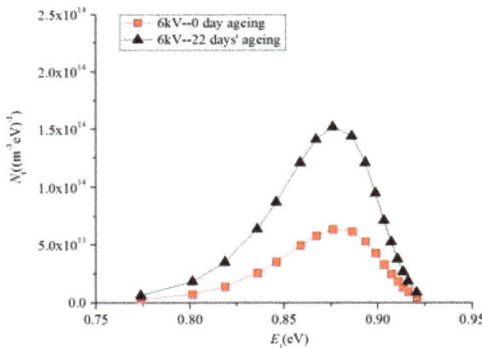

Figure 10. Trap energy distributions for samples with new oil and seriously aged oil under different voltages at 15 °C [20].

3.4.3. Aged Oil-Paper

In 2004, Ciobanu tried to identify the evolution of space charges and fields in thermally aged oil-paper systems using the PEA method. The measurements were carried out with oil-immersed paper specimens, with a thickness of 70 μm and 0.43% mineral content, submitted to a poling field of about 80% of breakdown strength [21]. The conclusions showed that homo-charge injection was clearly noticed, and the charge packet formation was triggered by the thermal stress, in conjunction with the value of the applied field.

The experiment results from the University of Southampton in 2008 (three layers, about 220 um in thickness, 35 kV/mm) showed that as the ageing time increased, the threshold voltage decreased which made the charge injection easier, the charge density increased and the total charge amount inside oil-paper increased as well. A clear exponential law was observed for the charge decay process, as shown in Figure 11 [22].

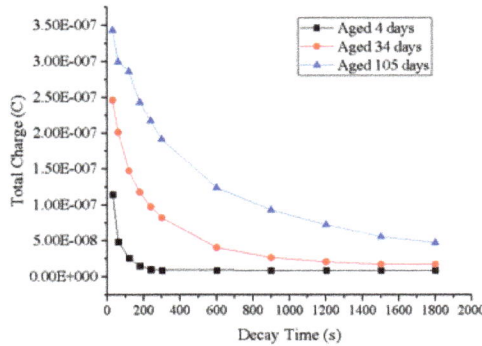

Figure 11. Total charge amount inside oil-paper with different ageing degrees.

In 2015, the most recent studies by Zhou *et al.* (single layer, 130 μm, 10 kV/mm) showed that the formation of space charge by unaged and aged oil-paper were consequently different under low electric field conditions [23]. Along with the degradation of cellulose, more traps inside paper samples were generated, more charge (especially positive charges) was trapped, and the electric field distortion was more severe as the ageing progressed (Figure 12).

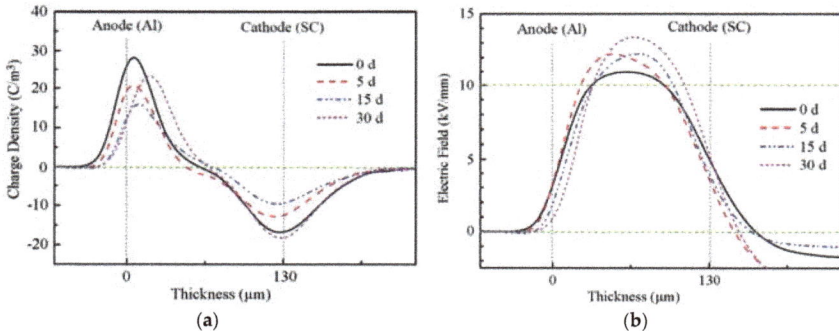

Figure 12. Space charge (**a**) and corrected electric field distribution profiles (**b**) of oil-paper aged for different days, measured at the end of 30 min polarization under 10 kV/mm electric field [23].

3.5. Interfaces

In HV insulation systems, there are different kinds of dielectric interfaces, such as solid-solid (cable accessories, insulation paper with paper, and paper with metallic conductor), solid-gas (gas-insulated high-voltage switchgear—GIS) and solid-liquid (insulation paper with oil). In the interface regions, the difference in permittivity and conductivity of the dielectric materials across the interface may lead to interfacial polarization and space charge formation [24,25]. Here, two kinds of interfaces that are closely associated with power transformers are discussed.

3.5.1. Paper-Oil Interface

The tests in Southampton reported that an interfacial charge peak was quickly formed at the interface between oil and pressboard upon the external voltage application [26]. However, the dynamics of interfacial charges in fresh oil and aged oil samples were quite different, which resulted from the difference in moisture content and oil conductivity. The PEA test research results from samples with a 500 μm oil gap and 200 μm fresh oil-impregnated insulation pressboard indicated that the charge decay rate was much slower than in single layer oil-immersed paper. The interface provided deeper traps and made it difficult for the trapped charges to dissipate [27]. However, compared with the new oil gap and oil-impregnated pressboard insulation, a higher charge migration rate was clearly observed in aged oil gap and oil-impregnated pressboard. There were nearly no charges observed in the sample after five mins of decay time (Figure 13). The main reason could be due to the higher conductivity of the aged samples.

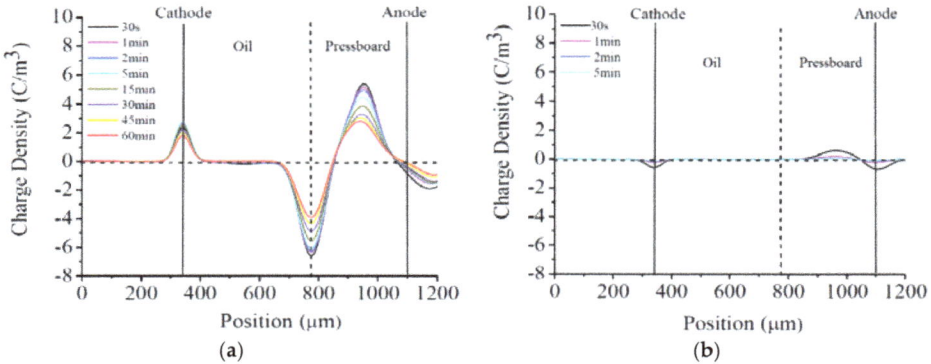

Figure 13. Space charge decay of new oil gap and oil impregnated pressboard ((a) new oil with 0.68% water content, (b) aged oil with 3.83% water content) [27].

A further study made by Wu *et al.* on the space charge properties of oil-immersed-paper with different oil gap thicknesses, revealed some rules of charges accumulation. The charges with the same polarity as the oil side electrode were accumulated at the interface and gradually increased with the increase of applied voltage (Figure 14). The amount of interface charge decreased with the increase of oil layer thickness because of the charge recombination in oil [28]. The results showed that interfaces have a direct effect of restraining charge migration inside the oil-paper insulation, which would lead to the electric field distortion. The interfacial charges proved to have the same polarity with the electrode close to the oil layer [28].

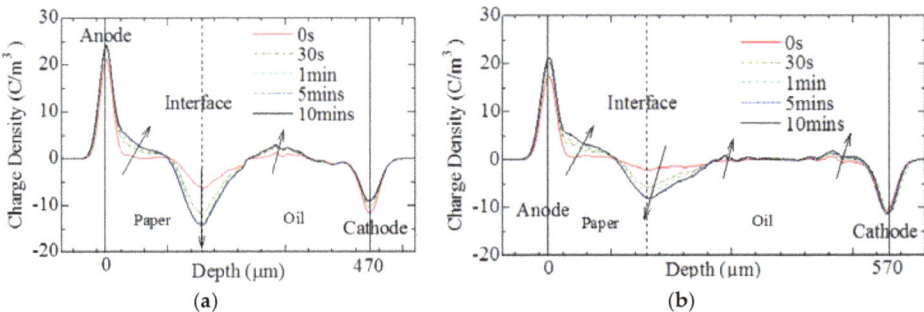

Figure 14. *Cont.*

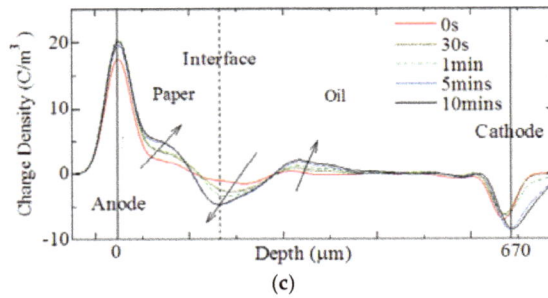

(c)

Figure 14. Space charge development under an average field of 20 kV/mm with different thickness of oil [28]. (**a**) 0.17 mm oil-immersed-paper with 0.3 mm oil (**b**) 0.17 mm oil-immersed-paper with 0.4 mm oil; (**c**) 0.17 mm oil-immersed-paper with 0.5 mm oil.

Moreover, the electric field measurement in the oil and oil/solid composite can be directly compared to an electro-optical measurement. The Kerr electro-optic effect has been applied to measure the electric field in insulation liquid since 1983 [29] and measured the oil/solid dielectrics composite insulation system in transformer under dc voltage in 1997 [30]. It offers a way to validate the PEA results and reveal the inner mechanism of charge behavior.

3.5.2. Paper-Paper Interface

As for the topic of paper-paper interface, these are interfaces in the multi-layer oil immersed paper without the tiny oil gap being taken into consideration. the space charge behaviors of up to four paper layers were tested at Southampton in 2008, using the PEA method [22]. The results (Figure 15) showed that homo-charge injections were observed in all cases considering the physical-chemical properties of oil-paper itself. In most conditions, space charges were accumulated at the interfaces, which indicated that the paper-paper interfaces have a significant effect on slowing down space charge migration (Figure 16). The interfacial charges were mainly supposed to be formed by ionic charges and polarization charges mainly.

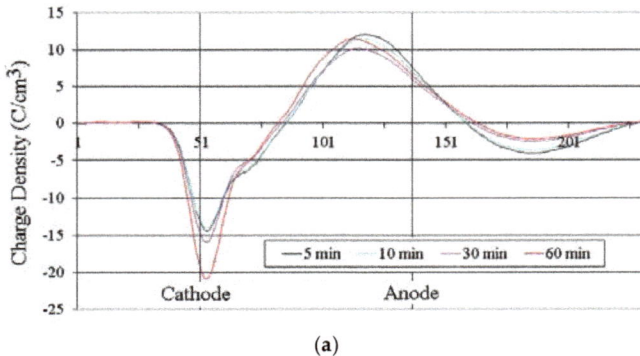

(a)

Figure 15. *Cont.*

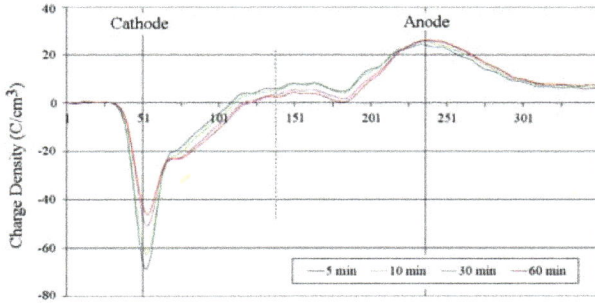

(b)

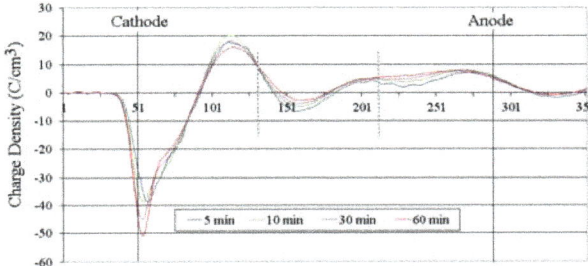

(c)

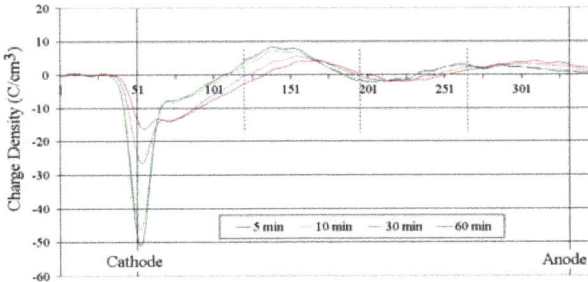

(d)

Figure 15. Space charge behaviour of oil-paper insulation with different layers under volt-on condition ((**a**) one layer, (**b**) two layers; (**c**) three layers; (**d**) four layers).

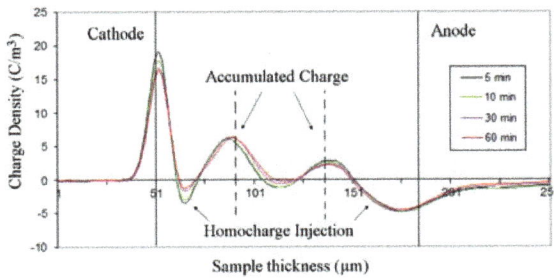

Figure 16. Space charge behaviour of oil-paper insulation with three layers under Volt-off condition.

The polarity of the applied DC voltage would affect the polarity of charge trapped at the interfaces. Under negative voltage, the negative charge accumulated at the interface. The positive charge could accumulate at the interface under the positive voltage, and the same phenomenon could be found in the literature [31–33]. Different from the oil-paper interfaces mentioned above, when homo-charge injection takes place, the polarity of charge accumulated in the paper-paper interface is usually opposite to the polarity of the nearest electrode in the vicinity of the PVDF sensor.

3.6. Polarity Reversal

The polarity reversal of DC voltage is an important operation in HVDC transmission (especially in the converter transformer) to control the direction of power flow (Figure 17). It is believed that a transient electric field enhancement within the oil happens immediately after the voltage reversal, as the accumulated charges in oil has the opposite polarity compared to the cellulose pressboard. This temporary voltage distribution is governed by the conductivity and permittivity of the dielectrics, which may also be affected by the value of applied voltage, moisture, temperature and so on. Early in 1995, Liu investigated the charge storage and transport in oil-impregnated pressboard (1 mm in thickness, ±15 kV) at polarity reversal under HVDC by using the pressure wave propagation (PWP) technique [34], and significant field distortion was observed when the polarity reversal occurs. In recent years, researchers have paid more attention to the charge dynamics under polarity reversal voltage in single layered oil impregnated paper/pressboard [35–37].

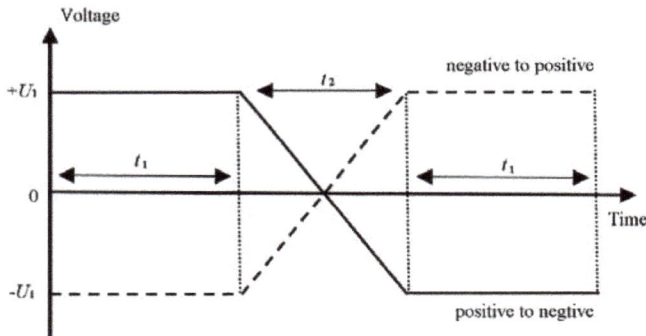

Figure 17. Polarity reversal of DC voltage.

Space charge dynamics in oil gap and thick pressboard combined system (1 mm thick pressboard with a 0.5 mm thick oil film) under polarity reversal voltage were researched in Southampton [35]. Three kinds of oil, which were fresh, medium aged and severely aged oil were used. Compared with the fresh and medium aged oil, the charge injection enhanced greatly in the severely aged oil samples. The electric field was significantly distorted during the first stage of DC stressing process for the aged oil. After polarity reversal, most of the space charges had dissipated. Therefore, only a small electric field enhancement in the oil could be observed. Then significant homo-charge injection occurred again and the "mirror image effect" was observed (Figure 18).

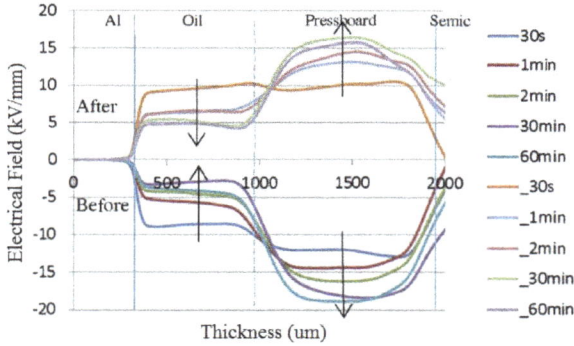

Figure 18. The "mirror image effect" of electric field distribution [35].

Further investigation of the impacts caused by the duration of polarity reversal process was performed on both the fresh oil immersed paper sample and the aged oil immersed paper sample. For the fresh oil sample, the electric field enhancement in the oil gap is smaller than 10% immediately after the application of the reversed voltage. Therefore, the polarity reversal durations have limited influence on the electric field enhancement. For the aged oil sample, the electric field across the oil gap could be significantly enhanced by voltage polarity reversal. A shorter reverse period could lead to a higher the electric stress enhancement (Table 1). The same conclusions could be found in [36], which indicates that the reversal period (reversal time) is proved to have an effect on space charge accumulation.

Table 1. Impacts of the duration of polarity reversal process in the aged oil sample under 20 kV/mm.

Duration t_2 (Min)	Peak value of the Ground Electrode (C/m^3)	Maximum Electric Field (kV/mm)	Field Enhancement in the Oil Gap (%)
0.5	15	42.1	110.5
2	9.3	27.2	36
5	8.5	26.6	33

3.7. AC Electric Field

Due to the complexity of the testing and the hardware restriction, the research on the space charge characteristics of insulating materials under AC stressing lags quite behind that under DC conditions. Especially for the oil-paper insulation, it has not been widely carried out, though it is quite an interesting and important topic and has been investigated in Southampton since 2010.

The sample was oil-impregnated insulation paper aged for 22 days, under an AC electric field of 60 kV/mm (peak to peak). According to the research results shown in Figure 19, the amount of space charge accumulated in the oil-paper insulation sample under sinusoidal AC conditions was reduced significantly compared to that under DC conditions [38]. However, there were some positive charges observed to accumulate in the paper layer near the Al electrode. The oil properties had an obvious impact on the charge distribution. The severe deterioration of the oil could lead to a larger amount of charges injected into the oil-impregnated insulation paper [39].

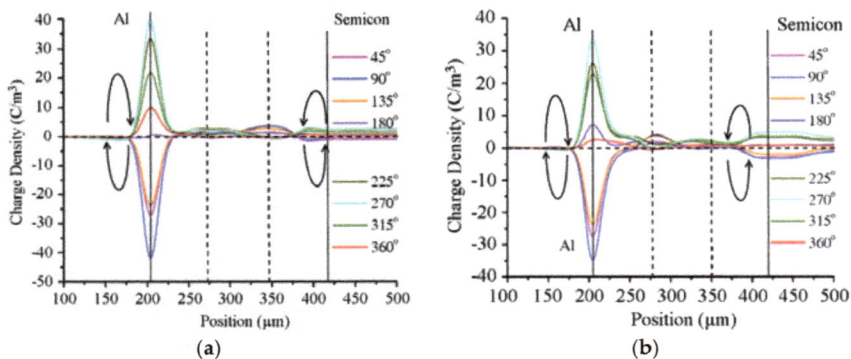

Figure 19. AC volt-on space charge behaviour in a sinusoidal cycle at 120 min for oil immersed paper sample (60 kV/mm, peak-peak) [36]. (a) new oil immersed paper; (b) 22 days' aged oil immersed paper.

4. Key Points for Space Charge Testing of Oil-Paper Insulation Systems

The PEA method was originally developed to measure space charge behaviors in polymer materials, and it has been applied to a broad variety of substances, such as XLPE, LDPE, polyimide and oil-paper, most of which are homogeneous solid materials [40–44]. However, for oil-paper insulation material, due to its loose, porous and hygroscopic structure, as well as multi-layer application, the space charge measurements are much more complicated than those in polymers. When discussing the possible errors that may occur in using the PEA method, much more attention must be paid to the test conditions, the charge density calibration, signal processing, waveform recovery, and charge distribution calculation. Here, some special concerns relating the key points of space charge tests on oil-paper insulation are discussed.

4.1. Test Condition Control

The oil-paper insulation consists of insulation paper (pressboard) and oil, which have high moisture absorption ability and their space charge behavior are strongly influenced by temperature. It is vitally important to control the space charge test conditions strictly so as to ensure the accuracy and reproducibility of test results. The test conditions include, on one hand, the environment parameters of short term testing which may last for hours to days, on the other hand, the relative uniformity of long term testing (from weeks to months).

4.1.1. Relative Humidity (Moisture Content)

For the space charge tests using PEA, the test procedure for one sample usually involves 30 min to 3 h of voltage stressing plus 30 min to 1 h decay, which makes the whole process take hours. Although the oil-paper sample is covered by theupper and lower electrodes, the commonly open to air PEA test cell of the oil-paper sample will not prevent the moisture absorption from the environment, especially for some kinds of oil with a high moisture saturation (Table 2). In that case, the moisture content inside the oil-paper will increase during the test process and cause some inaccuracy in the test results.

Table 2. The maximum moisture content in some kinds of insulating oils.

	Karamay 25#	**Gemini X**	**MIDEL 7131**	**BIOTEMP**
Maximum moisture content	⩾50 ppm	⩾50 ppm	⩾1000 ppm	⩾150 ppm

In most laboratory experiments, oil and paper samples are pre-processed to limit the moisture content to be consistent with a real transformer. However, during the experiment, insulation paper (pressboard) and oil will rapidly absorb moisture until they reach equilibrium with the ambient relative humidity. A simple test on the moisture absorbing ability of preprocessed insulation paper (Weidmann, transformer board TIV/IEC, 1 mm in thickness with an original moisture content of less than 0.5%) placed in an uncovered beaker in the laboratory is shown in Figure 20. It suggests that once open to the air, the dry paper sample would quickly absorb moisture, and the moisture content increases rapidly within the first few hours. The same goes for oil and oil-paper though the distribution and equilibrium inside oil-paper are quite complicated. The unexpected increase of moisture in oil-paper during the test will influence the signal processing and subsequent analysis of space charge behavior.

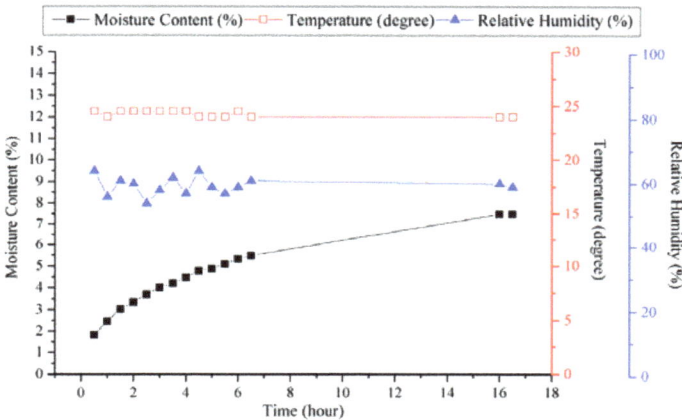

Figure 20. The moisture absorbing ability of pre-processed insulation paper.

(1) Influence on the space charge behavior

Results from Southampton in [14] show that the moisture content, even within 5%, has a great influence on the charge injection, movement and accumulation. The higher the moisture content of the oil-paper sample, the higher the mobility of the charges, and more positive charge injection and negative charge injection were observed. Moreover, the higher mobility of the charges leads to less slow moving charges trapped in the sample with higher moisture content. While for the sample with 4.96% moisture content, due to its higher conductivity, the charges injected in the sample could transport to the opposite electrode rapidly, thus fewer charges were trapped and could be measured. According to Figure 20, under room temperature and a normal relative humidity, the time for the preprocessed insulation paper sample to reach a moisture content of 5% is less than 6 h. Therefore, more attention should be paid to the influence of an unexpected increase in moisture content.

(2) Influence on the signal processing of space charge test

In the PEA test, an electric pulse is applied to the test sample, resulting in a perturbation force at the space charge location, which generates an acoustic wave. The final output space charge information is calculated from the voltage signal provided by the piezoelectric sensor, which is originally transferred by the detected acoustic wave. Therefore, the propagation of the acoustic wave inside the specimen, the oil-paper insulation, in this case, should be carefully investigated.

In general, the acoustic velocity V in solids and liquids (one dimensional) are given by the Newton-Laplace equation:

$$V_{solid} = \sqrt{E/\rho}, \ V_{fluid} = \sqrt{K/\rho} \tag{2}$$

where E is the Young's modulus, K is the bulk modulus of the fluid.

The relationship between acoustic velocity V (m/s) in mineral oil and water content P (%) is given below:

$$V = a_0 + a_1 P \tag{3}$$

where, a_0 and a_1 are constant for a specific fluid under a certain temperature.

As it can be seen in Equations (2) and (3), the variation in moisture content also has an influence on the acoustic velocity in the oil-paper insulation material. A higher water content can lead to a higher acoustic velocity. Therefore, the moisture will lead to a variation of space charge distribution in the time domain.

4.1.2. Environment Temperature

For scientific work, room temperature is normally taken to be about 20 °C to 26 °C with an average of 23 °C. In the uncontrolled environment of the indoor laboratory, the temperature variation from lowest to highest in a test period could reach 15–20 °C. For example, a long term ageing experiment (which may last for months) implies a long duration of the space charge tests on samples with different degrees of ageing. Therefore, the relative humidity and the variation in temperature have an influence on both the space charge behavior and the signal processing of space charges in oil-paper.

The speed of sound in mineral oil in the pressure range of 0–1400 bar and the temperature range of 10–121 °C is shown in Figure 21 [45]. An increase in temperature could lead to a decrease of the magnitude of the acoustic wave within the test sample. Besides, the PVDF, which is used as an important component in the PEA test cell to convert the acoustic signal into electrical signal is also sensitive to temperature variations. For example, the pyro-electrical coefficient for a biaxially oriented PVDF film is $-24 \ \mu C/m^2 \cdot K$ [46]. Though the PVDF characteristics have improved a lot in recent years, the influence of conversion efficiency for PVDF caused by the variation of temperature may still require more attention.

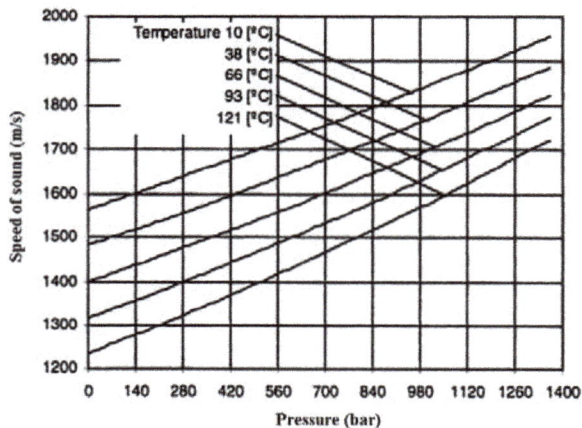

Figure 21. The speed curve of sound in mineral oil [45].

4.2. Signal Processing and Recovery

4.2.1. Acoustic Impedance

The PEA method is based on the generation and propagation of acoustic waves [47]. In the case of different sample layers or multi-layers, a key point is the acoustical mismatching, which is the difference between acoustic impedances of the materials contacted with each other. This needs to be paid more attention in the calculation of wave generation, transmission and reflection. Particularly, to evaluate the space charge distribution in a multi-layer dielectric using the PEA method the relation between the detected acoustic and the attenuation of acoustic propagation must also be taken into consideration. The attenuation could be divided into two kinds, one happens when the acoustic wave transmits through the interface (from one dielectric to another dielectric, or from one layer to another layer), the other happens during the propagation of the acoustic wave inside the dielectric material.

When an acoustic pulse generates and propagates in the material, it is reflected from the boundary of different layers. The acoustic impedance Z, which is the characteristic property of a material when an acoustic pulse travels through, is defined as:

$$Z = \rho \times V \tag{4}$$

where, ρ is the material density, V is the acoustic velocity in the material.

Considering the waves traveling through the multi-dielectric as planar waves, the generation coefficient G, the transmission coefficient T and reflection coefficient R can be calculated as [48]:

$$G_{i-j} = \frac{Z_j}{Z_i + Z_j} \tag{5}$$

$$T_{i-j} = \frac{2 \times Z_j}{Z_i + Z_j} \tag{6}$$

$$R_{i-j} = \frac{Z_j - Z_i}{Z_i + Z_j} \tag{7}$$

where, "i" is the medium from which the wave comes from, "j" is the medium toward which the wave is traveling.

Therefore, the greater the impedance mismatch, the larger the percentage of the sound wave energy that will be reflected at the interface or boundary between one layer and another. Especially for oil and paper, the difference in acoustic impedance between oil and paper is the main reason for the wave attenuation. Furthermore, the change of speed sound will lead to the change of acoustic impedance in different material, which will affect the transmission coefficient and the space charge signal eventually.

4.2.2. Sound Wave Propagation in Multi-Layer Oil-Paper

As mentioned above, besides the interface, when sound travels through a medium, its intensity (energy of the sound wave) decreases as the distance increases. In idealized materials, sound pressure (signal amplitude) is only reduced by the spreading of the wave. As for natural materials, however, all produce an effect that further weakens the energy of the sound wave. This kind of further weakening results from scattering and absorption of the medium during sound wave propagation. Scattering is the reflection of the sound in directions other than its original propagation direction in porous materials, and absorption is the conversion of the sound energy to other forms due to the energy loss of heat conduction and viscosity. The combined effect of scattering and absorption is called attenuation, which can be calculated by the decay rate of the wave as it propagates through the material. Here, taken the sample with two layers (one oil immersed paper layer and one oil layer, Figure 22) for an example, the sound wave propagation and the calculation of attenuation and dissipation are presented.

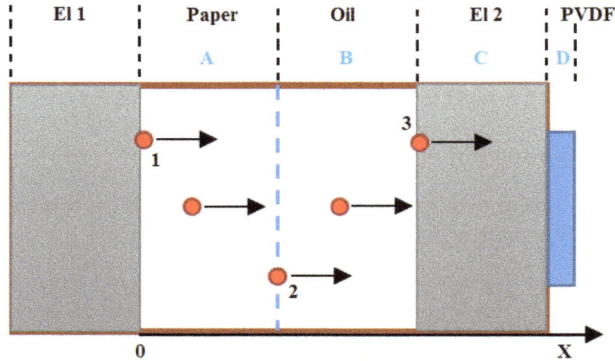

Figure 22. Sound wave propagation in oil and oil immersed paper.

When the attenuation and dissipation are ignored, the pressure wave P_0 (expansion wave or compression wave) generated at the position 1 ($x = 0$) travels through layer A (insulation paper), layer B (insulating oil), electrode 2 (layer C, EL 2), and finally reaches the PVDF (layer D), the final pressure wave P_1 received by PVDF can be calculated by:

$$P_1 = P_0 \times T_{AB} \times T_{BC} \times T_{CD} \tag{8}$$

where, T_{AB} is the transmission coefficient from layer A to B, T_{BC} is the transmission coefficient from layer B to C, T_{CD} is the transmission coefficient from layer C to D.

The amplitude change of a decaying plane wave can be expressed as considering attenuation factor:

$$A = A_0 e^{-\alpha x} \tag{9}$$

where A_0 is the unattenuated amplitude of the propagating wave at the initial location ($x = 0$). The amplitude a is the reduced amplitude after the wave has traveled a distance x from that initial location. The quantity is the attenuation coefficient of the wave traveling in the x-direction. The term e is the exponential (or Napier's constant) which is equal to approximately 2.71828.

Then the pressure wave P_1' which received by PVDF after attenuation can be calculated by:

$$P_1' = P_0 \times e^{-\alpha_A x} \times T_{AB} \times e^{-\alpha_B x} \times T_{BC} \times e^{-\alpha_C x} \times T_{CD} \tag{10}$$

where, α_A is the attenuation factor of layer A, α_B is the attenuation factor of layer B, α_C is the attenuation factor of layer C.

If the dispassion factor is taken into consideration, the final pressure wave P_1'' can be calculated as follows:

$$P_1'' = P_0 \times e^{-\alpha_A x} \times e^{-j\beta_A x} \times T_{AB} \times e^{-\alpha_B x} \times e^{-j\beta_B x} \times T_{BC} \times e^{-\alpha_C x} \times e^{-j\beta_C x} \times T_{CD} \tag{11}$$

where, β_A is the dispassion factor of layer A, β_B is the dispassion factor of layer B, β_C the dispassion factor of layer C.

In fluids, the classical equation for calculation of attenuation factor is:

$$\alpha = \frac{2\pi^2 f^2}{\rho V^3} \left[\frac{4}{3}\eta + (\gamma - 1)\frac{k}{c_P} \right] \tag{12}$$

where, f is the frequency of sound wave, ρ is the density of material, V is the speed of sound, η is the shear viscosity of material, γ is the ratio of specific heat capacities, k is heat conductivity, and cₚ is the constant-pressure specific heat.

The calculation of dispassion factor is [49]:

$$(f) = \frac{2\pi f}{V} \tag{13}$$

In general, to calculate the space charge revolution inside oil-paper precisely, the attenuation and dissipation of acoustic wave propagation should be taken into consideration, and the transmission attenuation at the interface as well. When a temperature gradient exists between the two electrodes, this will be quite complicated since the density of the material is not homogeneous anymore and the acoustic velocity is not a constant but varies with the temperature gradient. This will be presented in future work.

5. Recent Research Results

5.1. Space Charge Dynamics in Pressboard-oil-pressboard Multilayer System

In the research at the University of Southampton, the space charge behavior of a sandwiched structure consisted of two layers of 0.5 mm impregnated pressboards and one layer of 0.5 mm mineral oil gap (Figure 23) is under investigation. It is used to simulate the space charge behavior within the multilayers configuration of the real converter transformer. The space charge characteristics are investigated by a purpose built PEA system at room temperature [50].

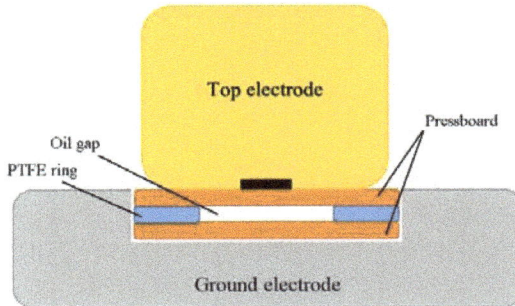

Figure 23. The structure of insulation system and electrode system [48].

Once the DC voltage is applied, charges accumulate at the interfaces between oil gap and pressboards gradually (Figure 24a). Positive charges accumulate at the first interface between the oil gap and the first layer of the pressboard, whilst negative charges accumulate at the other interface between the oil gap and the second layer of the pressboard. It satisfies the Maxwell-Wagner polarization that charges could form at the interfaces on the condition that there was discontinuity of permittivity and conductivity for different materials. The decay experiments are realized by removing the external voltage. The results reveal the real space charge profile within the insulation. As shown in Figure 24b, with one hour of depolarization time, the accumulated charges decrease slowly, suggesting the mobility of the accumulated charges is small in multilayer fresh oil and oil-impregnated pressboard.

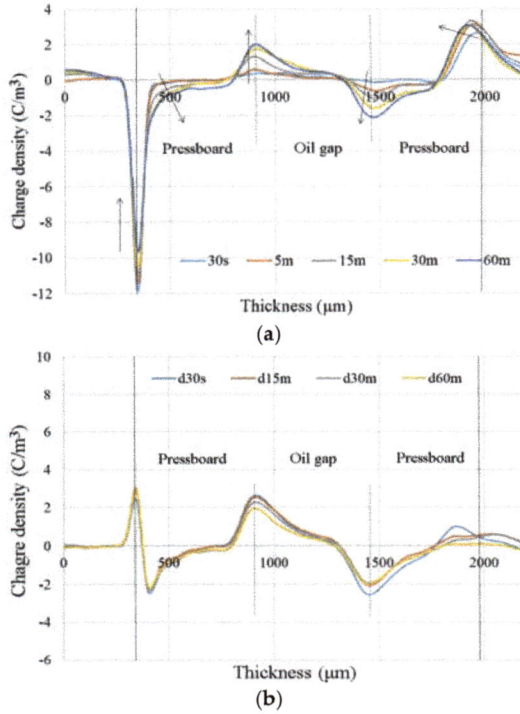

Figure 24. Volt-on (20 kV/mm) (**a**) and decay (**b**) results in multilayer oil and oil-impregnated pressboard [50].

It is worth noting that in insulation liquid (insulation oil), the concept of mobility is limited [51]. The limitations are largely due to fluid motion and the range of species that can be positive and negative carriers. Therefore, from charge mobility perspective, more attention should be paid to the analysis in insulation liquid.

5.2. Space Charge Dynamics of Oil-Paper and Oil Gap under Combined AC and DC Voltages

5.2.1. Cellulose Particles

Before further presenting the space charge dynamics, a series of tests performed at the University of Southampton which were about the cellulose particles accumulation in mineral oil under AC, DC and DC combined AC electric field are introduced. The results shown in Figure 25 are quite interesting and illustrate the bridge formation and electric field distribution between electrodes [52].

A pair of spherical brass electrodes with 13 mm diameter are used for the experiments. The distance between the electrodes is kept constant at 10 mm. Once the 15 kV DC voltage is applied to the sample, the particles start to become polarized. Moreover, the fiber particles align themselves parallel to external electric field lines. After 60 s, a thick bridge is created.

Under 15 kV AC voltage, it is clearly seen that the particles accumulate evenly on the surface of the electrodes. This is mainly attributed to the alternation of the electric field. When the particles make contact with the electrodes, they become charged. Other particles may also attach to these charged particles. Therefore, particle chains are elongated and distribute parallel to external electric field lines.

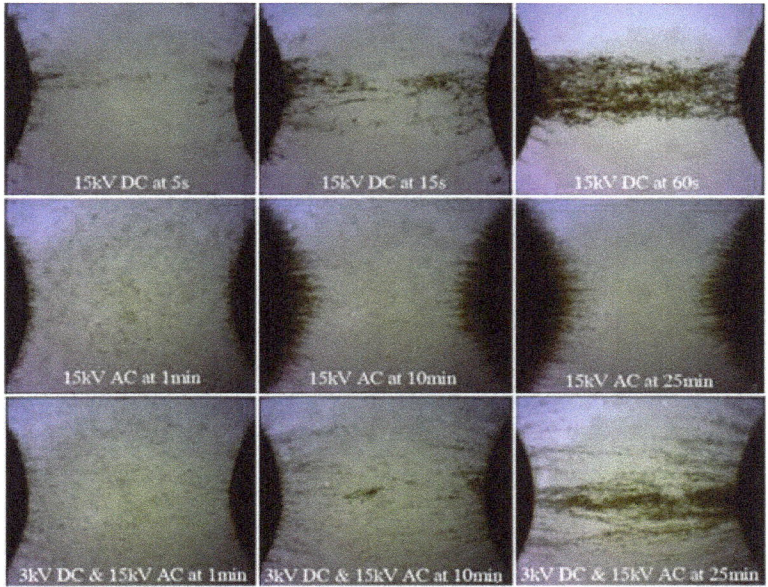

Figure 25. Optical microscopic images for bridging under influence of DC, AC and DC biased AC tests [52].

Under 3 kV DC combined 15 kV AC, a complete bridge was formed between electrodes after 10 min. Although the particle accumulation and the bridging process is much slower compared to the pure 15 kV DC electric field, the formed bridges are denser under the combined voltage.

5.2.2. Oil-Paper and Oil Gap

To correlate with particle movement under AC, DC, and DC combined AC voltage, the space charge profiles in mineral oil gap and oil-impregnated pressboards are also investigated under AC, DC, and DC combined AC voltage conditions [53]. Under 50 Hz AC voltage at room temperature, the sample consists of 0.5 mm pressboard and 0.5 mm oil gap. The results (Figure 26) indicate that no accumulated space charge can be observed in the insulation system. There are only oscillations within the insulation bulk. This may be due to the relatively low AC field, which is only 9.6 kV/mm in r.m.s. It is proved that the space charge injection and accumulation under AC is far less than that under DC. Under AC conditions, when the oil gap is applied, in which both positive charges and negative charges are believed to drift much faster than in the pressboard. Therefore, the injected charges may keep drifting within the oil gap rather than being trapped by the oil/pressboard interface. Moreover, from the cellulose particles experiment, the particles under AC voltage accumulated at the surface of electrodes instead of forming the bridge with the oil gap. That may be the reason that there is no obvious charge injection within the oil and pressboard insulation system.

Figure 27 shows the space charge after instantaneous removal of the applied voltage. In the fresh oil sample, no obvious space charge accumulation can be observed in the insulation bulk under such a low electric field, only a small amount of the positive charges were located in the vicinity of the interface between the top electrode and the pressboard.

For the converter transformer, the valve winding stands the superposition of both AC and DC voltages in the HVDC transmission system. The dielectric performance under combined AC and DC stress is usually obtained by combining the calculation of AC and DC components separately [54].

However, this may not be accurate as the dielectric materials are usually non-linear systems. In fact, the research in [55] has shown the significant space charge accumulation under the superimposed electric fields in the LDPE, which was quite different compared with the sum of the DC impact and AC impact separately.

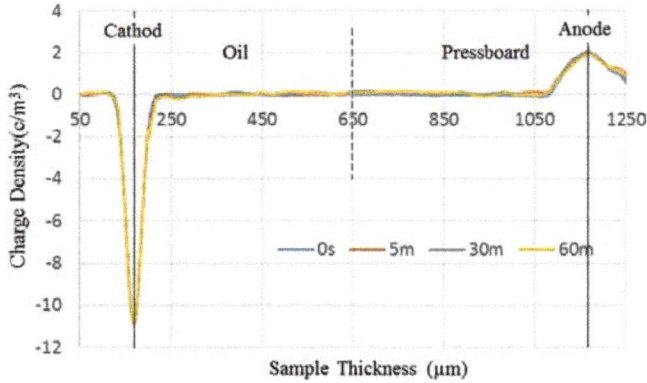

Figure 26. Volt-on results of space charge in fresh oil combined with impregnated pressboard insulation system under 9.6 kV/mm AC field at 81° [53].

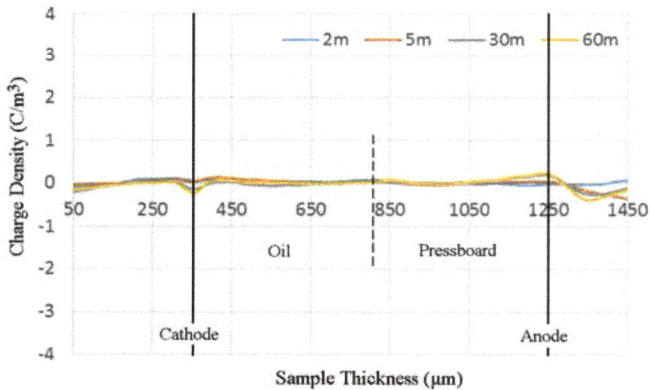

Figure 27. Volt-off results of space charge in fresh oil combined with impregnated pressboard insulation system under 4.8 kV/mm DC field.

The space charge behavior in the one layer oil impregnated pressboard with the one layer oil under superimposed electric field (+4.8 kV/mm DC stress combined with 9.6 kV/mm AC stress) was investigated. As shown in Figure 28, the amount of space charge at a phase angle of 81° is greatly increased after the combination of the AC and DC stress. When a small DC stress +4.8 kV/mm (much smaller than the threshold) is combined with as AC stress of 9.6 kV/mm, the presence of large amounts of interfacial negative charges is observed at the oil/pressboard interface. This negative interfacial charge density increases quickly to the maximum value (about 4.3 C/m^3) within the first 5 min, and that value is much higher in comparison to the space charge under pure DC voltage conditions. Then the peak value keeps decreasing which may result from the neutralization by the positive charges injected from the top electrode. Correspondingly, as shown in Figure 29 (the space charge dynamics at a phase angle of 261°), the peak value of the ground electrode increases to the maximum value (about 7.3 C/m^3) for 5 min then gradually decreases to about 6.1 C/m^3 at 60 min. The high amount of space charge on the ground electrode may result from significant negative charge accumulated as the interface. The negative interfacial charge could induce the positive charge on the ground electrode. Moreover, with the addition of the capacitive charge on the ground electrode, the maximum charge density occurs at 5 min on the ground electrode. After that, the decrease of the charge on the ground correlates with the charge neutralization at the interface between oil and the pressboard. It may also indicate that the electric field distributed across the oil gap could be greatly enhanced for 5 min. After that, this enhancement starts to decrease.

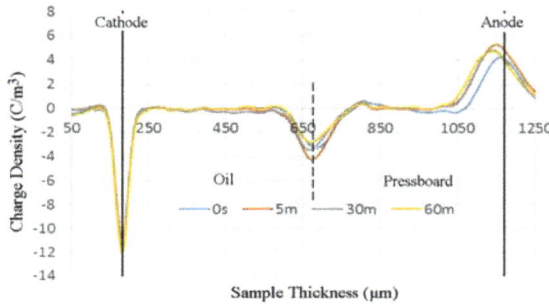

Figure 28. Volt-on results of space charge in fresh oil combined with impregnated pressboard insulation system under AC/DC combined stresses at 81°.

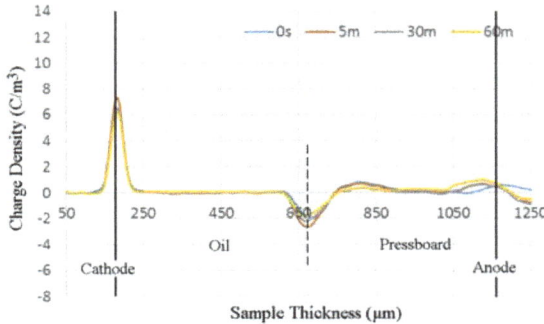

Figure 29. Volt-on results of space charge in fresh oil combined with impregnated pressboard insulation system under AC/DC combined stresses at 261°.

The previous results indicate that the amount of space charge generated from the superimposition of the DC and AC electric field is higher than the simple addition of space charge generated from the individual DC and AC components. This indicates the space charge dynamics can be accelerated by the superposition of the DC and AC components for the fresh oil and oil-impregnated pressboard sample.

5.3. New Oil-Paper Combination

Apart from the previous understanding of the space charge behavior in traditional oil-paper insulation materials, other methods of reducing the space charge injection, accumulation, and improving the insulating properties, are also under investigation. There are two methods. One is the optimization of insulation combination. The other one is the application of new modified insulation material, including the modified cellulose pressboard and the new types of insulating oil.

5.3.1. Space Charge in the Polypropylene Laminated Paper (PPLP)

Polypropylene Laminated Paper (PPLP) has been used in some commercial HVDC projects such as underground transmission cables [56,57]. The advantages of using PPLP are higher AC and DC breakdown strength and lower dielectric loss advantage compared to standard Kraft paper. However, the mechanism that leads to this phenomenon is still unknown. Therefore, at the University of Southampton, the lapped PPLP has been investigated to analyze the space charge behavior.

Figure 30 shows the space charge distribution in a PPLP sample (220 um in total thickness) under an applied voltage of 1 kV. The dashed line is the signal of the sample under the pulse electric field, which can give the location of the cathode and the anode. The negative peak captured from the cathode was very small after 1 kV was applied. The expected positive peak at the anode cannot be observed. This is not simply due to the attenuation of the paper. The net charge captured by PEA is the resultant charge from the injected homo-charge, electrode induced charge and possible ions caused by the applied electric field. The obvious negative and positive peaks in the bulk are believed to be the charge accumulated in the interface zone between the Kraft paper and polypropylene.

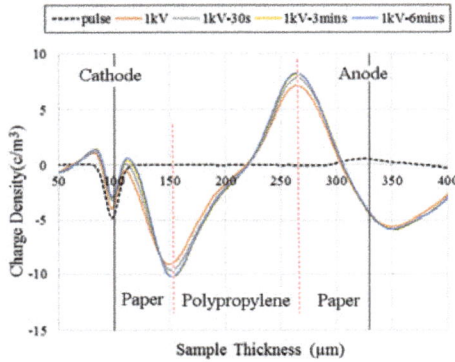

Figure 30. Space charge distribution in PPLP film under 1 kV applied voltage (Volt-on).

Volt-off results after 6 min of 1 kV applied voltage are shown in Figure 31. It shows the information about space charges that remain in the sample. More importantly, the interface regions and charge polarity close to the electrodes can be clearly seen as the capacitive charge due to elimination of the applied voltage. Hetero-charges can be found in the lower paper area next to the cathode.

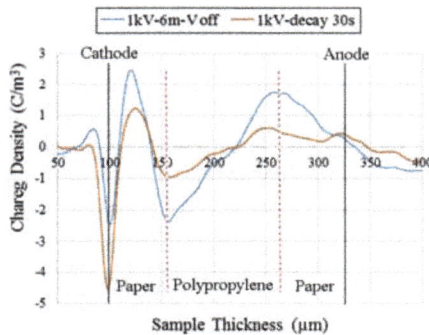

Figure 31. Space charge distribution in PPLP film under 1 kV applied voltage (volt-off).

The same space charge distribution can be observed from Figures 32 and 33 which are the results measured under 8 kV. Charge injection from the electrode takes place at the very low field when the Kraft paper is in contact with the electrode. The ionization in the Kraft paper is also a major concern for the lapped sample. The interfacial zones in the lapped samples can trap/slow down charge resulting in electric field enhancement in PP film.

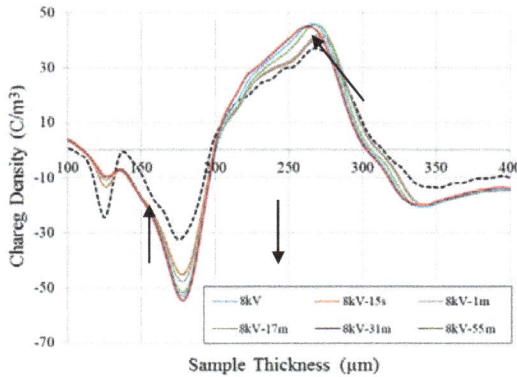

Figure 32. Space charge distribution in PPLP film under 8 kV applied voltage (volt-on).

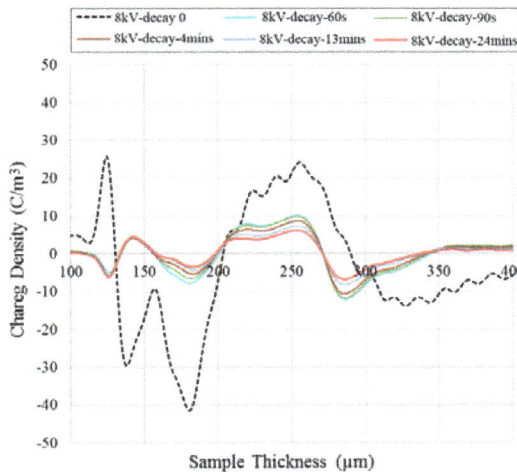

Figure 33. Space charge distribution of PPLP sample under 8 kV applied voltage (volt-off).

5.3.2. Space Charge on Nano-TiO$_2$ Modified Cellulose Paper

To improve the accumulation and dissipation properties of space charge in oil-paper insulation, Lv *et al.* modified cellulose insulation paper using nano-TiO$_2$ [58]. The accumulation and dissipation characteristics of space charge of oil-paper were tested using PEA. The results show that there is no negative space charge accumulation near the anode of the nano-TiO$_2$ mixed sample observed under 10 kV/mm and 30 kV/mm. The reason could be the addition of nano-TiO$_2$ enhanced the threshold voltage of charge injection from the cathode and then slowed down the movement of electrons.

Under 10 kV/mm, the ratios of electrical field distortions of P0 (without the nano-TiO$_2$), P1 (with a nano-TiO$_2$ mass fraction of 1%) and P2 (with a nano-TiO$_2$ mass fraction of 3%) were 50%, 20%, and 10%, respectively. While under 30 kV/mm (Figure 34), the ratios were 60%, 20%, and 10%. We may reach the conclusion that the addition of nano-TiO$_2$ to insulation paper is quite effective in improving the accumulation and dissipation properties of space charge, relieving the electric field distortion, though further research is still required.

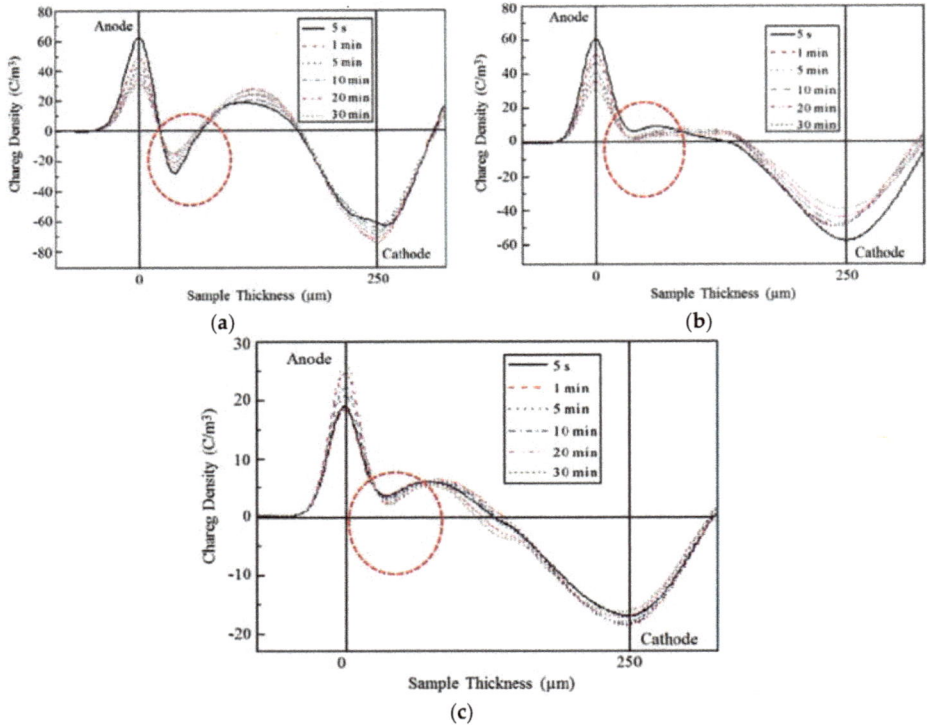

Figure 34. Space charge distribution of samples P0 (**a**), P1 (**b**) and P2 (**c**) under 30 kV/mm applied electric field [58].

5.4. Simulation

5.4.1. COMSOL for Electric Field Simulation

As the converter transformer may experience polarity reversal in operation, it is necessary to simulate the electric field of the oil and oil-impregnated pressboard with the emphasis on the polarity reversal operation. Traditionally, the electric field simulation is based on the Maxwell-Wagner theory. However, considering the existence of charge traps and surface states, an accurate method is required to introduce the space charge effect on the electric field estimation. The electric field caused by the space charge was simulated at Southampton for different polarity reversal operation times using the COMSOL software.

For circuit representation of Maxwell-Wagner theory, the oil and oil-impregnated pressboard could be regarded as a parallel configuration of the resistor and capacitor. The electric field and voltage distribution could be calculated based on the equations below. U$_1$ and U$_2$ are the applied voltage for pressboard and oil, R_1 and R_2 are the resistance of the pressboard and oil. C_1 and C_2 are the capacitance of the pressboard and oil, respectively:

$$U_1(t) = \frac{R_1 U}{R_1 + R_2} + \left(\frac{C_2}{C_1 + C_2} - \frac{R_1}{R_1 + R_2}\right) U \times e^{-\frac{t}{\tau}} \tag{14}$$

$$E_1(t) = \frac{R_1 U}{(R_1 + R_2)d_1} + \left(\frac{C_2}{C_1 + C_2} - \frac{R_1}{R_1 + R_2}\right)\frac{U}{d_1} \times e^{-\frac{t}{\tau}} \tag{15}$$

$$U_2(t) = \frac{R_2 U}{R_1 + R_2} + \left(\frac{C_1}{C_1 + C_2} - \frac{R_2}{R_1 + R_2}\right) U \times e^{-\frac{t}{\tau}} \tag{16}$$

$$E_2(t) = \frac{R_2 U}{(R_1 + R_2)d_2} + \left(\frac{C_1}{C_1 + C_2} - \frac{R_2}{R_1 + R_2}\right)\frac{U}{d_2} \times e^{-\frac{t}{\tau}} \tag{17}$$

$$\tau = \frac{C_1 + C_2}{\frac{1}{R_1} + \frac{1}{R_2}} \tag{18}$$

To interpolate the space charge into the COMSOL software, the oil and oil-impregnated pressboard are divided into different layers for adding to the space charge [59]. After the interpolation of the space charge into the COMSOL software, the electric field within the oil and oil-impregnated pressboard could be simulated based on the Poisson equation:

$$E = \int_0^d \frac{\rho}{\varepsilon_0 \varepsilon_r} dx \tag{19}$$

Figure 35 shows the electric field of oil and oil-impregnated pressboard based on the Maxwell-Wagner theory. After the polarity reversal operation time of 60 s, the transient electric field distribution meets the capacitive distribution. From the Equations (15), the transient electric field of the pressboard is proportional to the capacitance of the oil, leading to the lower electric field of pressboard due to the lower permittivity of the oil.

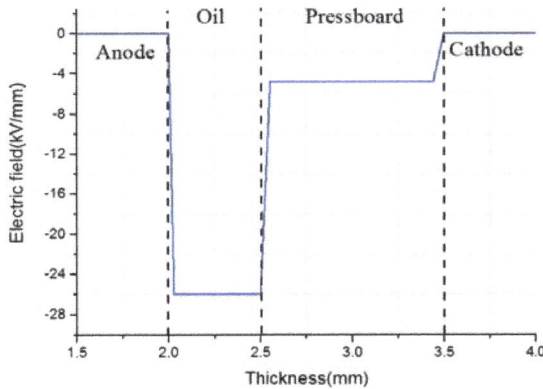

Figure 35. Electric field distribution for fresh oil and oil-impregnated pressboard based on the Maxwell-Wagner theory for polarity reversal operation time of the 60 s.

After the interpolation of the space charge, the electric field distribution within the oil and oil-impregnated pressboard is shown in Figure 36. It is noticed that there is a concave region for the electric field of the oil-impregnated pressboard. The electric field in the vicinity of electrode and interface of the oil-impregnated pressboard is enhanced. There are two reasons. Firstly, the homo-charge injection within pressboard could be converted into hetero-charge after the polarity reversal operation. The electric field for two sides of pressboard caused by the hetero-charge is added to the external electric field, leading to the electric field enhancement. Moreover, the hetero-charge could induce the same polarity charge compared to the electrode, which could also enhance the electric field for two sides of the oil-impregnated pressboard. For the oil part, the electric field distribution could be attributed to the existence of the space charge, the charge injection previously could be converted into homo-charge leading to the electric field enhancement in the center.

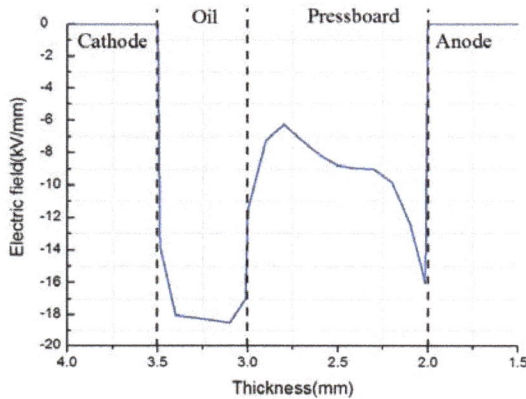

Figure 36. Electric field of fresh oil and oil-impregnated pressboard adding space charge for polarity reversal operation time of the 60 s.

The electric field caused by space charge and Maxwell-Wagner theory after the different polarity reversal operation time could be summarized in Figure 37. Both fresh and aged oil-impregnated pressboards are considered. It has been found that electric field caused by the space charge is higher in comparison to the electric field calculated from the Maxwell-Wagner theory, and the difference between them is higher for the fresh sample compared to the aged sample. The electric field based on the Maxwell-Wagner theory increases while the electric field caused by the space charge decreases after a longer polarity reversal operation time. Moreover, the electric field of the aged sample caused by the space charge decreases faster compared to the fresh sample, which results from fast space charge dissipation rate of the aged sample. After the comparison between the electric field resulted from space charge after polarity reversal operation and the electric field based on the Maxwell-Wagner theory for the steady-state condition, it is suggested that the current 2 min polarity reversal operation time could be safely reduced for both fresh and aged oil and oil-impregnated pressboard samples.

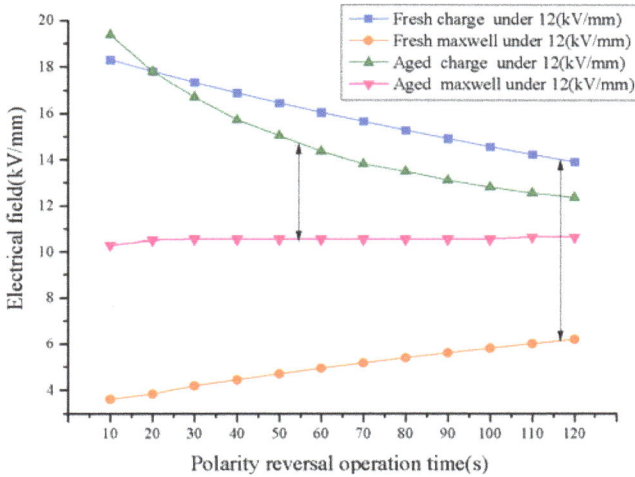

Figure 37. Electric field distribution of both fresh and aged oil-impregnated pressboard caused by space charge and Maxwell theory for different polarity reversal operation time.

5.4.2. Molecular Simulation for Material Modification

Molecular simulation technology can explain the mechanism of cellulose's thermal ageing improvement from the perspective of interactions between molecules. Quite a few works have showed that the molecular simulation method is a research field with great potential in the study of microscopic mechanisms [60–62]. However, few studies on nanomaterial-modified insulation paper cellulose using a molecular simulation method have been reported.

Nano-Al_2O_3 particles have been used to modify insulation paper fiber, and molecular simulation and experimental methods were utilized to analyze the changes in the mechanical properties of the modified insulation paper after addition of the nano-Al_2O_3. We also compare microscopic molecular simulation results and macroscopic experiment results, and explore the mechanism of nano-Al_2O_3 modification of the thermal ageing of insulation paper, and thus provide some theoretical support for further study of nano-modified insulation paper (Figure 38).

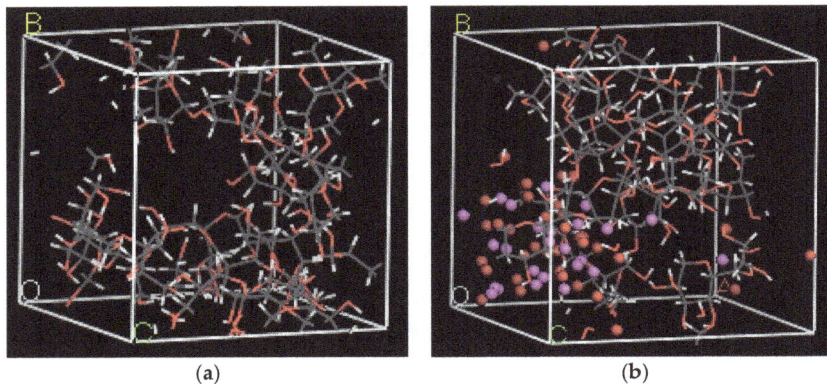

Figure 38. Unmodified cellulose model (a) and modified cellulose model (b) with addition of nano-Al_2O_3 [60].

From Figure 39, after adding nano-Al_2O_3 particles to paper fiber, the rate of decrease of the degree of polymerization of insulation paper is obviously slower than that of unmodified insulation paper. This may also indicate that the addition of 1% nano-Al_2O_3 particles can improve the mechanical strength and also decrease the rate of aging of insulation paper. This improvement may also correlate with the increase of hydrogen bonds surrounding the cellulose. The nano-Al_2O_3 particles fill some voids in the amorphous region of cellulose, forming hydrogen bonds surrounding the cellulose. As the result of more hydrogen bonds attached to the cellulose chain, the reaction intensity of cellulose chain is modified and it becomes less compared to the unmodified model. Therefore, this could decrease the rate of the degree of polymerization of insulation paper and also the ageing rate. The space charge behavior using both unmodified cellulose and modified cellulose paper to verify its polymerization degree (DP) characteristics property will be presented in the future work.

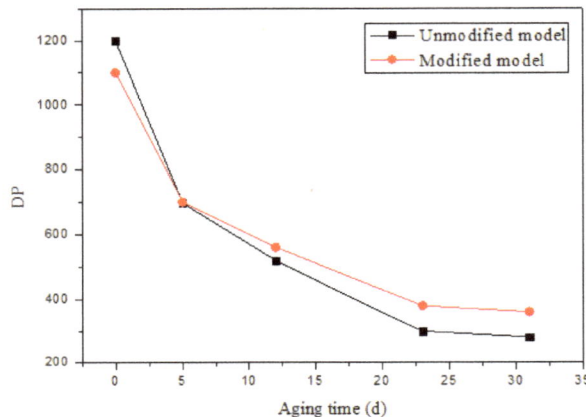

Figure 39. Variation of polymerization degree (DP) of insulation paper with ageing time.

6. Conclusions and Prospects

It has been more than half century since in 1950 a 400 kV electrical power transformer was first introduced in a high voltage electrical power system. The fast expansion of HVDC networks nowadays requires more secure and stable DC power equipment. Oil-paper is used as the main insulation material of the key DC power equipment, and its space charge behavior is proved to have a great influence on the insulating properties, therefore, the research on space charge behaviors of oil-paper is vitally important for the sustainable operation of power grids as well as the improvement of the physical-chemical properties and electrical performances of insulation materials.

This paper focuses on PEA technology, where research on space charge in oil-paper insulation in the past twenty years have been classified and reviewed. Oil-paper insulation is subject to the combined stresses of electrical, thermal and mechanical, possesses complex physical and chemical properties, and exhibits complicated and various insulation structures inside the power transformer, all of which make research on space charge evolution in oil-paper insulation a difficult topic to study.

Our reviewing of the existing research indicates that temperature (both environmental and test), moisture content, and applied voltage have a great influence on the space charge evolution inside oil-paper. The connections between space charge and other electrical parameters such as permittivity, conductivity, partial discharge, breakdown voltage and so on are still not so clear. The mechanisms behind the observed phenomena need further investigation. For all that, some points that need special attention are emphasized below:

(1) Control of the test environment. As PEA was not designed for oil-paper in the first place, it is essential to ensure a uniform test environment through all the experimental procedures, which means that space charge testing should be conducted under the same temperature, humidity, and the consistent pressure from the upper electrode to the sample.

(2) Precise signal and data processing. As for multilayer oil-paper, the traditional signal process and recovery methods have some defects because of the attenuation, dissipation, recovery algorithm and so on. Thus, a further study on the progress of sound wave propagation and the signal recovery algorithm are quite important.

(3) Conformity to practical operation situations. The normal working temperature in a converter transformer is usually around 70 °C, which may also dramatically increase to a higher value due to the variable loads. Besides a high temperature, temperature gradients also exist in converter transformers from the conductor to the cooling system. Furthermore, metal ions such as copper, iron, zinc and so on, which exist in the real transformer with a certain degree will affect the space charge behavior. Therefore, to acquire scientific and useful results, the experimental conditions should be consistent with the practical operation situation.

(4) PEA test set-up. There is still some room for hardware improvement to achieve a better signal, especially for complicated combinations of oil and paper. Besides, the development of simulations provides another way to better understand of the kinetics of space charge within oil and oil-impregnated paper/pressboard. The space charge simulations could be further interpolated into the COMSOL software for the electric field simulation, which will be beneficial for the electric field simulation for multi-layers and even the whole converter transformer.

According to the research results, an electric field distortion results from the space charge accumulation in oil-paper insulation, and the thermal effects caused by fast charge transportation inside the material are the main reason for electrical faults. To reduce the influence of space charge, decrease the charge accumulation, limit the fast charge transportation and even the charge distribution inside oil-paper could predict the trends of the future research.

Acknowledgments: The authors wish to thank the editors of *Energies*, and Issouf Fofana for their kind invitation to present this feature article. One of the authors, Chao Tang, wishes to thank the National Natural Science Foundation of China (Project for Young Scientists Fund, Grant No. 51107103), the Fundamental Research Funds for the Central Universities (Grant No. XDJK2014B031) and the CSC Scholarship (Grant No. 201406995060) for their financial support.

Author Contributions: Chao Tang and Bo Huang completed writing of the manuscript. George Chen and Jian Hao reviewed and edited the manuscript. Zhiqiang Xu and Miao Hao were involved in conceiving the aims, objectives, scope and structure of the paper. All authors have therefore been involved in the preparation and have approved the submitted manuscript.

Conflicts of Interest: The authors declare no conflict of interest.

References

1. JWG A2/B4. 28. HVDC Converter Transformers Design Review, Test Procedures, Ageing Evaluation and Reliability in Service. 2010. Availible online: http://www.e-cigre.org/Publications/file.asp (accessed on 18 November 2015).
2. Heathcote, M.J. *J & P Transformer Book*, 13th ed.; Elsevier Ltd.: Oxford, UK, 2007.
3. Mazzanti, G.; Montanari, G.C.; Alison, J.M. A space-charge based method for the estimation of apparent mobility and trap depth as markers for insulation degradation-theoretical basis and experimental validation. *IEEE Trans. Dielectr. Electr. Insul.* **2003**, *10*, 187–197. [CrossRef]
4. Chen, G.; Chong, Y.L.; Fu, M. Calibration of the pulsed electroacoustic technique in the presence of trapped charge. *Meas. Sci. Technol.* **2006**, *17*, 1974–1980. [CrossRef]
5. Li, Y.; Yasuda, M.; Takada, T. Pulsed electroacoustic method for measurement of charge accumulation in solid dielectrics. *IEEE Trans. Dielectr. Electr. Insul.* **1994**, *1*, 188–195.

6. Liu, R.; Tornkvist, C.; Johansson, K. Space charge distribution in composite oil cellulose insulation. In Proceedings of the IEEE Annual Report of the Conference on Electrical Insulation and Dielectric Phenomena (CEIDP), Arlington, VA, USA, 23–26 October 1994; pp. 316–321.

7. Liu, R.; Wahlstrom, G. Measurements of the DC electric field in liquid impregnated pressboard using the pressure wave propagation technique. In Proceedings of the Conference Record of the IEEE International Symposium on Electrical Insulation (ISEI), Pittsburgh, PA, USA, 5–8 June 1994; pp. 103–106.

8. Liu, R.; Tornkvist, C.; Gafvert, U. Pressure wave propagation technique to measure the space charge distribution in pressboard impregnated with aged transformer oil. In Proceedings of the 4th International Conference on Properties and Applications of Dielectric Materials (ICPADM), Brisbane, Australia, 3–8 July 1994; pp. 139–142.

9. Morshuis, P.; Jeroense, M. Space charge measurements on impregnated paper: A review of the PEA method and a discussion of results. *IEEE Trans. Dielectr. Electr. Insul.* **1997**, *13*, 26–35. [CrossRef]

10. Ciobanu, R.; Schreiner, C.; Pfeiffer, W.; Baraboi, B. Space charge evolution in oil-paper insulation for DC cables application. In Proceedings of the IEEE 14th International Conference on Dielectric Liquids (ICDL), Graz, Austria, 7–12 July 2002; pp. 321–324.

11. Tang, C.; Chen, G.; Fu, M.; Liao, R. Space charge behavior in multi-layer oil-paper insulation under different DC voltages and temperatures. *IEEE Trans. Dielectr. Electr. Insul.* **2010**, *17*, 775–784. [CrossRef]

12. Wang, D.; Wang, S.Q.; Lei, M.; Mu, H.B.; Zhang, G.J. Temperature effect on space charge behavior in oil-impregnated paper insulation. In Proceedings of the 2011 International Conference on Electrical Insulating Materials (ISEIM), Kyoto, Japan, 6–10 September 2011; pp. 378–382.

13. Hao, J.; Liao, R.J.; Yang, L.J. Space charge dynamics in oil-paper insulation under the combination influence of moisture and temperature. In Proceedings of the 2012 International Conference on High Voltage Engineering and Application (ICHVE), Shanghai, China, 17–20 September 2012; pp. 294–297.

14. Judendorfer, T.; Muhr, M.; Andritsch, T.; Smit, J.J. Assessment of space charge behavior of oil-cellulose insulation systems by means of the PEA method. In Proceedings of the IEEE International Conference on Solid Dielectrics (ICSD), Bologna, Italy, 30 June–4 July 2013; pp. 401–404.

15. Hao, J.; Chen, G.; Liao, R.J.; Yang, L.J.; Tang, C. Influence of moisture on space charge dynamics in multilayer oil-paper insulation. *IEEE Trans. Dielectr. Electr Insul.* **2012**, *19*, 1456–1464. [CrossRef]

16. Zhou, Y.X.; Huang, M.; Chen, W.J.; Jin, F.B. Space charge behavior of oil-paper insulation thermally aged under different temperatures and moistures. *J. Electr. Eng. Technol.* **2015**, *10*, 1124–1130. [CrossRef]

17. Fofana, I.; Borsi, H.; Gockenbach, E.; Farzaneh, M. Aging of transformer insulating materials under selective conditions. *Eur. Trans. Electr. Power Eng.* **2007**, *17*, 450–470. [CrossRef]

18. Fofana, I.; Bouaïcha, A.; Farzaneh, M. Characterization of ageing transformer oil–pressboard insulation using some modern diagnostic techniques. *Eur. Trans. Electr. Power* **2011**, *21*, 1110–1127. [CrossRef]

19. Fu, J.; Hao, J.; Liu, H.; Li, K.; Cui, H.; Zhang, W. Influence of paper ageing on space charge dynamics in oil impregnated insulation paper under DC electric field. In Proceedings of the International Symposium on Electrical Insulating Materials (ISEIM), Chuo-ku Niigata City, Japan, 1–5 June 2014; pp. 385–388.

20. Hao, J.; Tang, C.; Fu, J.; Chen, G.; Wu, G.L.; Wang, Q. Influence of oil aging on the space charge dynamics of oil-immersed paper insulation under a DC electric field. *IEEJ Trans. Electr. Electron. Eng.* **2015**, *10*, 1–11. [CrossRef]

21. Ciobanu, R.; Prisecaru, I.; Schreiner, C. Space charge evolution in thermally aged cellulose materials. In Proceedings of the IEEE International Conference on Solid Dielectrics (ICSD), Toulouse, France, 5–9 July 2004; pp. 221–224.

22. Tang, C. Studies on the DC space charge characteristics of oil-paper insulation materials. Ph.D. Thesis, Chongqiang Univeristy, Chongqing, China, 2010.

23. Zhou, Y.; Huang, M.; Chen, W.; Lu, L. Space charge behavior evolution with thermal aging of oil-paper insulation. *IEEE Trans. Dielectr. Electr. Insul.* **2015**, *22*, 1381–1388. [CrossRef]

24. Bodega, R.; Morshuis, P.H.F.; Smit, J.J. Space charge measurements on multi-dielectrics by means of the pulsed electroacoustic method. *IEEE Trans. Dielectr. Electr. Insul.* **2006**, *13*, 272–281. [CrossRef]

25. Bodega, R.; Morshuis, P.H.F.; Redjosentono, E.; Smit, J.J. Dielectric interface characterization by means of space charge measurements. In Proceedings of the Annual Report Conference on Electrical Insulation and Dielectric Phenomena (CEIDP), Albuquerque, NM, USA, 19–22 October 2003; pp. 728–733.

26. Hao, M.; Zhou, Y.; Chen, G.; Wilson, G.; Jarman, P. Space charge behaviour in oil and impregnated pressboard combined insulation system. In Proceedings of the IEEE International Conference on Liquid Dielectrics (ICLD), Bled, Slovenia, 29 June–3 July 2014; pp. 1–4.
27. Hao, J.; Fu, J.; Tang, C.; Wu, G.; Wang, Q.; Yao, Q. Space charge characteristics of oil gap and pressboard mixed insulation based on the pulsed electro-acoustic measurement. In Proceedings of the International Conference on High Voltage Engineering and Application (ICHVE), Poznan, Poland, 8–11 September 2014; pp. 1–4.
28. Wu, K.; Zhu, Q.; Wang, H.; Wang, X.; Li, S. Space charge behavior in the sample with two layers of oil-immersed-paper and oil. *IEEE Trans. Dielectr. Electr. Insul.* **2014**, *21*, 1857–1865. [CrossRef]
29. Kelley, E.F.; Robert, E.H. Electro-optic measurement of the electric field distribution in transformer oil. *IEEE Trans. Power Appar. Syst.* **1983**, *102*, 2092–2097. [CrossRef]
30. Okubo, H.; Shimizu, R.; Sawada, A.; Kato, K.; Hayakawa, N.; Hikita, M. Kerr electro-optic field measurement and charge dynamics in transformer-oil/solid composite insulation systems. *IEEE Trans. Dielectr. Electr. Insul.* **1997**, *4*, 64–70. [CrossRef]
31. Zhou, Y.X.; Huang, M.; Sun, Q.H.; Sha, Y.C.; Jin, F.B.; Zhang, L. Space charge characteristics in two-layer oil-paper insulation. *J. Electrostat.* **2013**, *71*, 413–417. [CrossRef]
32. Huang, M.; Zhou, Y.X.; Sun, Q.H.; Sha, Y.C.; Zhang, L. Effect of interface on space charge behavior in multi-layer oil-paper insulation. In Proceedings of the IEEE Conference on Electrical Insulation and Dielectric Phenomena (CEIDP), Montreal, QC, Canada, 14–17 October 2012; pp. 654–657.
33. Huang, M.; Zhou, Y.X.; Chen, W.; Lu, L.C.; Jin, F.; Huang, J.W. Space charge dynamics at the physical interface in oil-paper insulation under DC voltage. *IEEE Trans. Dielectr. Electr. Insul.* **2015**, *22*, 1739–1746. [CrossRef]
34. Liu, R.S.; Tornkvist, C. Charge storage and transport in oil-impregnated pressboard at polarity reversal under HVDC. In Proceedings of the Conference on Electrical Insulation and Dielectric Phenomena (CEIDP), Virginia Beach, VA, USA, 22–25 October 1995; pp. 33–36.
35. Hao, M.; Zhou, Y.; Chen, G.; Wilson, G.; Jarman, P. Space charge dynamics in oil and thick pressboard combined system under polarity reversal voltage. In Proceedings of the IEEE Conference on Electrical Insulation and Dielectric Phenomena (CEIDP), Des Moines, IA, USA, 19–22 October 2014; pp. 867–870.
36. Huang, M.; Zhou, Y.X.; Chen, W.J.; Sha, Y.C.; Jin, F.B. Influence of voltage reversal on space charge behavior in oil-paper insulation. *IEEE Trans. Dielectr. Electr. Insul.* **2014**, *21*, 331–339. [CrossRef]
37. Wang, D.; Wang, S.Q.; Lei, M.; Mu, H.B.; Zhang, G.J. Space charge behavior in oil-paper insulation under polarity reversed voltage. In Proceedings of the IEEE International Conference on Condition Monitoring and Diagnosis (CMD), Bali, Indonesia, 23–27 September 2012; pp. 265–268.
38. Hao, J.; Chen, G.; Wu, G.L.; Fu, J.; Wang, Q.; Yao, Q.; Peng, H.D. Space charge characteristics of oil impregnated insulation paper under the power frequency voltage. In Proceedings of the IEEE Conference on Electrical Insulation and Dielectric Phenomena (CEIDP), Shenzhen, China, 20–23 October 2013; pp. 1314–1317.
39. Wu, G.L.; Hao, J.; Wang, Q.; Fu, J.; Yao, Q. Influence of oil property on space charge dynamics in oil-paper insulation under DC and AC electric field. In Proceedings of the IEEE Conference on Electrical Insulation and Dielectric Phenomena (CEIDP), Shenzhen, China, 20–23 October 2013; pp. 218–221.
40. Holé, S.; Ditchi, T.; Lewiner, J. Non-destructive Methods for Space Charge Distribution Measurements: What are the Differences? *IEEE Trans. Dielectr. Electr. Insul.* **2003**, *4*, 670–677. [CrossRef]
41. Tanaka, Y.; Takada, T.; Shinoda, C. Temperature dependence of space charge distribution in XLPE cable. In Proceedings of the IEEE Conference on Electrical Insulation and Dielectric Phenomena (CEIDP), Arlington, VA, USA, 23–26 October 1994; pp. 334–339.
42. Dissado, L.A.; Mazzanti, G.; Montanari, G.C. The role of trapped space charges in the electrical aging of insulating materials. *IEEE Trans. Dielectr. Electr. Insul.* **1997**, *4*, 496–506. [CrossRef]
43. Chen, G.; Banford, H.M.; Davies, A.E. Influence of radiation environments on space charge formation in γ-irradiated LDPE. In Proceedings of the International Symposium on Electrical Insulating Materials (ISEIM), Toyohashi, Japan, 27–30 Sepember 1998; pp. 113–116.
44. Chen, G.; Davies, A.E.; Xi, B. Charge formation and decay in γ-irradiated low-density polyethylene. In Proceedings of the 6th International Conference on Properties and Applications of Dielectric Materials (ICPADM), Xi'an, China, 21–26 June 2000; pp. 443–446.

45. Trostmann, E. *Tap Water as a Hydraulic Pressure Medium*, 1st ed.; CRC Press: Boca Raton, FL, USA, 2000; p. 63.

46. Nalwa, H.S. *Ferroelectric Polymers: Chemistry: Physics, and Applications*; CRC Press: Boca Raton, FL, USA, 1995; p. 208.

47. Bodega, R.; Morshuis, P.H.F.; Smit, J.J. Space charge signal interpretation in a multi-layer dielectric tested by means of the PEA method. In Proceedings of the IEEE International Conference on Solid Dielectrics (ICSD), Toulouse, France, 5–9 July 2004; pp. 240–243.

48. Blitz, J. *Fundamentals of Ultrasonic*, 2nd ed.; Butterworths: London, UK, 1967; p. 100.

49. Li, Y.; Murata, K.; Tanaka, Y.; Takada, T.; Aihara, M. Space charge distribution measurement in lossy dielectric materials by pulsed electroacoustic method. In Proceedings of the 4th International Conference on Properties and Applications of Dielectric Materials (ICPADM), Brisbane, Australia, 3–8 July 1994; pp. 725–728.

50. Fu, M.; Luo, B.; Hou, S.; Liao, Y.; Hao, M.; Chen, G. Space charge dynamics in pressboard-oil-pressboard multilayer system under DC voltages. In Proceedings of the IEEE 11th International Conference on the Properties and Applications of Dielectric Materials (ICPADM), Sydney, Australia, 19–22 July 2015; pp. 112–115.

51. Michael, B.; Michael, D.C. Conduction and breakdown mechanisms in transformer oil. *IEEE Trans. Plasma Sci.* **2006**, *34*, 467–475.

52. Mahmud, S.; Chen, G.; Golosnoy, I.; Wilson, G.; Jarman, P. Experimental studies of influence of DC and AC electric fields on bridging in contaminated transformer oil. *IEEE Trans. Dielectr. Electr. Insul.* **2015**, *22*, 152–160. [CrossRef]

53. Hao, M.; Zhou, Y.; Chen, G.; Wilson, G.; Jarman, P. Space charge dynamics in oil-impregnated pressboard under AC electric field. In Proceedings of the Annual Report Conference on Electrical Insulation and Dielectric Phenomena (CEIDP), Des Moines, IA, USA, 19–22 October 2014; pp. 1–4.

54. The International Electrotechnical Commission (IEC). *IEC 61378-3: Converter Transformers Part 3: Application Guide*, 2nd ed.; IEC: Geneva, Switzerland, 2015.

55. Zhao, J.; Chen, G.; Zhong, L. Space charge in polyethylene under combined AC and DC voltages. *IEEE Trans. Dielectr. Electr. Insul.* **2014**, *21*, 1757–1763. [CrossRef]

56. Nakagawa, T. Measurement of space charge accumulation in PPLP. In Proceedings of the IEEE 13th International Conference on Dielectric Liquids (ICDL), Nara, Japan, 20–25 July 1999; pp. 533–536.

57. Kim, W.J.; Kim, S.H.; Kim, H.J.; Cho, J.W.; Lee, J.S.; Lee, H.G. The fundamental characteristics of PPLP as insulating material for HTS DC cable. *IEEE Trans. Appl. Superconduct.* **2013**, *23*, 3–6.

58. Cheng, L.; Ruijin, L.; Weiqiang, W.; Tuan, L. Influence of nano-TiO$_2$ on DC space charge characteristics of oil-paper insulation material. *High Volt. Eng.* **2015**, *2*, 417–423.

59. Huang, B.; Hao, M.; Chen, G.; Hao, J.; Fu, J.; Wang, Q. Space charge characteristics and the electric field distortion after polarity reversal operation in two layers of oil-impregnated paper and oil. In Proceedings of the 19th International Symposium on High Voltage Engineering (ISH), Pilsen, Czech Republic, 23–28 August 2015; pp. 1–4.

60. Liao, R.J.; Zhu, M.Z.; Yang, L.J. Analysis of interaction between transformer oil and cellulosic insulation paper using molecular simulation method. *High Volt. Eng.* **2011**, *37*, 268–275.

61. Liao, R.J.; Zhu, M.Z.; Zhou, X. Molecular dynamics simulation of the diffusion behavior of water molecules in oil and cellulose composite media. *Acta Phys. Chim. Sin.* **2011**, *27*, 815–824.

62. Cheng, Y.H.; Xie, X.J.; Chen, X.L. Research on dielectric properties at ultra-high temperature based on molecular simulation technique. *Trans. China Electrotech. Soc.* **2006**, *21*, 1–6.

energies

MDPI

Article

Streamer Propagation and Breakdown in a Very Small Point-Insulating Plate Gap in Mineral Oil and Ester Liquids at Positive Lightning Impulse Voltage

Pawel Rozga

Institute of Electrical Power Engineering, Lodz University of Technology, Stefanowskiego 18/22, 90-924 Lodz, Poland; pawel.rozga@p.lodz.pl; Tel.: +48-42-631-2676

Academic Editor: Issouf Fofana
Received: 4 May 2016; Accepted: 7 June 2016; Published: 17 June 2016

Abstract: This article presents the results of comparative studies on streamer propagation and breakdown in a point-insulating plate electrode system in mineral oil and two ester liquids. The studies were performed for a 10-mm gap and a positive standard lightning impulse. The work was focused on the comparison of light waveforms registered using the photomultiplier technique. The results indicated that both esters demonstrate a lower resistance against the appearance of fast energetic streamers than mineral oil. The reason for such a conclusion is that the number of lightning impulses supplied to the electrode system for which the above-mentioned fast streamers appeared at a given voltage level was always higher in the case of ester liquids than mineral oil. In terms of breakdown, the esters tested were assessed as more susceptible to the appearance of breakdown in the investigated electrode system. The number of breakdowns recorded in the case of esters was always greater than the corresponding number of breakdowns in mineral oil. This may be supposed on the basis of the obtained results that imply that, in both synthetic and natural ester, the formed breakdown channel, which bridged the gap through the surface of pressboard plate, is characterized by higher energy than in the case of mineral oil.

Keywords: streamer propagation; mineral oil; synthetic ester; natural ester; lightning impulse; breakdown

1. Introduction

Synthetic and natural esters as alternative liquids for mineral oils have become more and more popular in transformer applications. This is primarily due to the fact that mineral oils, commonly used as insulating and cooling medium in transformers, are not neutral to the environment and may constitute a potential threat to the soil and watercourses when they release into the environment. The synthetic and natural esters, from the point of view of environmental hazards, are friendlier to the environment because of their better properties connected with biodegradability and flammability. In comparison to the mineral oils, esters are characterized by biodegradability of about 90% compared to only 10% characteristic of mineral oils, with a fire point (above 300 °C) higher than mineral oils, which provides their fire-resistant nature [1–7].

Both esters, apart from having environmentally friendly properties, should fulfill some requirements concerning their dielectric characteristics. In terms of electrical strength at AC voltage, synthetic and natural esters are more resistant to the influence of moisture content on this electrical strength. For example, for synthetic ester, even up to 600 ppm of moisture content, its AC breakdown voltage does not change, while for mineral oils a small amount of water in the oil volume (*circa* 20–30 ppm) decreases AC breakdown voltage significantly. Besides, both esters are characterized by the ability to absorb water from the insulating paper, which is desirable from the point of view of paper aging. Additionally, higher electrical permittivity of esters (3.2–3.3) compared with that of mineral oils (2.2–2.4) results in a more uniform electrical field distribution in a paper-dielectric liquid insulating system [4,5,8–12].

Despite many positive features of the esters, the studies concerning streamer propagation and breakdown under lightning impulse (LI) voltage have indicated that esters may behave worse than mineral oils at such types of voltage stresses [13–17]. Because the number of the studies in this field is still limited, and knowledge is still regarded as insufficient to clearly determine which of the liquids (esters or mineral oils) behave better under LI stresses and why, the authors' studies have only been focused on the above-mentioned aspect and are presented in this paper in terms of a very short (10 mm) point-plate gap. The studies have been focused on a positive polarity due to a well-known fact that this polarity is more dangerous for the real insulating systems with solid components. In contrast to the majority of published works [13–16,18–21], the author used an insulating plate placed on the grounded electrode. This allowed for closer alignment of the electrode system tested with real systems, where the inhomogeneity caused by the point electrode may constitute a place of locally increased intensity of the electric field stress and where the discharge develops only from this point to the electrode, which is usually insulated [17,22,23].

The commonly adopted approach in the assessment of esters is based on the comparison of ester features with features of mineral oil registered in the same testing conditions [2–4,8–11,13–17]. Among the features of the streamers developing in dielectric liquids, the most important are the streamer shapes, currents, and light waveforms, as well as propagation velocity. All of these indicators change with the so-called propagation modes which occur together consecutively with voltage increases in the given electrode configuration. In view of the propagation velocity of the streamers, these modes are divided into slow and fast. However, within these main modes, there are some sub-modes, such as 1st and 2nd mode (characterized by propagation velocity of a few mm/µs, commonly referred to as slow) and 3rd and 4th mode (having propagation velocity from a dozen to tens of mm/µs, commonly referred to as fast) [18–21]. Recognition between distinctive modes may be also identified on the basis of light and current characteristics, where the differences between the modes are clearly visible. Generally, it is a well-known fact that the 1st and 2nd propagation modes concern the streamers of relative low energies, while 3rd and 4th modes concern higher energies. Which propagation mode occurs depends on the value of testing voltage and thus on the value of the local electrical field, also resulting from the geometry of the electrode system. This may be said that lower values of electrical field stress (from tenths of MV/cm to few MV/cm) cause the development of slow propagating streamers, while higher values of electrical field stress (from tens to even 100 MV/cm) may contribute to the propagation of the fast, high-energy streamers. However, the moment of the appearance of fast streamers with an increase of testing voltage is also connected with the type of liquid in which the streamers develop. Ionization and excitation of the molecules in the given liquids are the molecular structure-dependent processes [13–22].

In the comparative assessment of the liquid behavior at lightning impulse stress, an especially important aspect is the determination of the value of voltage, at which a change in propagation mode from slow to fast occurs. This value has been called the acceleration voltage (and marked commonly as V_a) and has been related to the value of inception or breakdown voltage for a given electrode setup. The accepted name "acceleration voltage" comes from the fact that the streamers rapidly change their propagation velocity from a few to tens of mm/µs after exceeding this value of voltage. As mentioned above, the change of propagation velocity entails the change of the spatial shape of the streamers and the recorded time-dependent courses of current and light. Simultaneously, this change is accompanied by a higher energy of the streamer channels. If breakdown takes place within the development of fast streamers, the energy of the breakdown channel is also much higher than the corresponding energy of the breakdown channel being a result of development of slow propagating streamers. Thus, the observation of pre-breakdown and breakdown phenomena for different dielectric liquids in the same testing conditions may allow for the assessment of the differences and similarities between them [14,15,17].

2. Measurement Setup

The laboratory setup, which is presented schematically in Figure 1, was used in the measurements. A source of testing voltage was a six-stage Marx generator of a rated voltage of 500 kV and a storage energy of 2.2 kJ. This generator produced a standard positive lightning impulse voltage of 1.2/50 μs. It was supplied by a testing transformer with a ratio of 230:110000 and a solid-state high voltage rectifier. Measurement of the peak value of voltage impulse was achieved using a resistive voltage divider and a peak value meter. The voltage waveform was also observed on the screen of the oscilloscope used in the experimental setup.

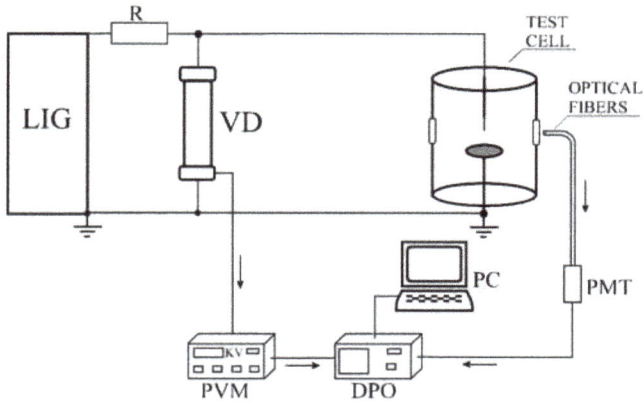

Figure 1. Laboratory setup used in the experiment: LIG—lightning impulse generator, VD—voltage divider, R—limiting resistor, PMT—photomultiplier, DPO—digital oscilloscope, PVM—peak value meter.

The voltage was supplied to the electrode system, which is presented in Figure 2.

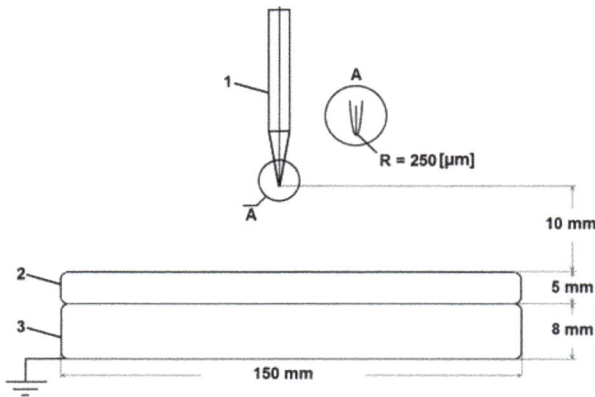

Figure 2. Electrode system used in the studies: 1—HV electrode, 2—insulating pressboard plate, 3—grounded electrode.

This system was placed in a test cell of 26 liters in volume. It consisted of a HV (high voltage) point electrode made of a tungsten needle with a 250-μm radius of curvature and a grounded electrode made of an aluminum plate 150 mm in diameter. On the surface of the grounded electrode, a 5-mm-thick pressboard plate was deposited. Before the beginning of the experiment, the pressboard plates were dried and impregnated in the liquid, in which the measurements were then performed. The procedure of drying and impregnation included the following:

- 24 h of drying in a vacuum at a temperature of 105 °C,
- impregnation with the given liquid in a vacuum at a temperature of 85 °C for 24 h, and
- lying in the vacuum at ambient temperature for 24 h.

The distance between the tip of the HV point and the surface of the insulating pressboard plate was set to 10 mm.

The research was focused on the assessment of the processes that occurred on the basis of the registration of light emitted by the streamers and the breakdown channel using the photomultiplier. It is assumed, in view of the experience gained during many years of studies, that the light pulses are strictly correlated with current pulses providing knowledge about the possible mode of streamer propagation and the level of ionization of streamer channels [13–15,17–19,21,23,24]. The choice of photomultiplier as a light detector resulted from the fact that light generated by the streamers is weak and the amount of light that reaches the side window of the test cell is limited by the absorption and dispersion phenomena, and only a photomultiplier (PMT) is a detector that is sensitive enough to register such a weak light. The light caught by the end of the optical fiber cable placed in the above-mentioned UV (of the lower wavelength range equal to 300 nm) side glass window of the test cell was transferred to the photomultiplier. The Hamamatsu R1925 photomultiplier with a wavelength range from 300 to 850 nm was used. The PMT output signal, after being amplified, was registered using the oscilloscope in the form of a waveform (temporal sequence of discrete negative pulses having the rise-times of a few nanoseconds). Simultaneously, the waveforms obtained were saved on a hard-disk of a PC-type computer where it could be analyzed and compared with other results of the measurements.

3. Measurement Assumptions

Three commercial dielectric liquids were used in the experiment: naphtenic type mineral oil, organic synthetic pentaerythritol ester, and natural ester produced from soya bean. All three liquids before the beginning of the experiment were defined in relation to their basic dielectric parameters. This was assumed that the liquids tested had to fulfill the requirements described in the standards corresponding to a given liquid [25–27]. The values of the parameters measured are set in Table 1.

Table 1. Basic dielectric parameters of the liquids tested.

Parameters	Synthetic Ester	Natural Ester	Mineral Oil
AC breakdown voltage—mean value [kV]	64	67	66
Dielectric dissipation factor at 90 °C and 50 Hz	0.0108	0.0446	0.004
Moisture content [ppm]	129	102	12

The next step was to define a measurement cycle. This cycle was related to previously estimated inception voltages of the streamers. A procedure of inception voltage estimation was described in detail in [28]. The calculations were performed using MOSTAT software where the maximum likelihood method was applied. This software is the authors' tool, which was created at the High Voltage Division of the Institute of Electrical Power Engineering of Lodz University of Technology, Poland, and has been tested from many years, solving both scientific and industry problems [17,24,29–31]. The results of this estimation for the considered gap distance of 10 mm are quoted in Table 2. The statistical distribution used for estimation was a three-parameter Weibull distribution described by Equation (1) presented below.

$$F(V) = 1 - \exp\left[-\left(\frac{V_i - V_0}{V_m - V_0}\right)^k\right]. \tag{1}$$

In this equation,

- V_0 is the location parameter for which $F(V_0) = 0$, meaning the threshold value of voltage below, in which discharge initiation in a given electrode configuration does not occur (expressed in kV);
- V_m is the scale parameter for which $F(V_m) = 1 - e^{-1} \approx 0.632$, representing the value of voltage below, in which 63.2% of the analyzed population of inception voltages is included (expressed in kV);
- k is the shape parameter, a measure of the dispersion of the data;
- V_i is the random variable (inception voltages measured in kV).

In addition to the main parameters of the Weibull distribution, the 0.5th percentile (median V_{Med}) of the measured values was added.

Table 2. Weibull distribution parameters for positive impulse inception voltages.

Type of Liquid	V_0 [kV]	V_m [kV]	k	V_{Med} [kV]
Synthetic ester	49.9	55.8	0.9	53.7
Natural ester	49.3	54.4	1.6	53.4
Mineral oil	43.2	55.3	4.2	54.3

On the basis of the results obtained, the reference value was determined as the starting value for the studies planned. This value was rounded up for an integer value taking into account the voltage step assumed. Hence, 55 kV was treated as a reference inception voltage V_i for all the liquids tested. This was done because similar values V_{Med} were obtained in each case. After the inception voltage estimation, it was assumed that, starting from this value of the testing voltage, the next voltage levels would be reached by increasing the voltage in 0.2 V_i steps.

For the inception voltage and subsequent inception voltage multipliers, 20 lightning impulses were supplied to the electrode system tested at each voltage level. The oscillograms of light were collected in each case, and the surface of insulating plate placed on the grounded electrode was simultaneously observed after every 5 impulses. Before beginning the experiment, it was assumed that the insulating plate would be changed after each voltage step. However, taking into account that significant changes were observed on the surface of the pressboard as a result of the impact of developing streamers, the plates were changed after every 10 lightning impulses supplied.

4. Results of the Measurements

Figure 3 presents the representative oscillograms registered for the reference inception voltage $V_i = 55$ kV. These oscillograms are similar to each other, showing a sequence of discrete light pulses rising in time. This means that the streamers developed step by step, and each step was connected with the next extension of the streamer channels, which occurred one by one with nanosecond intervals. After reaching some distance from the HV point, electrode streamers probably disappeared in the space between the electrodes since the light pulses suddenly ended. Confirmation of this fact was reached by observation of the insulating plates used. There were no traces on the surface of these plates. Thus, the propagation mode observed was assessed as a propagation of the so-called "stopping length" streamers, probably of the second propagation mode. Alternatively, the streamers finished their propagation, reaching the insulating plate placed on the grounded electrode but without the breakdown and without any other similar phenomena. The disappearance of the streamers in the electrode space was the result of a low electrical field stress, existing in some distance from the HV point and too weak an impact of space charge that cannot maintain the ionization processes. In all of the liquids tested, this disappearance followed after a few µs from the moment of the lightning impulse supplied [13–15,21].

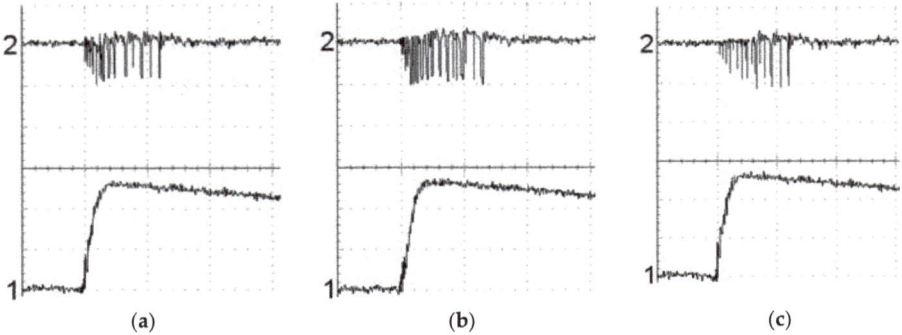

Figure 3. Oscillograms registered at testing voltage equal to $V_i = 55$ kV: (**a**) synthetic ester, (**b**) natural ester, (**c**) mineral oil; 1—voltage [20 kV/div.], 2—light [arb. units], $t = 4$ µs/div.

A comparison of the oscillograms registered for the tested liquids showed significant visible differences of higher frequency of the light pulses registered for streamers developing in esters. Simultaneously, slightly higher peak values of these pulses were observed in such cases. The observed phenomenon may be explained as an easier way for the next step of propagation when the streamers develop in one of the esters. Because such a step represents the extension of the streamer channels resulting from the influence of actual electrical field stress and space charge left by the previous discharge, it may be supposed that re-ignition of the streamers, which requires restoration of the former field stress to the value able to cause the next ionization and excitation processes, for the individual liquids tested occurs in a slightly different way. Re-ignition happens more easily when streamers develop in esters with simultaneous intensification of the ionization processes.

Increase of the testing voltage caused the changes in the oscillograms registered. For all the liquids tested, the sequence of light pulses ended as a wide light pulse saturated the photomultiplier. This took place after 5–6 µs from the moment at which lightning impulse was supplied to the electrode system. Because intense flash finishing streamer propagation was also observed, the wide light pulse from the oscillograms may be identified solely with this flash. The voltage waveform, however, did not indicate a breakdown (voltage collapse was not observed); thus, it may be supposed that the streamers touched the insulating plate placed on the grounded electrode and that surface discharges started to develop with the creation of a return channel, a result of capacitive coupling between the HV point and the grounded plate [17,24]. The intensity of the processes connected with streamer propagation was, as in the case of the measurements at inception voltage, higher in the case where one of the esters was the liquid under the test. In such cases, the frequency of light pulses registered was higher, and the width of the pulse finishing the process of streamer propagation was greater. An additional fact in favor of the more intense processes occurring during the development of the streamers in esters was the observation of the insulating pressboard plate after emptying a test cell from the given liquid. The tracks left on the plate used during the measurements in the ester liquids indicated a more intense penetration of the surface of the plate with a simultaneous greater number of channels in comparison with the analogically observed channels formed during the measurements in mineral oil.

Figure 4 presents the representative oscillograms concerning the above-mentioned testing voltage equal to 1.2 V_i (66 kV).

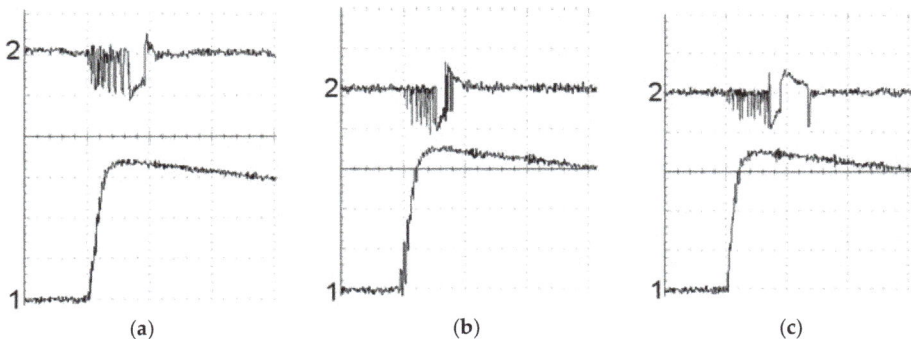

Figure 4. Oscillograms registered at testing voltage equal to 1.2 V_i = 66 kV: (**a**) synthetic ester, (**b**) natural ester, (**c**) mineral oil; 1—voltage [20 kV/div.], 2—light [arb. units], t = 4 μs/div.

The subsequent testing voltages caused many problems during measurements. In all cases at the inception voltage multipliers in the range between 1.4 and 1.8 V_i, a more intense streamer propagation started to be observed. This was deduced from the fact that a wide light pulse finishing the streamer development appeared after *circa* 1 μs, thus at least four times faster than at a voltage equal to 1.2 V_i. A simple calculation of the propagation velocity considering gap distance and time to appearance of wide light pulse indicated a minimum 10 mm/μs of propagation velocity, which may allow for the identification of the propagation mode as a propagation of fast streamers in very small gaps [13–15,18–22,24]. The appearance of such a phenomenon in synthetic and natural ester was observed for all the cases concerning the inception voltage multipliers equal to 1.8 V_i. For the multiplier of 1.4 V_i, such a situation took place for synthetic ester in 13 of 20 supplied lightning impulses and for natural ester in 14 of 20 impulses. In turn for 1.6 V_i, 18 of 20 supplied impulses caused fast streamer propagation in the case of the synthetic ester and in all 20 cases when the tested liquid was natural ester. Contrary to the results obtained for ester liquids in the case of mineral oil, only 11 of 20 oscillograms registered at 1.4 V_i concerned the propagation of fast streamers, 14 of 20 at voltage level equal to 1.6 V_i, and all for 1.8 V_i. In addition, the development of streamers was accompanied in many cases with breakdown, during which the light was emitted more intensely than in the case of the above-mentioned return channel. The breakdown phenomena were visible in the voltage waveforms in the form of a sudden voltage collapse. For 20 lightning impulses at a voltage level equal to 1.4 V_i, breakdown in synthetic ester took place seven times, in natural ester nine times, but in mineral oil not once. For the testing voltage equal to 1.6 V_i, breakdown was observed 14 times in synthetic ester and 18 times in natural ester. At 1.8 V_i, breakdown was, however, identified in all the cases concerning both synthetic and natural ester. In mineral oil, breakdown occurred 6 times at 1.6 V_i and 13 times at 1.8 V_i. This confirmed the assumption that the variety of phenomena in the point-insulating plate electrode system is greater than in the classical experimental electrode system, including only bare electrodes. A summary of the data collected during the measurements is presented collectively in Table 3 and graphically in Figures 5 and 6.

In order to assess whether bridging the electrodes took place along the surface of the insulating plate or with its inclusion, each plate was tested under AC voltage in the parallel electrode system in accordance with Standard IEC 60243 [32]. If the increased AC voltage did not cause the short circuit, it was recognized that breakdown through the plate did not occur. In all of the cases, the tests performed did not indicate a breakdown of the insulating plates used, thus showing a way for an inductive plasma channel that bridges the electrodes followed, as shown in Figure 7, along the surface of the plate.

Table 3. Number of fast streamers and number of breakdowns per 20 lightning impulses (LI) supplied to the electrode system tested.

Inception Voltage Multiplier	Liquid Type					
	Synthetic Ester		Natural Ester		Mineral Oil	
	Number of Fast Streamers per 20 LI Supplied	Number of Breakdowns per 20 LI Supplied	Number of Fast Streamers per 20 LI Supplied	Number of Breakdowns per 20 LI Supplied	Number of Fast Streamers per 20 LI Supplied	Number of Breakdowns per 20 LI Supplied
1.4 V_i	13	7	14	9	11	0
1.6 V_i	18	14	20	18	14	6
1.8 V_i	20	20	20	20	20	13

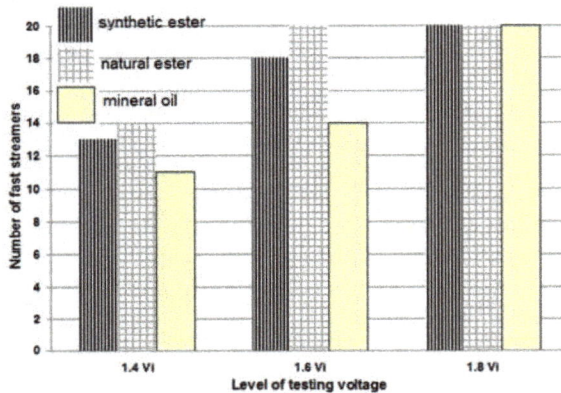

Figure 5. Number of fast streamers per 20 lightning impulses supplied to the electrode setup tested at a given value of testing voltage.

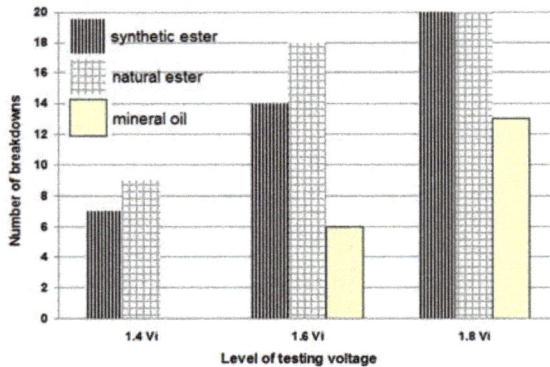

Figure 6. Number of breakdowns per 20 lightning impulses supplied to the electrode setup tested at a given value of testing voltage.

Similar to the case of lower testing voltages, the intensity of the processes connected with the streamers developing in esters was greater, which was confirmed again both on the basis of oscillograms registered and by observation of the pressboard plates after being removed from the test cell. The channels on the plates were again more intense in the case of the ester liquids.

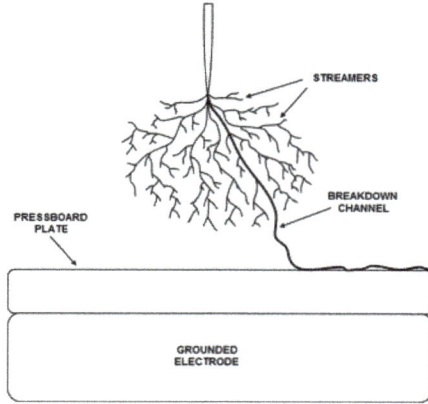

Figure 7. The way of breakdown channel formed.

Figure 8 presents the selected oscillograms concerning the development of fast streamers at a voltage level equal to 1.4 V_i (77 kV). Figure 9 shows, however, the oscillograms registered for breakdowns at 1.8 V_i. For all the liquids tested, breakdown occurred after a time shorter than 1 µs; thus, the lightning impulse supplied did not achieve its peak value.

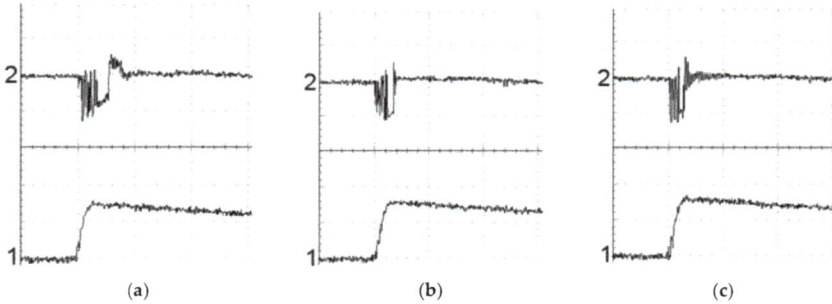

Figure 8. Oscillograms registered at testing voltage equal to 1.4 V_i = 77 kV: (**a**) synthetic ester, (**b**) natural ester, (**c**) mineral oil; 1—voltage [50 kV/div.], 2—light [arb. units], t = 4 µs/div.

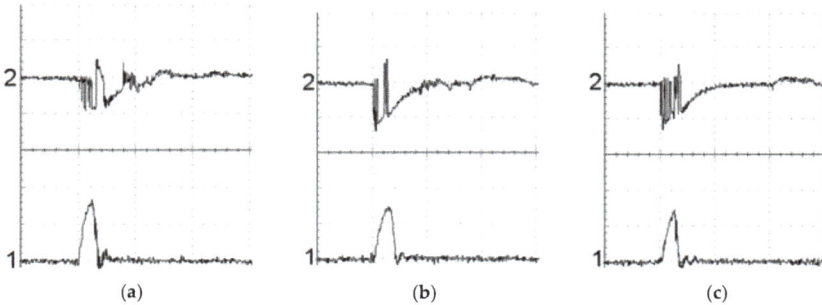

Figure 9. Oscillograms registered at testing voltage equal to 1.8 V_i = 99 kV: (**a**) synthetic ester, (**b**) natural ester, (**c**) mineral oil; 1—voltage [50 kV/div.], 2—light [arb. units], t = 2 µs/div.

Due to the fact that, at a testing voltage equal to 1.8 V_i in synthetic ester and natural ester, breakdown occurred each time and always at the front of the lightning impulse, studies at higher values of voltage ceased. This resulted from the assumption that, with a large probability, such studies would not have brought more valuable information about the comparison of the pre-breakdown and breakdown processes in esters and mineral oil. It is, however, difficult to observe, beyond these differences indicated in the macro scale (number of fast discharges or breakdowns per 20 impulses supplied), any additional aspects in favor of one of the liquids tested when the time of discharge development from the initiation up to breakdown is less than 1 μs. Simultaneously, seeking the limitation in mineral oil at which, for 20 supplied impulses, 20 breakdowns occur also does not seem to make sense because better properties of the mineral oil have been clearly specified for the lower voltage multipliers on the basis of the studies performed.

5. Conclusions

On the basis of the studies performed, the following conclusions can be drawn:

1. In the point-insulating plate electrode systems investigated in these studies, the variety of phenomena which are possible to observe at a given voltage level is greater than that in classically applied electrode systems, including bare electrodes. The unambiguous inference is therefore much more difficult in the considered case.

2. The measurements performed demonstrated that, in the case of the propagation of already-initiated streamers in the tested point-insulating plate electrode system, ester liquids, as in the case of the systems with bare electrodes, demonstrate a lower resistance against the appearance of fast and energetic streamers than mineral oil. Although the inception voltage and the threshold value of the testing voltage for the appearance of fast streamers are similar, for both of the liquids tested, the differences in the results obtained are clearly indicated. The number of fast streamers observed for the voltages between 1.4 and 1.8 of V_i was always much higher in the case of synthetic and natural ester than that of mineral oil.

3. The ability to form a breakdown channel was also higher in the case of the ester liquids, where breakdown occurred almost always, only at the voltage level equal to 1.6 V_i. For mineral oil, for this voltage level, the different types of streamer propagation modes were registered from slow propagating streamers, through fast streamers that did not lead to the breakdown, up to breakdown similar to this observed in the esters. Intensification of the differences between the liquids tested at testing voltages equal to 1.8 V_i definitely strengthened the above-formed conclusion.

4. Limiting the comparison only to the esters tested, it was found that synthetic ester behaved a little better under lightning stresses. Both for 1.4 and 1.6 V_i, the number of fast streamers registered and the number of breakdowns occurring at the 20 lightning impulses supplied were lower than the corresponding numbers concerning natural ester. However, comparing the oscillograms collected, there were no obvious differences between the esters under consideration.

5. Relating the observations quoted to the theory of propagation of the streamers in liquid dielectrics, it may be supposed that both esters in small point-insulating plate electrode systems are similarly more susceptible on the appearance of such types of the streamers, which propagate as a result of liquid phase ionization (3rd or 4th propagation mode). The channels of such streamers seem to be more energetic than channels of the streamers propagating slowly (2nd mode). In turn, if the breakdown occurs in the gap that is filled with one of the esters, it is characterized by a more intense impact on solid insulation that may be damaged easier.

Acknowledgments: The studies presented in this article were supported in part by the Polish National Science Centre under Grant ST8/03549 and within statutory works realized in Institute of Electrical Power Engineering at Faculty of Electrical, Electronic, Computer and Control Engineering of Lodz University of Technology.

Author Contributions: The research presented in this paper is a result of the sole effort of the author Pawel Rozga who prepared the assumption for the studies, performed the studies, analyzed their results, and formed the final conclusions.

Conflicts of Interest: The author declares no conflict of interest.

References

1. McShane, C.P. Vegetable-oil-based dielectric coolants. *IEEE Ind. Appl. Mag.* **2002**, *2*, 34–41. [CrossRef]
2. Borsi, H.; Gockenbach, E. Properties of ester liquid Midel 7131 as an alternative liquid to mineral oil for transformers. *IEEE Int. Conf. Dielectr. Liq.* **2005**, 377–380. [CrossRef]
3. Gockenbach, E.; Borsi, H. Natural and synthetic ester liquids as alternative to mineral oil for power transformers. *IEEE Conf. Electr. Insul. Dielectr. Phenom.* **2008**, 521–524. [CrossRef]
4. Perrier, C.; Beroual, A. Experimental investigations on insulating liquids for power transformers: Mineral, ester and silicone oils. *IEEE Elect. Insul. Mag.* **2009**, *25*, 6–13. [CrossRef]
5. CIGRE brochure 436. *Experiences in Service with New Insulating Liquids*; International Council on Large Electric Systems: Paris, France, 2011.
6. Lashbrook, M.; Kuhn, M. The use of ester transformer fluids for increased fire safety and reduced costs. *CIGRE Tech. Progr.* **2012**, A2–A210.
7. Fernández, I.; Ortiz, A.; Delgado, F.; Renedo, C.; Pérez, S. Comparative evaluation of alternative fluids for power transformers. *Electr. Power Syst. Res.* **2013**, *98*, 58–69. [CrossRef]
8. Liao, R.J.; Hao, J.; Chen, G.; Ma, Z.Q.; Yang, L.J. A comparative study of physicochemical, dielectric and thermal properties of pressboard insulation impregnated with natural ester and mineral oil. *IEEE Trans. Dielectr. Electr. Insul.* **2011**, *18*, 1626–1637. [CrossRef]
9. Martins, M.A.G.; Gomes, A.R. Comparative study of the thermal degradation of synthetic and natural esters and mineral oil: effect of oil type in the thermal degradation of insulating Kraft paper. *IEEE Electr. Insul. Mag.* **2012**, *28*, 22–28. [CrossRef]
10. Talhi, M.; Fofana, I.; Flazi, S. Comparative study of the electrostatic charging tendency between synthetic ester and mineral oil. *IEEE Trans. Dielectr. Electr. Insul.* **2013**, *20*, 1598–1606. [CrossRef]
11. Loiselle, L.; Fofana, I.; Sabau, J.; Magdaleno-Adame, S.; Olivares-Galvan, J.C. Comparative studies of the stability of various fluids under electrical discharge and thermal stresses. *IEEE Trans. Dielectr. Electr. Insul.* **2015**, *22*, 2491–2499. [CrossRef]
12. Bandara, K.; Ekanayake, C.; Saha, T.; Ma, H. Performance of natural ester as a transformer oil in moisture-rich environments. *Energies* **2016**, *9*, 258. [CrossRef]
13. Duy, C.T.; Denat, A.; Lesaint, O.; Bonifaci, N. Streamer propagation and breakdown in natural ester at high voltage. *IEEE Trans. Dielectr. Electr. Insul.* **2009**, *16*, 1582–1594. [CrossRef]
14. Dang, V-H.; Beroual, A.; Perrier, C. Comparative study of streamer phenomena in mineral, synthetic and natural ester oils under lightning impulse voltage. *Int. Conf. High Volt. Eng. Appl.* **2010**, 560–563. [CrossRef]
15. Liu, Q.; Wang, Z.D. Streamer characteristic and breakdown in synthetic and natural ester transformer liquids under standard lightning impulse. *IEEE Trans. Dielectr. Electr. Insul.* **2011**, *18*, 285–294. [CrossRef]
16. Liu, Q.; Wang, Z.D. Secondary reverse streamer observed in an ester insulating liquid under negative impulse voltage. *J. Phys. D: Appl. Phys.* **2011**, *44*. [CrossRef]
17. Rozga, P. Streamer propagation in small gaps of synthetic ester and mineral oil under lightning impulse. *IEEE Trans. Dielectr. Electr. Insul.* **2015**, *22*, 2754–2762. [CrossRef]
18. Devins, J.C.; Rzad, S.J.; Schwabe, R.J. Breakdown and prebreakdown phenomena in liquids. *J. Appl. Phys.* **1981**, *52*, 4531–4545. [CrossRef]
19. Beroual, A. Electronic and gaseous processes in prebreakdown phenomena of dielectric liquids. *J. Appl. Phys.* **1993**, *73*, 4528–4532. [CrossRef]
20. Tobazcon, R. Prebreakdown phenomena in dielectric liquids. *IEEE Trans. Dielectr. Electr. Insul.* **1996**, *1*, 1132–1147. [CrossRef]
21. Lesaint, O.; Massala, G. Positive streamer propagation in large oil gaps: Experimental characterization of propagation mode. *IEEE Trans. Dielectr. Electr. Insul.* **1998**, *5*, 360–370. [CrossRef]
22. Galczak, J. Electrical discharges in mineral oil developing from insulated transformer wire to plane. *Arch. Electr. Eng.* **2004**, *73*, 353–367.

23. Lundgaard, L.; Linhjell, D.; Berg, G.; Sigmond, S. Propagation of positive and negative streamers in oil with and without pressboard interfaces. *IEEE Trans. Dielectr. Electr. Insul.* **1998**, *5*, 388–395. [CrossRef]

24. Rozga, P. The influence of paper insulation on the prebreakdown phenomena in mineral oil under lightning impulse. *IEEE Trans. Dielectr. Electr. Insul.* **2011**, *11*, 720–727. [CrossRef]

25. *IEC 60296 Standard: Fluids for Electrotechnical Applications—Unused Mineral Insulating Oils for Transformers and Switchgears*; International Electrotechnical Commission: Geneva, Switzerland, 2012.

26. *IEC 61099 Standard: Insulating liquids – Specifications for Unused Synthetic Organic Esters for Electrical Purposes*; International Electrotechnical Commission: Geneva, Switzerland, 2011.

27. *IEC 62770 Standard: Fluids for Electrotechnical Applications - Unused Natural Esters for Transformers and Similar Electrical Equipment*; International Electrotechnical Commission: Geneva, Switzerland, 2014.

28. Rozga, P.; Stanek, M.; Cieslinski, D. Comparison of properties of electrical discharges developing in natural and synthetic ester at inception voltage. *2013 IEEE Annual Report Conf. Electr. Insul. Diel. Phenom.* **2013**, 891–894. [CrossRef]

29. Mosinski, F.; Wodzinski, J.; Sikorski, L.; Ziencikiewicz, J. Electrical strength of paper-oil insulation subjected to composite voltages. *IEEE Trans. Dielectr. Electr. Insul.* **1994**, *1*, 615–623. [CrossRef]

30. Mosinski, F.; Piotrowski, T. New statistical methods for evaluation of DGA data. *IEEE Trans. Dielectr. Electr. Insul.* **2003**, *10*, 260–265. [CrossRef]

31. Piotrowski, T. Probability distribution of gases dissolved in oil of failed power transformers. *Int. Conf. High Volt. Eng. Applic.* **2014**, 1–4. [CrossRef]

32. *IEC 60243–1 Standard: Electric Strength of Insulating Materials - Test Methods - Part 1: Tests at Power Frequencies*; International Electrotechnical Commission: Geneva, Switzerland, 2013.

Article

Moisture Migration in an Oil-Paper Insulation System in Relation to Online Partial Discharge Monitoring of Power Transformers

Wojciech Sikorski *, Krzysztof Walczak and Piotr Przybylek

Institute of Electrical Power Engineering, Poznan University of Technology, Piotrowo 3A, 60-965 Poznan, Poland; krzysztof.walczak@put.poznan.pl (K.W.); piotr.przybylek@put.poznan.pl (P.P.)
* Correspondence: wojciech.sikorski@put.poznan.pl; Tel.: +48-61-665-2035

Academic Editor: Issouf Fofana
Received: 10 October 2016; Accepted: 13 December 2016; Published: 17 December 2016

Abstract: Most power transformers operating in a power system possess oil-paper insulation. A serious defect of this type of insulation, which is associated with long operation time, is an increase in the moisture content. Moisture introduces a number of threats to proper operation of the transformer, e.g., ignition of partial discharges (PDs). Due to the varying temperature of the insulation system during the unit's normal operation, a dynamic change (migration of water) takes place, precipitating the oil-paper system from a state of hydrodynamic equilibrium. This causes the PDs to be variable in time, and they may intensify or extinguish. Studies on model objects have been conducted to determine the conditions (temperature, humidity, time) that will have an impact on the ignition and intensity of the observed phenomenon of PDs. The conclusions of this study will have a practical application in the evaluation of measurements conducted in the field, especially in relation to the registration of an online PD monitoring system.

Keywords: partial discharge (PD); online monitoring; power transformer; oil-paper insulation; water migration

---

1. Introduction

The last few years have brought a clear shift in the strategy of network asset management, including large power transformers. The overall aging of the transformer population, manifesting itself, e.g., in an increase in the average moisture content [1], and the more often occurring catastrophic failures have forced the introduction of new regulations and recommendations for the operation and diagnosis of strategic importance devices to ensure a continuity of energy supply. Additionally, the growing demands of insurance companies concerning an aged network infrastructure, and thus burdened with a high risk of failure, have forced operators to change the current policy. One of the symptoms of these changes is the introduction of more complex diagnosis of particular transformer components and shorter intervals between successive periodic inspections.

The increasing outlays for periodic diagnostics seriously enhance the overall operating costs without bringing a 100% guarantee to avoid damaging of the unit, e.g., due to the rapidly developing defects. Therefore, currently, an alternative to periodic diagnosis is more often the use of a transformer monitoring in the short-term (e.g., weekly monitoring of partial discharge (PD)) or continuous mode (the measurement system is installed permanently). With the rising costs of operation and due to the increasing reliability of these solutions, it seems that the use of online systems is advantageous from both a technical and economical point of view. It should also be noted that continuous monitoring systems very well fit into the strategy that assumes resignation from manned substations in the near future to those that are fully automated and remotely managed.

The primary task of the monitoring system of any electric power device is to assess its technical condition and to generate an alarm or a warning signal if some anomaly is to occur in its functioning. In the case of such a large and complex device such as a power transformer, it is very difficult to provide a clear, synthetic answer regarding its condition (e.g., in the form of a three-stage classification: normal, warning or alarm), especially if we are aware that defects in the insulation may develop at different rates, in different places and have different levels of importance to the risk of failure of a given unit.

One of the ways to assess the condition of power transformer insulation is to track changes in the activity of PDs. The presence of PDs in the transformer insulation system is an alarming signal about the development of dangerous defects that can lead to serious consequences, including damage of the unit. The main causes of PD activity are: (i) the electrical or mechanical weakening of insulation; (ii) the presence of voids (delaminations), gas bubbles or conductive particles; and (iii) the excessive moisture. The moisture migration and its impact on the PD activity in oil-paper insulation will be the subject of this article.

One of the currently used methods of online measurement of PDs is a method of detection and localisation of acoustic emission (AE) signal sources and the ultra-high frequency (UHF) signal, both of which belong to a group called unconventional methods [2–4]. In these methods, the recorded measuring signal, based on different physical phenomena, is associated with the effect of PD generation in a way that prevents its calibration, e.g., correlation with the apparent charge, which is a widely accepted parameter describing the phenomenon of PD generation. In practice, this means that generally accepted normative criteria expressed in pico/nano Coulombs cannot be used for an assessment of the power transformer, and only quantities describing parameter changes over time, the trends of these changes, etc. are used. Implementation of a monitoring system that will take into account all of these factors and also carefully protect the object is extremely difficult. It requires the creation of complex algorithms of inference that should be verified based on the system's operation as installed on the units in service.

In 2011, as a result of a four-year research project, the Institute of Electrical Power Engineering at the Poznan University of Technology (Poznan, Poland) developed a prototype system (called PDtracker), which was one of the first in Europe for PD online monitoring of power transformers (Figure 1). PDtracker was intensively tested and developed for almost two years at one of the power substations belonging to a Polish Transmission System Operator (PSE) [5]. After this time, PDtracker was used for PD detection and monitoring in numerous power transformers and allowed the authors to expand their knowledge on this important issue [6].

1. Industrial power supply
2. Signal conditioning unit for partial discharge sensors
3. Signal acquisition unit
4. Temperature and humidity control modules
5. Circuit breakers
6. Liquid crystal display and light-emitting diode indicators module
7. Electromagnetic interference (EMI) shielded chassis
8. Contactless module for high voltage measurement

Figure 1. Hardware architecture of a prototype online partial discharge (PD) monitoring system for power transformers.

The PDtracker system can operate autonomously or as an integrated part of the overall substation monitoring system. This approach enables a wide range of correlation analysis that allows for combining PD activity with selected parameters of unit functioning (e.g., oil temperature, voltage, load). This, in turn, creates conditions for observation of a scientific nature.

The experience gained from implementation of PDtracker, which was the basis for the laboratory tests undertaken by this team of authors, is discussed in detail in the next sections of this paper.

2. Prototype Online Partial Discharge Monitoring System for Power Transformers

PDtracker works based on the detection of AE pulses registered by piezoelectric contact transducers, which are mounted on the transformer tank wall. The mounting places are usually chosen on the basis of results obtained with the auscultatory technique (PD activity regions can be easily identified by taking acoustic measurements in a number of places on the transformer tank) [7]. To reduce the influence of external electromagnetic and acoustic interference, the piezoelectric transducer and preamplifier circuit (40 dB) are mounted in a combined metal housing equipped with magnetic holders and passive vibration absorbers. The pre-amplified signals are transmitted to a signal conditioning unit that consists of adjustable-gain amplifiers and band-pass (20–800 kHz) filters. The conditioned signals are then streamed into a signal acquisition unit that includes a powerful, fan-less industrial PC with a high-speed acquisition card (simultaneous-sampling rate up to 20 MS/s). Procedures for data acquisition and signal processing were implemented in a LabVIEW 2009 (National Instruments, Austin, TX, USA) programming environment and are done in real time.

The PDtracker system was designed for continuous, multi-month fieldwork. Therefore, the specialised firmware not only allows for continuous registration of PD activity but also for correct work of the system itself (e.g., temperature and humidity inside the enclosure or operation of the electronic measuring circuits). The firmware is equipped with advanced data processing modules that make it easier to evaluate events and noise filtering (wavelet-based denoising). In addition to registration and calculation of basic parameters (e.g., AE hits rate, energy and amplitude of AE pulses, dominant frequency), the program also creates an event log whose goal is to inform, with a specified frequency (service station or the superior system), about the work of the PD monitoring system or about a threat to the transformer resulting from intensity discharge growth [8]. External communication is provided using a GSM (Global System for Mobile Communications) modem with an additional antenna or LAN/WLAN network (Local/Wireless Local Area Network). Optionally, in order to increase the reliability of PD detection and to determine the source of the AE signals (internal PDs or external acoustic disturbances), the PDtracker system can be equipped with high-frequency current transformers (split ferrite core; bandwidth from 400 kHz to 10 MHz) installed around the ground wire, from neutral bushing to ground or around the grounded test tap of bushing [9]. The system can also be equipped with Rogowski Coils installed around the base of the bushing (just above where the porcelain and metal flange join). Currently, work is underway to deploy the UHF module with probes installed in the transformer via the oil drain valve or in the mounting flanges [10]. A typical arrangement of the sensors for PD monitoring is shown in Figure 2.

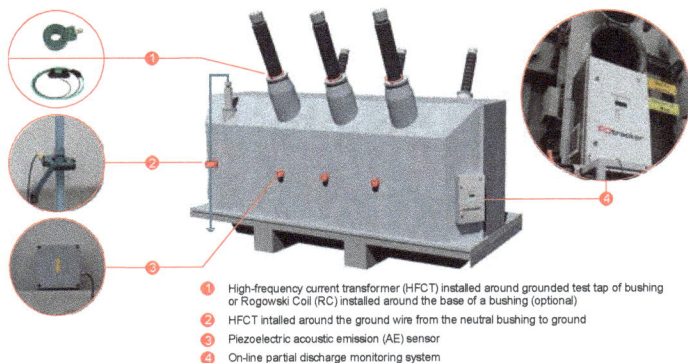

① High-frequency current transformer (HFCT) installed around grounded test tap of bushing or Rogowski Coil (RC) installed around the base of a bushing (optional)
② HFCT intalled around the ground wire from the neutral bushing to ground
③ Piezoelectric acoustic emission (AE) sensor
④ On-line partial discharge monitoring system

Figure 2. Arrangement of PD sensors on the monitored power transformer.

3. Experience with Online Partial Discharge Monitoring of Power Transformers

The PDtracker system was implemented in short- or long-term monitoring mode on a dozen power transformers. Most of the transformers were chosen by the power grid operator on the basis of negative results during a periodical diagnosis (the most common cause was a growing level of dissolved gases in oil). In most cases, analysis of the measurement data recorded by the system confirmed the stochastic nature of the PD phenomenon, which is affected by the complexity of the mechanisms of its generation and development (e.g., local electrical stress concentrations in the insulation or on the surface of the insulation, thermal and electrochemical ageing of the insulation). This fact is well illustrated in Figure 3, which summarises the activity of PD (AE hits rate per minute) as a function of voltage registered for one of the monitored power transformers (330 MVA, 400/110 kV). In the analysed period (18 days), it may be observed that it was not always increased electric field intensity (in Figure 3, the voltage peaks are marked by arrows) that determined the moment of initiation of PD phenomena and its activity level.

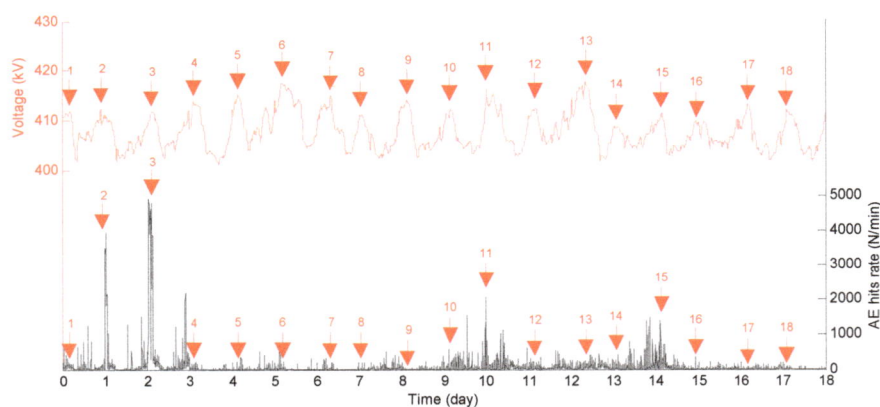

Figure 3. Relation between PD activity (AE hits rate per minute) and voltage changes (voltage peaks are marked by arrows) during 18 days of monitoring a 330 MVA/400 kV power transformer.

In the case of the transformer as discussed above, an interesting relationship was observed between the intensity of the PD and the top-oil temperature estimated based on the thermal model of the power transformer (according to IEC 60076-7 Loading Guide for Oil-Immersed Power Transformers [11]) implemented in the substation superior monitoring system (supervisory control and data acquisition (SCADA)) and temperature measurements carried out by the thirteen industrial PT100 sensors (two sensors were installed under the top cover of the transformer tank, ten sensors were installed at the inlet and outlet of the radiators and one sensor was used to monitor the ambient temperature).

An analysis of the measurement data shows that PDs were generated not only in the periods in which the voltage was increasing but also when its value was decreasing or relatively low. What is important to note is that, especially in the context of the research discussed in this article, it was observed that the periods of increased intensity of PDs often coincided with the local maxima and minima of top-oil temperature.

Figure 4 shows the results of measurements worked out for a selected period (February 2012) during which the monitoring system reported the highest activity of PDs. The largest differences between the minimum and maximum top-oil temperature (over 30 °C) were recorded periodically during periods including the Saturday (or Sunday) minimum and the Monday maximum power demand. It can be noticed that the monitoring system was recording high PD activity during these periods.

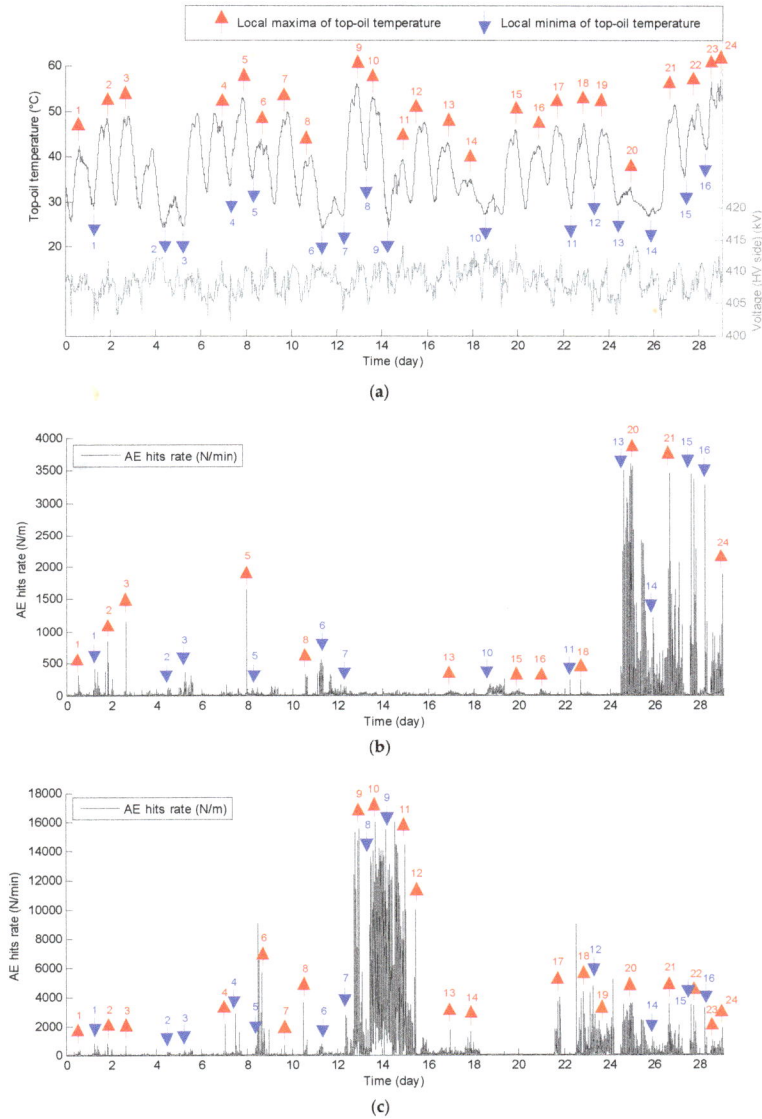

Figure 4. (**a**) Comparison of voltage, top-oil temperature (peaks and troughs are marked by arrows); (**b**) PD activity (AE hits rate per minute) registered in the high voltage HV1 phase; and (**c**) PD activity (AE hits rate per minute) registered in the high voltage HV2 phase during monthly monitoring of a 330 MVA/400 kV/110 kV power transformer.

A similar correlation between PD intensity and changes in the temperature of oil was also observed during monitoring of the 250 MVA transformer (the system was running for five days), for which the periodic DGA (dissolved gas analysis) tests (Table 1) and the AE inspection indicated the presence of PD phenomena (Figure 5).

Table 1. Results of the periodic dissolved gas analysis (DGA) tests. Measurements were taken using KELMAN Transport X Portable Dissolve Gas Analyzer (General Electric, Fairfield, CT, USA).

Gas Description		Date in 2011 of Sampling and Gas Concentration (in ppm)				
		2 December	9 December	16 December	22 December	30 December
Hydrogen	H_2	512	452	647	853	1248
Methane	CH_4	45	25	68	134	146
Acetylene	C_2H_2	1	1	<0.5	<0.5	0.5
Ethylene	C_2H_4	9	7	8	19	18
Ethane	C_2H_6	28	12	16	72	37
Carbon monoxide	CO	524	426	881	1018	1225
Carbon dioxide	CO_2	5937	5248	8444	9187	10,459
Total dissolved combustible gases		1119	923	1620	2098	2675

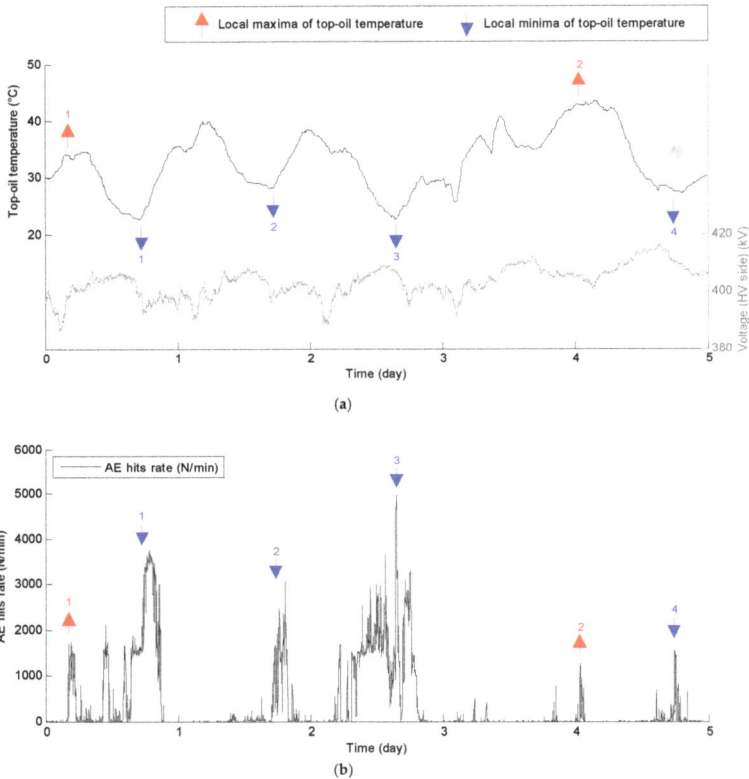

Figure 5. (**a**) Comparison of voltage, top-oil temperature (peaks and troughs are marked by arrows); and (**b**) PD activity (AE hits rate per minute) registered in the low voltage LV1 phase during five-day monitoring of a 250 MVA/400 kV/110 kV power transformer.

An analysis of the literature shows that the physical mechanism describing the detected correlation has not been studied and well understood yet. The authors, based on their own experience in the field of testing the degree of moisture of oil-paper insulation and the PD phenomenon, put forth the hypothesis that migration of water (from cellulose to oil and vice versa) occurring during a cycle of cooling and heating the transformer oil may be responsible for this state of affairs. It was also assumed that this could have a direct impact on the decrease in electrical strength at the cellulose–oil interface, which, in turn, should facilitate the initiation and development of PDs.

4. Water Migration in an Oil-Paper Insulation System in the Context of Partial Discharge Phenomena

In the transformer insulation system, water migrates between cellulose materials and mineral oil or other liquid insulation. It is well known that an increase in the insulation temperature is the cause of water migration from paper to oil, whereas its decrease is the cause of migration in the opposite direction. The direction of water migration is due to the fact that hygroscopicity of cellulose decreases and water solubility in dielectric liquids increases along with a temperature rise [12–15]. Water migration in a transformer in service is mainly caused by: (i) load changes; (ii) non-uniform temperature distribution inside the insulation; and (iii) ambient temperature changes.

Moreover, according to [16–18], the thickness of the cellulose materials also strongly affects the process of water migration. In a brochure [17], distinguishing the insulating system components into three insulation structures such as: "thick structures", "thin and cold structures" and "thin and hot structures" can be found. Due to the high temperature and small thickness of the cellulose materials, water migration in the areas of the "thin and hot structure" is the most dynamic.

Issues related to the influence of temperature changes and water migration on the development of PDs and electrical strength of the insulating system were analysed in several scientific centers. The main conclusions of these analyses are shown below.

Based on a research study, the authors of [19] demonstrated that the breakdown voltage of pressboard impregnated with mineral oil depends not only on insulation temperature changes, but, first of all, on water content. The authors of this paper noted that the temperature changes of a dry pressboard with a water content equal to 0.5% insignificantly affected its electrical strength, whereas with moistened pressboard (3.5%), a 25% decrease in breakdown voltage was observed in the case of a small temperature gradient (0.08 °C/min) and a 40% decrease in the case of a high temperature gradient (0.13 °C/min). According to the authors of this paper, the decrease in electric strength of the pressboard should be explained by the transient state and a disturbance of the moisture equilibrium in the oil-paper insulation system. Similar conclusions can be found in [20].

The authors of [21] also noted that the exposure time of the temperature influenced the intensity of PDs, i.e., the higher the temperature, the more dynamic the phenomenon. This relationship is associated with the fact that the higher the temperature and the longer the exposure time, the more intensive the water migration is from the cellulose materials to the electro-insulating liquid.

Water saturation of oil increases and significantly decreases its electrical strength as a consequence of water migration from cellulose to dielectric liquid [22,23]. Such a situation is particularly dangerous when the water saturation limit is exceeded and dispersed and free water occurs. The increase in water saturation of oil affects PD activity, which was confirmed in [24]. In the literature, information indicating the dependence of water content in the insulation system on PD activity is described by means of inception voltage of PDs [25] and the number of impulses [26]. Such a situation can be explained by a local weakening of oil insulation due to the presence of water.

The authors of this paper, based on the literature analysis and their experience gained during PD monitoring of power transformers, assumed that a local increase in the water content can appear at the interface of cellulose and oil, which can then lead to surface discharges. Undoubtedly, the electric field intensity contributes to the local increase in moisture. Information concerning the influence of the electric field on the motion of water to the area of the highest electric field intensity may be found in [24,27]. Such a field will occur exactly at the materials' interface, which is caused due to the different electric permittivity of mineral oil ($\varepsilon = 2.2$) and the cellulose material impregnated with mineral oil ($\varepsilon = 4.4$). Pollution particles of electric permittivity significantly different from the permittivity of mineral oil are particularly easily drawn into the area of the highest electric field intensity. An example of such a contamination is water ($\varepsilon = 80.1$ at 20 °C). In particular, contaminants with relatively large dimensions are drawn to the area of the highest electric field intensity. However, in [27], it was demonstrated that also water dissolved in oil could migrate to the area of the highest electric field intensity. The author of [27] noticed that the water content at the interface area increases to a certain limit value, beyond which the concentration of water definitely decreases. For the conditions of the experiment assumed in [27], the highest increase of the water content occurred at an electric field intensity in the range between 15 kV/cm and 20 kV/cm. Such an electric field occurs in a real transformer insulation system. It should be pointed out that an even lower electric field intensity leads to the motion of water molecules moving to the area of the highest electric field.

According to the authors of this paper, during insulation, temperature growth as a consequence of water migration from cellulose to the oil and its concentration at the interface of these materials, surface resistivity of cellulose is considerably reduced, which can lead to the appearance of surface discharges. The situation is not improved in the case of a temperature drop. Surface discharges may still occur and even their intensification is possible. This is due to a decrease in oil electric strength resulting from the increase in water saturation of oil. This increase is caused by a decrease in the water saturation limit due to a temperature drop.

The assumptions presented above result from the literature analysis and the experience of the authors gained during PD monitoring of power transformers as described in Section 3. An extensive experiment was conducted in order to confirm the crucial influence of the presence of water in an oil-paper insulation system on the possibility of the appearance of PDs. The results of these research studies are presented in the next section.

5. Experiment

5.1. Measurement Set-Up

A measurement set-up was designed and compiled for the experiment. It allowed for simultaneous realisation of multiple tasks, i.e., (i) the generation of a surface PD in the model of an oil-paper insulation system; (ii) PD detection by means of the conventional electrical method according to norm IEC 60270 [28]; (iii) controlling and monitoring of the oil temperature; (iv) monitoring of moisture content in oil; and (v) oil-circulation forcing in the test chamber. The temperature of oil was measured by means of three sensors. Two of them (Pt1000 sensors) were connected to the temperature controller (TC). These sensors were used to control of the heating procedure and to monitor the top (T_T) and the bottom (T_B) oil temperature. Moreover, the temperature of the oil in the middle part of the chamber was measured using a Vaisala probe (humidity and temperature sensor (HS), Vaisala, Helsinki, Finland). The humidity and the temperature sensors were placed directly above the magnetic stirrer (700 rpm) to improve their response time. A schematic diagram of the measurement set-up is presented in Figure 6.

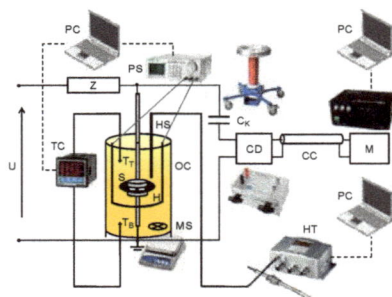

Figure 6. Schematic diagram of the measurement set-up: U: high-voltage supply; Z: short-circuit current limiting resistor; TC: temperature controller; T_T: top-oil temperature sensor; T_B: bottom-oil temperature sensor; H: immersion heater; PS: immersion heater power supply; S: oil-impregnated pressboard sample with electrodes; OC: hermetic glass chamber filled with mineral oil; MS: magnetic stirrer; HS: humidity and temperature sensor; HT: humidity transmitter; C_K: coupling capacitor; CD: coupling device (measuring impedance); CC: connecting cable; and M: conventional PD measuring instrument (in accordance with standard IEC 60270 [28]).

5.2. Electrode System for Partial Discharge Generation

Generally, all insulation systems of the transformer can be treated as systems of the oil-barrier type in which the initiation and development of PDs always takes place in the oil. In an ideal set-up of this type, the electric field is perpendicular to the barrier surface and parallel (tangential) to the spacer elements (strips, spacers, etc.). In this configuration, the ratio of electric field strength in the barrier to electric field strength in the oil channels is inversely proportional to the ratio of electrical permittivity of the barrier ($\varepsilon = 3.6$–4.7) and oil ($\varepsilon = 2.2$). Thus, the electric field strength in the compartments does not exceed 60%–70% of the electric field strength in the oil channels. A breakdown of barriers that are located perpendicularly to the force lines of the electric field can only be the result of discharges in oil. Spacers in oil ducts in the ideal oil-barrier system are "unbreakable" because the cross-stress here is almost the same as stress in the oil channels. The cross-strength of the spacer elements is always greater than their surface strength. Therefore, the development of PD on strips or spacers can be caused almost exclusively by a loss of surface strength. According to the previously outlined theoretical assumptions, this may happen as a result of the migration of water caused by a local increase in moisture (both at the surface of the spacer and at the interface of the oil-pressboard). An important factor may also be the process of entanglement of water molecules in the area of higher electric field strengths (e.g., in the oil gap created by the rounded edge of the pressboard strip).

Based on these assumptions, the authors decided to use the electrode arrangement presented in Figure 7a, which approximately reproduces the part of the transformer insulation, i.e., the oil duct-strip-barrier (Figure 7b).

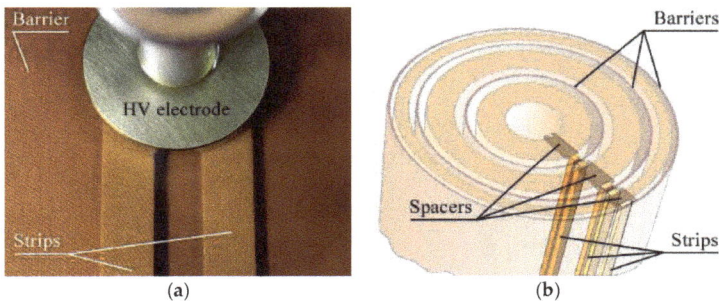

Figure 7. (**a**) Schematic diagram of the transformer paper-oil insulation system; and (**b**) arrangement of the insulation samples used in the experiment.

This electrode system allows for generating surface discharges in a uniform electric field where the normal component of the field is negligible. In the experiment, it was decided to investigate this type of PD for two reasons. First, for PD initiation a deterioration of the dielectric properties of the surface of the pressboard or area at the interface of the oil–pressboard must take place (according to the hypothesis put forward in this paper, migration of water may be responsible for this state of affairs). Second, this type of discharge has, in its initial stage, relatively low energy, which ensured that the test samples would not degrade rapidly. Of course, creeping discharges are more dangerous to the transformer insulation system (surface discharges in a non-uniform electric field with a large normal component of the electric field strength vector). Unfortunately, with regard to the research assumptions, they are characterised by too high energy (at an early stage of development), and, usually, within a short period of time, this leads to a breakdown of the sample. Additionally, their ignition depends much more on the set-up geometry and the field conditions related to them.

Figure 8 shows the analysis of the distribution of the electric field for the electrodes used in the experiment. The voltage applied to the system was 30 kVrms. The simulation results show that the greatest electric field intensity is in oil gaps created by the rounded edge of the pressboard strips.

The authors hypothesised that, during the process of moisture migration, water molecules are drawn into this area and may help to initiate the surface discharge.

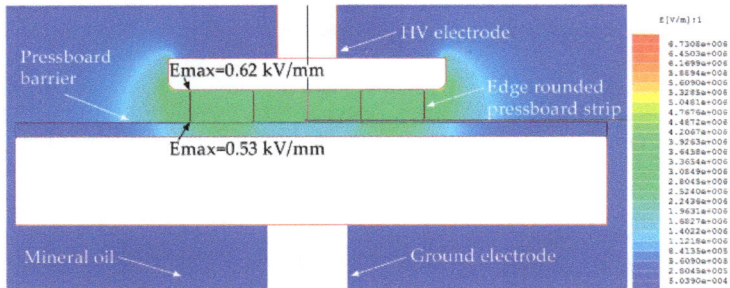

Figure 8. Analysis of electric field distribution in the oil-paper insulation model investigated here (U = 30 kVrms).

5.3. Sample Preparation

For this research study, the authors used two kinds of pressboard, both made of sulphate wood pulp. One of the pressboards was used in a transformer insulation system as a barrier and the second one as a strip. In order to achieve different water content, the samples were dried in a vacuum chamber at a pressure of 5 mbar and in a temperature equal to 90 ± 5 °C for a time period equal to 24 h. After drying, the samples were placed in a climatic chamber. To achieve the required moisture, the samples were conditioned in contact with air of different relative humidity according to isotherms of water sorption as presented in [29] for a period equal to about 30 days. After conditioning, the samples were impregnated with uninhibited naphthenic transformer oil—Nytro Taurus (Nynas, Stockholm, Sweden), in a vacuum chamber, and the water content was measured by means of the Karl Fischer titration method according to the standard [30]. The following levels of water content were obtained in the pressboard samples: 0.4%, 1.6%, 2.5%, and 5.7%. According to the guidelines for interpreting the percentage of moisture as proposed in [31], the first two values correspond to dry insulation. The next two values correspond to wet paper (2.5%) and excessively wet paper (5.7%). Samples prepared in this manner were stored in hermetically sealed vessels for a period equal to about 30 days. After that, the samples were tested according to the procedure described below.

5.4. Experimental Procedure

The experimental procedure involved the following steps:

Step 1 Three-day conditioning of the test chamber with new mineral oil at a temperature of 25 °C.
Step 2 Placement of the insulation sample in the test chamber.
Step 3 Calibration of the PD measuring system.
Step 4 Application of high voltage (30 kVrms) to the electrode system.
Step 5 Oil heating in a temperature range from 25 °C to 75 °C for two days under a linear temperature-rising programme.
Step 6 Oil cooling in a temperature range from 75 °C to 25 °C for the next two days.

The temperature was monitored during the experiment in the following points: (i) top-oil; (ii) bottom-oil; (iii) near the pressboard barrier; and (iv) external wall of the test chamber. Moreover, the PD apparent charge, water activity (amount of water in a substance relative to the total amount of water it can hold) and moisture content of oil expressed in ppm were simultaneously registered. The water activity of mineral oil was measured by means of Vaisala MMT 330 moisture and temperature transmitter equipped with capacitive sensor. The water content in oil expressed in ppm by weight was calculated on the basis of water activity and temperature measurement results.

5.5. Experimental Results

In the first stage of the research, measurements for insulation samples with a moisture content of 2.5% were performed. Typical results representative of all the measurement attempts are shown in Figure 9.

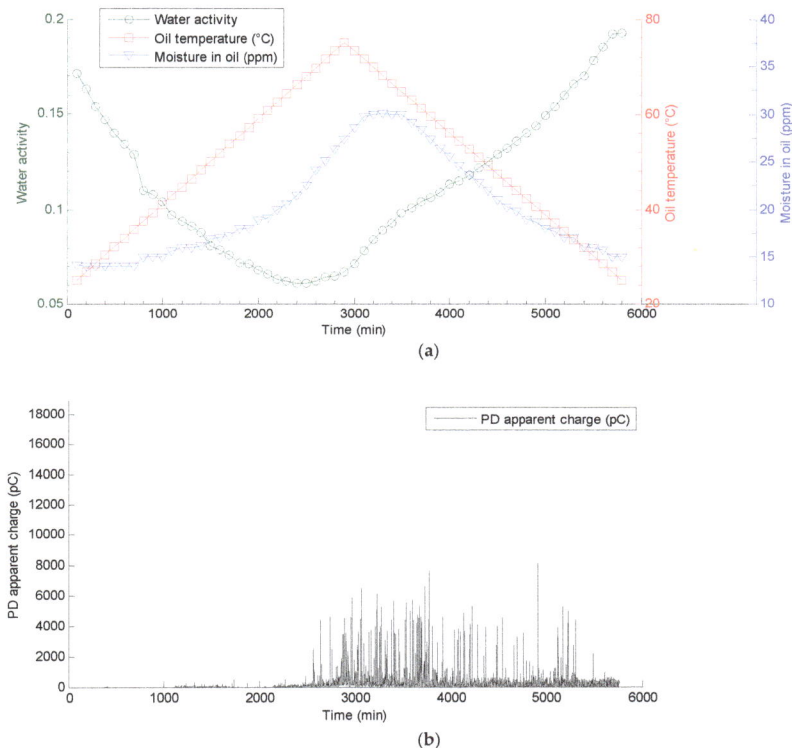

Figure 9. Typical experimental results obtained for an insulation sample with a moisture content of 2.5%: (**a**) water activity, temperature and moisture content of oil; and (**b**) PD apparent charge.

For all of these samples, a repeatable scenario of PD activity was observed. PD pulses were not registered during the first 1000–1200 min of the experiment (which corresponded to an oil temperature near the pressboard sample equal to about 42–45 °C). Afterwards, the inception of stable PDs with a relatively low energy was found. Except for single PD events, its apparent charge did not exceed 250 pC. This state of affairs persisted for 2300–2500 min of the experiment, when the measured oil temperature reached a level of 66−70 °C. Shortly after this time period, a step change of the apparent charge level of PD (q > 500 pC) and simultaneous dynamics growth of water migration from cellulose insulation to oil were noted. From that moment onwards, a general upward trend in PD activity was observed that lasted for about 3800−4000 min of the experiment. At that time, the maximal values of the apparent charge reached a very high level of a few nC. In this time interval, the oil had already been cooled down and the analysis of the data from the humidity sensor (decrease of the moisture content in the oil) indicated a process of "reverse moisture migration" (from oil to cellulose). In the later part of the experiment, the discharges remained at a relatively high level; however, the general trend was a diminishing one. The PDs were not completely extinguished and remained at a level of 100−600 pC until the end of the experiment. It is worth underlining that none of the investigated insulation samples with a moisture content of 2.5% were broken down.

At the second stage of the investigation, measurements for dry insulation samples (0.4% and 1.6%) were conducted. During the whole four-day experiment, no PD pulses were registered for any of the investigated samples with a moisture content of 0.4%.

For samples with a moisture content of 1.6%, stable PDs were initiated in a very similar time frame as samples with a moisture content of 2.5% (i.e., after about 1000−1200 min) and with equally low energy ($q < 500$ pC) (Figure 10). It should be pointed out that, in contrast to samples with a moisture content of 2.5%, a rapid increase in PD activity was not observed. In most cases, in the second part of the experiment, when the oil temperature decreased, the discharges were completely extinguished.

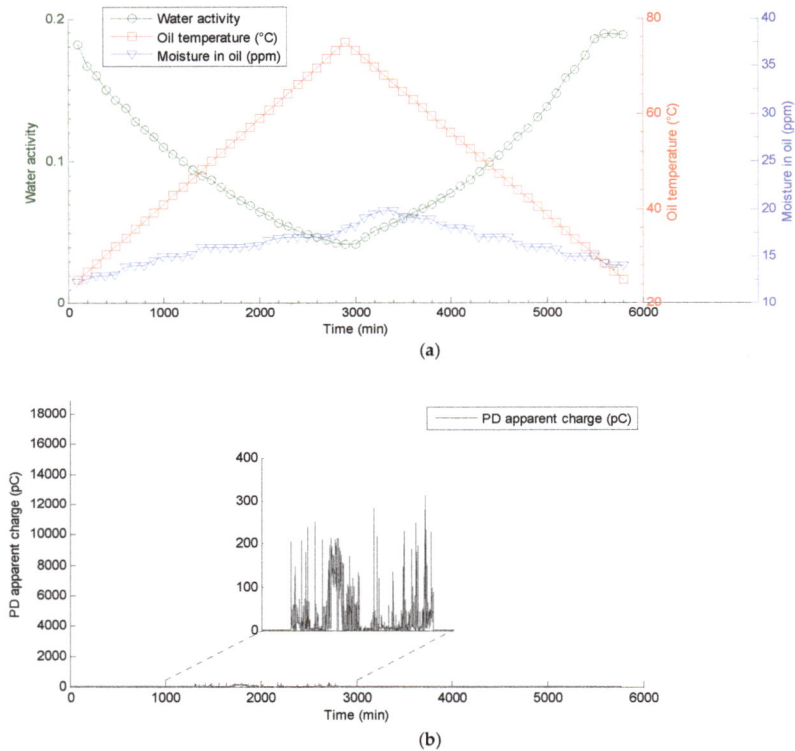

Figure 10. Typical experimental results obtained for an insulation sample with a moisture content of 1.6%: (**a**) water activity, temperature and moisture content of oil; and (**b**) PD apparent charge.

Samples with the highest moisture content (5.7%) were investigated during the last stage of the experiment. Compared to samples with a 1.6% and 2.5% moisture content, the first PD pulses were registered slightly earlier, i.e., after the first 500−800 min. Up to about 1800−2000 min of the experiment, unstable PDs were registered whose apparent charge was in the range from 50 pC to 1–2 nC. After that time, ignition of stable (continuous) PDs whose apparent charge dynamically grew, exceeding a level of 15 nC (Figure 11), took place.

A period of high-energy discharges, mostly in a shorter time period (from a few to over a dozen min), leads to sample breakdown (Figure 12). For such extreme moisture sample, it was not possible to carry out the experiment in the full four-day time period.

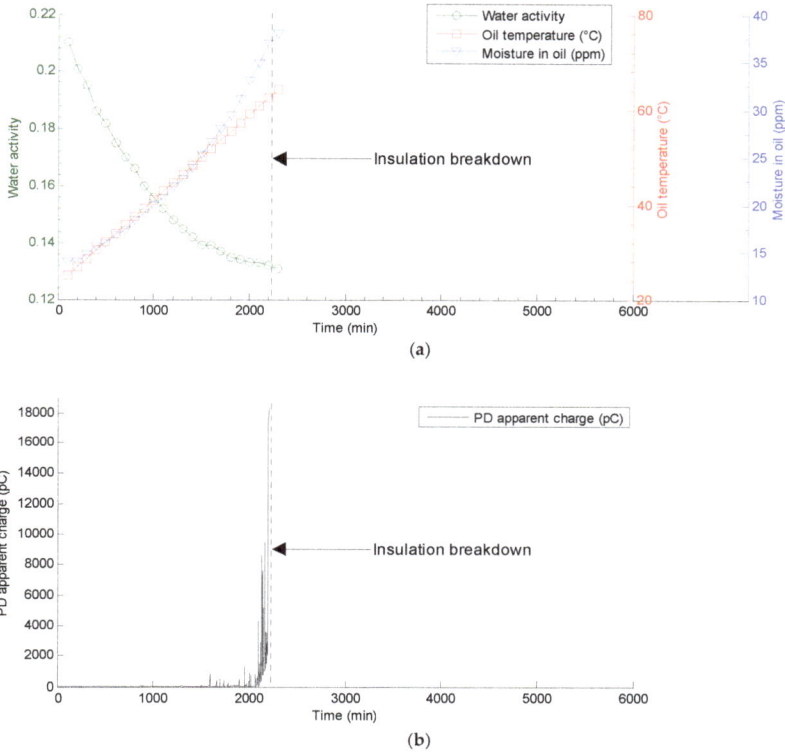

(a)

(b)

Figure 11. Typical experimental results obtained for an insulation sample with a moisture content of 5.7%: (**a**) water activity, temperature and moisture content of oil; and (**b**) PD apparent charge.

Figure 12. Traces of surface PD on an insulation sample with a moisture content of 5.7%.

121

6. Conclusions

The test results presented in Section 5.5 show that the ignition of PDs in the case of temperature changes should be associated with a higher level of moisture of the insulating system. In the case of very dry insulation (0.4%), changes in temperature insulation did not lead to ignition of PDs. However, at a higher moisture level (above 1%), it was found that the intensity of the PDs increased along with the moisture; in the case of wet samples (5.7%), the system was broken down every time after reaching the critical parameters (temperature, moisture oil). A similar relationship was observed when analysing the dynamics changes of moisture content in oil on the temperature, i.e., the higher the output of humidity of the sample, the greater the rate of change of the water content in the oil and therefore at the interface of the oil-pressboard.

According to the authors, the test results obtained in the laboratory model (Section 5.5) can be applied to results obtained during monitoring of PDs on power transformers (Section 3). In both cases, ignition of PDs occurred along with the growth of temperature insulation, and the discharges did not extinguish despite a drop in the temperature. In Section 4, the authors of the article explain this state of affairs according to phenomena occurring at the interface of cellulose and oil. As a result of temperature growth, migration of water from the cellulose to the oil takes place, which was also observed during the experiment. A strengthening of the electric field occurring at the interface contributes to the concentration of water in this area. A consequence of the increase in moisture at the interface of the materials is a decrease in surface resistivity of cellulose, which leads to PD ignition of surface type. The drop in temperature insulation does not quickly dry the interfacial area, which favours the duration of PDs. This is due to the continuous impact of the electric field on the molecules of water and the time needed for migration of water from oil to cellulose.

When referring to the results of the experiment to operational conditions, it can be observed that, in the case of dry or moderately moistened (to less than 2%) insulation, even large temperature fluctuations do not cause an increase in PD activity to dangerous levels, which, in a short period of time, would damage the insulation. An increase in moisture above 3% seems to be of great importance for the transformer's working conditions and causes significant reductions in the range of unit load, and thus in the temperature of the insulation system.

The results of the experiment, which confirmed the hypothesis that was made on the basis of registrations of the PDtracker monitoring system, indicate another important conclusion. If a clear correlation between the activity of PD and temperature changes in the monitored transformer is observed, strict control of the unit's moisture level should be introduced, and, in extreme cases, it should be confirmed by other methods [32] in order to allocate it to the drying process.

Acknowledgments: The research was financed from resources of the Ministry of Science and Higher Education for Statutory Activities No 04/41/DS-PB/4235, name of the task: Development of advanced measurement methods to evaluate the technical condition of the electric power devices.

Author Contributions: Section 1 was prepared by Krzysztof Walczak. Section 2 was prepared by Wojciech Sikorski. The data used in Section 3 were collected by Wojciech Sikorski and Krzysztof Walczak, and Section 3 was prepared by Wojciech Sikorski. Section 4 was prepared by Piotr Przybylek. All the authors jointly planned the experiment described in Section 5 by Wojciech Sikorski. The samples of different water content used in the experiment were prepared by Piotr Przybylek. The experiment control software and analysis of electric field distribution was prepared by Wojciech Sikorski. Temperature measurement and control was realized using software created by Krzysztof Walczak. The experiment was conducted by Wojciech Sikorski and Krzysztof Walczak. Conclusions were prepared jointly by all the authors.

Conflicts of Interest: The authors declare no conflict of interest.

References

1. Gielniak, J.; Graczkowski, A.; Moranda, H.; Przybylek, P.; Walczak, K.; Nadolny, Z.; Moscicka-Grzesiak, H.; Feser, K.; Gubanski, S.M. Moisture in cellulose insulation of power transformers-statistics. *IEEE Trans. Dielectr. Electr. Insul.* **2013**, *20*, 982–987. [CrossRef]
2. *Guidelines for Unconventional Partial Discharge Measurements*; Cigré Technical Brochure 444; International Council on Large Electric Systems (CIGRE): Paris, France, 2010.
3. Tenbohlen, S.; Coenen, S.; Mohammad, D.; Müller, A.; Samimi, M.H.; Siegel, M. Diagnostic measurements for power transformers. *Energies* **2016**, *9*, 347. [CrossRef]
4. Fofana, I.; Hadjadj, Y. Electrical-based diagnostic techniques for assessing insulation condition in aged transformers. *Energies* **2016**, *9*, 679. [CrossRef]
5. Walczak, K.; Sikorski, W.; Siodla, K.; Andrzejewski, M.; Gil, W. Online condition monitoring and expert system for power transformers. In Proceedings of the 3rd Advanced Research Workshop on Transformers, Santiago de Compostella, Spain, 3–10 October 2010; pp. 433–438.
6. Sikorski, W.; Walczak, K.; Moranda, H.; Gil, W.; Andrzejewski, M. Partial discharge on-line monitoring system based on acoustic emission method—operational experiences. *Prz. Elektrotech.* **2012**, *88*, 117–121. (In Polish)
7. Sikorski, W.; Siodla, K.; Moranda, H.; Ziomek, W. Location of partial discharge sources in power transformers based on advanced auscultatory technique. *IEEE Trans. Dielectr. Electr. Insul.* **2012**, *19*, 1948–1956. [CrossRef]
8. Sikorski, W.; Walczak, K. Trend analysis of partial discharge parameters implemented by monitoring system of power transformers PDtracker. *Prz. Elektrotech.* **2014**, *90*, 168–171. (In Polish)
9. Sikorski, W.; Walczak, K. PDtracker—On-line partial discharge monitoring system for power transformers. *Prz. Elektrotech.* **2014**, *90*, 45–49. (In Polish)
10. Walczak, K.; Sikorski, W.; Gil, W. Multi-module system for partial discharge monitoring using AE, HF and UHF methods. *Prz. Elektrotech.* **2016**, *92*, 5–9. (In Polish)
11. *IEC 60076-7: Loading Guide for Oil-Immersed Power Transformers*; International Electrotechnical Commission (IEC): New York, NY, USA, 2005.
12. Du, Y.; Zahn, M.; Lesieutre, B.C.; Mamishev, A.V.; Lindgren, S.R. Moisture equilibrium in transformer paper-oil systems. *IEEE Electr. Insul. Mag.* **1999**, *15*, 11–20. [CrossRef]
13. Przybylek, P. The influence of temperature and aging of cellulose on water distribution in oil-paper insulation. *IEEE Trans. Dielectr. Electr. Insul.* **2013**, *20*, 552–556. [CrossRef]
14. Fofana, I.; Arakelian, V.G. Water in oil-filled high-voltage equipment, Part I: States, solubility, and equilibrium in insulating materials. *IEEE Electr. Insul. Mag.* **2007**, *23*, 15–27.
15. Przybylek, P. Investigations of the temperature of bubble effect initiation oil-paper insulation. *Prz. Elektrotech.* **2010**, *86*, 166–169. (In Polish)
16. Gasser, H.P.; Krause, C.; Prevost, T. Water absorption of cellulosic insulating materials used in power transformers. In Proceedings of the 2007 IEEE International Conference on Solid Dielectrics, Winchester, UK, 8–13 July 2007; pp. 289–293.
17. *Moisture Equilibrium and Moisture Migration within Transformer Insulation Systems*; Cigré Technical Brochure 349; International Council on Large Electric Systems (CIGRE): Paris, France, 2008.
18. Garcia, D.F.; Garcia, B.; Burgos, J.C. A Review of moisture diffusion coefficients in transformer solid insulation—Part 1: Coefficients for paper and pressboard. *IEEE Electr. Insul. Mag.* **2013**, *29*, 46–54. [CrossRef]
19. Buerschaper, B.; Kleboth-Lugova, O.; Leibfried, T. The electrical strength of transformer oil in a transformerboard-oil system during moisture non-equilibrium. In Proceedings of the Conference on Electrical Insulation and Dielectric Phenomena (CEIDP), Albuquerque, NM, USA, 19–22 October 2003; pp. 269–272.
20. Sokolov, V.; Berler, Z.; Rashkes, V. Effective methods of assessment of insulation system conditions in power transformers: A view based on practical experience. In Proceedings of the Electrical Insulation Conference and Electrical Manufacturing & Coil Winding Conference, Cincinnati, OH, USA, 26–28 October 1999; pp. 659–667.
21. Wang, H.; Li, C.; He, H. Influence of temperature to developing processes of surface discharges in oil-paper insulation. In Proceedings of the IEEE International Symposium on Electrical Insulation (ISEI), San Diego, CA, USA, 6–9 June 2010.

22. *Experiences in Service with New Insulating Liquids*; Cigré Technical Brochure 436; International Council on Large Electric Systems (CIGRE): Paris, France, 2010.

23. The Effect of Moisture on the Breakdown Voltage of Transformer Oil, White Paper of Vaisala. Available online: http://www.vaisala.com/Vaisala%20Documents/White%20Papers/CEN-TIA-power-whitepaper-Moisture-and-Breakdown-Voltage-B211282EN-A-LOW.pdf (accessed on 5 October 2016).

24. Borsi, H.; Schroder, U. Initiation and formation of partial discharges in mineral-based insulating oil. *IEEE Trans. Dielectr. Electr. Insul.* **1994**, *1*, 419–425. [CrossRef]

25. Dai, J.; Wang, Z.D.; Jarman, P. Moisture and aging effect on the creepage discharge characteristics at the oil/transformer-board interface under divergent field. In Proceedings of the Conference on Electrical Insulation and Dielectric Phenomena (CEIDP), Québec City, QC, Canada, 26–29 October 2008; pp. 662–665.

26. *Partial Discharges in Transformer Insulation*; CIGRE Task Force 15.01.04; International Council on Large Electric Systems (CIGRE): Paris, France, 2000.

27. Lutyński, B. *The Effect of the Field Stress on the Variation of Water Concentration in the Oil in the Electrode Gap*; Wrocław University of Science and Technology: Wrocław, Poland, 1970; pp. 41–47.

28. *IEC 60270: High-Voltage Test Techniques—Partial Discharge Measurements*; International Electrotechnical Commission (IEC): New York, NY, USA, 2000.

29. Przybylek, P. Water saturation limit of insulating liquids and hygroscopicity of cellulose in aspect of moisture determination in oil-paper insulation. *IEEE Trans. Dielectr. Electr. Insul.* **2016**, *23*, 1886–1893. [CrossRef]

30. *IEC 60814: Insulating Liquids—Oil-Impregnated Paper and Pressboard—Determination of Water by Automatic Coulometric Karl Fischer Titration*; International Electrotechnical Commission (IEC): New York, NY, USA, 1997.

31. 62-1995-IEEE Guide for Diagnostic Field Testing of Electric Power Apparatus–Part 1: Oil Filled Power Transformers, Regulators, and Reactors. Available online: http://ieeexplore.ieee.org/document/467562 (accessed on 5 October 2016).

32. Ekanayake, C.; Gubański, S.M.; Graczkowski, A.; Walczak, K. Frequency response of oil impregnated pressboard and paper samples for estimating moisture in transformer insulation. *IEEE Trans. Power Deliv.* **2006**, *21*, 1309–1317. [CrossRef]

energies

MDPI

Article

An Intelligent Sensor for the Ultra-High-Frequency Partial Discharge Online Monitoring of Power Transformers

Jian Li [1], Xudong Li [1], Lin Du [1,*], Min Cao [2] and Guochao Qian [2]

[1] State Key Laboratory of Power Transmission Equipment and System Security and New Technology, Chongqing University, Chongqing 400044, China; lijian@cqu.edu.cn (J.L.); lixudong@cqu.edu.cn (X.L.)

[2] Yunnan Electric Power Research Institute, Kunming 650217, China; cm1961@sohu.com (M.C.); qianguochao@im.yn.csg (G.Q.)

* Correspondence: dulin@cqu.edu.cn; Tel.: +86-23-6510-2442

Academic Editor: Issouf Fofana
Received: 15 February 2016; Accepted: 11 May 2016; Published: 19 May 2016

Abstract: Ultra-high-frequency (UHF) partial discharge (PD) online monitoring is an effective way to inspect potential faults and insulation defects in power transformers. The construction of UHF PD online monitoring system is a challenge because of the high-frequency and wide-frequency band of the UHF PD signal. This paper presents a novel, intelligent sensor for UHF PD online monitoring based on a new method, namely a level scanning method. The intelligent sensor can directly acquire the statistical characteristic quantities and is characterized by low cost, few data to output and transmit, Ethernet functionality, and small size for easy installation. The prototype of an intelligent sensor was made. Actual UHF PD experiments with three typical artificial defect models of power transformers were carried out in a laboratory, and the waveform recording method and intelligent sensor proposed were simultaneously used for UHF PD measurement for comparison. The results show that the proposed intelligent sensor is qualified for the UHF PD online monitoring of power transformers. Additionally, three methods to improve the performance of intelligent sensors were proposed according to the principle of the level scanning method.

Keywords: ultra-high-frequency (UHF); partial discharge (PD); online monitoring; intelligent sensor; level scanning method; field programmable gate array (FPGA); high-speed voltage comparator

1. Introduction

Power transformers are key equipment in power systems. Faults and insulation defects may happen under electrical, thermal, and mechanical stress with the increase in operation time. Partial discharge (PD) online monitoring is an effective way to identify potential faults and inspect insulation defects in power transformers [1–8]. PD is generally a transient phenomenon accompanied by physical and chemical phenomena, such as electrical pulse, electromagnetic wave, ultrasonic signal, mechanical vibration, and light and gas components, which can be detected by corresponding sensors [9–16]. Among those methods, the ultra-high-frequency (UHF) PD detection method becomes an international, advanced research hotspot because of its advantages such as high sensitivity, strong anti-interference ability, high reliability, and ability to recognize and locate discharge sources [17–22].

The frequency of UHF PD detection ranges from 300 MHz to 3 GHz [23]. The acquisition of UHF PD signal is a challenge because of its high frequency and wide frequency band. The waveform recording method is the simplest method to acquire UHF PD signal, but the sampling rate of acquisition device must be several GHz according to the sampling theorem, which is beyond an ordinary data acquisition card's ability. There are several high-performance high-speed data acquisition cards and digital oscilloscopes satisfying the requirement, but they are not suitable for the online continuous monitoring of the UHF PD signal and are mostly used in laboratory research because of such disadvantages as high cost, large amounts of data to store and transmit, and complex data post-processing [24,25]. In order to construct the UHF PD online monitoring system, a peak value recording method was presented in [26] in which the peak-value-detect-and-hold circuit was designed to maintain the maximum magnitude of the UHF PD signal in each phase interval for further data processing, but the low sampling rate and error of the peak-valve-detect-and-hold circuit will cause a large loss of information in the UHF PD signal, which leads to less accurate detection results. Moreover, there are other methods proposed to acquire the UHF PD signal: In [27], increasing a frequency mixing circuit in the signal preprocessing module to decrease the frequency of the UHF PD signal to that of an ordinary data acquisition card was proposed, but the error of signal magnitude is large in this method; in [28] a method using the UHF envelope detection circuit and high-speed data acquisition system to acquire UHF PD signal was demonstrated, but it had the same disadvantages as the waveform recording method. There are also several commercial products available for UHF PD online monitoring, but taking into consideration their high price, the mass data transmission, and specialized transport protocol, those commercial products are not cost-effective and not suitable for a wide application of constructing a UHF PD online monitoring system in power transformers.

The present paper proposes a novel, intelligent senor for continuous online UHF PD monitoring of power transformers in substations. It is characterized by low cost, little data for output and transmission, and Ethernet functionality, which is suitable for wide use. Section 2 proposes a new method, namely the level scanning method, to acquire the statistical characteristic quantities of the UHF PD signal, which is the base of the intelligent sensor. Section 3 introduces the implementation of the intelligent sensor. Section 4 presents the comparative experiment between intelligent sensors and the waveform recording method, and the results are presented and discussed. Section 5 presents a further analysis of the experiment results and proposes three methods to improve the performance of the intelligent sensor. The use of the proposed intelligent sensor for UHF PD detection in other electrical components is also discussed in Section 5. The last section offers conclusions.

2. The Level Scanning Method

The PD activity has statistical characteristic quantities. The most fundamental and important statistical characteristic quantities are the magnitude of discharge, the number of discharges, and the corresponding phase distribution, from which we can obtain ϕ-V_{max}, ϕ-n_{tot}, ϕ-V-n, and other pattern charts, where ϕ is phase, V is the magnitude of PD signal, V_{max} is the maximum magnitude of the PD signal in a phase interval, n is number of discharges, and n_{tot} is the total number of discharges in a phase interval. Some statistical characteristic quantities can be extracted from these patterns charts to recognize the PD pattern or to monitor the evolution of insulation detects long-term to avoid insulation failure. A novel method, namely the level scanning method, is proposed in this paper to obtain the magnitude of discharge, the number of discharges, and the corresponding phase distribution directly without the post-processing of data.

Figure 1 shows the basic principle of the level scanning method. In this figure, the distribution of discharges within a power frequency cycle is shown. The UHF PD pulses appear in both the positive and negative half cycles of the AC voltage. Note that the UHF PD pulses are actually waves with positive parts and negative parts because of decaying oscillation, and the positive pulses here are used to represent actual UHF PD pulses for simplicity in Figure 1. In order to obtain the magnitude of discharge, a set of increasing levels, V_1–V_5, namely the reference levels, are compared with the UHF PD pulses. Initially, the power frequency cycle is divided into several equal phase intervals. Then, the UHF PD pulses, whose magnitudes are larger than a set reference level within several power frequency cycles, are counted and stored for each phase interval according to the time UHF PD pulses appeared on. In this way, the corresponding number of discharges for different reference levels is obtained. Moreover, it can be observed that the number of discharges counted becomes smaller when reference levels increase. If the step of reference level is small enough, the magnitude and number of discharges can be precisely extracted. It should be emphasized that, in this method, the number of discharges for a specific magnitude of discharge in a phase interval represents the number of all discharge pulses whose magnitude are greater than the corresponding reference level in this phase interval, and the corresponding reference level is regarded as the magnitude of discharge in this method, which is different from the traditional method.

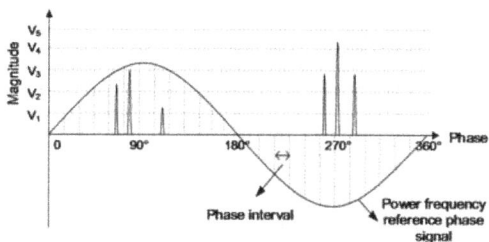

Figure 1. The principle of the level scanning method.

In order to implement this method, the configuration of the designed intelligent sensor is shown in Figure 2. The dotted lines signify analog signals, and the solid lines signify digital signals. Four antennas are used to receive the UHF PD signal and connect to the data processing module via cables. Note that the UHF PD measurement for a power transformer only uses one antenna in our design. The advantage of the four-antenna design is that the intelligent sensor can measure UHF PD for four power transformers at most, which can lower the cost for the construction of the UHF PD online monitoring system for power transformers in substations. The UHF PD signals from the selected channel are input into an ultra-fast voltage comparator (UFVC) after being filtered and amplified for comparison with an analog reference signal output by a digital analog converter (DAC). The input signal of DAC, namely the reference level, is controlled by a field programmable gate array (FPGA). After the comparison, if the magnitude of the UHF PD signal is greater than the reference level, the UFVC will output a square signal that will be scanned by the FPGA, and then the number of discharges for this reference level in corresponding phase interval will add 1 in FPGA's memory. This process continues until the scanning cycles reach the set value, and this process goes on with the next reference level, which is changed by the algorithm in FPGA. The whole process continues until there is no more UHF PD signal that is larger than the reference level.

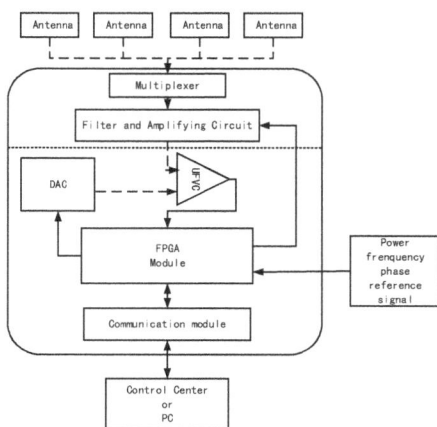

Figure 2. The configuration of the intelligent sensor.

3. Implementation of the Intelligent Sensor

3.1. Ultra-High-Frequency Antanas

The UHF antenna is one of the core parts of the proposed intelligent sensor. There are several kinds of antennas designed for UHF PD detection in [29–32]. In this work, the optimal third order Peano fractal antenna designed in our previous work [33] is used as the UHF antenna of the intelligent sensor for its good properties and small size—90 mm × 90 mm. The voltage standing wave ratio (VSWR) curve of the antenna is shown in Figure 3a, which shows that the antenna has a wide pass band where VSWR < 5 between 0.3 GHz and 1 GHz. The three-dimensional radiation patterns at 0.4 GHz and 0.7 GHz are shown in Figure 3c,d, respectively. The patterns at the two frequencies are both near a hemisphere, which shows that the antenna has a good direction. The prototype of the antenna is shown in Figure 3b.

For the installation of this antenna, it is not installed in a transformer drain valve. An alternative way to install PD antennas in power transformers was presented in [32], and the installation of antenna in the proposed intelligent sensor also uses this method. Specifically, a hole will be opened at the wall of the transformer, and a dielectric window made of polytetrafluoroethylene (PTFE) will be welded to install the antenna container. There is a shell of the antenna container made of cast iron that can prevent outside noises from coming into the antenna system.

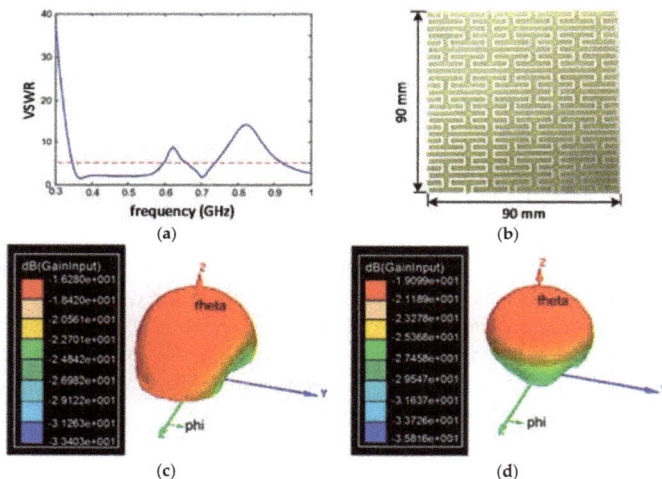

Figure 3. The third Peano fractal antenna: (**a**) Voltage standing wave ratio (VSWR) curve of the third Peano fractal antenna; (**b**) the prototype of the third Peano fractal antenna; (**c**) the 3-D radiation patterns of the third Peano fractal antenna at 370 MHz; and (**d**) the 3-D radiation patterns of the third Peano fractal antenna at 700 MHz.

3.2. Hardware of the Data Processing Module

The data processing module is another core part of the proposed intelligent sensor. In our work, the data processing module is divided into two parts, namely the signal pre-processing module and the data acquisition module.

3.2.1. The Signal Pre-Processing Module

The signal pre-processing module comprised of a multiplexer, a band-pass filter, and an amplifier circuit is integrated in a printed circuit board (PCB). The analog multiplexer CD452 by Fairchild

(Semiconductor Corporation, Sunnyvale, CA, USA) is used as a 4-channel multiplexer to choose the signal channel. Considering the interference such as the corona discharge (with the upper frequency below 300 MHz) and the signals of cell phones (880–960 MHz) [29], the band-pass filter is designed with a pass band from 300–800 MHz. The amplifier circuit composed of two CLC425s (National Semiconductor Corporation, Santa Clara, CA, USA) has an alternative gain according to signal intensity, namely 20 dB and 40 dB. The operation of the multiplexer and the amplifier is controlled by FPGA.

3.2.2. The Data Acquisition Module

The data acquisition module is also integrated in a PCB. As shown in Figure 2, the level scanning process is accomplished by FPGA, DAC, and UFVC. In our design, FPGA controls all of the functions of the intelligent sensor, which contains the control of the signal pre-processing module, the level scanning process, and the communication module. In particular, an Altera FPGA, model EP2S30 of the Stratix II device family, is utilized, which is characterized by a mass equivalent logic element up to 180 k, 9 Mbits of on-chip, supporting various Input/Output standards along with support for 1-gigabit per second (Gbps) source synchronous signaling with DPA circuitry. Moreover, an UFVC ADCMP567 (Analog Devices, Inc., Norwood, MA, USA) is used, which is characterized by a 250-ps propagation delay input to output, 50-ps propagation delay dispersion, and a 5-GHz equivalent input rise time bandwidth, which is enough to compare the signal with the frequency range from 300 MHz to 3 GHz.

3.3. Software of the Data Processing Module

The program in the data processing module controls all of the functions of the intelligent sensor, which contains UHF PD signal reception, pre-processing, comparison and scanning, data storage, and data transmission, as shown in Figure 4. The specific steps are as follows:

Step 1　Initialization. In this step, the signal channel, the gain of amplifier, the initial reference level, and the number of scanning cycles are set. Moreover, a frequency cycle is divided into several equal phase intervals, and the corresponding memory addresses to store the number of discharges within each phase interval are assigned in FPGA.

Step 2　Signal comparison, data storage, and transmission. The start of the module is first triggered by the zero crossing point in the rising edge of the power frequency phase inference signal after being initialized, and the scanning time is counted from this moment. UHF PD signals are compared with the reference level and then scanned by FPGA, and the phase of UHF PD signals are calculated simultaneously. If the UHF PD signal is greater than the reference level, the number of discharges within the corresponding phase interval in the memory address add 1. If the counted scanning cycle reaches the set valve t_s, stop scanning and transmitting the data to the PC or control center. The data is a row of numbers, which is shown in Table 1.

Step 3　Comparison with variable reference level. FPGA automatically changes the value of the reference level according to the algorithm. Repeat Step 2.

Step 4　Stop operation. Judge the number of discharges in each phase interval; if they are totally equal to zero, which means there is no discharge whose magnitude is greater than the reference level, stop scanning and exit the loop.

The final statistical parameters of PD collected by the intelligent sensor are reserved as a table in the PC or control center, as shown in Table 1, where V_i is the reference level, j is the serial number of phase interval, and n_{ij} is the number of discharges whose magnitude is greater than V_i within phase interval j. From this table, we can plot the pattern charts of ϕ-V_{max}, ϕ-n_{tot}, ϕ-V-n, and other exact statistical characteristic quantities for PD pattern recognition and fault diagnosis.

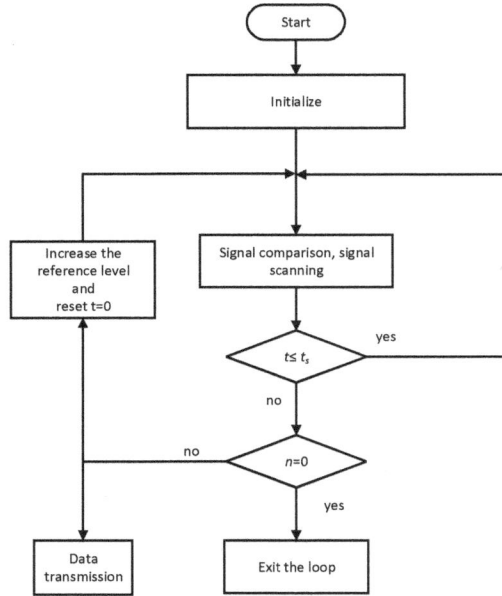

Figure 4. Flowchart of the data processing program.

Table 1. The table of data output from the intelligent sensor.

Reference Level	Phase Interval			
	1	2	...	j
V_1	n_{11}	n_{12}	...	n_{1j}
V_2	n_{21}	n_{22}	...	n_{2j}
V_3	n_{31}	n_{32}	...	n_{3j}
...	...	...	...	...
V_{i-1}	$n_{(i-1)1}$	$n_{(i-1)2}$	...	$n_{(i-1)j}$
V_i	n_{i1}	n_{i2}	...	n_{ij}

4. Experiment and Results

4.1. Experiment

The case study is used to assess the performance of the proposed intelligent sensor for UHF PD detection of the power transformer. For comparison, the waveform recording method of UHF PD signal is also used at the same time.

Figure 5 shows the UHF PD detection experiment setup. The experiments are carried out in an electromagnetic shielded laboratory at room temperature (20 °C). The PD free power source consists of a function generator and a high voltage amplifier (TREK 50 kV/12 mA, TREK, Inc., Lockport, NY, USA). The function generator generates the AC voltage, and the high voltage amplifier raises the AC voltage to the required level. A PC is connected to the intelligent sensor to store the PD data and perform other data processing tasks. Moreover, the UHF PD signal output from the signal pre-processing module is directly input into oscilloscope (DPO 7104, Tektronix Inc., Beaverton, OR, USA) to record the UHF PD signal. The record length of the oscilloscope reaches up to the 400-M point, and its real-time sampling rate reach up to 10 GS/s in 4 channels, which is sufficient to collect the UHF PD signal for a power frequency cycle (20 ms).

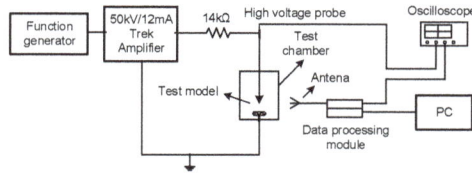

Figure 5. The experiment setup.

There were three typical artificial defect models built in the experiment to generate UHF PD signals. Figure 6a shows an air-void discharge model, including three layers of oil-impregnated paper and a sphere-to-board electrode system. A disc-shaped void with a diameter of 20 mm was bounded with oil-impregnated paper in the air-void discharge model. Figure 6b shows an experiment model of a cylinder-to-board electrode for surface discharge defects. Figure 6c shows the corona discharge model, which is basically a needle-plate electrode system. The thickness of the pressboard in each model is 0.5 mm. When performing the experiments, the artificial defect models were placed into a test chamber that was made out of organic glass and was filled with insulation oil. The UHF antenna was placed beside the test chamber.

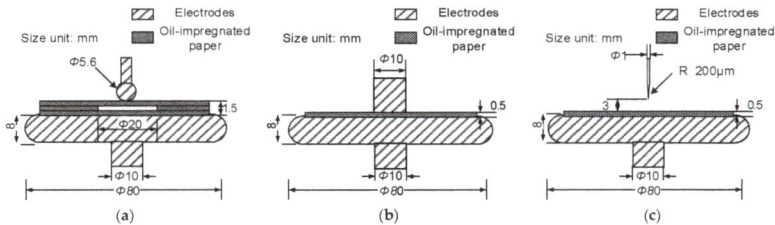

Figure 6. Three types of artificial defect models in insulation oil: (**a**) the air-void discharge model; (**b**) the surface discharge model; and (**c**) the corona discharge model.

Table 2 shows the inception voltages, breakdown voltages, and test voltages of the three types of artificial defect models in the experiment. During the experiment, the amplification factor of the amplifier is set at 40 dB, and the power frequency cycle is divided into 128 equal phase intervals. The UHF PD signals of 200 power frequency cycles are scanned under each reference level for the surface discharge model and the air-void discharge model. The UHF PD signals of 400 power frequency cycles are scanned under each reference level for the corona discharge model because its discharge frequency is small compared to the other two discharge models. The applied voltage for each discharge model increases gradually from 0 kV. When the applied voltage for each discharge model reaches the corresponding test voltage shown in Table 2, stop increasing the applied voltage. When the corresponding test voltage is applied to each discharge model for 15 min, start the intelligent sensor and oscilloscope to collect the UHF PD signals at the same time. Moreover, the magnitude of the background interference signal, which is distributed in the whole cycle, is about 20 mV. In order to avoid the background interference signal, the initial reference level is set at 20 mV, and the step of reference level is set at 10 mV.

Table 2. Partial discharge (PD) experiment conditions.

Defect Model	Incepetion Voltage (kV)	Breakdown Voltage (kV)	Test Voltage (kV)
Air-void discharge	6.1	12.3	9.7
Surface discharge	8.4	13.2	10.5
Corona discharge	5.7	12.5	9.0

4.2. Results

The acquired data of the intelligent sensor are integrated in a data table similar to Table 1. The ϕ-n_{tot}, ϕ-V_{max}, and ϕ-V-n pattern charts of the three types of discharge models are plotted by the drawing program according to the corresponding data tables. For comparison, the UHF PD signals acquired by the oscilloscope for the three types of discharge models are also processed by the level scanning method. The ϕ-n_{tot}, ϕ-V_{max}, and ϕ-V-n pattern charts of the two methods for the air-void discharge model, the surface discharge model, and the corona discharge model are shown in Figures 7–9 respectively. Because the initial reference level is set at 20 mV, the signals whose magnitude are below 20 mV have been reset to 0 in all ϕ-V_{max} and ϕ-V-n pattern charts.

From Figures 7–9 it can be seen that the data acquired by the intelligent sensor can strongly reflect the corresponding characteristics of the three types of discharge models as well as the data acquired by the oscilloscope, which validates the effectiveness of the proposed intelligent sensor. The discharge of the air-void discharge model under the given test voltage mainly distributed in the rising and falling edges of the positive and negative half cycles, respectively (0°–90° and 180°–270°), and the PD phase distributions in the positive and negative half cycles were basically symmetrical. The discharge of the surface discharge model under the given test voltage mainly distributed in the range of 30°–130° in the positive half cycle and 180°–290° in the negative half cycle. The discharge of the corona discharge model under the given test voltage both concentrated on the peaks in the positive half cycle and the negative half cycle, and the magnitude and number of discharges in the negative half cycle were greater than those in the positive half cycle. However, there are differences in the magnitude and number of discharges between the two methods. The magnitudes of discharges for the three types of discharge models collected by the oscilloscope are all greater than those collected by the intelligent sensor. The number of discharges collected by the intelligent sensor are all much greater than those collected by the oscilloscope, especially for the number of discharges with low magnitude. These differences will be discussed in the next section.

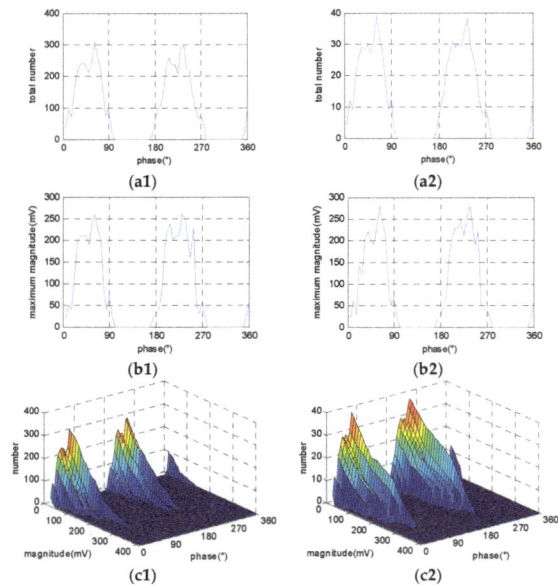

Figure 7. PD pattern charts of the air-void discharge model. (**a1**)–(**c1**) are the ϕ-n_{tot}, ϕ-V_{max}, and ϕ-V-n pattern charts of data acquired by the intelligent sensor, respectively; (**a2**)–(**c2**) are the ϕ-n_{tot}, ϕ-V_{max}, and ϕ-V-n pattern charts of data acquired by the oscilloscope, respectively.

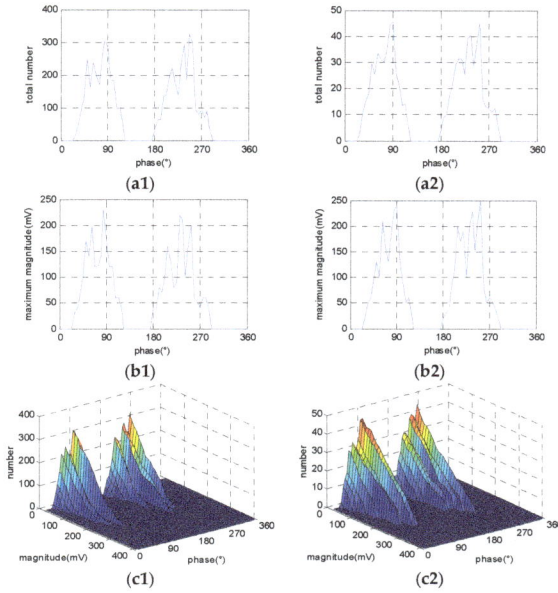

Figure 8. PD pattern charts of the surface discharge model. (**a1**)–(**c1**) are the ϕ-n_{tot}, ϕ-V_{max}, and ϕ-V-n pattern charts of data acquired by the intelligent sensor, respectively; (**a2**)–(**c2**) are the ϕ-n_{tot}, ϕ-V_{max}, and ϕ-V-n pattern charts of data acquired by the oscilloscope, respectively.

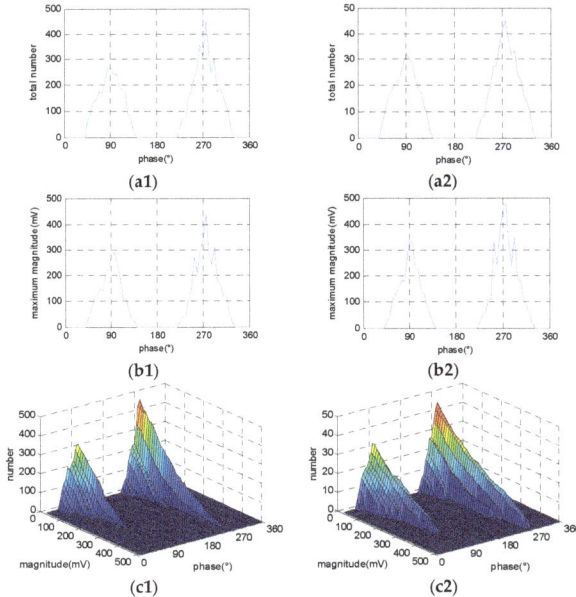

Figure 9. PD pattern charts of the corona discharge model. (**a1**)–(**c1**) are the ϕ-n_{tot}, ϕ-V_{max}, and ϕ-V-n pattern charts of data acquired by the intelligent sensor, respectively; (**a2**)–(**c2**) are the ϕ-n_{tot}, ϕ-V_{max}, and ϕ-V-n pattern charts of data acquired by the oscilloscope, respectively.

V_{max} is an important parameter in PD, which in general can reflect the severity of defects. In order to quantitatively analyze the differences between V_{max} acquired by the intelligent sensor and that by the oscilloscope, the correlation of the φ-V_{max} pattern charts of the two methods of the three types of discharge models were analyzed, respectively. The correlation of the two figures is always expressed as a correlation coefficient, and the greater the absolute value of the correlation coefficient is, the stronger the correlation is. In our work, Pearson's correlation coefficient was chosen, which was proposed by British statistician Pearson. The formula of Pearson's correlation coefficient between variable X and variable Y is as follows:

$$\rho_{X,Y} = \frac{\sum XY - \frac{\sum X \sum Y}{N}}{\sqrt{(\sum X^2 - \frac{(\sum X)^2}{N})(\sum Y^2 - \frac{(\sum Y)^2}{N})}} \tag{1}$$

The correlation coefficients of the φ-V_{max} pattern charts of the two methods of the air-void discharge model, the surface discharge model and the corona discharge model calculated by the above formula are 0.9025, 0.8913, and 0.9127, respectively, which all show strong correlation. This shows that the intelligent sensor can accurately acquire the UHF PD signals' magnitude.

5. Discussion

5.1. The Influence Factors of the Number of Discharges

As mentioned previously, the level scanning method counts the number of discharge pulses instead of the number of discharges. Comparing Figures 7b1,b2, 8b1,b2 and 9b1,b2, respectively, it can be seen that the number of discharges counted by the intelligent sensor is greater than that by the waveform recording method. In order to analyze the reason, a typical UHF PD signal in insulation oil was measured by the oscilloscope, as shown in Figure 10. It can be seen that a UHF discharge signal contains several discharge pulses because of the decaying oscillation of the discharge signal. Therefore, when using the intelligent sensor to count the number of discharges, a UHF PD signal may be counted multiple times. Moreover, the repeated counting times depend on the value of the reference level and the magnitude of the UHF PD signal. For UHF PD signals with same magnitude, the smaller the reference level is, the greater the counted number of discharge pulses is; for a fixed reference level, the greater the magnitude of the UHF PD signal is, the greater the counted number of discharge pulses is.

From the analysis above, it can be seen that, when using the intelligent sensor, the number of discharges with low magnitude is influenced significantly, but the number of discharges with high magnitude is hardly influenced. It is difficult to quantitatively compare the number of discharges by the two methods for their different principles. However, the number of discharges counted by the intelligent sensor can also accurately reflect the characteristics of the PD as the waveform recording method.

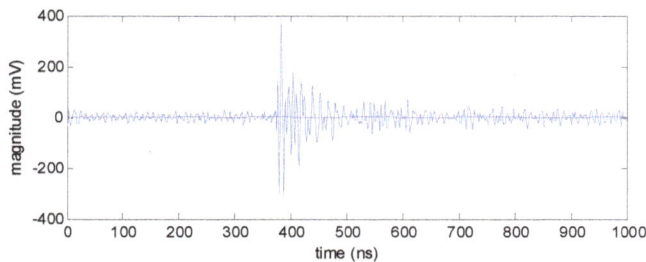

Figure 10. A typical ultra-high-frequency (UHF) PD signal measured by an oscilloscope.

5.2. Methods to Improve the Performance of the Intelligent Sensor

From the experiment result, it is found that the magnitude of discharge acquired by the oscilloscope is greater than that acquired by the intelligent sensor. In order to analyze the reason, the data acquisition theory of the level scanning method is further analyzed.

As shown in Figure 11, S_1, S_2, S_3, and S_4 represent the UHF PD pulse; V_1 and V_2 are two reference levels with a different value. When doing a level comparison, the parts of S_1, S_2, S_3, and S_4 that are greater than the reference level are converted into the corresponding square wave in Sq_1 and Sq_2. If the width of the square wave is greater than the scanning cycle of FPGA, this UHF PD pulse can be counted. It can be seen that, if the width of discharge pulse is narrow or its duration time is short, the width of the corresponding square wave is narrow; for a same discharge pulse, the part that is greater than the reference level becomes narrower when the reference level increases.

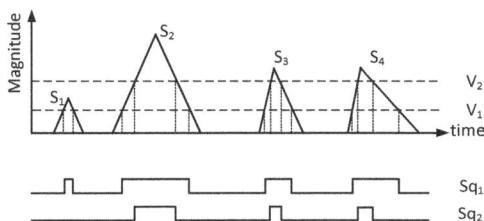

Figure 11. Data acquisition theory of the level scanning method.

In order to quantitatively analyze the performance of the intelligent sensor, we use high-frequency sinusoidal pulses as test signals. A function generator is used to generate high-frequency sinusoidal pulses with different magnitudes and frequencies. Because the core part of the intelligent sensor is the data acquisition module, the high-frequency sinusoidal pulses are directly input into the data acquisition module to obtain the number and the magnitude of the high-frequency sinusoidal pulses.

When doing the test, the function generator is adjusted to output high-frequency sinusoidal pulses whose magnitudes are 250, 500 and 1000 mV and whose frequencies are 50, 80 and 100 MHz, respectively. Table 3 includes the results obtained by the data acquisition module, where V_t is the theoretical magnitude of the sine wave, f is the frequency of the sine wave, N_1 is the detection number of the sine waves and N_2 is the theoretical number of the sine waves. In particular, V_{off} is the maximum reference level where N_1 nearly equals N_2, and W_{off} is the corresponding width of the part of the sine wave that is greater than V_{off}. Therefore, W_{off} is the smallest width of the square wave that can be counted by the intelligent sensor. The number of the scanning cycle is 10 power frequency cycles, namely 0.2 s. Table 3 shows W_{off} is about 2–3 ns. Therefore, for a certain reference level, the discharge pulse may not be detected if its width of the part that is greater than the reference level is smaller than 2 ns.

Table 3. Statistics of sinusoidal pulse by the data acquisition module.

V_t (mV)	f (MHz)	N_1	N_2	V_{off} (mV)	W_{off} (ns)
1000	100	312,500	312,508	725	2.4184
1000	80	250,000	250,007	785	2.6583
1000	50	156,250	156,255	870	3.2824
500	100	312,500	312,510	390	2.0483
500	80	250,000	250,005	420	2.2819
500	50	156,250	156,253	450	2.8713
250	100	312,500	312,506	190	2.2520
250	80	250,000	250,003	210	2.2819
250	50	156,250	156,253	230	2.5638

From the analysis above, the width of the discharge pulse, the scanning frequency of the FPGA, and the step of the reference level influence the performance of the intelligent sensor. In order to improve the performance of the intelligent sensor, three methods are proposed:

- Increase the gain of the amplifier. For a UHF PD signal, the width of the discharge pulse becomes larger after being amplified, and the larger the gain of the amplifier is, the greater the width of the discharge pulse is, which makes the discharge pulse easier to detect.
- Increase the scanning frequency of the FPGA. W_{off} of the proposed intelligent sensor is decided by the scanning frequency used to count the square wave in the FPGA; the smaller the W_{off} is, the more accurate the data is. This method can be realized with the rapid development of the FPGA in the future.
- Decrease the step of the reference level. According to the theory of the level scanning method, the detection accuracy of the magnitude will increase with the decrease in the step of the reference level, especially when the reference level is near the peak of the discharge pulse.

When using the proposed intelligent sensor to detect PD in power transformers on-site, the initial reference level is usually set at the magnitude of the background interference signal. The installation location of the antenna on the power transformer is fixed, so the magnitude of the UHF PD electromagnetic wave, which is generated far from the antenna, may become small because of the signal attenuation. In order to sensitively detect the PD generated far from the antenna, the amplification factor of the amplifier is recommended to be set at 40 dB. For the step of the reference level, as mentioned above, the smaller the step of the reference level is, the more accurate the detection of the magnitude is. However, the smaller the step of the reference level is, the longer the time to finish a detection is. Therefore, the selection of the step of the reference level depends on the users' demands for accuracy and efficiency.

5.3. The Use of the Intelligent Sensor for Ultra-High-Frequency Partial Discharge Detection in Other Electrical Components

The UHF PD detection method is also used to detect PD in gas-insulation substations (GIS's) and cables because of its high sensitivity and strong anti-interference ability. The proposed intelligent sensor can used to detect UHF PD for GIS's. Because the UHF PD electromagnetic wave in GIS's can leak out at the spacers of a GIS, the Peano fractal antenna can be fixed at the spacer of a GIS and used as an external antenna. However, the intelligent sensor only acquires statistical characteristic quantities of the UHF PD signal and does not acquire the parameters of a single UHF PD electromagnetic wave, so the intelligent sensor cannot be used to localize PD in GIS's.

As for cable, in contrast to the cable itself, insulation failures are more likely happen at the cable connectors that have a higher risk of defects and contamination. As for UHF PD online monitoring for cable connectors, the Peano fractal antenna cannot be used as a coupler, and the inductive UHF sensor and the capacitive UHF sensor are usually used [19]. If the antennas in an intelligent sensor are replaced with inductive UHF sensors or capacitive UHF sensors, which are used for the UHF PD detection of cables, the intelligent sensor can be used to detect UHF PD in cable connectors.

6. Conclusions

In this paper, a novel, intelligent senor for UHF PD online monitoring of power transformers based on the proposed level scanning method is introduced. The proposed intelligent sensor accurately acquires and directly outputs statistical characteristic quantities of UHF PD signals containing the distribution of magnitude and number of discharges in power frequency phase intervals without data post-processing, which avoids the error caused by signal delays and achieves low storage and fast real-time commutation for its small data quantity. The intelligent sensor is composed of UHF antennas and integrated circuits with universal chips, which is cheaper compared to the traditional method using high-speed data acquisition cards or an oscilloscope and other industrial products. Moreover, the intelligent sensor is easy to install because it is of small volume and is easy to maintain for its high reliability. Because of these advantages, the proposed intelligent sensor can be widely used for UHF PD online monitoring of power transformers and can be used to achieve a distributed PD monitoring system in substations. The main results of the work can be summarized as follows:

(1) A new method to directly acquire the statistical characteristic quantities of UHF PD, namely the level scanning method, is proposed.
(2) The corresponding data processing module of the level canning method was designed, and a prototype was made. Combined with the antenna designed in our previous work, the intelligent sensor was made.
(3) Actual UHF PD experiments with three typical artificial defect models of power transformers were carried out to verify the performance of the intelligent sensor in a laboratory, and the waveform recording method and the intelligent sensor proposed were simultaneously used for UHF PD measurement. The results show that the intelligent sensor can accurately acquire statistical characteristic quantities of the UHF PD signal, which indicates the proposed intelligent sensor is qualified for UHF PD online monitoring.
(4) In order to improve the accuracy of the intelligent sensor, three methods to improve the performance of the intelligent sensor are proposed according to the principle of the proposed level scanning method.

For future works, there is still much work to do to construct a complete UHF PD online monitoring system. Because the level scanning method is different from traditional methods, the corresponding filter methods should be researched, as should the methods of pattern recognition and fault diagnosis.

Acknowledgments: The authors acknowledge the National High-Tech Research and Development Program of China (863 Program) (2011AA05A120). We also appreciate the funding provided by the National Natural Science Foundation of China (No. 51321063) and the National "111" Project of the Ministry of Education of China (No. B08036).

Author Contributions: The research presented in this paper was a collaborative effort among all authors. Jian Li, Xudong Li, and Lin Du proposed the methodology of the intelligent sensor, implemented the intelligent sensor, and wrote the paper. Min Cao and Guochao Qian designed and performed the experiment, discussed the results, and critically revised the manuscript.

Conflicts of Interest: The authors declare no conflict of interest.

References

1. Barbieri, L.; Villa, A.; Malgesini, R. A step forward in the characterization of the partial discharge phenomenon and the degradation of insulating materials through nonlinear analysis of time series. *IEEE Trans. Dielectr. Electr. Insul.* **2012**, *28*, 14–21. [CrossRef]
2. Kiiza, R.C.; Niasar, M.G.; Nikjoo, R.; Wang, X.; Edin, H. Change in partial discharge activity as related to degradation level in oil-impregnated paper insulation: Effect of high voltage impulses. *IEEE Trans. Dielectr. Electr. Insul.* **2014**, *21*, 1243–1250. [CrossRef]
3. Sellars, A.G.; Farish, O.; Hampton, B.F.; Pritchard, L.S. Using the uhf technique to investigate PD produced by defects in solid insulation. *IEEE Trans. Dielectr. Electr. Insul.* **1995**, *2*, 448–459. [CrossRef]
4. Haida, T.; Wakabayashi, S.; Tsuge, R.; Sakakibara, T. Development of partial discharge monitoring technique using a neural network in a gas insulated substation. *IEEE Trans. Power Syst.* **1997**, *12*, 1014–1021.
5. Hikita, M.; Okabe, S.; Murase, H.; Okubo, H. Cross-equipment evaluation of partial discharge measurement and diagnosis techniques in electric power apparatus for transmission and distribution. *IEEE Trans. Dielectr. Electr. Insul.* **2008**, *15*, 505–518. [CrossRef]
6. Jacob, N.D.; Mcdermid, W.M.; Kordi, B. On-line monitoring of partial discharges in a HVDC station environment. *IEEE Trans. Dielectr. Electr. Insul.* **2012**, *19*, 925–935. [CrossRef]
7. Yao, C.G.; Zhou, D.B.; Chen, P.; Xing, L.; Sun, C.X. UHF-based monitoring for equipment PD within the substation and early warning. *High Volt. Eng.* **2011**, *37*, 1670–1676.

8. Jiang, T.; Li, J.; Zheng, Y.; Sun, C. Improved bagging algorithm for pattern recognition in uhf signals of partial discharges. *Energies* **2011**, *4*, 1087–1101. [CrossRef]

9. De Kock, N.; Coric, B.; Pietsch, R. UHF PD detection in gas-insulated switchgear-suitability and sensitivity of the UHF method in comparison with the IEC 270 method. *IEEE Electr. Insul. Mag.* **1996**, *6*, 20–26. [CrossRef]

10. Wang, M.; Vandermaar, A.J.; Srivastava, K.D. Review of condition assessment of power transformers in service. *IEEE Electr. Insul. Mag.* **2002**, *18*, 12–25. [CrossRef]

11. Chen, M.; Chen, J.; Cheng, C. Partial discharge detection by rf coil in 161 kv power transformer. *IEEE Trans. Dielectr. Electr. Insul.* **2014**, *21*, 1405–1414. [CrossRef]

12. Zargari, A.; Blackburn, T.R. Application of optical fibre sensor for partial discharge detection in high-voltage power equipment. In Proceedings of the IEEE 1996 Annual Report of the Conference on Electrical Insulation and Dielectric Phenomena, Millbrae, CA, USA, 20–23 October 1996.

13. Sharkawy, R.M.; Abdel-Galil, T.K.; Mangoubi, R.S.; Salama, M.M.; Bartnikas, R. Particle identification in terms of acoustic partial discharge measurements in transformer oils. *IEEE Trans. Dielectr. Electr. Insul.* **2008**, *15*, 1649–1656. [CrossRef]

14. Tang, J.; Zhou, J.; Zhang, X.; Liu, F. A transformer partial discharge measurement system based on fluorescent fiber. *Energies* **2012**, *5*, 1490–1502. [CrossRef]

15. Chen, W.; Chen, X.; Peng, S.; Li, J. Canonical correlation between partial discharges and gas formation in transformer oil paper insulation. *Energies* **2012**, *5*, 1081–1097. [CrossRef]

16. Sima, W.; Jiang, C.; Lewin, P.; Yang, Q.; Yuan, T. Modeling of the partial discharge process in a liquid dielectric: effect of applied voltage, gap distance, and electrode type. *Energies* **2013**, *6*, 934–952. [CrossRef]

17. Meijer, S.; Agoris, P.D.; Smit, J.J.; Judd, M.D.; Yang, L. Application of UHF diagnostics to detect PD during power transformer acceptance tests. In Proceedings of the Conference Record of the 2006 IEEE International Symposium on Electrical Insulation, Toronto, ON, Canada, 11–14 June 2006.

18. Cleary, G.P.; Judd, M.D. UHF and current pulse measurements of partial discharge activity in mineral oil. *IEE Proc. Sci. Meas. Technol.* **2006**, *153*, 47–54. [CrossRef]

19. Tenbohlen, S.; Denissov, D.; Hoek, S.M.; Markalous, S.M. Partial discharge measurement in the ultra-high frequency (UHF) range. *IEEE Trans. Dielectr. Electr. Insul.* **2008**, *15*, 1544–1552. [CrossRef]

20. Yoshida, M.; Kojima, H.; Hayakawa, N.; Endo, F.; Okubo, H. Evaluation of UHF method for partial discharge measurement by simultaneous observation of UHF signal and current pulse waveforms. *IEEE Trans. Dielectr. Electr. Insul.* **2011**, *18*, 425–431. [CrossRef]

21. Beltle, M.; Mueller, A.; Tenbohlen, S. Statistical analysis of online ultrahigh-frequency partial-discharge measurement of power transformers. *IEEE Trans. Dielectr. Electr. Insul.* **2012**, *28*, 17–22. [CrossRef]

22. Wang, Y.; Wu, J.; Li, Z.; Yin, Y. Research on a practical de-noising method and the characterization of partial discharge UHF signals. *IEEE Trans. Dielectr. Electr. Insul.* **2014**, *21*, 2206–2216. [CrossRef]

23. Judd, M.D.; Yang, L.; Hunter, I. Partial discharge monitoring for power transformers using UHF sensors Part 1: Sensors and signal interpretation. *IEEE Electr. Insul. Mag.* **2005**, *21*, 5–14. [CrossRef]

24. Zhang, X.X.; Wang, Z.; Tang, J.; Liu, L.; Wei, Y. GIT partial discharge UHF on-line monitoring system. *High Volt. Eng.* **2010**, *36*, 1692–1697.

25. Xie, Y.; Tang, J.; Zhang, X. Development of GIT partial discharge UHF online monitoring system. In Proceedings of the 2010 International Conference on High Voltage Engineering and Application (ICHVE), New Orleans, LA, USA, 11–14 October 2010.

26. Capponi, G.; Schifani, R. Measurement of partial discharge in solid dielectrics with a microprocessor-based system. *IEEE Trans. Dielectr. Electr. Insul.* **1992**, *27*, 106–113. [CrossRef]

27. Wang, G.; Hao, Y.; Peng, Y. Application of frequency mixing technique to ultra-high-frequency PD detection for transformers. *Proc. CSEE* **2013**, *24*, 115–120.

28. Lixue, L.; Letian, T.; Chengjun, H. Envelope analysis and defects identification of partial discharge UHF signals in GIS. *High Volt. Eng.* **2009**, *35*, 260–265.

29. Ye, H.; Qian, Y.; Dong, Y.; Sheng, G.; Jiang, X. Development of multi-band ultra-high-frequency sensor for partial discharge monitoring based on the meandering technique. *IET Sci. Meas. Technol.* **2014**, *8*, 327–335.

30. Shibuya, Y.; Matsumoto, S.; Tanaka, M.; Muto, H.; Kaneda, Y. Electromagnetic waves from partial discharges and their detection using patch antenna. *IEEE Trans. Dielectr. Electr. Insul.* **2010**, *17*, 862–871. [CrossRef]

31. Li, T.; Rong, M.; Zheng, C.; Wang, X. Development simulation and experiment study on UHF partial discharge sensor in GIS. *IEEE Trans. Dielectr. Electr. Insul.* **2012**, *19*, 1421–1430. [CrossRef]

32. Li, J.; Jiang, T.; Wang, C.; Cheng, C. Optimization of UHF Hilbert antenna for partial discharge detection of transformers. *IEEE Trans. Antennas Propag.* **2012**, *60*, 2536–2540.
33. Li, J.; Cheng, C.; Bao, L.; Jiang, T. Resonant frequency calculation and optimal design of peano fractal antenna for partial discharge detection. *Int. J. Antennas Propag.* **2012**, *2012*. [CrossRef]

energies

MDPI

Article

Raman Spectral Characteristics of Oil-Paper Insulation and Its Application to Ageing Stage Assessment of Oil-Immersed Transformers

Jingxin Zou, Weigen Chen *, Fu Wan, Zhou Fan and Lingling Du

State Key Laboratory of Power Transmission Equipment & System Security and New Technology,
Chongqing University, Chongqing 400044, China; zoujingxin@cqu.edu.cn (J.Z.); wanfuhappy@163.com (F.W.);
fanzhou@cqu.edu.cn (Z.F.); dulingling2014@163.com (L.D.)
* Correspondence: weigench@cqu.edu.cn; Tel.: +86-23-65111098

Academic Editor: Vijay Kumar Thakur
Received: 9 August 2016; Accepted: 8 November 2016; Published: 12 November 2016

Abstract: The aging of oil-paper insulation in power transformers may cause serious power failures. Thus, effective monitoring of the condition of the transformer insulation is the key to prevent major accidents. The purpose of this study was to explore the feasibility of confocal laser Raman spectroscopy (CLRS) for assessing the aging condition of oil-paper insulation. Oil-paper insulation samples were subjected to thermal accelerated ageing at 120 °C for up to 160 days according to the procedure described in the IEEE Guide. Meanwhile, the dimension of the Raman spectrum of the insulation oil was reduced by principal component analysis (PCA). The 160 oil-paper insulation samples were divided into five aging stages as training samples by clustering analysis and with the use of the degree of polymerization of the insulating papers. In addition, the features of the Raman spectrum were used as the inputs of a multi-classification support vector machine. Finally, 105 oil-paper insulation testing samples aged at a temperature of 130 °C were used to further test the diagnostic capability and universality of the established algorithm. Results demonstrated that CLRS in conjunction with the PCA-SVM technique provides a new way for aging stage assessment of oil-paper insulation equipment in the field.

Keywords: Raman spectroscopy; power transformers; aging stage; principal component analysis; clustering analysis; degree of polymerization; support vector machine

1. Introduction

Transformers are essential components of a power transmission and distribution system. According to the reports of the International Council of Large Electric Systems (CIGRE), the operating life of transformers in most countries averages 30 years, and it is influenced by various factors, including load, manufacturing process, and operating environment [1]. The condition of a transformer is critical to the safety and reliability of the power system. The probability of an accident from transformers increases with the deterioration of the insulation. Oil-paper insulation, which is the main insulation type for oil-immersed transformers, suffers from thermal and electrical aging during long-term operation. Thus, the identification of the different aging stages of oil-paper insulation, particularly for transformers running for more than 20 years, becomes particularly critical and important. Given that the degradation of insulation performance is a major and direct threat to the reliability of transformer, a study on aging condition monitoring is of considerable importance in the subject of insulation. Such a study can contribute to insulation diagnosis and lifetime prediction several years in advance.

The degree of polymerization (DP) in insulation paper is commonly used to characterize the aging degree of the insulation paper and has been regarded as a basic parameter to evaluate the aging stage of oil-paper insulation by the IEEE Guide [2]. On the basis of the massive body of research on the aging mechanism and aging characteristic of insulation paper, Emsley introduced and improved the kinetic equation for the degradation reaction of insulation paper to describe the development law of the DP in the aging process [3–5]. Although DP has been accepted worldwide as the most effective indicator for the discriminant analysis of the aging stages of insulation paper, it necessitates cutting the power and hanging the cover of the transformer during sampling and measurement; as a result, the field application of DP is restricted. For this reason, the aging state of the transformer insulation is mainly indirectly reflected by the aging characteristics of the oil-paper insulation, namely its degradation and dissolution in insulation oil [6].

Shroff studied the formation of furfural in the paper aging process and confirmed that an approximate logarithmic relationship exists between the furfural content and the DP of the insulation paper [7]. Thus, the concentration of furfural can serve as an essential characteristic to assess the aging condition of the insulation [8–11]. Currently, high performance liquid chromatography (HPLC), ultraviolet (UV) spectrophotometry and the colorimetric method are the major methods to detect the concentration of furfural dissolved in oil. However, these methods have their respective disadvantages. The drawbacks of HPLC include complex operation, difficult elution, and extra-column effect existence [12]. UV spectrophotometry has poor stability and is susceptible to the organic matter in the transformer oil [13]. Toluidine, which is used in the colorimetric method, is recognized as one of the most potent carcinogens in the world; furthermore, the colorimetric method has lower measurement accuracy than the other methods [14].

The thermal and electrical faults that develop in an oil-immersed power transformer are typically associated with the formation of dissolved gases, including CO, CO_2, CH_4, C_2H_4, C_2H_2, C_2H_6 and H_2 [15–17]. Used for several decades in testing and monitoring oil-immersed transformers, dissolved gas analysis (DGA) has been accepted worldwide as an effective method for the diagnosis of the aging stage of power transformers [18–20]. Various gas-in-oil detection methods have been developed, including gas chromatography (GC), which is a well-known diagnostic method for accurately determining the concentrations of nine different gases [21,22]. However, the performance of chromatograph columns degrades with time, and GC monitoring systems need to be operated in a laboratory by highly qualified personnel.

Raman spectroscopy has been widely used in food, materials, chemistry, biochemistry and other fields for qualitative or quantitative analyses [23–27]. It shows considerable potential in the early failure diagnosis for transformers. Furfural was previously characterized by the Raman signal at 1707 cm^{-1} and reached a detection limit of 14.4 mg/L [28]. In recent years, Raman detection for dissolved gases in oil has also been proposed [29]. However, the application of Raman spectra to the assessment of the aging condition of a transformer has been rarely reported. Accordingly, the primary objectives of this study are to explore the Raman spectral characteristics of oil-paper insulation, and to establish a method of its application to aging stage assessment of oil-immersed transformers.

In this study, thermal accelerated aging experiments were conducted at 120 °C for up to 160 days in order to obtain oil-paper samples [2]. The mapping relationship between the Raman signal of the insulation oil and the DP of the insulation paper was investigated. Firstly, a principal component analysis (PCA) was conducted to extract the representative features from the Raman signal for use in the aging condition diagnosis. Secondly, the dimension-reduced spectral data were utilized in the clustering analysis to divide the sample into five categories, which correspond to the five aging stages according to the average DP of the insulation paper immersed in oil. Next, a genetic algorithm (GA)-optimized multi-classification support vector machine (SVM) was employed to develop a suitable diagnostic algorithm for assessing the aging condition of the oil-paper insulation. Finally, 105 more insulation samples were aged at 130 °C and used to further test the diagnosis performance of the established algorithm model.

2. Materials and Methods

2.1. Raman Instrumentation

The working principle of the platform used in the Raman spectroscopic studies of insulation oil is illustrated in Figure 1, the excitation source is focused on the oil sample by confocal microscopy to excite Raman scattering. Subsequently, the scattered light is collected by an objective and guided into a charge-coupled device (CCD), which is connected to the spectrometer controlled by a personal computer. The Raman spectra of the insulation oil associated is displayed on the computer screen in real time and can be saved for further analysis.

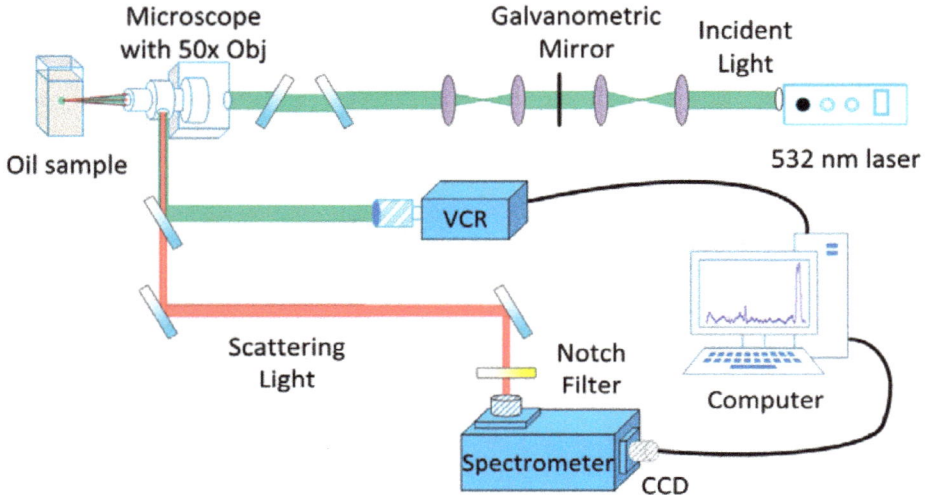

Figure 1. Schematic diagram of the CLRS liquid detection test platform.

On the basis of the given operating principle, a Raman detection platform was constructed to study the Raman spectra of the insulation oil. The system mainly consists of a 532 nm CW laser with a power of 500 mW as the excitation source, and its current controller (LDX-3232) and temperature controller (TCU151); a 50× long-focal-length objective used for laser convergence and signal collection, which has a high spatial resolution to avoid the interferences produced by the entrance window; a Video Cassette Recorder (VCR) helping to adjust the facula; a back-thinned CCD (refrigeration temperature: −85 °C, distinguishability: 2000 × 256, quantum efficiency: >90%), an Andor 500i series spectrometer with three blazed gratings (600 lines per 500 nm, 1800 lines per 500 nm, and 1200 lines per 750 nm) and the focal length of the spectrometer was 500 mm. The system acquired the Raman spectra with light intensity on the oil sample stabilized at 35 mW, the spectrum over the wavenumber range of 390–3082 cm^{-1}. Exposure time and the number of accumulations were respectively set to 5 s and three times to avoid signal oversaturation and light degradation of the oil characteristics. Moreover, the width of the entrance slit of the spectrometer was set to 100 µm.

2.2. Thermal Accelerated Aging Experiment

Thermal accelerated aging experiments were conducted to obtain oil-paper samples at different aging stages in a short time. Performing accelerated aging in sealed systems is recommended in the IEEE loading guide to simulate the real aging of modern sealed transformers [2]. The 25# transformer mineral oil was provided by Chuanrun Lubricant Company, China. The cellulose papers samples provided by Baoqing Paper Co. Ltd. (Hunan, China) had a thickness of 0.3 mm and a diameter of

32 mm. The samples were pretreated as follows: Firstly, 17.6 g of papers samples were taken out every time and placed in a glass bottle (250 mL), all papers samples were placed in a vacuum box and dried at 90 °C for 48 h. The temperature of the vacuum box was then adjusted to 40 °C. Secondly, fresh mineral oil was then added into each bottle at an oil/paper mass weight ratio of 10:1 (each bottle contains 176 g of oil and 17.6 g of paper). Thirdly, all the bottles were placed back to the vacuum box. The temperature of the vacuum box was maintained at 90 °C for another 48 h and then cooled down to room temperature. Subsequently, each bottle was filled with dry nitrogen gas and then sealed (1 atm). Finally, the 160 samples were placed in aging ovens and heated to 120 °C for the accelerated thermal aging of up to 160 days. Twenty samples were collected in days 1, 10, 20, 40, 70, 102, 110, and 160 to obtain oil-paper insulation samples with different aging states.

Before CLRS measurement was performed, the oil samples were cooled naturally to room temperature (28 °C). For the analysis of aging condition of the oil-paper insulation, the DP of the oil-impregnated papers aged with the oil was measured according to ASTM D4243-99.

2.3. Data Pre-Processing

The average spectral data set of five repeated Raman measurements on each insulation oil sample was used for oil classification to reduce the spectral measurement errors in this study. The raw spectra acquired from the insulation oil in the 390–3082 cm^{-1} range represented a combination of prominent oil fluorescence, oil Raman scattering signals, and noise. Baseline commonly exists in the spectrum detection, and it is mainly caused by fluorescent substance generated during the aging process, the fluorescence of oil, impurities in oil and the detecting equipment. The baseline will bring a very adverse impact on the extraction of spectral features. Accordingly, baseline correction is important means to solve this problem, and is an important part of Raman spectrum signal preprocessing. The raw spectra were preprocessed by adjacent five-point smoothing to reduce the noise. For the polynomial baseline correction method, the baseline was estimated using cubic spline functions [30–32], which were obtained by the least-squares criterion. As shown in Figure 2, the function fitted by the points was then subtracted from the raw spectrum to obtain pure Raman spectrum of each oil sample. Each of the baseline-subtracted Raman spectra was normalized to the integrated area under the curve in the wavenumber range of 390–3082 cm^{-1} to enable a better comparison of the spectral shapes and relative peak intensities among the different oil samples.

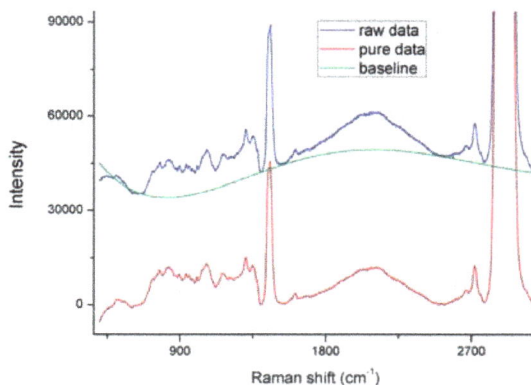

Figure 2. Data pre-processing for Raman spectra of oil samples.

2.4. Empirical Approach

Oil color is one of the important indicators of insulation performance. In this study, the color of the insulation oil produced by the same company became darker as aging time is extended, as shown in Figure 3a. Fresh oil is usually pale yellow and transparent. The mechanical mixture and free carbon generated the aging characteristic groups, such as C=C and C=O, which were responsible for darkening and browning of oil in the process of aging experiment. As shown in Figure 3b, the deepening of the color of the insulation oil resulted in an increase in the baseline noise; as a result, some details of the spectra were covered, and the signal-to-noise ratio was reduced.

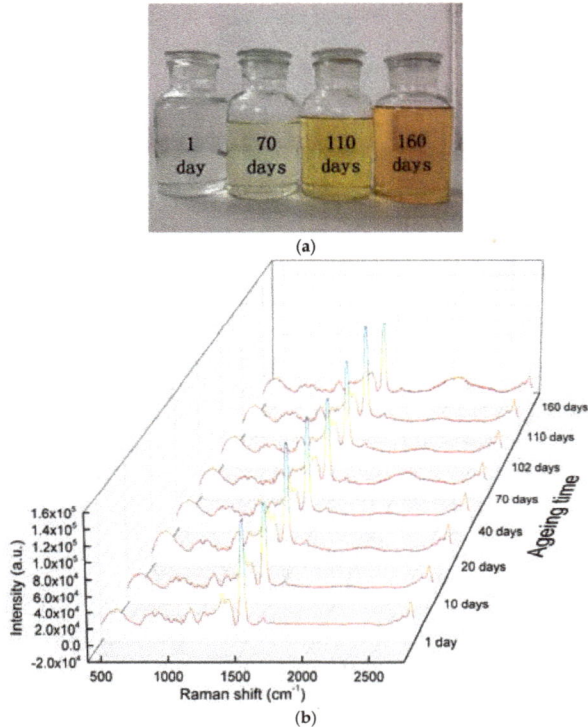

Figure 3. Oil samples and the shape of Raman spectra: (**a**) Four oil samples collected at different aging times; (**b**) Raw Raman spectra of the insulation oil samples for different aging times.

2.5. Multivariate Analysis

A high dimension of the Raman spectral space (each Raman spectrum had 2000 data points) results in the complexity of computation and inefficiency of optimization [33]. Thus, in this study, PCA was first performed on the insulation oil Raman data set to reduce the dimension of the Raman spectral space whilst retaining the most diagnostically significant information for oil classification. The entire spectrum was standardized so that the mean of the spectrum was zero and the standard deviation of all the spectral intensities was one to eliminate the influence of inter- and intra-subject spectral variability on PCA. Mean centering ensured that the principal components (PCs) form an orthogonal basis [34,35]. The standardized Raman data sets were assembled into data matrices with feature columns and instance case rows. Thus, PCA was performed on the standardized spectral data matrices to generate PCs comprising a reduced number of orthogonal variables, which accounted for most of the total variance in the original spectra. PC scores reflected the differences between each class. These significant PC scores were applied to select the training samples for clustering analysis and develop the SVM algorithm for multiclass classification.

The SVM used was a binary classifier that assessed the aging stage of the oil-paper insulation in this study as a multi-classification problem. A multi-classification method called one-against-one is constructed to solve the multi-classification problem and recognize the aging stage of the oil-paper insulation in transformers [36]. The basic principle of the "one-against-one" method is that $k(k-1)/2$ classifiers can be constructed to solve a k-class discrimination problem and each of these classifiers is trained to distinguish two classes. With the training data assumed to belong to the mth and the nth class, the multi-classifier can be derived by solving the binary classifier problem:

$$\min_{\omega,b,\xi} \quad \frac{1}{2}\left(\omega^{mn}\right)^T\left(\omega^{mn}\right) + C\sum_{i=1}^{k}\left(\xi_i^{mn}\right)\left(\omega^{mn}\right)^T \qquad \xi_i \geq 0$$
$$if \quad y_i = m, \qquad \left(\omega^{mn}\right)^T \phi(x_t) + b^{mn} \geq 1 - \xi_i^{mn} \tag{1}$$
$$if \quad y_i = n, \qquad \left(\omega^{mn}\right)^T \phi(x_t) + b^{mn} \leq -1 + \xi_i^{mn}$$

where $(x_1, y_1), \cdots, (x_l, y_l)$ denote the training data; x_i represents the attributes (features); $y_i \in \{1, \cdots, k\}$ is the target value (class labels); ϕ is the function used to map x_i to a higher dimensional space; $\omega = [\omega_1, \omega_2, \cdots, \omega_N]^T$ is the linear weight vector which links the feature space to output space; b is the threshold; and C is the penalty parameter of the error term. The training samples were mapped from the input space into a higher dimensional feature space via a mapping function ϕ. The scalar product $\phi(x_i) \cdot \phi(x_j)$ is calculated directly by computing the kernel function $k(x_i, x_j)$ for given training data in an input space. Radial basis function (RBF) is a common kernel function as the follows.

$$k(x_i, x_j) = \exp\left(-\gamma\|x_i - x_j\|^2\right) \tag{2}$$

where γ is the kernel parameter, and $\gamma > 0$.

3. Results

3.1. Classification of the Training Samples

We employed the entire Raman spectrum (390–3082 cm^{-1}) to determine the most diagnostically significant Raman features and to improve the analysis and classification of the insulation oil. Firstly, the raw spectra were treated using the baseline correction and denoising method. After normalization, PCA was employed to observe the latent distribution of the samples subjected to the spectral pre-processing methods. As shown in Figure 4, the obtained PC scores indicate that the cumulative variance proportion of the first 12 PCs (PC1, PC2, ... , PC12) reaches about 95%, which is diagnostically significant for discriminating oil-paper insulation of different aging conditions.

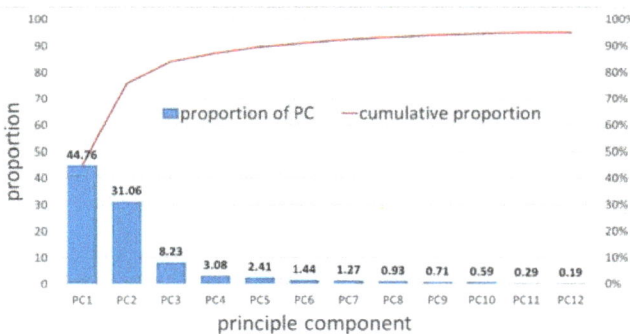

Figure 4. Cumulative variance of the first 12 principal components.

Although PCA analysis does not provide the answer for what the physical meaning of the PC component is, the loading plot can provide some hints related to the characteristic vibrational frequencies giving the dominant contribution to the components. Figure 5 is PCA loading plots 1, 2, 3 and 4 on the Raman spectra of the insulation oil; the loading indicated the variable's contribution to the principal component. The vibration characteristics of the loading weight are closely related to the contribution of the chemical composition to the principal components. Thus, the loading plots show us which vibrational bands have significantly contributed to the differences seen in the PCA plot, and provide more information on the Raman spectra of oil in each aging stage.

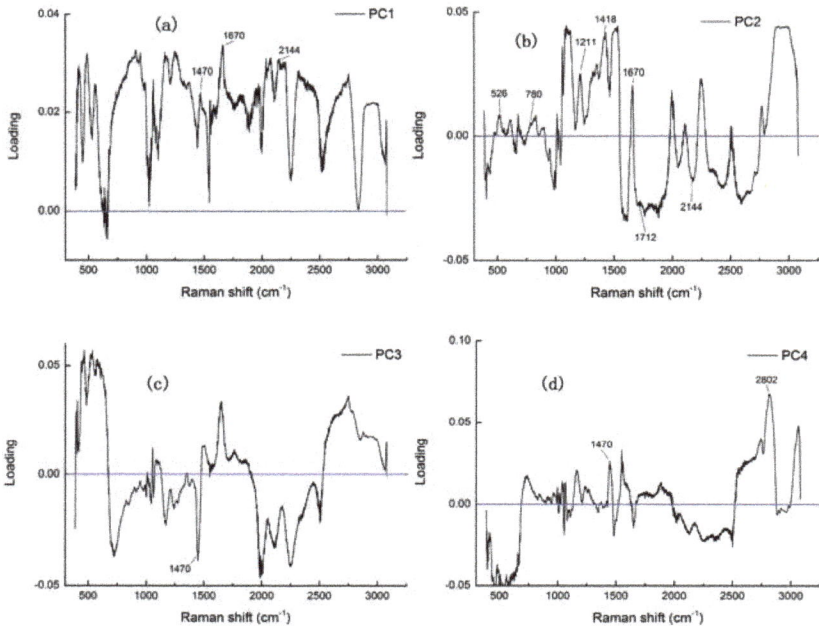

Figure 5. The first four diagnostically significant principal components (PCs). PCA loading plot for (a) PC1; (b) PC2; (c) PC3 and (d) PC4.

Some relatively high (positive and negative) values are marked and associated with their corresponding variables in the Raman spectra, such as peaks from furfural (1418 cm^{-1}, 1470 cm^{-1} and 1670 cm^{-1}), CO (2144 cm^{-1}), CO_2 (2802 cm^{-1}); acetone, which is the recently proposed aging characteristic, generated peaks at 526 cm^{-1}, 780 cm^{-1}, 1211 cm^{-1} and 1712 cm^{-1} [29,37]. From the loading plot we can see that PC1 has a high correlation ranging all the Raman bands. PC2 has a positive correlation in the Raman bands of 1000–1500 cm^{-1} and 2750–3000 cm^{-1}; PC3 has a high correlation in the Raman bands of 400–600 cm^{-1}, 1900–2500 cm^{-1} and 2750–3000 cm^{-1}; and PC4 has a high correlation in the Raman bands of 400–600 cm^{-1} and 2000–2800 cm^{-1}.

Every 20 thermal accelerated aging samples were taken out from the aging ovens at eight time points of one, 10, 20, 40, 70, 102, 110 and 160 days and numbered from #1 to #160. The samples were divided into eight groups: A, B, C, D, E, F, G and H. The DP of the oil-impregnated papers was measured and the clustering analysis was conducted on the low-dimension features of all 160 oil samples. The clustering results of oil at different aging times provided the basis for the classification of the training samples. Mahalanobis distance and shortest distance methods were employed in clustering the characterization factors without any prior knowledge [38]. The clustering results are shown in Figure 6.

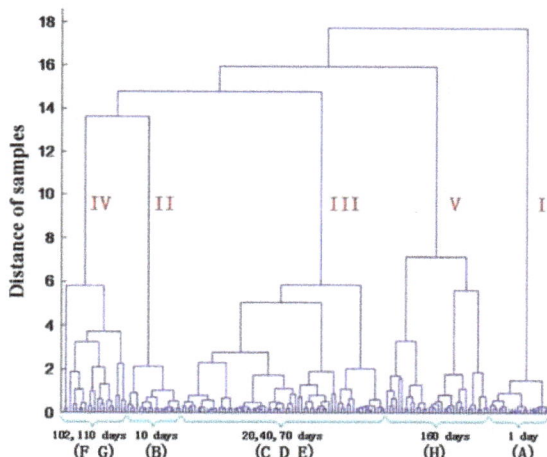

Figure 6. Clustering results of the oil samples.

Observing the clustering spectra without any prior reference, we arrived at the following conclusions: firstly, the 160 samples could be divided into two classes when the distance of the samples was approximately 16.5. The samples aged for only one day (nearly fresh) were separated from those aged for more than 10 days. Secondly, when the distance of the samples was reduced to 15.5, the seriously aged (160 days) samples could be separated from the others. When the distance was set to 5–13, the samples aged for 10 days; 20, 40 and 70 days; 102 and 110 days belonged to three different aging stages, respectively. However, certain crosses occurred between classes in the clustering result. For instance, a few samples in group E (70 days) joined class IV with groups F (102 days) and G (110 days). Furthermore, some samples in group D (40 days) even jumped to class V and were classified together with group H (160 days). Nevertheless, we still divided the 160 training samples into five classes according to the real aging time. Corresponding to the average DPs of the oil-impregnated papers in the groups, these five classes represented the five aging stages.

According to the guide for the diagnosis of insulation aging in oil-immersed power transformers [39,40], the five training classes of the clustering results in Figure 7a represented five aging stages: fresh condition (DP > 800), early age (500 < DP < 800), medium age (250 < DP < 500), late age (150 < DP < 250) and terminal age (DP < 150). Figure 7b illustrated the utility of the first three PCs for the classification of the training samples. PC1, PC2 and PC3 retained high percentages of the total variance (44.77%, 31.06% and 8.23%, respectively). With the information on PC1, PC2 and PC3, classes I, II and V were clearly distinguished; however, the identification of class III and class IV initially did not achieve an ideal effect. By combined analysis of the loading plot (Figure 5) and the scores plot (Figure 7b), we can see that the aging process has a positive correlation with PC2, which can be largely ascribed to the generation of the typical aging characteristics (furfural, CO and CO_2). Besides, the acetone shows a clear contribution to PC2. During the aging process, the break and formation of C–C and C=C may influence the contribution of bands 400–600 cm^{-1} and 2750–3000 cm^{-1}. The information in the loading plot can also be used to discriminate the aging stage of the oil-paper insulation.

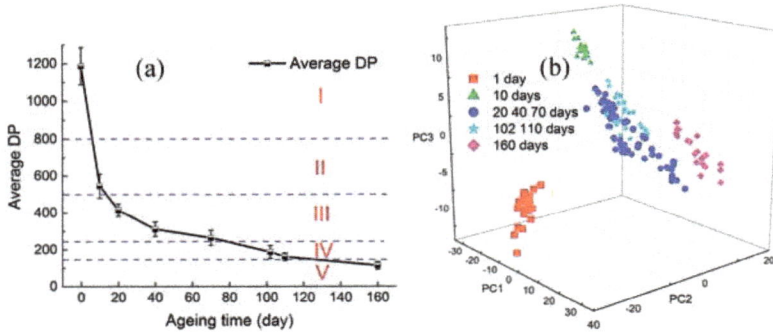

Figure 7. Classification result of training samples: (**a**) Relationship between DP and aging time; (**b**) Scatter plots of the PC scores for five classes of oil samples, with the PC scores derived from the Raman spectra.

3.2. Results of the Multi-Classification SVM

Accordingly, all 12 diagnostically significant PCs were loaded into the multi-classification SVM model to generate a suitable diagnostic algorithm for aging stage classification and to improve oil diagnosis. Table 1 shows the classification results based on the PCA-SVM technique coupled with the 10-fold cross-validation method.

Table 1. Confusion matrix for the support vector machine.

True Class	Predicted Class					True Positive Rates	Positive Predictive Values
	I	**II**	**III**	**IV**	**V**		
I	19	0	1	0	0	95.0%	100%
II	0	17	3	0	0	85.0%	94.4%
III	0	1	59	0	0	98.3%	84.3%
IV	0	0	6	34	0	85.0%	100%
V	0	0	1	0	19	95.0%	100%

The classification results indicated that the PCA-SVM diagnostic algorithm demonstrated a significantly good capability in diagnosing the oil-paper insulation aging stage. In the 10-fold cross-validation for the original cases, the average accuracy of the 10 instances of training and testing was 92.5%. The method had the capability to distinguish fresh oil and serious aged oil clearly, but had a slight difficulty with the middle three aging stages.

In this study, the penalty parameter C and the kernel function parameters γ for SVM can be optimized by a genetic algorithm [40]. After being trained with the feature quality of the historic training data, the best parameters C and γ for SVM can be determined. For each chromosome representing C, γ and selected features, the training dataset is used to train the SVM classifier, while the testing dataset is used to calculate the classification accuracy. When the classification accuracy is obtained, each chromosome is evaluated by fitness function [41]. The fitness curve of seeking for the best C and γ of the SVM by GA is shown in Figure 8a. The best C and γ are 17.3 and 1.44, respectively. It can be seen from Figure 8b that the accuracy of the 10-fold cross-validation [42] has been raised to 99.37% (159/160).

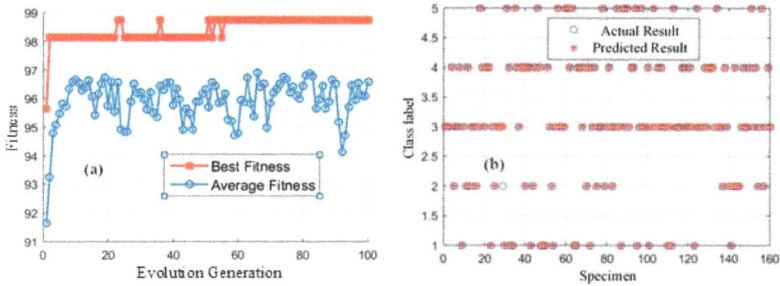

Figure 8. GA-optimized PCA-SVM for aging stage assessment of oil-paper insulation: (**a**) The fitness curve of seeking the best C and γ by GA; (**b**) Classification results of the training samples.

3.3. Testing for the Established Diagnostic Method

In order to test the diagnostic capability and universality of the established algorithm, 105 testing samples with another weight ratio of oil and paper were accelerated for aging at 130 °C. The samples were prepared and aged following the procedure mentioned before. Every 15 samples were taken out from the aging ovens at aging times of zero, three, 11, 20, 30, 38 and 70 days. The average DP of the oil-impregnated papers at each aging time was measured. Although detecting results for the DPs of samples in same aging time may fluctuate a lot, the seven groups of samples were divided into five aging stages according to the average DP of each group. The classification result was shown in Figure 9a; there are 30, 15, 30, 15, 15 samples in each class.

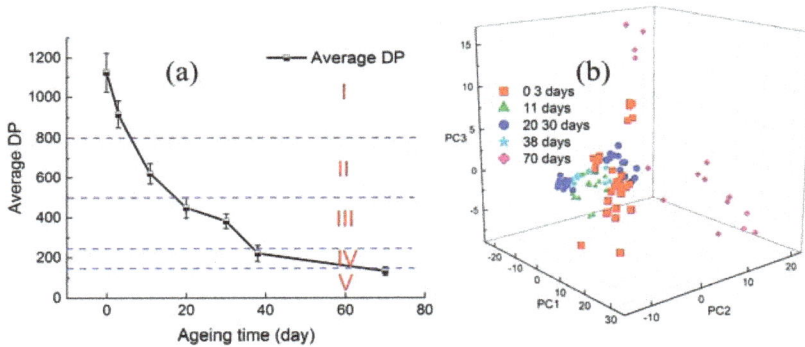

Figure 9. Classification results of testing samples: (**a**) Relationship between DP and aging time; (**b**) Scatter plots of the PC scores for five classes of oil samples, with the PC scores derived from the Raman spectra.

The Raman spectrum of every oil sample was detected using the same experimental procedure. Firstly, each raw Raman spectrum was pre-treated by smoothing and baseline correction. Then, the dimension was reduced to 12 features by using the same transfer matrix obtained and used for the training samples in the PCA process. Figure 9b demonstrated the first three PCs of the 105 samples; it indicated that the testing samples, especially the middle three classes, were more confusing than the training samples. However, the fresh condition and serious aging still had high identification. Finally, the processed spectral data set was recognized by our multi-classification SVM trained by the 160 training samples mentioned before. Table 2 shows the testing diagnosis results by the established algorithm.

Table 2. Results of the testing experiment using GA-SVM.

Aging Time (Day)	Average DP	True Class	Predicted Class					Accuracy
			I	II	III	IV	V	
0	1124	I	14	0	1	0	0	93.3%
3	916	I	12	1	1	1	0	80.0%
11	621	II	2	9	2	1	1	60.0%
20	449	III	1	3	10	1	0	66.7%
30	382	III	0	1	12	0	2	80.0%
38	221	IV	1	1	3	8	2	53.3%
70	132	V	0	0	1	2	12	80.0%

The results of the testing experiment were evaluated by the classification result of the average DP, which showed a decrease in the accuracy of the data set (73.3%). Results of the DP measurement indicated that the aging stages of the tested samples were more confusing than those of the training samples. The aging stage of some individual samples (e.g., samples aged for 20, 30 and 38 days) between two adjacent aging times was hardly identified even though the two groups had a clear difference in average DP. Furthermore, the errors in the DP measurement and spectral detection also had an impact on the accuracy of the testing experiment.

4. Discussion

Given that the oil-paper insulation aging process is part of a widely accepted multistep, continuum progression cascade from fresh insulation oil to insulation deterioration, the component and content distinction of insulation oils at each aging stage is vague, rendering the characterization and discrimination of these oils by Raman spectral analysis more challenging. The Raman spectral pattern between oil samples at each aging stage could be very similar. For these reasons, accurately classified training samples should be obtained to develop a robust diagnostic algorithm. In this study, the training samples were classified by clustering analysis and defined by the widely accepted gold standard for assessing the transformer aging stage, i.e., the DP of the papers aged together with oil.

However, this study did not focus on any specific characteristic products of oil-paper insulation aging for the following reasons: (1) The concentration of furfural in oil will fluctuate with a change in the operating temperature of a transformer; (2) Different weight ratio of oil and paper in a transformer will lead to different furfural content detection results for equipment at the same aging stage; (3) Even if gases are detected accurately, the employment of the most used methods (e.g., Rogers, International Electrotechnical Commission (IEC)ratio and Duval triangle) for DGA data may yield a certain percentage of incorrect diagnoses, and their significance is also easily misinterpreted [6]. In a Raman fingerprint information analysis, the quantitative detection of the specific components of the sample is not required; only the contents of the chemical components and the proportion relationship in the form of a macroscopic spectral signal are needed. Thus, the problem resulting from the presence of numerous components in transformer oil and the difficulties in qualitative and quantitative analyses are mitigated.

Although this study has provided milestone contributions, further work may focus on the following aspects. Firstly, the in situ detection based on Raman technology has not yet realized a precise quantitative analysis for the aging characteristics of substances in mineral oil. With the development of Raman detecting technology, such as the use of surface-enhanced Raman spectroscopy, the difference between insulation oil in every aging stage may be highlighted, and may ultimately realize quantitative analysis for characteristics in oil. Secondly, all the materials in this study are provided by the same company, prepared in the same mode, and aged in the same environment, whereas real operating transformers have different materials, structures, aging environments, and other conditions. Thirdly, the related data processing method and classification algorithm can still be optimized to improve the accuracy of the diagnosis. In order to make this diagnostic method suitable for field application, a great deal of work is required to collect oil-paper samples from transformer substations, which is helpful for the growth of the diagnostic model.

5. Conclusions

In summary, for the purpose of using more information contained in the Raman spectra for spectral analysis, a multivariate statistical analysis using an entire spectrum to determine the most diagnostically significant spectral features was proposed. The training samples were divided into five classes by cluster analysis and defined as five aging stages according to the DP of the insulating paper. The final accuracy of multi-classification SVM is 99.37% by 10-fold cross-validation. Although the algorithm did not perform as expected in the final test, the accuracy can principally meet the demand of engineering applications. The diagnosis accuracy can be further improved by enhancing the detection technology, adopting a higher laser power, classifying training samples accurately, adopting surface enhanced Raman scattering (SERS) and optimizing the algorithm. Therefore, the CLRS method can provide a new mode for realizing a fast, non-destructive, and comprehensive assessment of the aging state of oil-paper insulation.

Acknowledgments: The authors are grateful for the financial support from the National "111" Project of the Ministry of Education of China (No. B08036) and the National Natural Science Foundation of China (No. 61605020).

Author Contributions: The research presented in this paper was a collaborative effort among all authors. Weigen Chen and Jingxin Zou conceived and designed the experiments; Jingxin Zou and Zhou Fan performed the experiments; Weigen Chen, Jingxin Zou and Fu Wan wrote the paper; Zhou Fan and Lingling Du discussed the results and revised the manuscript critically.

Conflicts of Interest: The authors declare no conflict of interest.

References

1. *Aging of Cellulose in Mineral-Oil Insulated Transformers*; Conseil International des Grands Réseaux Électriques (CIGRÉ): Paris, France, 2007.
2. *IEEE Guide for Loading Mineral Oil Immersed Transformers*; IEEE: New York, NY, USA, 1995.
3. Emsley, A.M. The kinetics and mechanisms of degradation of cellulosic insulation in power transformers. *Polym. Degrad. Stab.* **1994**, *44*, 343–349. [CrossRef]
4. Emsley, A.M.; Xiao, X.; Heywood, R.J.; Ali, M. Degradation of cellulosic insulation in power transformers. Part 2: Formation of furan products in insulating oil. *IEE Proc. Sci. Meas. Technol.* **2000**, *147*, 110–114. [CrossRef]
5. Emsley, A.M.; Xiao, X.; Heywood, R.J.; Ali, M. Degradation of cellulosic insulation in power transformers. Part 3: Effects of oxygen and water on aging in oil. *IEE Proc. Sci. Meas. Technol.* **2000**, *147*, 115–119. [CrossRef]
6. N'cho, J.S.; Fofana, I.; Hadjadj, Y.; Beroual, A. Review of physicochemical-based diagnostic techniques for assessing insulation condition in aged transformers. *Energies* **2016**, *9*, 367. [CrossRef]
7. Shroff, D.H.; Stannett, A.W. A review of paper aging in power transformers. *IEE Proc. C Gener. Transm. Distrib.* **1985**, *132*, 312–319. [CrossRef]
8. Scheirs, J.; Camino, G.; Avidano, M.; Tumiatti, W. Origin of furanic compounds in thermal degradation of cellulosic insulating paper. *J. Appl. Polym. Sci.* **1998**, *69*, 2541–2547.
9. Morais, R.M.; Mannheimer, W.A.; Carballeira, M.; Noualhaguet, J.C. Furfural analysis for assessing degradation of thermally upgraded papers in transformer insulation. *IEEE Trans. Dielectr. Electr. Insul.* **1999**, *6*, 159–163. [CrossRef]
10. Höhlein, I.; Kachler, A.J. Aging of cellulose at transformer service temperatures. Part 2. Influence of moisture and temperature on degree of polymerization and formation of furanic compounds in free-breathing systems. *IEEE Electr. Insul. Mag.* **2005**, *21*, 20–24. [CrossRef]
11. Okabe, S.; Ueta, G.; Tsuboi, T. Investigation of aging degradation status of insulating elements in oil-immersed transformer and its diagnostic method based on field measurement data. *IEEE Trans. Dielectr. Electr. Insul.* **2013**, *20*, 346–355. [CrossRef]

12. Bruzzoniti, M.C.; Maina, R.; De Carlo, R.M.; Sarzanini, C.; Tumiatti, V. GC methods for the determination of methanol and ethanol in insulating mineral oils as markers of cellulose degradation in power transformers. *Chromatographia* **2014**, *77*, 1081–1089. [CrossRef]

13. Ren, M.; Dong, M.; Liu, J. Statistical analysis of partial discharges in SF6 gas via optical detection in various spectral ranges. *Energies* **2016**, *9*, 152. [CrossRef]

14. DuBois, M.; Gilles, K.A.; Hamilton, J.K.; Rebers, P.A.; Smith, F. Colorimetric method for determination of sugars and related substances. *Anal. Chem.* **1956**, *28*, 350–356. [CrossRef]

15. Zheng, Y.; Sun, C.; Li, J.; Yang, Q.; Chen, W. Entropy-based bagging for fault prediction of transformers using oil-dissolved gas data. *Energies* **2011**, *4*, 1138–1147. [CrossRef]

16. Xiang, C.; Zhou, Q.; Li, J.; Huang, Q.; Song, H.; Zhang, Z. Comparison of dissolved gases in mineral and vegetable insulating oils under typical electrical and thermal faults. *Energies* **2016**, *9*, 312. [CrossRef]

17. *Guide to the Interpretation of Dissolved and Free Gases Analysis*; IEC Publication: Geneva, Switzerland, 2007.

18. Shintemirov, A.; Tang, W.; Wu, Q.H. Power transformer fault classification based on dissolved gas analysis by implementing bootstrap and genetic programming. *IEEE Trans. Syst. Man Cybern. Part C* **2009**, *39*, 69–79. [CrossRef]

19. Su, Q.; Mi, C.; Lai, L.L.; Austin, P. A fuzzy dissolved gas analysis method for the diagnosis of multiple incipient faults in a transformer. *IEEE Trans. Power Syst.* **2000**, *15*, 593–598. [CrossRef]

20. Kelly, J.J. Transformer fault diagnosis by dissolved-gas analysis. *IEEE Trans. Ind. Appl.* **1980**, *IA-16*, 777–782. [CrossRef]

21. Arakelian, V.G. The long way to the automatic chromatographic analysis of gases dissolved in insulating oil. *IEEE Electr. Insul. Mag.* **2004**, *20*, 8–25. [CrossRef]

22. Terry, S.C.; Jerman, J.H.; Angell, J.B. A gas chromatographic air analyzer fabricated on a silicon wafer. *IEEE Trans. Electron Devices* **1979**, *26*, 1880–1886. [CrossRef]

23. Bateni, A.; Erdem, E.; Repp, S.; Weber, S.; Somer, M. Al-doped MgB2 materials studied using electron paramagnetic resonance and Raman spectroscopy. *Appl. Phys. Lett.* **2016**, *108*, 202601. [CrossRef]

24. Schicks, J.M.; Spangenberg, E.; Giese, R.; Steinhauer, B.; Klump, J.; Luzi, M. New approaches for the production of hydrocarbons from hydrate bearing sediments. *Energies* **2011**, *4*, 151–172. [CrossRef]

25. Kiefer, J. Recent advances in the characterization of gaseous and liquid fuels by vibrational spectroscopy. *Energies* **2015**, *8*, 3165–3197. [CrossRef]

26. Kong, W.D.; Wu, S.F.; Richard, P.; Lian, C.S.; Wang, J.T.; Yang, C.L.; Shi, Y.G.; Ding, H. Raman scattering investigation of large positive magnetoresistance material WTe2. *Appl. Phys. Lett.* **2015**, *106*, 081906. [CrossRef]

27. Teh, S.K.; Zheng, W.; Ho, K.Y.; Teh, M.; Yeoh, K.G.; Huang, Z. Diagnostic potential of near-infrared Raman spectroscopy in the stomach: Differentiating dysplasia from normal tissue. *Br. J. Cancer* **2008**, *98*, 457–465. [CrossRef] [PubMed]

28. Somekawa, T.; Fujita, M.; Izawa, Y.; Kasaoka, M.; Nagano, Y. Furfural analysis in transformer oils using laser raman spectroscopy. *IEEE Trans. Dielectr. Electr. Insul.* **2015**, *22*, 229–231. [CrossRef]

29. Li, X.Y.; Xia, Y.X.; Huang, J.M.; Zhan, L. A Raman system for multi-gas-species analysis in power transformer. *Appl. Phys. B* **2008**, *93*, 665–669. [CrossRef]

30. Reinsch, C.H. Smoothing by spline functions. *Numer. Math.* **1967**, *10*, 177–183. [CrossRef]

31. Smith, R., Jr.; Price, J.; Howser, L. *A Smoothing Algorithm Using Cubic Spline Functions*; NASA-TN-D-7397; NASA: Washington, WA, USA, 1974.

32. Zhang, Z.-M.; Chen, S.; Liang, Y.-Z. Baseline correction using adaptive iteratively reweighted penalized least squares. *Analyst* **2010**, *135*, 1138–1146. [CrossRef] [PubMed]

33. Jiang, X.; Xia, Y.; Hu, J.; Zhang, Z.; Shu, L.; Sun, C. An S-transform and support vector machine (SVM)-based online method for diagnosing broken strands in transmission lines. *Energies* **2011**, *4*, 1278–1300. [CrossRef]

34. Lachenbruch, P.A.; Mickey, M.R. Estimation of error rates in discriminant analysis. *Technometrics* **1968**, *10*, 1–11. [CrossRef]

35. Devore, J.L. *Probability and Statistics for Engineering and the Sciences*; Cengage Learning: Boston, MA, USA, 2015.

36. Hsu, C.; Lin, C. A comparison of methods for multiclass support vector machines. *IEEE Trans. Neural Netw.* **2002**, *13*, 415–425. [PubMed]

37. Chen, W.; Gu, Z.; Zou, J.; Wan, F.; Xiang, Y. Analysis of furfural dissolved in transformer oil based on confocal laser Raman spectroscopy. *IEEE Trans. Dielect. Electr. Insul.* **2016**, *23*, 915–921. [CrossRef]

38. De Maesschalck, R.; Jouan-Rimbaud, D.; Massart, D.L.L. The Mahalanobis distance. *Chemom. Intell. Lab. Syst.* **2000**, *50*, 1–18. [CrossRef]

39. Saha, T.K. Review of modern diagnostic techniques for assessing insulation condition in aged transformers. *IEEE Trans. Dielect. Electr. Insul.* **2003**, *10*, 903–917. [CrossRef]

40. Van Bolhuis, J.P.; Gulski, E.; Smit, J.J. Monitoring and diagnostic of transformer solid insulation. *IEEE Trans. Power Deliv.* **2002**, *17*, 528–536. [CrossRef]

41. Huang, C.; Wang, C. A GA-based feature selection and parameters optimization for support vector machines. *Expert Syst. Appl.* **2006**, *31*, 231–240. [CrossRef]

42. Kohavi, R. A study of cross-validation and bootstrap for accuracy estimation and model selection. In Proceedings of the 14th International Joint Conference on Artificial intelligence, San Francisco, CA, USA, 20–25 August 1995; Volume 2, pp. 1137–1143.

![energies logo] *energies*

MDPI

Article

An Integrated Decision-Making Model for Transformer Condition Assessment Using Game Theory and Modified Evidence Combination Extended by D Numbers

Lingjie Sun [1,2], Yingyi Liu [1,*], Boyang Zhang [1], Yuwei Shang [3], Haiwen Yuan [1] and Zhao Ma [3]

[1]   School of Automation Science and Electrical Engineering, Beihang University, Beijing 100191, China;
      sunlingjie@buaa.edu.cn (L.S.); zbyang@buaa.edu.cn (B.Z.); yhw@buaa.edu.cn (H.Y.)
[2]   School of telecommunications, Taizhou Vocational & Technical College, Taizhou 318000, China
[3]   China Electric Power Research Institute, Beijing 100192, China;
      shangyuwei@epri.sgcc.com.cn (Y.S.); ma_zhao@hotmail.co.uk (Z.M.)
*   Correspondence: 09339@buaa.edu.cn; Tel.: +86-10-8231-6147

Academic Editor: Issouf Fofana
Received: 29 April 2016; Accepted: 18 August 2016; Published: 31 August 2016

Abstract: The power transformer is one of the most critical and expensive components for the stable operation of the power system. Hence, how to obtain the health condition of transformer is of great importance for power utilities. Multi-attribute decision-making (MADM), due to its ability of solving multi-source information problems, has become a quite effective tool to evaluate the health condition of transformers. Currently, the analytic hierarchy process (AHP) and Dempster–Shafer theory are two popular methods to solve MADM problems; however, these techniques rarely consider one-sidedness of the single weighting method and the exclusiveness hypothesis of the Dempster–Shafer theory. To overcome these limitations, this paper introduces a novel decision-making model, which integrates the merits of fuzzy set theory, game theory and modified evidence combination extended by D numbers, to evaluate the health condition of transformers. A four-level framework, which includes three factors and seventeen sub-factors, is put forward to facilitate the evaluation model. The model points out the following: First, the fuzzy set theory is employed to obtain the original basic probability assignments for all indices. Second, the subjective and objective weights of indices, which are calculated by fuzzy AHP and entropy weight, respectively, are integrated to generate the comprehensive weights based on game theory. Finally, based on the above two steps, the modified evidence combination extended by D numbers, which avoids the limitation of the exclusiveness hypothesis in the application of Dempster–Shafer theory, is proposed to obtain the final assessment results of transformers. Case studies are given to demonstrate the proposed modeling process. The results show the effectiveness and engineering practicability of the model in transformer condition assessment.

Keywords: power transformer; multi-attribute decision-making (MADM); game theory; fuzzy analytic hierarchy process (AHP); D numbers

---

1. Introduction

As a key piece of equipment in power systems, the power transformer comprises up to 60% of the total investment in substations and affects the safety and stability of power supply [1,2]. With the rapid expansion of the power system network, sudden failures of transformers will affect the security of life and property more seriously than before [3]. Therefore, grasping the health condition of transformers accurately is of significant importance, which involves transformers' operation and maintenance [4]. Health diagnosis methods provide feasibility for changing the maintenance strategy and, accordingly, maximizing the practicable operating efficiency and optimum life, while minimizing the risk of premature failure [5,6].

In past years, many techniques, such as neural network [7], support vector machine [8] and fuzzy logic [9], were applied to transformer fault diagnosis. These approaches usually focused on a single factor (e.g., DGA analysis, thermal modeling, winding fault analysis, etc.). Results indicated that these research works could evaluate the transformer fault condition effectively to a certain extent. Nevertheless, these attempts were not sufficient to obtain an overall and precise health condition of the transformers [5,6]. They usually gave a qualitative description of transformers whether in good or bad condition. In fact, the transformer health condition is affected by many factors, which reflect its condition from different aspects, degrees and levels. The health condition of power transformers is often somewhere between good and bad. For example, some indices may have deviated from their permissible thresholds, but the overall condition is still acceptable. On the other hand, some indices may be below the thresholds, but the overall condition is bad, since timely maintenance is required. Therefore, it is difficult for power utilities to obtain accurate evaluation results due to varied information sources from transformers, which can be regarded as an MADM problem [5,6].

To address such MADM problems, some researchers have attempted to integrate the merits of AHP and evidence theory to evaluate the electric primary devices including diverse condition information [5,10]. The AHP method, established by Satty, which has been successfully employed under many actual decision-making situations [11–14], is a popular approach for determining the weights of alternatives in MADM problems involving qualitative data [15,16]. In addition, the Dempster–Shafer theory (also called evidence theory), initially presented by Dempster [17] and then developed by Shafer [18], is applied to handle the uncertain information in MADM problems [5,6]. The kernel of evidence theory is the combination rule, which can be adopted to obtain an evaluation result considering various kinds of condition information [19].

However, these previous studies are still one-sided and unsystematic because of several challenges or drawbacks remaining.

- For the classical AHP approach, the scale of pair-wise comparison judgment, derived from experts, is confined to crisp numbers [20]. However, in many practical applications, such as condition assessment of transformers, expert objective predilection may be fuzzy [21], and the experts may not be willing to provide exact values for pair comparisons [22].
- For the calculation of weights, determining a suitable weight is a very important step in the decision process. However, both objective and subjective weight have limitations. The objective weight neglects the decision maker's knowledge and actual situation. On the contrary, the subjective weight is heavily influenced by expert experiences and prejudices, resulting in high subjectivity [23].
- For the traditional evidence theory, it is strongly confined to the definition of exclusiveness hypothesis and the completeness constraint [24]. Therefore, this limits the actual application of evidence theory, especially the application in the health condition assessment of transformers, including five intersection grades (health, sub-health, minor defect, major defect and critical defect) based on human judgment [25,26]. Unfortunately, little attention has been paid to the rigorous mathematical definition of evidence theory.

To effectively overcome these shortcomings of existing methods, several techniques, such as fuzzy extended AHP, game theory and D numbers, have been developed. The fuzzy extended AHP, extending the classical AHP by using a triangular fuzzy number [27], has become an outstandingly effective tool to determine the weights of evaluation criteria in an actual complex system. Recently, it has been successfully applied in many fields, like green product designs [28], ship selection [29] and teaching performance evaluation [30]. Game theory, a strategic bargaining behavior [31], has been developed and employed for various fields from economics to engineering [32]. It can play a better role when it comes to dealing with the conflicts among two or more participants [23]. Similarly, subjective and objective weight can be considered as two participants of a game, and the comprehensive weight is the result of the 'weight' game [23]. D numbers, a novel theory initially proposed by Deng [24], has become a powerful method to deal with the uncertainty in actual engineering applications due to its capacity of avoiding the mutually-exclusive hypothesis of the frame of discernment [25,26,33,34].

Herein, a novel MADM model, which integrates the merits of fuzzy set theory, game theory and modified evidence combination extended by D numbers, is adopted to evaluate the health condition of transformers in this paper. Three factors, (i) dissolved gas analysis (DGA) date; (ii) electrical testing; (iii) oil testing and seventeen sub-indices are involved in the evaluate framework. The followings have been investigated in this paper: (i) adopting the fuzzy set theory to generate the original basic probability assignments for all indices; (ii) applying the game theory to obtain a comprehensive weight based on the subjective and objective weight, which are calculated by fuzzy extended AHP and the entropy weight, respectively; (iii) employing the distance of D numbers to modify original basic probability assignments and obtain final assessment results for transformers. The proposed model is verified by evaluating a realistic transformer and compared to a typical method. The results indicate that the model can evaluate the transformer health condition effectively.

This paper unfolds in the following fashion. Section 2 presents the framework for transformer condition assessment. Section 3 demonstrates the detailed procedures of the condition assessment model, including the fuzzy set theory, game theory and modified evidence combination extended by D numbers. Section 4 takes two cases for example to show the efficiency of the model, and final conclusions are illustrated in Section 5.

2. Framework for Transformer Condition Assessment

During the whole service period of the power transformer, various subsystems of the power transformer are aging gradually. Although the health condition of the power transformer cannot be observed directly, it can be reflected by all kinds of condition information [5,6]. Thus, diverse evaluation indices are acquired to evaluate the health condition of the transformer, which is regarded as an MADM problem. The selected evaluation indices should be typical and reasonable, so as to the reflect health condition of the transformer. Based on the aging mechanisms and fault properties of the transformer, three factors, DGA data, electrical testing and oil testing, are chosen in the evaluation framework.

The evaluation framework, a four-layer structure, is established as shown in Figure 1. Level 1, the objective level, represents the final condition evaluation result of the power transformer. Level 2, the factor level, describes the condition information of the transformer from three aspects. Level 3, the sub-factors' level, involves corresponding indices' information. For example, $f_1 = \{f_{11}, f_{12}, f_{13}, f_{14}, f_{15}\}$ represents the DGA data with five indices. Level 4, the assessment result level, indicates the evaluation grades of each index.

Based on previous research [6,21] and experts' experiences, the evaluation grades, relating to maintenance purposes, can be divided into five grades (health, sub-health, minor defect, major defect and critical defect) and are given by:

$$H = \{H_1, H_2, H_3, H_4, H_5\}$$
$$= \{health, sub - health, minor\ defect, major\ defect, critical\ defect\} \qquad (1)$$

The relationship between the assessment grades and maintenance strategy is described in Table 1.

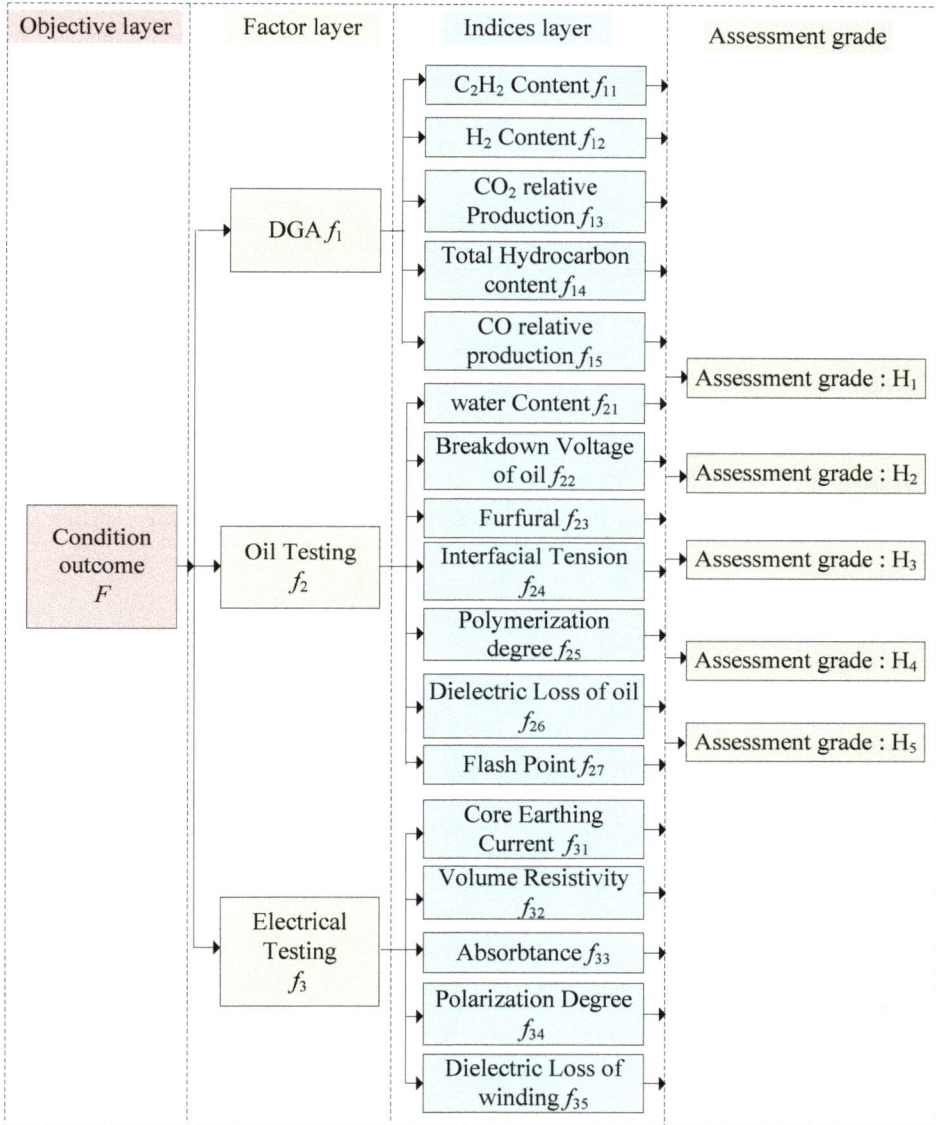

Figure 1. Condition information framework of the power transformer.

Table 1. Assessment grades' relation to the maintenance.

Grade	Condition Description	Maintenance Schedule
Health	Each property reaches the standard level, with a sufficient margin for all of the corresponding critical characteristic quantities and a strong ability to resist risks and adapt to the environment.	One may properly delay the maintenance schedule.
Sub-health	All of the properties can reach the standard level, but some of the critical characteristic quantities' values are close to the standard limit values. Additionally, the ability to resist risks and adapt to the environment declines.	Conduct maintenance as originally planned. Pay attention to the parts that are close to standard limit values of the characteristic quantities.
Minor defect	Some of the critical characteristic quantities are out of limit, but the comprehensive influence is small. There appear slight defects of the ability to resist risks and adapt to the environment.	Arrange to carry out the maintenance schedule in advance; intensify tour inspection, operation monitoring, on-ling inspection, etc.
Major defect	There appears serious degeneration of some properties, and corresponding critical characteristic quantities are out of the limit. The comprehensive influence is large, and there exist obvious defects of the ability to resist risks and adapt to the environment.	Timely arrange to carry out the maintenance schedule; intensify tour inspection, operation monitoring, on-ling inspection, etc. The defect elimination time is recommended to not exceed one week.
Critical defect	The transformer cannot normally carry out the regulated functions, but its functions can be recovered after overhaul.	Promptly arrange maintenance, and the defect elimination time is recommended to not exceed 24 h.

3. Methodology

A novel hybrid MADM model, which integrates the merits of fuzzy set theory, game theory and modified evidence combination extended by D numbers, has been proposed in this paper. The assessment process consists of three key steps. First, the original basic probability assignments for all indices are obtained by the fuzzy set theory. Second, based on game theory, the subjective and objective weights of indices, which are calculated by fuzzy AHP and the entropy weight, respectively, are integrated to generate the comprehensive weights. Third, the modified evidence combination extended by D numbers is proposed to obtain the final assessing result.

3.1. Fuzzy Set Theory

Due to different dimensions or magnitudes, various indices need to be first normalized so as to obtain the membership grades for quantitative indices. Let x_{ij} be the j-th index of the i-th factor, and the normalization mapping $x_{ij} : f \rightarrow [0,1]$ is given as follows [6].

If the indices are benefit attributes, the standardization process is:

$$\gamma_{ij} = \frac{x_{ij} - \min\left(x_{ij}\right)}{\max\left(x_{ij}\right) - \min\left(x_{ij}\right)} \tag{2}$$

If the indices are cost attributes, the standardization process is:

$$\gamma_{ij} = \frac{\max\left(x_{ij}\right) - x_{ij}}{\max\left(x_{ij}\right) - \min\left(x_{ij}\right)} \tag{3}$$

where γ_{ij} is the standardized value.

The membership function is adopted widely in the condition assessment of electrical equipment. Nonetheless, there is no unified standard within fuzzy theory for constructing suitable membership functions [10]. Recently, a trapezoidal membership function is usually employed in the health diagnosis of transformers [35,36], and the trapezoidal model is also in accordance with the health condition of transformers [21]. Hence, the trapezoidal model is adopted to obtain the assessing grades in this paper. The design of the membership function is shown in Figure 2 [21] and can be described as follows.

$$
\begin{cases}
f_r\left(x_{ij}\right) = \dfrac{\left(Z_{r+1}-x_{ij}\right)}{\left(Z_{r+1}-Z_r\right)} & r = 1,3,5,7 \\
f_r\left(x_{ij}\right) = \dfrac{\left(x_{ij}-Z_{r-1}\right)}{\left(Z_r-Z_{r-1}\right)} & r = 2,4,6,8
\end{cases}
\tag{4}
$$

$$
\begin{cases}
\mu_1\left(x_{ij}\right) = \begin{cases} 1 & x_{ij} \leq Z_1 \\ f_1\left(x_{ij}\right) & Z_1 \leq x_{ij} \leq Z_2 \\ 0 & x_{ij} > Z_2 \end{cases} \\[2ex]
\mu_2\left(x_{ij}\right) = \begin{cases} f_2\left(x_{ij}\right) & Z_1 \leq x_{ij} \leq Z_2 \\ 1 & Z_2 \leq x_{ij} \leq Z_3 \\ f_3\left(x_{ij}\right) & Z_3 < x_{ij} < Z_4 \end{cases} \\[2ex]
\mu_3\left(x_{ij}\right) = \begin{cases} f_4\left(x_{ij}\right) & Z_3 < x_{ij} < Z_4 \\ 1 & Z_4 \leq x_{ij} \leq Z_5 \\ f_5\left(x_{ij}\right) & Z_5 < x_{ij} < Z_6 \end{cases} \\[2ex]
\mu_4\left(x_{ij}\right) = \begin{cases} f_6\left(x_{ij}\right) & Z_5 < x_{ij} < Z_6 \\ 1 & Z_6 \leq x_{ij} \leq Z_7 \\ f_7\left(x_{ij}\right) & Z_7 \leq x_{ij} \leq Z_8 \end{cases} \\[2ex]
\mu_5\left(x_{ij}\right) = \begin{cases} 0 & x_{ij} \leq Z_7 \\ f_8\left(x_{ij}\right) & Z_7 \leq x_{ij} \leq Z_8 \\ 1 & x_{ij} \geq Z_8 \end{cases}
\end{cases}
\tag{5}
$$

After extensive field testing and validations, the interval values are given as: $Z_1 = 0.05$, $Z_2 = 0.25$, $Z_3 = 0.3$, $Z_4 = 0.45$, $Z_5 = 0.5$, $Z_6 = 0.75$, $Z_7 = 0.8$, $Z_8 = 0.95$, respectively.

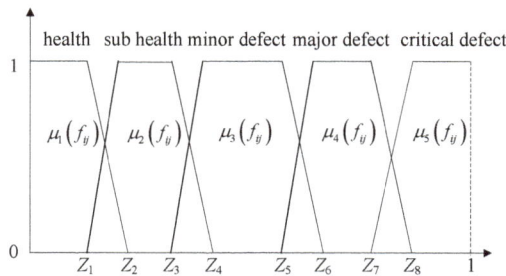

Figure 2. Membership function for the condition evaluation of indices.

By using Equations (2)–(5), the fuzzy membership matrix is then:

$$
Y_i\left(H\right) = \begin{bmatrix}
\mu_1\left(x_{i1}\right) & \mu_2\left(x_{i1}\right) & \cdots & \mu_5\left(x_{i1}\right) \\
\mu_1\left(x_{i2}\right) & \mu_2\left(x_{i2}\right) & \cdots & \mu_5\left(x_{i2}\right) \\
\vdots & \vdots & \vdots & \vdots \\
\mu_1\left(x_{im}\right) & \mu_2\left(x_{im}\right) & \cdots & \mu_5\left(x_{im}\right)
\end{bmatrix}
\tag{6}
$$

where $Y_i(H)$ stands for the index membership matrix of the evaluation level of the i-th factor.

3.2. Comprehensive Weights Based on Game Theory

3.2.1. Fuzzy Extended AHP

Several fuzzy AHP methods have been developed to determine the weights of alternatives [37]. Among these methods, the fuzzy extended AHP, proposed by Chang [27], is employed widely in different application areas due to its lower computation complexity than the other methods [30]. In this paper, the fuzzy extended AHP is adopted to calculate the weights of alternatives based on experts' opinions.

Since the hierarchical structure is constructed, the triangular fuzzy comparison matrix [27], based on expert judgments, is given by:

$$A = \left(a_{ij}\right)_{n \times n} = \begin{bmatrix} (1,1,1) & (l_{12}, m_{12}, u_{12}) & \cdots & (l_{1n}, m_{1n}, u_{1n}) \\ (l_{21}, m_{21}, u_{21}) & (1,1,1) & \cdots & (l_{2n}, m_{2n}, u_{2n}) \\ \vdots & \vdots & \vdots & \vdots \\ (l_{n1}, m_{n1}, u_{n1}) & (l_{n2}, m_{n2}, u_{n2}) & \cdots & (1,1,1) \end{bmatrix} \tag{7}$$

where:

$$a_{ij} = \left(l_{ij}, m_{ij}, u_{ij}\right), \quad a_{ij}^{-1} = \left(l_{ij}, m_{ij}, u_{ij}\right)^{-1} = \left(\tfrac{1}{u_{ij}}, \tfrac{1}{m_{ij}}, \tfrac{1}{l_{ij}}\right)$$
$$i, j = 1, \cdots, n \text{ and } i \neq j$$

The triangular fuzzy numbers and corresponding linguistic description are illustrated in Table 2. The linguistic description should be converted into fuzzy scales, which aims to be convenient for mathematical operation. The steps of fuzzy extended AHP are demonstrated as follows [27].

Table 2. Scale values of triangular fuzzy numbers.

Triangular Fuzzy Numbers	Linguistic Description
$(1, 1, 1)$	Equally important
$(2, 3, 4)$	Moderately important
$(4, 5, 6)$	Fairly important
$(6, 7, 8)$	Strongly important
$(9, 9, 9)$	Absolutely important
$(1, 2, 3)\ (3, 4, 5)\ (5, 6, 7)\ (7, 8, 9)$	Intermediate preference values

Step 1: Sum up each row of the fuzzy comparison matrix A, then normalize the row sums. The fuzzy synthetic extent values of the i-th object are:

$$S_i = \frac{RS_i}{\sum\limits_{j=1}^{n} RS_j} = \frac{\sum\limits_{j=1}^{n} a_{ij}}{\sum\limits_{k=1}^{n}\sum\limits_{j=1}^{n} a_{kj}} = \left[\frac{\sum\limits_{j=1}^{n} l_{ij}}{\sum\limits_{k=1}^{n}\sum\limits_{j=1}^{n} u_{kj}}, \frac{\sum\limits_{j=1}^{n} m_{ij}}{\sum\limits_{k=1}^{n}\sum\limits_{j=1}^{n} m_{kj}}, \frac{\sum\limits_{j=1}^{n} u_{ij}}{\sum\limits_{k=1}^{n}\sum\limits_{j=1}^{n} l_{kj}} \right], i = 1, 2, \cdots, n \tag{8}$$

Step 2: Compare the degree of possibility $(S_i \geq S_j)$. Thus:

$$V(S_1 \geq S_2) = 1 \quad iff \ m_1 \geq m_2$$
$$V(S_2 \geq S_1) = hgt(S_1 \cap S_2) = \mu_{S_1}(d) = \frac{l_1 - u_2}{(m_2 - u_2) - (m_1 - l_1)} \tag{9}$$

where $S_1 = (l_1, m_1, u_1)$, $S_2 = (l_2, m_2, u_2)$ and d is the intersection point between μ_{S_1} and μ_{S_2} (Figure 3).

Step 3: Compute the minimum degree of possibility. We have:

$$V(S_i \geq S_j | j = 1, \cdots, n; j \neq i) = \min_{j \in \{1, \cdots, n\} j \neq i} V(S_i \geq S_j), i = 1, \cdots, n \tag{10}$$

Assume that:

$$d(A_i) = \min_{j \in \{1, \cdots, n\} j \neq i} V(S_i \geq S_j), \ i = 1, \cdots, n \tag{11}$$

Then, the weight vector is:

$$\mathbf{W}' = (d(A_1), d(A_2), \cdots, d(A_n))^T \tag{12}$$

where A_i $(i = 1, 2, \ldots, n)$ are n design alternatives.

Step 4: Normalize the weight vectors. The final weight vector is given by:

$$\mathbf{W} = (W_1, W_2, \ldots, W_n) \tag{13}$$

where $W_1, W_2, \ldots, W_n$ are non-fuzzy numbers.

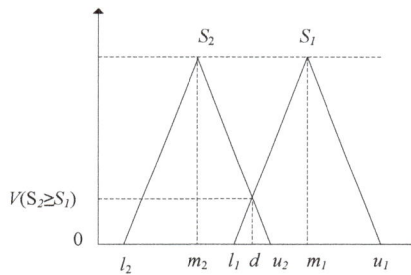

Figure 3. The degree of possibility $V(S_2 \geq S_1)$.

3.2.2. Entropy Weight

The information entropy theory was first set forth from thermodynamics to information systems by Shannon [38]. Based on the information entropy theory, the entropy weight can reflect the useful quantitative information of evaluation indices [39]. Assume that there are m evaluation objects and n indices for decision-making problems. The procedures are demonstrated as follows [40].

Step 1: Calculation of the entropy. Information entropy of index j is:

$$f_{ij} = \frac{\gamma_{ij}}{\sum\limits_{j=1}^{m} \gamma_{ij}}$$
$$H_j = -(\ln m)^{-1} \sum\limits_{j=1}^{m} f_{ij} \ln f_{ij} \tag{14}$$

where γ_{ij} is the normalization value of the quantitative index.

Step 2: Acquisition of the weight. The weight acquired from information entropy is:

$$\omega_{oj} = \frac{(1 - H_j)}{\left(n - \sum\limits_{j=1}^{m} H_j\right)} \tag{15}$$

where $0 \leq \omega_{oj} \leq 1$, $\sum\limits_{j=1}^{n} \omega_{oj} = 1$.

3.2.3. Game Theory

As discussed previously, there are certain limitations to consider a single weighting method under many situations. The objective weight neglects the decision-maker's knowledge and actual situation. On the contrary, the subjective weight is heavily influenced by expert experiences and some prejudices, resulting in high subjectivity. Therefore, the comprehensive weight, combining the subjective and objective weight with an effective algorithm, is more reasonable in the decision-making process.

Game theory, the research of strategic interaction, is an important branch of modern mathematics. Specifically, game theory is adopted to obtain the optimum equilibrium solution among two or more conflicts. In game theory, a decision is made either individually or collectively. Additionally, the decision can maximize the utility payoffs out of participants' expectations. Thus, a decision of either a consensus or compromise is suggested. Analogously, the comprehensive weight, which reaches a compromise between the subjective weight and the objective weight, can be regarded as an optimum equilibrium solution. The calculation steps of comprehensive weight based on game theory are described as below [23].

Step 1: Generate m weights using m kinds of weighting approaches. Then, establish a basic weight vector set $\mathbf{w} = \{\mathbf{w_1}, \mathbf{w_2}, \cdots, \mathbf{w_m}\}$. Thus, a possible weight set is formed by m vectors with the form of an arbitrary linear combination, expressed as:

$$\mathbf{W} = \sum_{j=1}^{m} \alpha_j \mathbf{w}_j^{\mathsf{T}} \ (\alpha_j > 0) \tag{16}$$

where $\mathbf{w}$ is a possible weight vector in set $\mathbf{W}$ and α_j is the weight coefficient.

Step 2: Calculate the optimum equilibrium weight vector $\mathbf{w}^*$ of the possible weight vector sets based on game theory, indicating that a consensus is reached among m weights. Such a consensus can be taken as the optimization of the weight coefficient α_j, which is a linear combination. The purpose of the optimization is to minimize the deviation between $\mathbf{w}$ and $\mathbf{w_j}$ using the following formula.

$$\min \left\| \sum_{k=1}^{n} \alpha_k \times \mathbf{w}_k^{\mathsf{T}} - \mathbf{w}_i^{\mathsf{T}} \right\|_2 \ (i = 1, 2, \cdots, n) \tag{17}$$

Based on the differentiation property of the matrix, the condition of the optimal first-order derivative in Equation (17) is determined as:

$$\sum_{k=1}^{n} \alpha_k \times \mathbf{w}_i \times \mathbf{w}_k^{\mathsf{T}} = \mathbf{w}_i \times \mathbf{w}_i^{\mathsf{T}} \ (i = 1, 2, \cdots, n) \tag{18}$$

Then, we have:

$$\begin{bmatrix} \mathbf{w_1} \cdot \mathbf{w}_1^{\mathsf{T}} & \mathbf{w_1} \cdot \mathbf{w}_2^{\mathsf{T}} & \cdots & \mathbf{w_1} \cdot \mathbf{w}_n^{\mathsf{T}} \\ \mathbf{w_2} \cdot \mathbf{w}_1^{\mathsf{T}} & \mathbf{w_2} \cdot \mathbf{w}_2^{\mathsf{T}} & \cdots & \mathbf{w_2} \cdot \mathbf{w}_n^{\mathsf{T}} \\ \vdots & \vdots & \vdots & \vdots \\ \mathbf{w_n} \cdot \mathbf{w}_1^{\mathsf{T}} & \mathbf{w_n} \cdot \mathbf{w}_2^{\mathsf{T}} & \cdots & \mathbf{w_n} \cdot \mathbf{w}_n^{\mathsf{T}} \end{bmatrix} \begin{bmatrix} \alpha_1 \\ \alpha_2 \\ \vdots \\ \alpha_n \end{bmatrix} = \begin{bmatrix} \mathbf{w_1} \cdot \mathbf{w}_1^{\mathsf{T}} \\ \mathbf{w_2} \cdot \mathbf{w}_2^{\mathsf{T}} \\ \vdots \\ \mathbf{w_n} \cdot \mathbf{w}_n^{\mathsf{T}} \end{bmatrix} \tag{19}$$

Step 3: Compute the weight coefficient $(\alpha_1, \alpha_2, \cdots, \alpha_n)$ by using Equation (19), then normalize them using the following equation.

$$\alpha_j^* = \alpha_j / \sum_{j=1}^{n} \alpha_j \tag{20}$$

Step 4: Obtain the final comprehensive weight with the following formula:

$$\mathbf{w}^* = \sum_{j=1}^{n} \alpha_j^* \cdot \mathbf{w}_j^{T} \tag{21}$$

3.3. Modified Evidence Combination Based on D Numbers

Although the evidence theory is widely applied to solve MADM problems, many issues are still unsolved in some situations. Among these problems, the definition of mutually-exclusive and conflict evidence have attracted more attention. Recently, two methods, D numbers and weighted average combination, are proposed by Deng et al. [24,41] to address the mentioned problems effectively. Inspired by the two methods, a modified evidence combination extended by D numbers is formulated as follows.

3.3.1. Dempster–Shafer Theory

Dempster–Shafer (D-S), also named evidence theory, is mainly introduced to solve the MADM problems with uncertainty. In the evidence theory, a sample set Θ that is collectively exhaustive and mutually exclusive, called a frame of discernment, is defined as [6]:

$$\Theta = (H_1, H_2, \cdots H_N) \tag{22}$$

The power set of Θ is described as 2^Θ, namely:

$$2^\Theta = \{\phi, \{H_1\}, \cdots, \{H_N\}, \{H_1, H_2\}, \cdots, \{H_1, H_2, \cdots, H_i\}, \cdots, \Theta\} \tag{23}$$

If $A \in 2^\Theta$, A is called a proposition. The combination rule is one of the most important performances in evidence theory. Suppose there are two pieces of evidence indicated by m_1 and m_2 on the same discernment framework Θ, and the combination rule is performed [6], with the following signs:

$$m(A) = \frac{1}{1-k} \sum_{A_1 \cap A_2 = A} m_1(A_1) m_2(A_2) \tag{24}$$

where:

$$k = \sum_{A_1 \cap A_2 = \Phi} m_1(A_1) m_2(A_2) \tag{25}$$

In (25), k is a conflict coefficient, which reflects the conflict degree between the two pieces of evidence $m_1(A_1)$ and $m_2(A_2)$.

3.3.2. D Numbers

As mentioned above, the frame of discernment is a strong hypothesis of being mutually exclusive. However, it is inevitable that linguistic assessments based on human judgment intersect each other, such as "health", "sub-health", "minor defect","major defect" and "critical defect". Therefore, it is not reasonable to apply D-S theory under such circumstances. To address this problem, a novel technique, D numbers, was proposed.

Let Θ be a finite nonempty set, and a D number is a mapping defined by [24,26]:

$$D : \Theta \rightarrow [0, 1] \tag{26}$$

with:

$$\sum_{A \subseteq \Theta} D(A) \leq 1 \quad \text{and} \quad D(\phi) = 0 \tag{27}$$

where ϕ is an empty set and A is a subset of Θ.

Since the frame of discernment does not need to be a mutually-exclusive set in D numbers theory, the five grades of transformer health condition from health to critical defect can be regarded as a frame of discernment of D numbers.

3.3.3. Distance between D Numbers

A relative matrix, explaining the relationship between each D number, is described as follows [26]. Let the number i and number j of m linguistic constants be expressed by M_i and M_j, the union region between M_i and M_j be U_{ij} and the intersection region between M_i and M_j be T_{ij}. The nonexclusive degree N_{ij} is expressed as below.

$$N_{ij} = \frac{T_{ij}}{U_{ij}} \tag{28}$$

The relative matrix is established as:

$$R = \begin{bmatrix} 1 & N_{12} & \cdots & N_{1i} & \cdots & N_{1n} \\ N_{21} & 1 & \cdots & N_{2i} & \cdots & N_{2n} \\ \vdots & \vdots & \vdots & \vdots & \vdots & \vdots \\ N_{i1} & N_{i2} & \cdots & 1 & \cdots & N_{in} \\ \vdots & \vdots & \vdots & \vdots & \vdots & \vdots \\ N_{n1} & N_{n2} & \cdots & N_{ni} & \cdots & 1 \end{bmatrix} \tag{29}$$

For instance, suppose m linguistic constants are shown in Figure 4. The non-exclusive degree N_{ij} is obtained to stand for the non-exclusive degree between two D numbers based on the region of union U_{ij} and intersection T_{ij} between M_i and M_j.

Then, an intersection degree of two subsets is described as below.

$$I(T_1, T_2) = \frac{\sum N_{ij}}{|T_1| \cdot |T_2|} \tag{30}$$

where $i \neq j, T_1, T_2 \in 2^\Theta$. In the relative matrix R, the variable i represents the row number of the first element of set T_1 and the variable j represents the column number of the first element of set T_2. $|T_1|$ shows the cardinality of T_1, and $|T_2|$ shows the cardinality of T_2. Note that when $i = j, I = 1$.

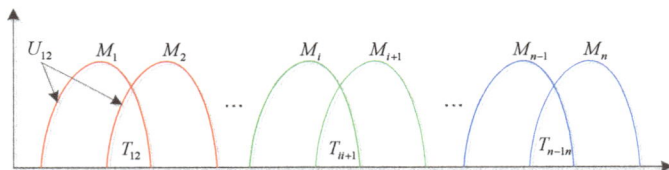

Figure 4. Example for linguistic constants.

Based on the above, the distance between two D numbers d_1 and d_2 is defined as:

$$d_{D-number(d_1, d_2)} = \sqrt{\frac{1}{2}\left(\overrightarrow{d_1} - \overrightarrow{d_2}\right)^T \underline{\underline{D}} \cdot \underline{\underline{I}} \left(\overrightarrow{d_1} - \overrightarrow{d_2}\right)} \tag{31}$$

where $\underline{\underline{D}}$ and $\underline{\underline{I}}$ are two $2^N \times 2^N$ matrices. Their elements are defined as:

$$\begin{aligned} \underline{\underline{D}}(A, B) &= \left|\frac{A \cap B}{A \cup B}\right|, \quad A, B \in 2^\Theta \\ \underline{\underline{I}}(A, B) &= \left|\frac{\sum E_{ij}}{|A| \cdot |B|}\right|, \quad A, B \in 2^\Theta (\text{when } i = j, I = 1) \end{aligned} \tag{32}$$

3.3.4. Modified Evidence Combination Based on D Numbers

After obtaining the distance of D numbers, we can construct a $n \times n$ matrix as:

$$
D = \begin{bmatrix}
0 & d_{12} & \cdots & d_{1j} & \cdots & d_{1n} \\
\vdots & \vdots & \vdots & \vdots & \vdots & \vdots \\
d_{i1} & d_{i2} & \cdots & d_{ij} & \cdots & d_{in} \\
\vdots & \vdots & \vdots & \vdots & \vdots & \vdots \\
d_{n1} & d_{n2} & \cdots & d_{nj} & \cdots & 0
\end{bmatrix}
\tag{33}
$$

Let $sim\left(m_i, m_j\right)$ be the similarity value between m_i and m_j, then the similarity value is given as [41]:

$$
Sim\left(m_i, m_j\right) = 1 - D\left(m_i, m_j\right)
\tag{34}
$$

It is obvious that the bigger the value of the distance is, the smaller the similarity of them will be, and vice versa. The similarity matrix is expressed as [41]:

$$
Sim = \begin{bmatrix}
1 & Sim_{12} & \cdots & Sim_{1j} & \cdots & Sim_{1n} \\
\vdots & \vdots & \vdots & \vdots & \vdots & \vdots \\
Sim_{i1} & Sim_{i2} & \cdots & Sim_{ij} & \cdots & Sim_{in} \\
\vdots & \vdots & \vdots & \vdots & \vdots & \vdots \\
Sim_{n1} & Sim_{n2} & \cdots & Sim_{nj} & \cdots & 1
\end{bmatrix}
\tag{35}
$$

The support degree of each evidence is illustrated as [41]:

$$
Sup\left(m_i\right) = \sum_{\substack{j=1 \\ j \neq i}}^{n} Sim\left(m_i, m_j\right)
\tag{36}
$$

To normalize $Sup\left(m_i\right)$, the objective weights of evidence are obtained as [41]:

$$
w\left(m_i\right) = \frac{Sup\left(m_i\right)}{\sum\limits_{i=1}^{n} Sup\left(m_i\right)}
\tag{37}
$$

where $\sum\limits_{i='}^{n} w\left(m_i\right) = 1$.

Considering the relative importance of different factors in the power transformer, the optimum equilibrium weights of evidence (three factors), by integrating the objective and subjective weights of evidence, are determined based on game theory, described as:

$$
w^* = w(m_i) \oplus w'\left(m_j\right)
\tag{38}
$$

where $w'\left(m_j\right)$ are the subjective weights of three factors (DGA date, electrical testing and oil testing).

After obtaining the optimum equilibrium weights of each piece of evidence, the new modified pieces of evidence are defined as [41]:

$$
MAE\left(m\right) = \sum_{i=1}^{n}\left(w^* \times m_i\right)
\tag{39}
$$

In this study, we take the modified pieces of evidence as independent of each other. If there are n pieces of evidence, we can apply the traditional Dempster–Shafer's combination rule to combine the new modified evidence $n - 1$ times.

3.4. Procedures for Transformer Condition Assessment

The detailed procedures of the novel multi-attribute decision-making model for transformer condition assessment are shown in Figure 5 and can be summarized as the following steps.

Step 1: Construct a framework of transformer condition assessment. Three factors and seventeen indices are involved in the assessment framework. The evaluation grades are divided into 5 grades (health, sub-health, minor defect, major defect, critical defect), defined by using Equation (1).

Step 2: Establish a fuzzy membership matrix. Due to the fact that various indices have different dimension values, a uniform standard, obtained by the fuzzy membership function, is needed in the assessment framework of the transformer. After determining the fuzzy membership function by using Equations (4) and (5), a fuzzy membership matrix for all of the indices is constructed in Equation (7).

Step 3: Calculate the subjective and the objective weight. The subjective weight is computed based on the fuzzy extended AHP by using Equations (8)–(14), and the objective weight is solved based on the entropy weight method by using Equations (15) and (16).

Step 4: Compute the comprehensive weight. As the subjective weight and objective weight are obtained, the comprehensive weight is generated based on the game theory by using Equations (17)–(22).

Step 5: Determine the original basic probability assignments. The original basic probability assignments are obtained through the additive weighting method, expressed as:

$$M_i(H) = \sum_{j=1}^{n} w_{ij} Y_i(H) \tag{40}$$

where $M_i(H)$ can be regarded as the original basic probability assignment of the i-th factor, $Y_i(H)$ stands for the index membership matrix of the evaluation level of the i-th factor and w_{ij} reflects the comprehensive weight of index f_{ij}.

Step 6: Combine the modified pieces of evidence to generate the evaluation results of the transformer health condition by using Equations (24) and (25).

Step 7: Judge the final evaluation results based on the decision-making rule. The decision rule is defined as [42]:

$$\begin{cases} M(H_1) = \max\{M(H_i), H_i \in \Theta\} \\ M(H_1) - M(H_2) > \varepsilon \end{cases} \tag{41}$$

where $\varepsilon = 0.04$.

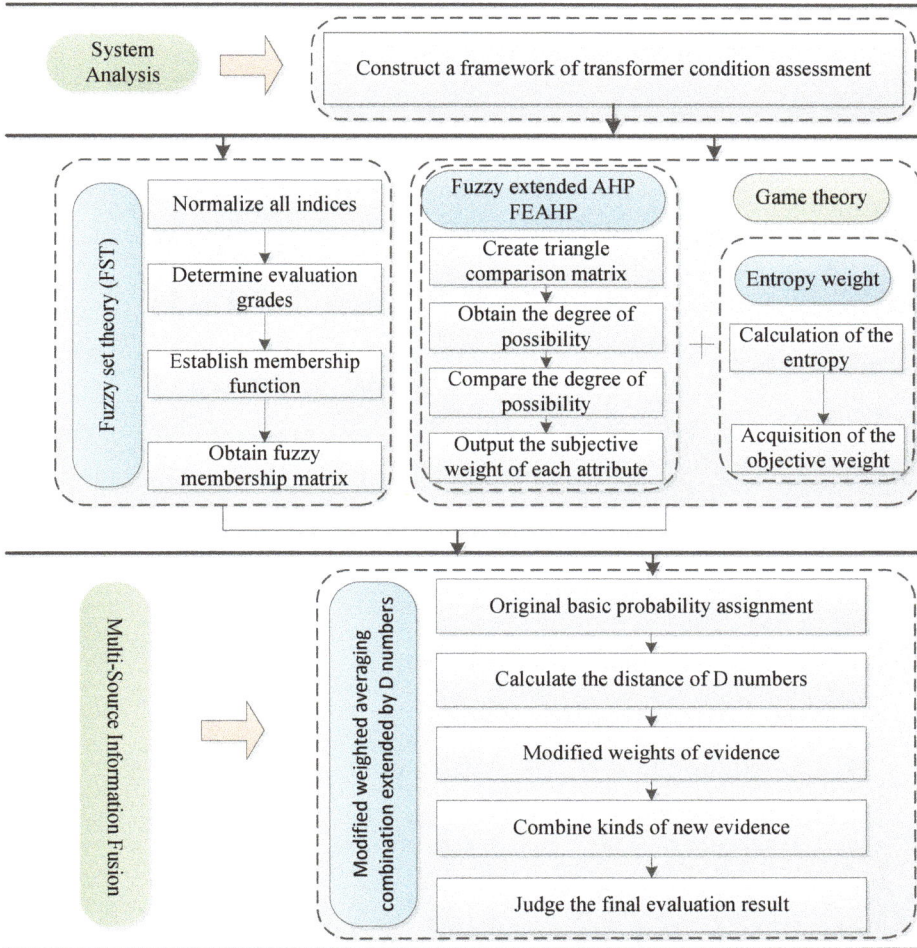

Figure 5. Flowchart of transformer condition assessment.

4. Case Study

4.1. Case 1

A 220-kV main transformer (SFPSZ7-120000/220) used in the substation of Beijing in China is taken as an example to verify the effectiveness of the proposed model. The preventive test data in 2014 and 2015 are shown in Table 3, and the evaluation procedures are demonstrated as follows.

4.1.1. Assessment Grades by Fuzzy Set Theory

From Table 3, the membership grades of indices are given by using Equations (2)–(5), and the results are shown in Table 4.

Table 3. Preventive test data of the transformer.

Index Term	12 December 2013	16 September 2015	Attention Values	Initial Value
C_2H_2	1.2 (μL/L)	2.1 (μL/L)	10 (μL/L)	0 (μL/L)
C_2H_4	10 (μL/L)	42 (μL/L)	50 (μL/L)	5.3 (μL/L)
CH_4	15.2 (μL/L)	68 (μL/L)	100 (μL/L)	8.7 (μL/L)
C_2H_6	23 (μL/L)	58 (μL/L)	65 (μL/L)	2.6 (μL/L)
H_2 (hydrogen content in oil)	48 (μL/L)	65 (μL/L)	150 (μL/L)	5.1 (μL/L)
Water content	7.2 (mg/L)	13.1 (mg/L)	25 (mg/L)	2.6 (mg/L)
Breakdown voltage of oil	49 (kV)	55 (kV)	35 (kV)	60 (kV)
Furfural	0.012 (mg/L)	0.032 (mg/L)	0.2 (mg/L)	0 (mg/L)
Interfacial tension	31 (mN/m)	35 (mN/m)	19 (mN/m)	45 (mN/m)
Polymerization degree	853	816	250	1000
Dielectric loss of oil	1.92%	2.51%	4%	0.21%
Flash point	153 (°C)	143 (°C)	130 (°C)	160 (°C)
Core earthing current	40 (mA)	72 (mA)	100 (mA)	10 (mA)
Volume resistivity	37×10^9 (Ω·m)	35×10^9 (Ω·m)	5×10^9 (Ω·m) (≤300 °C)	65×10^9 (Ω·m)
Absorptance	2.12	1.88	1.3	2.5
Polarization index	2.21	1.96	1.5	2.9
Dielectric loss of winding	0.38%	0.42%	0.6%	0.15%

Table 4. Membership degrees to assess grades.

Membership Degrees of Indices	Assessment Grades				
	H_1	H_2	H_3	H_4	H_5
f_{11}	0.2	0.8	0	0	0
f_{12}	0	0	0	0.87	0.13
f_{13}	0	0	0.4	0.6	0
f_{14}	0	0	0	0.4	0.6
f_{15}	0	0.27	0.73	0	0
f_{21}	0	0	1	0	0
f_{22}	0.25	0.75	0	0	0
f_{23}	0.45	0.55	0	0	0
f_{24}	0	0.47	0.53	0	0
f_{25}	0	1	0	0	0
f_{26}	0	0	0.7	0.3	0
f_{27}	0	0	0.72	0.28	0
f_{31}	0	0	0.24	0.76	0
f_{32}	0	0	1	0	0
f_{33}	0	0	1	0	0
f_{34}	0	0	0.32	0.68	0
f_{35}	0	0	0.6	0.4	0

4.1.2. Calculation of Weights

Based on the fuzzy extended AHP and entropy weight, the subjective and objective weights of indices are calculated by using Equations (7)–(15). Then, combining the subjective and objective weights based on game theory, the comprehensive weights are obtained by using Equations (16)–(21). All types of weights of indices are shown in Table 5. For fuzzy AHP, the fuzzy comparison matrices of corresponding indices are provided in Appendix A (see Tables A1–A3).

Figure 6 describes the results in Table 5. As shown in Figure 6, the laws of the curves for the subjective and the objective weight, which are calculated by the fuzzy AHP and entropy weight, respectively, are not consistent, and the comprehensive weights based on game theory are optimum equilibrium values between the subjective and the objective weights. Actually, the weight coefficient reaching the Nash equilibrium decides the proportion of subjective and objective weight. Therefore, the comprehensive weights based on game theory are more reasonable to apply to determine the weights of indices in the evaluation process.

Table 5. Weights of indices.

Indices	Fuzzy AHP	Entropy Weight	Game Theory
f_{11}	0.3800	0.0300	0.1653
f_{12}	0.2800	0.4000	0.3536
f_{13}	0.1000	0.4300	0.3024
f_{14}	0.0900	0.1300	0.1145
f_{15}	0.1500	0.0100	0.0641
f_{21}	0.1600	0.1500	0.1515
f_{22}	0.2400	0.3700	0.3507
f_{23}	0.2800	0.2400	0.2460
f_{24}	0.0200	0.0100	0.0115
f_{25}	0.1300	0.0100	0.0279
f_{26}	0.1300	0.0100	0.0279
f_{27}	0.0200	0.2000	0.1732
f_{31}	0.4500	0.5300	0.5200
f_{32}	0.3000	0.0500	0.1000
f_{33}	0.0400	0.3200	0.2300
f_{34}	0.0400	0.0500	0.0500
f_{35}	0.1600	0.0500	0.0800

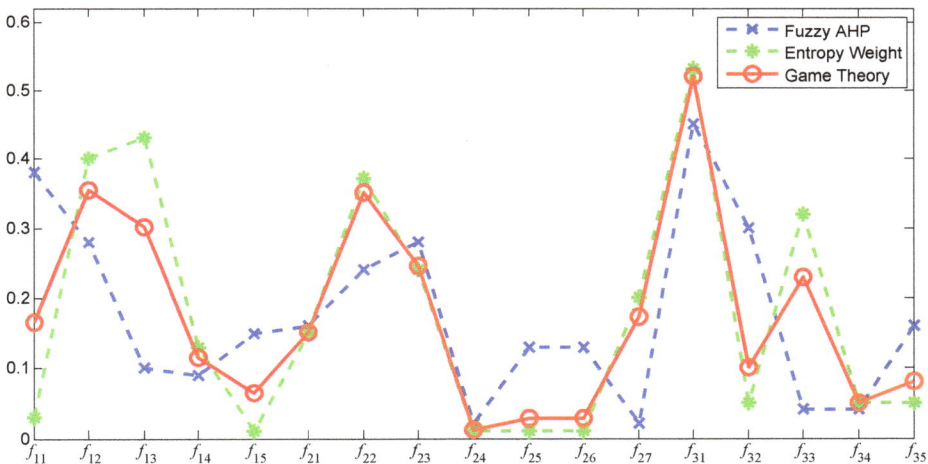

Figure 6. The calculation method of weights.

4.1.3. Modified Evidence Combination Based on D Numbers

From Tables 4 and 5, the original basic probability assignment matrix is obtained by using Equation (39):

$$M(H) = \begin{bmatrix} H_1 & H_2 & H_3 & H_4 & H_5 \\ 0.03 & 0.15 & 0.17 & 0.53 & 0.12 \\ 0.2 & 0.43 & 0.3 & 0.07 & 0 \\ 0 & 0 & 0.51 & 0.49 & 0 \end{bmatrix}$$

Based on the decision-making rule, the evaluation results of three factors are shown in Table 6. Figure 7 indicates the results in Table 6. As shown in Figure 7, the three curves corresponding to three different factors are various. Obviously, the evaluation results, considering an individual factor, are not accurate. Therefore, a multi-source information fusion is needed to determine the final health condition of the transformer.

Table 6. Basic probability assignment.

Evidence	$M(H)$					Assessing Results
	H_1	H_2	H_3	H_4	H_5	
f_1	0.03	0.15	0.17	**0.53**	0.12	H_4
f_2	0.2	**0.43**	0.3	0.07	0	H_2
f_3	0	0	**0.51**	**0.49**	0	unknown

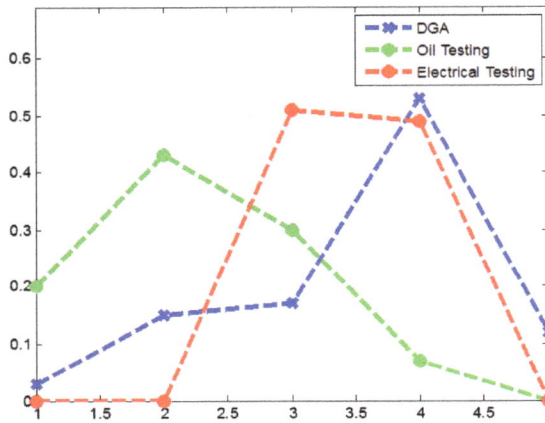

Figure 7. Evaluation grades of three factors.

As previously discussed, the basic probability assignment is regarded as three groups of D numbers. Therefore, we have:

$$d_1(H_1) = 0.03,\ d_1(H_2) = 0.15,\ d_1(H_3) = 0.17,\ d_1(H_4) = 0.53,\ d_1(H_5) = 0.12.$$
$$d_2(H_1) = 0.2,\ d_2(H_2) = 0.43,\ d_2(H_3) = 0.3,\ d_2(H_4) = 0.07.$$
$$d_3(H_3) = 0.51,\ d_3(H_4) = 0.49.$$

From Figure 3, in order to facilitate the calculation, the union region (U_{ij}) and the intersection region (T_{ij}) are given as:

$$U_{H_1 H_2} = 0.45,\ U_{H_2 H_3} = 0.7,\ U_{H_3 H_4} = 0.65,\ U_{H_4 H_5} = 0.5\ ;$$
$$T_{H_1 H_2} = 0.2,\ T_{H_2 H_3} = 0.15,\ T_{H_3 H_4} = 0.25,\ T_{H_4 H_5} = 0.15\ .$$

Therefore, we have:

$$
\underline{\underline{D}} = \begin{bmatrix} 1 & 0 & 0 & 0 & 0 \\ 0 & 1 & 0 & 0 & 0 \\ 0 & 0 & 1 & 0 & 0 \\ 0 & 0 & 0 & 1 & 0 \\ 0 & 0 & 0 & 0 & 1 \end{bmatrix}, \ \underline{\underline{I}} = \begin{bmatrix} 1 & 0.44 & 0 & 0 & 0 \\ 0.44 & 1 & 0.21 & 0 & 0 \\ 0 & 0.21 & 1 & 0.38 & 0 \\ 0 & 0 & 0.38 & 1 & 0.3 \\ 0 & 0 & 0 & 0.3 & 1 \end{bmatrix}
$$

Based on the distance function method of D numbers, the distance matrix can be calculated by using Equations (28)–(33), given as:

$$
D = \begin{bmatrix} 0 & 0.44 & 0.25 \\ 0.44 & 0 & 0.52 \\ 0.25 & 0.52 & 0 \end{bmatrix}
$$

By using Equations (34)–(37), the objective weights of evidence are generated as:

$$
w\,(m_1) = 0.37; \ w\,(m_2) = 0.29; \ w\,(m_3) = 0.34
$$

In addition, from Table A4 in Appendix A, the subjective weights of evidence (three factors) are computed based on the fuzzy AHP, denoted as:

$$
w'\,(m_1) = 0.446; \ w'\,(m_2) = 0.329; \ w'\,(m_3) = 0.225
$$

Therefore, based on game theory, the optimum equilibrium weights of each piece of evidence are given as:

$$
w_1^* = 0.44; \ w_2^* = 0.32; \ w_3^* = 0.23
$$

Then, using Equation (39), the modified pieces of evidence are calculated as:

$$
M\,(H) = [0.08, 0.2, 0.29, 0.37, 0.06]
$$

Finally, there are three pieces of evidence, and we take the traditional D-S combination rule two times. By using Equations (24) and (25), the final results are obtained as:

$$
M(H) = [0.01, 0.1, 0.29, 0.61, 0]
$$

4.1.4. Analysis of the Evaluation Results

The final evaluation results are shown in Table 7. As shown in Table 7, when two factors are combined, such as f_1 and f_2, the evaluation results indicate that the transformer health condition can be either good or bad, which gives little information on the maintenance schedule. Finally, when all three factors are combined and analyzed using the proposed method, the evaluation result clearly suggests a major defect since H_4 is far greater than the rest of the three evaluation grades.

The accuracy of this evaluation result is further consolidated by investigating the factual transformer condition. A field test suggests that the core is connected to the clamping pieces. Therefore, under the action of magnetic flux, the ring current is formed between the core and the clamping pieces. This leads to the deterioration of the insulation.

To conclude, the proposed method can effectively evaluate the health condition of the power transformer.

Table 7. Result of evidence combination.

Evidence	M(H)					Assessing Results
	H_1	H_2	H_3	H_4	H_5	
$f_1 \oplus f_2$	0.05	0.34	0.23	0.36	0.012	unknown
$f_1 \oplus f_2 \oplus f_3$	0.01	0.1	0.29	0.61	0	H_4

4.2. Case 2

The performance of the presented model is further compared with the method proposed in the literature [6]. From [6], the original basic probability assignment matrix is given as:

$$M(H) = \begin{bmatrix} H_1 & H_2 & H_3 & H_4 & H_5 \\ 0.0042 & 0.1112 & 0.3942 & 0.4904 & 0 \\ 0 & 0.4152 & 0.2513 & 0.1452 & 0.1883 \\ 0 & 0.4293 & 0.1867 & 0.2981 & 0.0859 \end{bmatrix}$$

Therefore, the D numbers are obtained as:

$$d_1(H_1) = 0.0042, \ d_1(H_2) = 0.1112, \ d_1(H_3) = 0.3942, \ d_1(H_4) = 0.4904$$
$$d_2(H_2) = 0.4152, \ d_2(H_3) = 0.2513, \ d_2(H_4) = 0.1452, \ d_2(H_5) = 0.1883$$
$$d_3(H_2) = 0.4293, \ d_3(H_3) = 0.1867, \ d_3(H_4) = 0.2981, \ d_3(H_5) = 0.0859$$

From the literature [6], the union region (U_{ij}) and the intersection region (T_{ij}) are given as:

$$U_{H_1 H_2} = \tfrac{4}{13}, \ U_{H_2 H_3} = \tfrac{8}{13}, \ U_{H_3 H_4} = \tfrac{8}{13}, \ U_{H_4 H_5} = \tfrac{6}{13};$$
$$T_{H_1 H_2} = \tfrac{2}{13}, \ T_{H_2 H_3} = \tfrac{2}{13}, \ T_{H_3 H_4} = \tfrac{2}{13}, \ T_{H_4 H_5} = \tfrac{2}{13}.$$

Then, we have:

$$\underline{\underline{D}} = \begin{bmatrix} 1 & 0 & 0 & 0 & 0 \\ 0 & 1 & 0 & 0 & 0 \\ 0 & 0 & 1 & 0 & 0 \\ 0 & 0 & 0 & 1 & 0 \\ 0 & 0 & 0 & 0 & 1 \end{bmatrix}, \ \underline{\underline{I}} = \begin{bmatrix} 1 & 0.5 & 0 & 0 & 0 \\ 0.5 & 1 & 0.25 & 0 & 0 \\ 0 & 0.25 & 1 & 0.25 & 0 \\ 0 & 0 & 0.25 & 1 & 0.33 \\ 0 & 0 & 0 & 0.33 & 1 \end{bmatrix}$$

By using Equations (28)–(33), the distance matrix of D numbers is obtained as:

$$D = \begin{bmatrix} 0 & 0.34 & 0.29 \\ 0.34 & 0 & 0.11 \\ 0.29 & 0.11 & 0 \end{bmatrix}$$

Based on Equations (34)–(37), the objective weights of evidence are computed as:

$$w(m_1) = 0.3; \ w(m_2) = 0.34; \ w(m_3) = 0.35$$

In addition, the subjective weights of factors are given as:

$$w'(m_1) = 0.446; \ w'(m_2) = 0.329; \ w'(m_3) = 0.225$$

Therefore, based on game theory, the optimum equilibrium weights of each piece of evidence are generated as:

$$w_1^* = 0.4343; \ w_2^* = 0.3332; \ w_3^* = 0.2405$$

By using Equation (39), the modified pieces of evidence can be given as:

$$M(H) = [0.002, 0.29, 0.3, 0.33, 0.08]$$

There are three pieces of evidence, and we combined the evidence two times. The final assessment results are given as:

$$M(H) = [0, 0.28, 0.3, 0.42, 0]$$

In the literature [6], the evaluation results are provided as:

$$M'(H) = [0.0011, 0.2445, 0.3432, 0.3472, 0.0336]$$

Figure 8 describes the comparison results between the proposed method and the compared method. As shown in Figure 8, the final assessing result of the proposed method is confirmed to be grade H_4 ($H_4 = 0.42$), which accurately reflects the actual condition of the transformer according to the literature [6]. Nevertheless, the evaluation results of the compared method indicated by grade H_3 ($H_3 = 0.3432$) and H_4 ($H_4 = 0.3472$) are very close to each other, which may lead to an ambiguous condition-assessing result. Therefore, the proposed model can evaluate the health condition of the transformer effectively without ambiguousness, which facilitates the implementation of the maintenance plan.

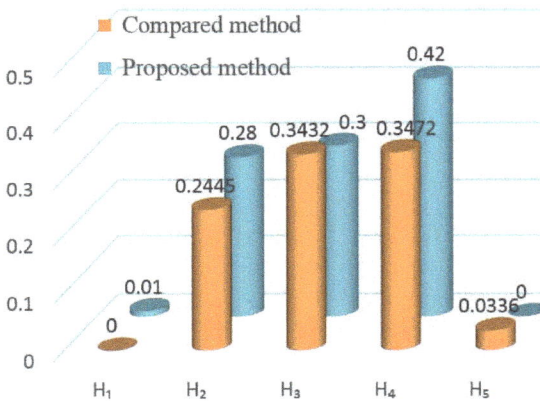

Figure 8. Comparison of the evaluation results of two methods.

5. Conclusions

A novel decision-making model, which integrates the merits of fuzzy set theory, game theory and modified evidence combination extended by D numbers, is proposed in this paper. The presented decision-making model provides a new scientific method for transformer condition assessment. The main results of this paper can be summarized in the following points.

- A four-level framework within three factors, DGA date, electrical testing and oil testing, as well as seventeen sub-indices, has been soundly established to facilitate the evaluation model.
- A comprehensive weight, determined by game theory, can be regarded as an optimum equilibrium solution by reaching a compromise between subjective and objective weight to overcome the limitations of the single weighting method. The subjective weight is given based on the fuzzy extended AHP, which extends traditional AHP and can better address the uncertainty existing in the comparison matrix given by experts. In addition, the objective weight is computed based on the entropy weight method. The final evaluation results can be obtained by the modified evidence

combination extended by D numbers. D numbers, a novel theory, can avoid the limitation of the exclusiveness hypothesis in the application of Dempster–Shafer theory.

- Case studies indicate that the proposed model can effectively reflect the actual health condition of the transformer. Furthermore, compared to the evidential reasoning-based method, the final evaluation result of the presented method can clearly show the health condition of the transformer.

- The proposed approach is not aiming at replacing the expert judgments in the test site or IEC standards. Instead, this paper offers a practical and effective approach for decision-makers, who do not necessarily have in-depth knowledge on power transformers, to evaluate the health condition of power transformers with uncertain and incomplete information.

In the future, several issues can be taken into consideration. First of all, developing a software assessment system based on the proposed model will be recommended. Secondly, some qualitative information could be further taken into consideration in the evaluation model, such as the on-load tap changer, breathing apparatus, etc. Finally, similar applications can be done under other criteria and jobs.

Acknowledgments: The research was supported by the SGCC (State Grid Corporation of China) Thousand program special support project (EPRIPDKJ (2014)2863).

Author Contributions: Lingjie Sun and Yingyi Liu conceived of the condition assessment model and wrote most parts of the manuscript. Yuwei Shang and Zhao Ma provided the required input data and wrote parts of the manuscript. Boyang Zhang and Haiwen Yuan analyzed the data and checked the whole paper.

Conflicts of Interest: The authors declare no conflict of interest.

Abbreviations

The following abbreviations are used in this manuscript:

MADM	multi-attribute decision-making
AHP	analytic hierarchy process
FAHP	fuzzy analytic hierarchy process
FEAHP	fuzzy extended analytic hierarchy process
DGA	dissolved gas analysis
D-S	Dempster–Shafer
FST	fuzzy set theory

Appendix A. Fuzzy Comparison Matrix

In this section, the fuzzy comparison matrices of three factors and corresponding indices are given as below. Tables A1–A3 give the corresponding fuzzy comparison matrix for the indices of different factors, and Table A4 shows the fuzzy comparison matrix of three factors (DGA data, oil testing and electrical testing).

Table A1. Fuzzy comparison matrix of the indices of DGA.

Indices	f_{11}	f_{12}	f_{13}	f_{14}	f_{15}
f_{11}	$(1, 1, 1)$	$(1, 3/2, 2)$	$(2, 5/2, 3)$	$(2, 5/2, 3)$	$(3/2, 2, 5/2)$
f_{12}	$(1/2, 2/3, 1)$	$(1, 1, 1)$	$(3/2, 2, 5/2)$	$(3/2, 2, 5/2)$	$(1, 3/2, 2)$
f_{13}	$(1/3, 2/5, 1/2)$	$(2/5, 1/2, 2/3)$	$(1, 1, 1)$	$(1/2, 3/2, 2)$	$(1/2, 1, 3/2)$
f_{14}	$(1/3, 2/5, 1/2)$	$(2/5, 1/2, 2/3)$	$(1/2, 2/3, 2)$	$(1, 1, 1)$	$(1/2, 1, 3/2)$
f_{15}	$(2/5, 1/2, 2/3)$	$(1/2, 2/3, 1)$	$(2/3, 1, 2)$	$(2/3, 1, 2)$	$(1, 1, 1)$

Table A2. Fuzzy comparison matrix of the indices of the oil testing factor.

Indices	f_{21}	f_{22}	f_{23}	f_{24}	f_{25}	f_{26}	f_{27}
f_{21}	(1, 1, 1)	(1/2, 2/3, 1)	(1/3, 1/2, 2/3)	(2, 5/2, 3)	(1/2, 1, 3/2)	(1/2, 1, 3/2)	(3/2, 2, 5/2)
f_{22}	(1, 3/2, 2)	(1, 1, 1)	(1/2, 1, 3/2)	(5/2, 3, 7/2)	(1, 3/2, 2)	(1, 3/2, 2)	(2, 5/2, 3)
f_{23}	(3/2, 2, 3)	(2/3, 1, 2)	(1, 1, 1)	(5/2, 3, 7/2)	(3/2, 2, 5/2)	(3/2, 2, 5/2)	(2, 5/2, 3)
f_{24}	(1/3, 2/5, 1/2)	(2/7, 1/3, 2/5)	(2/7, 1/3, 2/5)	(1, 1, 1)	(1/2, 2/3, 1)	(1/2, 1, 1)	(1/2, 1, 3/2)
f_{25}	(2/3, 1, 2)	(1/2, 2/3, 1)	(2/5, 1/2, 2/3)	(1, 3/2, 2)	(1, 1, 1)	(1, 1, 1)	(3/2, 2, 5/2)
f_{26}	(2/3, 1, 2)	(1/2, 2/3, 1)	(2/5, 1/2, 2/3)	(1, 3/2, 2)	(1, 1, 1)	(1, 1, 1)	(3/2, 2, 5/2)
f_{27}	(2/5, 1/2, 2/3)	(1/3, 2/5, 1/2)	(1/3, 2/5, 1/2)	(2/3, 1, 2)	(2/5, 1/2, 2/3)	(2/5, 1/2, 2/3)	(1, 1, 1)

Table A3. Fuzzy comparison matrix of the indices of the electrical testing factor.

Indices	f_{31}	f_{32}	f_{33}	f_{34}	f_{35}
f_{31}	(1, 1, 1)	(1, 3/2, 2)	(2, 5/2, 3)	(2, 5/2, 3)	(3/2, 2, 2)
f_{32}	(1/2, 2/3, 1)	(1, 1, 1)	(3/2, 2, 5/2)	(3/2, 2, 5/2)	(1, 3/2, 2)
f_{33}	(1/3, 2/5, 1/2)	(2/5, 1/2, 2/3)	(1, 1, 1)	(1/2, 3/2, 2)	(1/2, 1, 1)
f_{34}	(1/3, 2/5, 1/2)	(2/5, 1/2, 2/3)	(1/2, 2/3, 1)	(1, 1, 1)	(1/2, 1, 1)
f_{35}	(1/2, 1/2, 2/3)	(1/2, 2/3, 1)	(1, 1, 2)	(1, 1, 2)	(1, 1, 1)

Table A4. Fuzzy comparison matrix of three factors.

Indices	f_{41}	f_{42}	f_{43}
f_{41}	(1, 1, 1)	(3/5, 1, 4/3)	(3/2, 2, 5/2)
f_{42}	(3/4, 1, 5/3)	(1, 1, 1)	(2/3, 1, 3/2)
f_{43}	(2/5, 1/2, 2/3)	(2/3, 1, 3/2)	(1, 1, 1)

References

1. Wang, C.; Wu, J.; Wang, J.; Zhao, W. Reliability analysis and overload capability assessment of oil-immersed power transformers. *Energies* **2016**, *9*, 43.
2. Jahromi, A.; Piercy, R.; Cress, S.; Fan, W. An approach to power transformer asset management using health index. *IEEE Electr. Insul. Mag.* **2009**, *2*, 20–34.
3. Murugan, R.; Ramasamy, R. Failure analysis of power transformer for effective maintenance planning in electric utilities. *Eng. Fail. Anal.* **2015**, *55*, 182–192.
4. Wang, M.; Vandermaar, A.J.; Srivastava, K.D. Review of condition assessment of power transformers in service. *IEEE Electr. Insul. Mag.* **2002**, *18*, 12–25.
5. Tang, W.H.; Spurgeon, K.; Wu, Q.H.; Richardson, Z.J. An evidential reasoning approach to transformer condition assessments. *IEEE Trans. Power Deliv.* **2004**, *19*, 1696–1703.
6. Liao, R.; Stanislaw Grzybowski, H.Z.; Yang, L.; Zhang, Y.; Liao, Y. An integrated decision-making model for condition assessment of power transformers using fuzzy approach and evidential reasoning. *IEEE Trans. Power Deliv.* **2011**, *26*, 1111–1118.
7. Illias, H.A.; Chai, X.R.; Mokhlis, H. Transformer incipient fault prediction using combined artificial neural network and various particle swarm optimisation techniques. *PLoS ONE* **2015**, *10*, e0129363.
8. Cui, Y.; Ma, H.; Saha, T. Improvement of power transformer insulation diagnosis using oil characteristics data preprocessed by smoteboost technique. *IEEE Trans. Dielectr. Electr. Insul.* **2014**, *21*, 2363–2373.
9. Abu-Siada, A.; Hmood, S. A new fuzzy logic approach to identify power transformer criticality using dissolved gas-in-oil analysis. *Int. J. Electr. Power* **2015**, *67*, 401–408.
10. Lin, P.-C.; Yang, M.-T.; Gu, J.-C. Intelligent maintenance model for condition assessment of circuit breakers using fuzzy set theory and evidential reasoning. *IET Gener. Transm. Distrib.* **2014**, *8*, 1244–1253.
11. Gaudenzi, B.; Borghesi, A. Managing risks in the supply chain using the AHP method. *Int. J. Logist. Manag.* **2006**, *17*, 114–136.

12. Al-Harbi, K.M.A.-S. Application of the AHP in project management. *Int. J. Proj. Manag.* **2001**, *19*, 19–27.

13. Okello, C.; Pindozzi, S.; Faugno, S.; Boccia, L. Appraising bioenergy alternatives in Uganda using strengths, weaknesses, opportunities and threats (SWOT)-analytical hierarchy process (AHP) and a desirability functions approach. *Energies* **2014**, *7*, 1171–1192.

14. Liu, K.-S.; Hsueh, S.-L.; Wu, W.-C.; Chen, Y.-L. A DFuzzy-DAHP decision-making model for evaluating energy-saving design strategies for residential buildings. *Energies* **2012**, *5*, 4462–4480.

15. Saaty, T.L. *The Analytic Hierarchy Process*; McGraw-Hill: New York, NY, USA, 1980.

16. Saaty, T.L. How to make a decision: The analytic hierarchy process. *Interfaces* **1994**, *24*, 19–43.

17. Dempster, A.P. Upper and lower probabilities induced by a multivalued mapping. *Ann. Math. Stat.* **1967**, *38*, 325–339.

18. Shafer, G. *A Mathematical Theory of Evidence*; Princeton University Press: Princeton, NJ, USA, 1976.

19. Wang, H.; Lin, D.; Qiu, J.; Ao, L.; Du, Z.; He, B. Research on multiobjective group decision-making in condition-based maintenance for transmission and transformation equipment based on D-S evidence theory. *IEEE Trans. Smart Grid* **2015**, *6*, 1035–1045.

20. Deng, H. Multicriteria analysis with fuzzy pairwise comparison. *Int. J. Approx. Reason.* **1999**, *21*, 215–231.

21. Abu-Elanien, A.E.B.; Salama, M.M.A.; Ibrahim, M. Calculation of a health index for oil-immersed transformers rated under 69 kV using fuzzy logic. *IEEE Trans. Power Deliv.* **2012**, *27*, 2029–2036.

22. Mikhailov, L.; Tsvetinov, P. Evaluation of services using a fuzzy analytic hierarchy process. *Appl. Soft Comput.* **2004**, *5*, 23–33.

23. Lai, C.; Chen, X.; Chen, X.; Wang, Z.; Wu, X.; Zhao, S. A fuzzy comprehensive evaluation model for flood risk based on the combination weight of game theory. *Nat. Hazards* **2015**, *77*, 1243–1259.

24. Deng, Y. D numbers: Theory and applications. *J. Inf. Comput. Sci.* **2012**, *9*, 2421–2428.

25. Deng, X.; Lu, X.; Chan, F.T.S.; Sadiq, R.; Mahadevan, S.; Deng, Y. D-CFPR: D numbers extended consistent fuzzy preference relations. *Knowl.-Based Syst.* **2015**, *73*, 61–68.

26. Li, M.; Hu, Y.; Zhang, Q.; Deng, Y. A novel distance function of D numbers and its application in product engineering. *Eng. Appl. Artif. Intell.* **2016**, *47*, 61–67.

27. Chang, D.-Y. Application of the extent analysis method on fuzzy AHP. *Eur. J. Oper. Res.* **1999**, *95*, 649–655.

28. Wang, X.; Chan, H.K.; Li, D. A case study of an integrated fuzzy methodology for green product development. *Eur. J. Oper. Res.* **2015**, *241*, 212–223.

29. Uğurlu, Ö. Application of fuzzy extended AHP methodology for selection of ideal ship for oceangoing watchkeeping officers. *Int. J. Ind. Ergon.* **2015**, *47*, 132–140.

30. Chen, J.-F.; Hsieh, H.-N.; Do, Q.H. Evaluating teaching performance based on fuzzy AHP and comprehensive evaluation approach. *Appl. Soft Comput.* **2015**, *28*, 100–108.

31. Sanfey, A.G. Social decision-making: Insights from game theory and neuroscience. *Science* **2007**, *318*, 598–602.

32. Frank, D.M.; Sarkar, S. Group decisions in biodiversity conservation: Implications form game theory. *PLoS ONE* **2010**, *5*, e10688.

33. Deng, X.; Hu, Y.; Deng, Y.; Mahadevan, S. Environmental impact assessment based on D numbers. *Expert Syst. Appl.* **2014**, *41*, 635–643.

34. Fan, G.; Zhong, D.; Yan, F.; Yue, P. A hybrid fuzzy evaluation method for curtain grouting efficiency assessment based on an AHP method extended by D numbers. *Expert Syst. Appl.* **2016**, *44*, 289–303.

35. Dhote, N.K.; Helonde, J.B. Improvement in transformer diagnosis by DGA using fuzzy logic. *J. Electr. Eng. Technol.* **2014**, *9*, 615–621.

36. Liu, C.H.; Lin, T.B.; Yao, L.; Wang, S.Y. Integrated power transformer diagnosis using hybrid fuzzy dissolved gas analysis. *IEEJ Trans. Electr. Electron. Eng.* **2015**, *10*, 689–698.

37. Buyukozkam, G.; Kahraman, C.; Ruan, C. A fuzzy multi-criteria decision approach for software development sratege selection. *Int. J. Gen. Syst* **2004**, *33*, 259–280.

38. Shannon, C. A mathematical theory of communication. *Bell Syst. Tech. J.* **1948**, *27*, 379–423, 623–656.

39. Li, L.H.; Mo, R. Production task queue optimization based on multi-attribute evaluation for complex product assembly workshop. *PLoS ONE* **2015**, *10*, e0134343.

40. Zhao, H.; Li, N. Optimal siting of charging stations for electric vehicles based on fuzzy Delphi and hybrid multi-criteria decision making approaches from an extended sustainability perspective. *Energies* **2016**, *9*, 270.

Energies **2016**, *9*, 697

41. Deng, Y.; Shi, W.; Zhu, Z.; Liu, Q. Combining belief functions based on distance of evidence. *Decis. Support Syst.* **2004**, *38*, 489–493.

42. Yasinzadeh, M.; Seyedi, H. Fake measurement identification in power substations based on correlation between data and distance of the evidence. *IET Gener. Transm. Distrib.* **2015**, *9*, 503–512.

energies

MDPI

Article

Reliability Analysis and Overload Capability Assessment of Oil-Immersed Power Transformers

Chen Wang [1], Jie Wu [2,*], Jianzhou Wang [3] and Weigang Zhao [4,5]

[1] School of Mathematics and Statistics, Lanzhou University, Lanzhou 730000, China; chenwang15@lzu.edu.cn
[2] School of Mathematics and Computer Science, Northwest University for Nationalities, Lanzhou 730030, China
[3] School of Statistics, Dongbei University of Finance and Economics, Dalian 116025, China; wjz@lzu.edu.cn
[4] Center for Energy and Environmental Policy Research, Beijing Institute of Technology, Beijing 100081, China; zwgstd@gmail.com
[5] School of Management and Economics, Beijing Institute of Technology, Beijing 100081, China
* Correspondence: wuj19870903@gmail.com; Tel./Fax: +86-931-451-2202

Academic Editor: Issouf Fofana
Received: 4 November 2015; Accepted: 5 January 2016; Published: 14 January 2016

Abstract: Smart grids have been constructed so as to guarantee the security and stability of the power grid in recent years. Power transformers are a most vital component in the complicated smart grid network. Any transformer failure can cause damage of the whole power system, within which the failures caused by overloading cannot be ignored. This research gives a new insight into overload capability assessment of transformers. The hot-spot temperature of the winding is the most critical factor in measuring the overload capacity of power transformers. Thus, the hot-spot temperature is calculated to obtain the duration running time of the power transformers under overloading conditions. Then the overloading probability is fitted with the mature and widely accepted Weibull probability density function. To guarantee the accuracy of this fitting, a new objective function is proposed to obtain the desired parameters in the Weibull distributions. In addition, ten different mutation scenarios are adopted in the differential evolutionary algorithm to optimize the parameter in the Weibull distribution. The final comprehensive overload capability of the power transformer is assessed by the duration running time as well as the overloading probability. Compared with the previous studies that take no account of the overloading probability, the assessment results obtained in this research are much more reliable.

Keywords: current measurement; losses; power transformers; reliability estimation; transformer windings

1. Introduction

The power grid is an important infrastructure for a nation's economic and social development, however, in recent years, the objective environment to guarantee the security and stability of the power grid is undergoing tremendous changes. Factors such as the rapid growth of the loads, the initial formation of the large area grid interconnection, as well as the influence of the global climate change all impact the electricity market and the effects on the power grid have become increasingly apparent, thus, guaranteeing the security and stability of the power grid represents a new challenge. To solve this problem, in recent years, smart grids have been constructed by comprehensively considering the market, safety, power quality and environmental factors. The term smart grid refers to a fully automated complicated power supply network, where each user and each node are monitored in real-time, to ensure a two-way flow of the current and information between the power plant and clients' appliances. The features of the smart grid can be summarized as: self-healing, compatibility, interaction, coordination, efficiency, quality, and integration.

Power transformers is one of the most vital pieces of equipment in the smart grid. In addition, it is a network equipment whose structure is the most complex and sophisticated. Any failure in transformers can cause damage to the power system, among which failures caused by overloading cannot be ignored. The consequences of overloaded operation of power transformers can be serious. As indicated, when the current flow in the windings exceeds the rated current stated on the nameplate, *i.e.*, the transformer operates under overload conditions, the load loss of transformers is proportional to the square of the current, conductor heating rises sharply, and the temperature of the windings and insulating oil surge accordingly. In this case, the transformer loss will increase due to the reason that power transformers are designed according to their rated capacity, so when the load of the transformer exceeds the rated capacity, the losses will increase. This will greatly affect the lifetime of the power transformer. In addition, transformers may fail due to the following two reasons: on the one hand, the transformer may be damaged since the overload operation would accelerate the cracking of insulating oil, generate bubbles, reduce the dielectric strength of the transformer, and cause an electrical breakdown. On the other hand, the excessive heat will reduce the mechanical strength of the windings, and when a short circuit occurs, coil deformation or mechanical instability will occur due to the external strong electric power. Therefore, overload capacity assessment is of particular importance in avoiding the catastrophic failure of power transformers and guaranteeing the normal operation of power grids.

Adequate and accurate assessment of power system reliability is a very challenging task that has been and still is under investigation. Previously developed power system reliability and security assessment models include the super components contingency model [1], the hybrid conditions-dependent outage model [2], and probability distribution based models such as the log-normal distribution [3] and the Weibull distribution [4]. As one of vital aspects in the power system reliability assessment, the overload capability of power transformers, has also been specifically surveyed by many researchers. For example, to make up the limitation of the American National Standards Instituteloading guide, which is only applicable to ambient temperatures above 0 °C, Aubin *et al.* [5] proposed a calculation method to assess the overload capacity of transformers for ambient temperatures below 0 °C. Tenbohlen *et al.* [6] developed on-line monitoring systems to assess the overload capacity of power transformers. Bosworth *et al.* [7] reported the development of electrochemical sensors for the measurement of phenol in transformer overloading evaluation. A stochastic differential equation was used by Edstrom *et al.* [8] to estimate the probability of transformer overloading. Estrada *et al.* [9] adopted magnetic flux entropy as a tool to predict transformer failures, and the overloading is just one aspect among the failures. Liu *et al.* [10] assessed the overload capacity of transformers through an online monitoring and overload factor calculated by a temperature reverse extrapolation approach. As known, when assessing network load capability, the hot-spot temperature is one the most significant factors. Thus, there are many studies devoted to hot-spot temperature forecasting such as the radial basis function network [11], a genetic algorithm based technique [12], and a local memory-based algorithm [13] provided by Galdi *et al.*, the Takagi-Sugeno-Kang fuzzy model presented by Siano [14], the optimal linear combination of artificial neural network approach used by Pradhan and Ramu [15], the grey-box model introduced by Domenico *et al.* [16], *etc.* Though these researches make tremendous contributions, efforts on overload capability assessments should not be stopped, and new overload capability measurement techniques with respect to power transformers still need to be developed and exploited to improve the accuracy of overload capability assessment and provide more techniques to prevent failure of transformers caused by emergency overloads.

This research gives a new insight into how to measure the overload probability of oil-immersed power transformers. As known, the hot-spot temperature is the most critical factor in measuring the overload capability of power transformers. Thus, the hot-spot temperature is first calculated to measure the duration of running time under overload conditions. Then, the overloading probability is fitted by a mature and attractive Weibull distribution. Finally, the comprehensive overload capability of the power transformer is assessed from both the duration of running time under the overload conditions and the overloading probability aspects. This research is innovative in the following aspects: (a) apart from the duration of running time under the overload conditions, the overload capability is also assessed according to the overloading probability of the power transformer, which is measured by the Weibull distribution in this paper; (b) though the Weibull distribution is a quite mature and attractive method for fitting the distribution of data series, this paper improves the fitting performance of the Weibull distribution by proposing a new objective function to obtain the parameters in the Weibull distribution; (c) different from other researches, the shape parameter in the Weibull distribution in this paper is determined according to the mean of the shape parameter values obtained under ten different mutation scenarios in the differential evolutionary (DE) algorithms, *i.e.*, the shape parameter is determined by taking results under different situations into account, this operation improves the accuracy of overload capability assessment further. The remainder of this paper is organized as follows: Section 2 introduces related techniques. Simulation results and discussions are presented in Section 3, while Section 4 concludes the whole research.

2. Related Techniques

2.1. Duration Running Time Calculation under Overloading Conditions

2.1.1. Steady-State Temperature Measurement

The final hot-spot temperature (θ_h) of the winding for power transformer is calculated by [17]:

$$\theta_h = \theta_a + \Delta\theta_{br} \left[\frac{1 + RK^2}{1 + R}\right]^x + 2\left[\Delta\theta_{imr} - \Delta\theta_{br}\right]K^y + Hg_rK^y \tag{1}$$

where θ_a is the air temperature (°C), $\Delta\theta_{br}$ is the temperature rise in bottom (K), $\Delta\theta_{imr}$ is the average winding temperature rise (K), R is the ratio between the load losses at the rated load and no-load losses, K is the load current per unit and y is the index of the winding.

For a forced-directed oil circulation and forced air circulation (ODAF) transformer, the oil flow in the windings is affected by the oil pump as well as the guide channel, the viscosity of the oil has little effect on the temperature change of the transformer, however, at this time, the temperature effect of the conductor resistance must be considered. Therefore, based on Equation (1), the final hot-spot temperature (θ'_h) of the winding for power transformer is corrected using [17]:

$$\theta'_h = \theta_h + 0.15(\theta_h - \theta_{hr}) \tag{2}$$

where θ_h is the final hot-spot temperature of the windings by not taking the effect of the conductor resistance into account and obtained by Equation (1), θ_{hr} is the hot-spot temperature under the rated operating conditions.

2.1.2. Transient Temperature Measurement

With the changes of the transformer load, the temperature of the transformer will change as well. It is found that the temperature rise stabilization time of the electric insulating oil, which is 1.5 h, is much longer than that of the conductor (usually 5–10 min). Thus the transient temperature is measured as follows:

$$\Delta\theta_{bt} = \Delta\theta_{bi} + (\Delta\theta_{bu} - \Delta\theta_{bi})(1 - e^{-t/\tau_0}) \tag{3}$$

where $\Delta\theta_{bi}$ is the initial bottom oil temperature rise, $\Delta\theta_{bu}$ is the bottom oil temperature rise of the applied load at the in the steady state, and τ_0 is the winding time constant.

Therefore, once the limit hot-spot temperature of the winding is determined, with the assistance of the thermal characterization parameters obtained in the factory test, and taking no account of the life lost, the overload capacity of the transformer can be calculated by Equations (1)–(3).

2.2. Overloading Probability Measurement

It is indicated that the relationship between the active power of the three-phase transformer and the current is as follows:

$$P = \sqrt{3}UI\cos\varphi \tag{4}$$

where P is the active power, U and I are the voltage and current respectively, and $\cos\varphi$ is called the power factor. Therefore, the probability value of the current located in the interval $[I_1, I_2)$ is as equal as that of the active power located in the interval $[\sqrt{3}UI_1\cos\varphi, \sqrt{3}UI_2\cos\varphi)$. This inspires us to carry out the overloading probability measurement by means of the active power probability fitting results, in the situation that the current values are unknown whereas the active power values are observed.

The Weibull distribution is one of the most commonly used the loss of life distributions in the reliability research of single samples. Its main feature is that the difference of shape parameters can reflect various failure mechanisms. Numerous experimental results demonstrate that the life of components, equipment, and systems that cause the global function to stop running owing to the failure or breakdown in certain parts obey the Weibull distribution [18]. Moreover, according to Reference [19], the life of liquid insulation obeys a Gumbel distribution, while the lifetime of solid insulation follows a two-parameter distribution or lognormal distribution. Therefore, this paper applies a two-parameter Weibull distribution to research the life distribution features of hot-spot absolute temperature insulation samples. The statistical analysis of Weibull life data is based on the following three assumptions [20]:

A1:   In each different stress level, the loss of life of hot-spot absolute temperature insulation samples all obeys the Weibull distribution. That is to say, the distribution type of life will not change with increasing stress level.

A2:   In each different stress level, the failure mechanism of hot-spot absolute temperature insulation samples mush keep consistent. However, owing to the randomness of experimental data, the shape parameters of Weibull distribution can be only approximately equal.

A3:   The life of hot-spot absolute temperature insulation samples that obeys the Weibull distribution should the function of trial voltage and temperature. If A1 and A2 are satisfied, the hot-spot absolute temperature insulation samples obey the Weibull distribution. Assume that the main aim of A3 is to realize the data extrapolation.

The three assumptions are built based on certain physics, and we can use professional knowledge and engineering experience to judge whether they are true. In the statistical analysis, both hypothesis testing and correlation coefficient test can be applied to confirm their existence.

The active power distribution of the transformer is surveyed with the assistance of the Weibull distribution in this paper. The probability density function of the Weibull distribution can be described by:

$$f(a) = \left(\frac{k}{c}\right)\left(\frac{a}{c}\right)^{k-1}\exp\left[-\left(\frac{a}{c}\right)^k\right] \tag{5}$$

where a is the active power with the unit of kW, k is the dimensionless shape parameter and c is the scale parameter with the same unit of the active power.

2.3. Objective Function

To obtain the unknown shape and scale parameters, in this research, a new objective function is constructed and the results obtained by this new objective function are compared with those obtained by two other frequently used objective functions.

2.3.1. The New Proposed Objective Function

According to the Probability Density Function (PDF) of the Weibull distribution, the expected value ($E(a)$) and the variance ($Var(a)$) of the active power can be obtained by:

$$E(a) = c\Gamma(1 + \frac{1}{k})$$ (6)

and:

$$Var(a) = c^2\Gamma(1 + \frac{2}{k}) - c^2\Gamma^2(1 + \frac{1}{k})$$ (7)

The new objective function constructed in this paper benefits from the following idea. As known, the mean square error (MSE) defined as follows is always been used as the objective function:

$$MSE = \frac{1}{n}\sum_{i=1}^{n}(x_i - \hat{x}_i)^2$$ (8)

where x_i and $\hat{x}_i$ are the observed and forecasted values, respectively. Let Y be a random variable and the possible values for Y are $y_1, y_2, \ldots, y_n$, where $y_i = x_i - \hat{x}_i$. Then Equation (8) can be written as:

$$MSE = \frac{1}{n}\sum_{i=1}^{n}y_i^2$$ (9)

which can be seen as:

$$MSE = E(Y^2)$$ (10)

where $E(Y^2)$ represents the expected value of the variable Y^2. According to the following formula:

$$Var(Y) = E(Y^2) - [E(Y)]^2$$ (11)

Equation (10) is equivalent to:

$$MSE = [E(Y)]^2 + Var(Y)$$ (12)

where $E(Y)$ and $Var(Y)$ denote the expected value and variance of the variable Y, respectively. Based on the calculation results obtained by Equations (6) and (7):

$$[E(a)]^2 + Var(a) = c^2\Gamma(1 + \frac{2}{k})$$ (13)

However, there is always some error between the left side and the right side of the Equation (13). Thus, the residual value ε defined as below is used as the objective function:

$$\varepsilon_1 = [E(a)]^2 + Var(a) - c^2\Gamma(1 + \frac{2}{k})$$ (14)

where $E(a)$ represents the mean value of the active power and $Var(a)$ denotes the variance of the active power. Then according to Equation (6), the scale parameter c can be obtained by:

$$c = \frac{E(a)}{\Gamma(1 + 1/k)}$$ (15)

So by substituting Equation (15) into Equation (14), the final objection function used to optimize the shape parameter k can be expressed as:

$$\varepsilon_1 = [E(a)]^2 + Var(a) - \frac{[E(a)]^2\Gamma(1 + 2/k)}{\Gamma^2(1 + 1/k)}$$ (16)

2.3.2. The First Comparison Objective Function

To verify the performance of the DE algorithm under different objective functions, the first objective function used to compare with the new one proposed in this paper is expressed as:

$$\varepsilon_2 = \frac{Var(a)}{[E(a)]^2} - \frac{\Gamma(1 + 2/k) - \Gamma^2(1 + 1/k)}{\Gamma^2(1 + 1/k)} \tag{17}$$

where $E(a)$ represents the mean value of the active power and $Var(a)$ denotes the variance of the active power. Similarly, Equation (17) is only used to optimize the shape parameter. The scale parameter in this comparison strategy is obtained by Equation (15) just as it did in the new proposed objective function. The construction of this objective function can be found in Appendix A.

2.3.3. The Second Comparison Objective Function

The second objective function, which used to compare with the new proposed one in this paper and is derived from the maximum likelihood estimation, can be expressed as:

$$\varepsilon_3 = k - \left[\frac{\sum_{i=1}^{n} a_i^k \ln a_i}{\sum_{i=1}^{n} a_i^k} - \frac{\sum_{i=1}^{n} \ln a_i}{n} \right]^{1/k} \tag{18}$$

where n is the active power sample number and $\{a_i\}_{i=1}^{n}$ is the active power series of the transformer. The construction of this objective function can be found in Appendix B. Once the value of the shape parameter k has been obtained, the scale parameter c is determined according to:

$$c = \left(\frac{1}{n} \sum_{i=1}^{n} a_i^k \right)^{1/k} \tag{19}$$

2.4. Intelligent Optimization Algorithms

To obtain the optimum shape and scale parameters, the differential evolution (DE) algorithm is used in this research. The usage of the DE algorithm is built on the basis of the three previous described objective functions. In general, the DE algorithm contains three procedures: mutation, crossover and selection [21].

Procedure 1 (mutation): In this step, ten different mutation scenarios are employed in this research to survey the performance of the three objective functions. Given a population with N parameter vectors X_i^G, $(i = 1, 2, 3, \ldots, N$ for each generation $G)$, these ten scenarios are expressed as follows:

$$\text{Scenario 1}: v_i^{G+1} = x_{r1}^G + F \times (x_{r2}^G - x_{r3}^G), r1 \neq r2 \neq r3 \neq i; \tag{20}$$

$$\text{Scenario 2}: v_i^{G+1} = x_i^G + F_1 \times (x_{best}^G - x_i^G) + F_2 \times (x_{r2}^G - x_{r3}^G); \tag{21}$$

$$\text{Scenario 3}: v_i^{G+1} = x_{best}^G + (x_{r1}^G - x_{r2}^G) \times ((1 - 0.9999) \times rand + F); \tag{22}$$

$$\text{Scenario 4}: v_i^{G+1} = x_{r1}^G + F_1 \times (x_{r2}^G - x_{r3}^G), F_1 = (1 - F) \times rand + F; \tag{23}$$

where the values of F_1 are the same for all of the parameters need to be estimated.

$$\text{Scenario 5}: v_i^{G+1} = x_{r1}^G + F_1 \times (x_{r2}^G - x_{r3}^G), F_1 = (1 - F) \times rand + F; \tag{24}$$

$$\text{Scenario 6}: v_i^{G+1} = x_i^G + F \times (x_{r2}^G - x_{r3}^G); \tag{25}$$

$$\text{Scenario 7}: v_i^{G+1} = x_{r1}^G + F \times (x_{r2}^G - x_{r3}^G + x_{r4}^G - x_{r5}^G); \tag{26}$$

$$\text{Scenario 8}: v_i^{G+1} = x_i^G + F \times (x_{r2}^G - x_{r3}^G + x_{r4}^G - x_{r5}^G); \tag{27}$$

$$\text{Scenario 9}: v_i^{G+1} = x_i^G + F \times (x_{best}^G - x_i^G) + 0.5 \times (x_{r2}^G - x_{r3}^G); \tag{28}$$

$$\text{Scenario 10}: v_i^{G+1} = \begin{cases} x_{r1}^G + F \times (x_{r2}^G - x_{r3}^G), & \text{if } rand < 0.5 \\ x_{r1}^G + 0.5 \times (F+1) \times (x_{r1}^G + x_{r2}^G - 2 \times x_{r3}^G), & \text{if } rand \geqslant 0.5 \end{cases} \tag{29}$$

where *r1*, *r2*, *r3*, *r4*, *r5* are integer numbers randomly selected from {1, 2, . . . , N}, F is the mutation factor chosen from the range [0, 1], and x_i^G and x_{best}^G are the *i*th and the best individuals in generation G, respectively.

Procedure 2 (Crossover): The exponential crossover approach is employed in this step. Component update in the trial vector $U_i^{G+1} = (u_{1i}^{G+1}, u_{2i}^{G+1}, \ldots, u_{Di}^{G+1})$ is described as:

$$u_{ji}^{G+1} = \begin{cases} v_{ji}^{G+1}, & \text{if } j \in \{k, \langle k+1 \rangle_n, \ldots, \langle k+L-1 \rangle_n\} \\ x_{ji}^G, & \text{otherwise} \end{cases}, \quad j=1,2,\ldots D \tag{30}$$

where *k* and *L* are random values selected from the set {1, 2, . . . , n}, and $\langle j \rangle_n$ is set to *j* in the case of $j \leqslant n$ while $j - n$ in the case of $j > n$.

Procedure 3 (Selection): This step is operated according to the following law:

$$X_i^{G+1} = \begin{cases} U_i^{G+1}, & \text{if } f(U_i^{G+1}) \leqslant f(X_i^G) \\ X_i^G, & \text{otherwise} \end{cases} \tag{31}$$

The DE algorithm is terminated in the case of the value of ε or the iteration number reaches the expected level.

2.5. New Proposed Overloading Probability Measurement Algorithm

Based on the above related techniques, a new proposed overloading probability measurement algorithm is proposed, the outline of this algorithm is shown in Algorithm 1.

Algorithm 1 New proposed overloading probability measurement algorithm

---

Input: Active power a—a sequence of sample data
Output: The probability density function of the active power
1. Initialize the shape parameter *k*
2. **WHILE** (ε > predefined error level) **DO**
3. Update the shape parameter *k* with the DE algorithm
4. Calculate $\varepsilon = [E(a)]^2 + Var(a) - [E(a)]^2 \Gamma(1 + 2/k)/\Gamma^2(1 + 1/k)$ by using the new obtained *k*
5. **END WHILE**
6. Calculate $c = E(a)/\Gamma(1 + 1/k)$ by using the final value of *k*
7. $f(a) = (k/c)(a/c)^{k-1} \exp\left[-(a/c)^k\right]$
8. **RETURN** *f*

2.6. Fitting Performance Evaluation Criteria

In this paper, two error evaluation criteria named the Kolmogorov-Smirnov test error (KSE) [22] and the root mean square error (RMSE) [23], are applied to the further comparison among the new proposed and the comparison objective functions. The related definitions are as follows:

$$\text{KSE} = \max |S(a) - O(a)| \tag{32}$$

$$\text{RMSE} = \left[\frac{1}{n} \sum_{i=1}^n (a_{oi} - a_{ci})^2\right]^{1/2} \tag{33}$$

where $S(a)$ and $O(a)$ are the Cumulative Distribution Function (CDF)values of the active power not exceeding *a* obtained by the selected function and by the actual data, respectively, $\{a_{oi}\}_{i=1}^n$ and $\{a_{ci}\}_{i=1}^n$

are the probability data series obtained by the observed data and the selected probability density function respectively, *n* represents the number of the data.

3. Results and Discussion

In this paper, the overload capability of oil-immersed power transformers is assessed by the data sampled from three residential areas named Lake Neighborhood, North Neighborhood and Sunshine Mediterranean Neighborhood. The three-phase transformer used in the first residential area is a model S11-M-200/10 (HengAnYuan, Beijing, China), and those in the other two residential areas are both S11-M-400/10 units (HengAnYuan, Beijing, China), *i.e.*, the rated capacity values of the transformers used in these three neighborhoods are 200, 400 and 400 kVA, respectively.

3.1. Overloading Probability Fitting Results

The DE algorithm is carried out and terminated when the objective function is no larger than 1×10^{-5} in this paper. Table 1 presents performance of the three objective functions by using different DE mutation scenarios in terms of the iteration number and the actual obtained objective function values when the termination condition is reached. For convenience, the new proposed objective function, the first comparison objective function and the second objective function are named the objective function 1, the objective function 2 and the objective function 3 in Table 1, respectively.

As seen from Table 1, when the new proposed objective function is applied to the shape parameter optimization, the iteration numbers of the DE algorithm needed to reach the objective function level are smaller than those obtained by the other two comparison objective functions under most of the mutation scenarios. For the Lake Neighborhood, the percentages by which the new proposed objective function outperforms the first comparison and the second comparison objective functions from the iteration numbers are 30% and 100%, respectively. For the North Neighborhood, these corresponding two values are 70% and 90%, respectively, while for the Sunshine Mediterranean Neighborhood, the values are both 100%. Note that in the case where the two objective functions have the same iteration numbers, the superior one is further selected by the actual obtained objective function values.

Furthermore, the shape parameter values obtained by the new proposed objective function is much closer to those obtained by the first comparison objective function. Since the iteration numbers need to reach the objective function level of the first comparison objective function are smaller than those obtained by the second comparison objective function, the first comparison objective function can be regarded as a better one as compared to the second comparison objective function from the iteration speed perspective. According to this, it can be concluded that the new proposed objective function is the best one among the three objective functions from the iteration speed perspective.

It can also be observed from Table 1 that the new proposed objective function is more sensitive to the change of the mutation scenarios as compared to the other two objective functions. This can be indicated by the ten shape parameter values under ten different mutation scenarios in the Sunshine Mediterranean Neighborhood, where those obtained by the new proposed objective function varied (though the variation is small) with the change of the mutation scenarios, while there are almost no change to the shape parameters obtained by the other two objective functions under different mutation scenarios). Thus, the new proposed objective function is better for its sensitivity.

As shown in Table 1, there is little difference among the shape parameter values obtained by the first objective function under the ten different mutation scenarios. Thus, to avoid the one-sidedness, the final shape parameter in this paper is determined by calculating the mean of the ten shape parameter values. As also seen from Table 1, the shape parameter values obtained by the new proposed and the first comparison objective functions are nearly equal. However, results obtained by the second comparison objective functions have larger difference as those gained by the new proposed objective functions. In the next section, this conclusion will be convinced by some statistics analysis and a test named the Moses Extreme Reactions (MER).

Table 1. Parameters obtained by three different objective functions.

Objective Function Type		Lake Neighborhood			Objective Function Type		North Neighborhood			Objective Function Type		Sunshine Mediterranean Neighborhood		
	Mutation Scenario	Iteration Number	Objective Function Value	k		Mutation Scenario	Iteration Number	Objective Function Value	k		Mutation Scenario	Iteration Number	Objective Function Value	k
1	1	18	6.9259×10^{-6}	1.7718	1	1	18	2.4220×10^{-6}	1.4420	1	1	13	3.8005×10^{-6}	1.5006
	2	13	9.2435×10^{-6}	1.7718		2	11	8.9312×10^{-6}	1.4420		2	4	6.9169×10^{-6}	1.5001
	3	10	7.4746×10^{-6}	1.7718		3	11	3.8947×10^{-6}	1.4420		3	6	5.8058×10^{-6}	1.5002
	4	16	6.9762×10^{-6}	1.7718		4	20	3.9435×10^{-6}	1.4420		4	11	6.5550×10^{-7}	1.5004
	5	20	5.6428×10^{-6}	1.7718		5	19	3.2357×10^{-6}	1.4420		5	14	9.6016×10^{-6}	1.5008
	6	19	9.4087×10^{-6}	1.7718		6	25	9.9202×10^{-6}	1.4420		6	23	4.2009×10^{-7}	1.5004
	7	17	4.6030×10^{-6}	1.7718		7	19	6.2421×10^{-6}	1.4420		7	9	4.0648×10^{-6}	1.5006
	8	34	4.9812×10^{-6}	1.7718		8	39	7.1700×10^{-6}	1.4420		8	7	2.6037×10^{-6}	1.5005
	9	13	7.4412×10^{-6}	1.7718		9	12	2.0244×10^{-6}	1.4420		9	7	6.3303×10^{-6}	1.5007
	10	13	9.7352×10^{-6}	1.7718		10	16	7.5910×10^{-7}	1.4420		10	12	5.6289×10^{-6}	1.5002
2	1	16	8.3027×10^{-7}	1.7718	2	1	18	8.4671×10^{-6}	1.4420	2	1	16	8.7020×10^{-8}	1.5004
	2	13	5.9090×10^{-6}	1.7718		2	14	7.8769×10^{-7}	1.4420		2	13	4.4437×10^{-6}	1.5004
	3	12	1.6624×10^{-6}	1.7718		3	12	8.9997×10^{-7}	1.4420		3	10	8.0433×10^{-6}	1.5004
	4	14	1.8828×10^{-6}	1.7718		4	19	3.1183×10^{-6}	1.4420		4	24	1.1569×10^{-6}	1.5004
	5	12	8.6969×10^{-6}	1.7718		5	18	5.0858×10^{-6}	1.4420		5	19	1.5519×10^{-6}	1.5004
	6	23	7.7303×10^{-6}	1.7718		6	38	6.8227×10^{-6}	1.4420		6	37	8.6291×10^{-6}	1.5004
	7	14	5.2478×10^{-6}	1.7718		7	19	5.2558×10^{-6}	1.4420		7	12	7.9567×10^{-6}	1.5004
	8	36	7.3341×10^{-6}	1.7718		8	40	3.7643×10^{-6}	1.4420		8	26	8.7335×10^{-6}	1.5004
	9	6	2.7901×10^{-6}	1.7718		9	17	5.2971×10^{-6}	1.4420		9	12	3.3013×10^{-6}	1.5004
	10	13	3.3655×10^{-6}	1.7718		10	18	1.6249×10^{-6}	1.4420		10	15	3.0078×10^{-6}	1.5004
3	1	21	5.5706×10^{-6}	1.8322	3	1	21	3.4492×10^{-6}	1.5010	3	1	21	9.1215×10^{-8}	1.5743
	2	16	6.0681×10^{-6}	1.8322		2	13	8.2479×10^{-6}	1.5010		2	13	9.8864×10^{-7}	1.5743
	3	15	2.6695×10^{-6}	1.8322		3	10	5.9725×10^{-6}	1.5010		3	13	7.4311×10^{-6}	1.5743
	4	19	8.4953×10^{-6}	1.8322		4	23	6.4584×10^{-6}	1.5010		4	23	5.0605×10^{-8}	1.5743
	5	23	2.9226×10^{-6}	1.8322		5	22	1.7365×10^{-6}	1.5010		5	19	1.0723×10^{-6}	1.5743
	6	50	2.9237×10^{-7}	1.8322		6	39	7.8088×10^{-6}	1.5010		6	42	4.8807×10^{-6}	1.5743
	7	26	1.4879×10^{-6}	1.8322		7	24	7.5942×10^{-6}	1.5010		7	18	3.6736×10^{-6}	1.5743
	8	43	4.7320×10^{-6}	1.8322		8	44	2.3022×10^{-6}	1.5010		8	50	8.4293×10^{-6}	1.5743
	9	16	9.1194×10^{-6}	1.8322		9	16	4.8699×10^{-7}	1.5010		9	15	9.2910×10^{-6}	1.5743
	10	18	8.8692×10^{-6}	1.8322		10	16	4.7118×10^{-6}	1.5010		10	24	3.0137×10^{-6}	1.5743

3.2. Three Objective Functions Comparison

In this section, the three objective functions are compared from the iteration number and the objective function value aspects. These three objective functions are firstly analyzed by comparing the corresponding results with regard to the three groups and two group pairs shown in Figure 1.

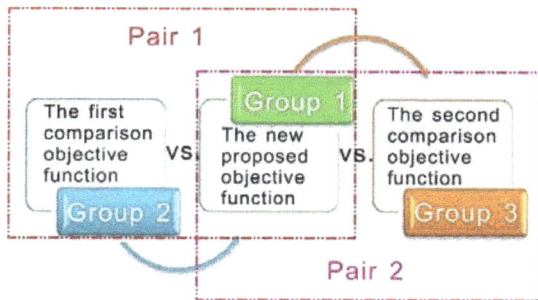

Figure 1. Groups and group pairs.

3.2.1. Analysis and Comparison Over the Three Groups

Boxplot Results Analysis

Figure 2(a1–c1) show the boxplots of the iteration number over the above defined three groups, where on each box, the central mark is the median, and the edges of the box are the lower quantile and the upper quantile, respectively. The lower quantile, the median and the upper quantile means the 0.25, 0.5 and 0.75 quantiles, respectively, where the f quantile corresponding to a datum $q(f)$ means that below this datum, approximately a decimal fraction f of the data can be found. It is calculated in this way: Sorting the data in a sequence $\{x_j\}_{j=1,2,\dots,n}$ in an ascending order. By this, the sorted data $\{x_{\langle i \rangle}\}_{i=1,2,\dots,n}$ have rank $i = 1, 2, \dots, n$. Then the quantile value f_i for the datum $x_{\langle i \rangle}$ (equal to $q(f_i)$) is computed as:

$$f_i = \frac{i - 0.5}{n}, i = 1, 2, \dots, n \tag{34}$$

While in the case of the desired quantile value f is equal to none of the f_i values shown in Equation (34), the f quantile $q(f)$ is found by linear interpolation, *i.e.*,:

$$q(f) = q(f_1) + \frac{f - f_1}{f_2 - f_1} [q(f_2) - q(f_1)] \tag{35}$$

where f_1 and f_2 are two unequal values selected from $\{0.5/n, 1.5/n, \dots, (n - 0.5)/n\}$. Note that in the case of the probability value f is less than $0.5)/n$, the value $q(f)$ is assigned to the first value $x_{\langle 1 \rangle}$, while the value $q(f)$ is assigned to the last value $x_{\langle n \rangle}$, when the probability value f is greater than $(n - 0.5)/n$.

In addition, Figure 2(a1–c1) also show the outliers beyond the whiskers which are displayed using +. The whiskers in this paper are specified as 1.0 times the interquartile range, *i.e.*, points larger than $q(0.75) + w[q(0.75) - q(0.25)]$ or smaller than $q(0.25) - w[q(0.75) - q(0.25)]$ are defined as outliers, where w is set to 1.0 in this paper.

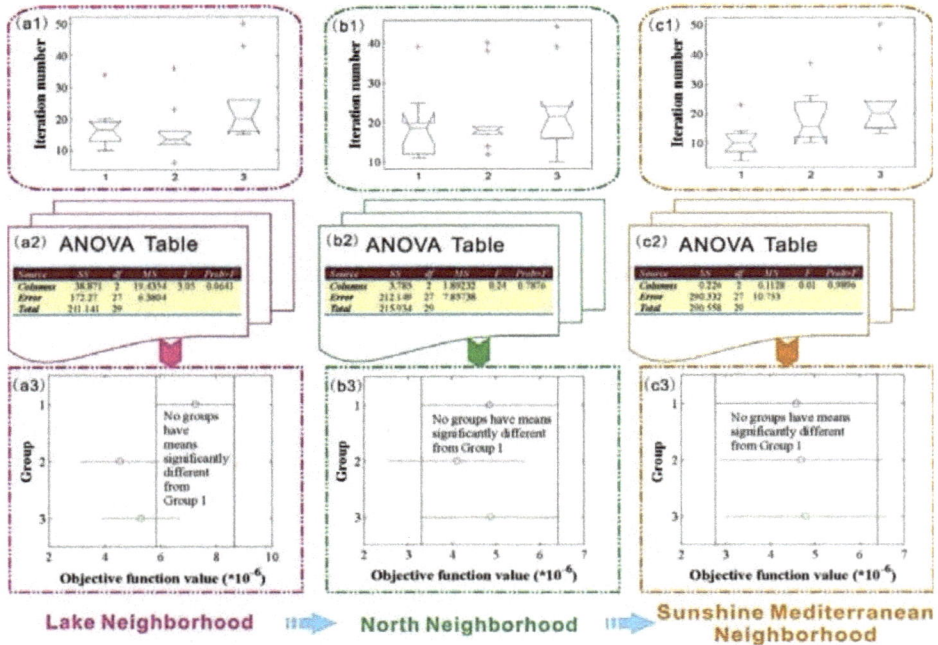

Figure 2. Boxplot and ANOVA comparison results of the three objective functions.

As seen from Figure 2(a1–c1), for the Lake Neighborhood, the number of outliers in the three groups are 1, 3, 2, respectively, while for the other two Neighborhoods, the number of outliers in Groups 1 and 3 remains the same, while values in Group 2 turns to 4 and 1 for the North Neighborhood and the Sunshine Mediterranean Neighborhood, respectively.

Analysis of Variance

Next one-way analysis of variance (ANOVA) was conducted to compare the objective function results of the three groups. Figure 2(a2–c2) provide the ANOVA results of the three neighborhoods, respectively, where *SS*, *df*, *MS* represent the sum of squares, degree of freedom and mean square, respectively, and *Columns*, *Error* mean the feature between groups and feature within groups, respectively, and *Total* indicates the sum of the *Columns* and the *Error*. Specifically, we have the following definitions:

$$SS \text{ of the } Columns = \sum_{i=1}^{k} n_i (\bar{x}_i - \bar{x})^2 \tag{36}$$

$$SS \text{ of the } Error = \sum_{i=1}^{k} \sum_{j=1}^{n_i} (x_{ij} - \bar{x}_i)^2 \tag{37}$$

and

$$SS \text{ of the } Total = \sum_{i=1}^{k} \sum_{j=1}^{n_i} (x_{ij} - \bar{x})^2 \tag{38}$$

where k is the number of the groups, x_{ij} denotes the jth sample in the ith group, n_i represents the number of the samples in the i th group, and $\bar{x}_i$ and $\bar{x}$ indicates the mean of the samples in the ith group and the mean of the samples in all of the groups, respectively. The one-way ANOVA can be conducted according to the following four steps:

Step 1: Determine the null hypothesis. The null hypothesis of the one-way ANOVA is that samples in all of the groups are drawn from populations with the same mean.

Step 2: Select the test statistic. The test statistic of the one-way ANOVA used is the F statistic, which is defined as:

$$F = \frac{SS \text{ of the } Columns/(k-1)}{SS \text{ of the } Error/(n-k)} \tag{39}$$

where n is the total number of the samples, and k–1 and n–k are the degree of freedom of the SS of the *Columns* and SS of the *Error*, respectively.

Step 3: Calculate the value of the test statistic as well as the corresponding probability value p.

Step 4: Make decisions according to the significance level α. In the case of $p < \alpha$, the null hypothesis should be rejected, and the decision that samples in all of the groups are not drawn from populations with the same mean is made; Otherwise, the null hypothesis should be accepted to demonstrate that samples in all of the groups are drawn from populations with the same mean.

As shown in Figure 2(a2–c2), all of the p values in the three neighborhoods are larger than the significance level α, which is set to 0.05 in this paper, this phenomenon indicates that for all of the three neighborhoods, the objective function samples in Groups 1–3 are drawn from populations with the same mean, Figure 2(a3–c3) display the mean comparison results of the three groups.

3.2.2. Test Over the Two Group Pairs

In this section, the three objective functions are analyzed by conducting the MER test over the two group pairs. The basic idea of the MER is that one group of the samples is regarded as the control group, while the other group of the samples is treated as the experimental group, then it is tested whether there are extreme reactions in the experimental group as compared to the control one. The conclusion of the MER is obtained by testing which one of the following hypothesis is accepted:

Null hypothesis: there is no significant difference between the distributions of samples in the control group and the experimental group; *vs.* Alternative hypothesis: there is significant difference between the distributions of samples in the control group and the experimental group.

If the experimental group has extreme reactions, it is assumed that there is no significant difference between the distributions of the control group and the experimental group; instead, there is significant difference between the distributions of these two groups. The detailed analysis process is as follows:

1. First of all, samples in the two groups are mixed and ordered by ascending;
2. Calculate the minimum rank R_{min} and the maximum rank R_{max} of the control group, and obtain the span by:

$$S = R_{\max} - R_{\min} + 1$$

3. To eliminate the effect of the extreme values of the sample data on the analysis results, a proportional (usually this value is set to 5%) of the samples close to the left and the right ends are removed from the control group, and the span of the remaining samples which is named the trimmed span is calculated.

The MERs focus on the analysis of the span and the trimmed span. Obviously, if the values of the span or the trimmed span are small, the two sample groups cannot be mixed fully, and sample values in one group are greater than those in the other group, therefore, it can be regarded that as compared to the control group, the experimental group contains the extreme reactions, and thus the conclusion that there is significant difference between the distributions of these two groups can be obtained; otherwise, if the values of the span or the trimmed span are great, the two sample groups are mixed fully, and the phenomenon that sample values in one group are greater than those in the other group does not exist, therefore, it can be regarded that as compared to the control group, the experimental group does not contain extreme reactions, and thus the conclusion that there is no significant difference between the distributions of these two groups is reached. In general, the H statistics defined as below is used to evaluate the span or the trimmed span:

$$H = \sum_{i=1}^{m} (R_i - \overline{R})^2$$

where m is the number of the samples in the control group, R_i is the rank of the ith control sample in the mixed samples, $\overline{R}$ is the average rank of the control samples. It can be proved that for small samples, the H statistics obey the Hollander distribution, while for large samples, the H statistics approximately obey a normal distribution.

If the value of p is smaller than the given confidence level α, then the null hypothesis should be rejected, and it is regarded that there is significant difference between the distributions of samples in the control group and the experimental group; otherwise, the null hypothesis should be accepted, and the conclusion that there is no significant difference between the distributions of samples in the control group and the experimental group can be obtained. In this paper, the MER technique is used to compare the difference of the three objective functions furthermore. Section 3.2.1 analyzed the three objective function mainly from the shape parameter aspect, in this section, the three objective functions will be analyzed through the iteration number as well as the objective function value.

Table 2 lists the descriptive statistics of Pair 1 and Pair 2, where N denotes the number of the samples in the pair and the hth percentile is equivalent to the $h/100$ quantile. As seen from Table 2, apart from the objective function value of the Lake Neighborhood, the standard deviation of which in Pair 2 is smaller than the one in Pair 1, for other items, the standard deviation values in Pair 2 are all larger than the corresponding values in Pair 1, *i.e.*, when Groups 1 and 3 are mixed, their deviation is larger than the one obtained by mixing Groups 1 and 2. In addition, the difference between the maximum and the minimum present similar phenomenon: apart from the objective function value of the Lake Neighborhood, the difference values for other items in Pair 2 are all larger than those in Pair 1. Based on the descriptive statistics results in Table 2, Table 3 presents the MER test results. Note that in Table 3, the term Outliers trimmed means outliers trimmed from each end. It can be observed from Table 3 that there is only one probability value which is smaller than the predefined confidence level $\alpha = 0.05$, which appears in the iteration number of the Sunshine Mediterranean Neighborhood in Pair 2. This indicates that there is significant difference between the distributions of the iteration number in Groups 1 and 3, while no significant difference can be observed between the corresponding distributions in Groups 1 and 2.

In summary, it can be concluded from these analysis results that the iteration number and the objective function value of the new proposed objective function and the first comparison objective function can be regarded to have nearly no difference between each other. In addition, the shape parameter values obtained by the new proposed and the first comparison objective functions are nearly equal, however, the same conclusion cannot be concluded with regard to the new proposed objective function and the second comparison objective function. Therefore, in the following sections, only the error values obtained by the new proposed and the second objective functions will be compared.

Table 2. Descriptive statistics of the two pairs.

Neighborhood	Item	Pair 1								Pair 2							
								Percentiles								Percentiles	
		N	Mean	Standard Deviation	Minimum	Maximum	25th	50th	75th	N	Mean	Standard Deviation	Minimum	Maximum	25th	50th	75th
Lake Neighborhood	Iteration number	20	16.6000	7.3155	6.0000	36.0000	13.0000	14.0000	18.7500	20	21.0000	10.2341	10.0000	50.0000	15.2500	18.0000	22.5000
	Objective function	20	5.8941	2.6892	0.8303	9.7352	3.6749	6.4175	7.6664	20	6.2645	2.5157	1.4879	9.7352	4.6353	6.4970	8.7757
North Neighborhood	Iteration number	20	20.1500	8.8274	11.0000	40.0000	14.5000	18.0000	19.7500	20	20.9000	9.6404	10.0000	44.0000	13.7500	19.0000	23.7500
	Objective function	20	4.4833	2.7723	0.7591	9.9202	2.1238	3.9191	6.6776	20	4.8656	2.8425	0.4870	9.9202	2.3322	4.3277	7.4882
Sunshine Mediterranean Neighborhood	Iteration number	20	14.5000	7.9637	4.0000	37.0000	9.2500	12.5000	18.2500	20	17.2000	11.5421	4.0000	50.0000	9.5000	13.5000	22.5000
	Objective function	20	4.6370	3.0436	0.0870	9.6016	1.8149	4.2543	7.6968	20	4.6890	3.1493	0.0506	9.6016	1.4552	4.4728	7.3026

Table 3. The Moses Extreme Reactions (MER) test results of the two pairs.

Neighborhood	Item	Pair 1								Pair 2							
		Frequencies			Untrimmed		Trimmed		Outliers Trimmed	Frequencies			Untrimmed		Trimmed		Outliers Trimmed
		Control Sample	Experimental Sample	Total	Span	p	Trimmed Span	p		Control Sample	Experimental Sample	Total	Span	p	Trimmed Span	p	
Lake Neighborhood	Iteration number	10	10	20	18	0.500	11	0.089	1	10	10	20	18	0.500	12	0.185	1
	Objective function	10	10	20	15	0.070	13	0.325	1	10	10	20	16	0.152	13	0.325	1
North Neighborhood	Iteration number	10	10	20	19	0.763	17	0.957	1	10	10	20	17	0.291	16	0.848	1
	Objective function	10	10	20	20	1.000	15	0.686	1	10	10	20	19	0.763	16	0.848	1
Sunshine Mediterranean Neighborhood	Iteration number	10	10	20	17	0.291	12	0.185	1	10	10	20	17	0.291	10	0.035	1
	Objective function	10	10	20	19	0.763	13	0.325	1	10	10	20	19	0.763	13	0.325	1

3.2.3. Fitting Error Comparison

The error comparison analysis in this section is built on final shape parameter, which is determined by the mean of the ten shape parameter values. Since the shape parameter obtained by the new proposed and the first comparison objective functions are quite the same, this section only present the error results of the new proposed and the second comparison objective functions, for which the shape parameters are different.

Let the minimum and the maximum active power values of the transformer are *MI* and *MA*, respectively. Then each interval [*k*, *k* + 1] can be divided into several subintervals with the same length, where *k* are the integers from *Floor*(*MI*) to *Ceil*(*MA*), and *Ceil*(*MA*) denotes the integer larger than *MA* which has the minimum distance with *MA*, similarly, *Floor*(*MI*) represents the integer smaller than or equal to *MI* which has the minimum distance with *MI*.

Figure 3 shows the PDF and CDF figures obtained by the new proposed and the second comparison objective functions where each unit interval [*k*, *k* + 1] is divided into different subintervals: Figure 3(a–c, a1–c1, a2–c2) show the figures of the three neighborhoods where each unit interval is divided into five subintervals, respectively, Figure 3(a1–c1) are the corresponding figures where each unit interval is divided into two subintervals, respectively, and Figure 3(a2–c2) provide the results with no division to the unit interval. The corresponding error values are listed in Table 4.

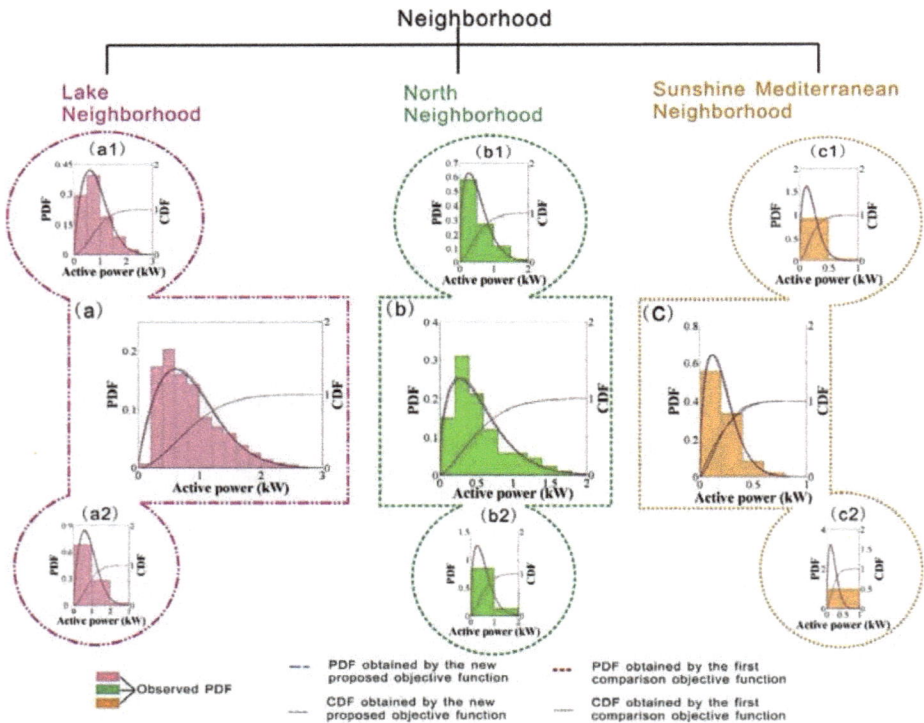

Figure 3. PDF and CDF results of the active power in the three neighborhoods by dividing the unit interval into different subintervals.

Table 4. Error values under different subinterval numbers. Kolmogorov-Smirnov test error (KSE); root mean square error (RMSE).

Neighborhood Name	Subinterval Numbers	The New Proposed Objective Function		The Second Comparison Objective Function	
		KSE	RMSE	KSE	RMSE
Lake Neighborhood	5 subintervals	0.05379	0.02199	0.04775	0.02236
	2 subintervals	0.02378	0.01916	0.03190	0.02414
	1 subinterval	0.02378	0.02190	0.02765	0.02646
North Neighborhood	5 subintervals	0.03878	0.02840	0.03896	0.02774
	2 subintervals	0.03739	0.03926	0.04639	0.04695
	1 subinterval	0.02687	0.02839	0.03079	0.03186
Sunshine Mediterranean Neighborhood	5 subintervals	0.00757	0.00518	0.01287	0.01247
	2 subintervals	0.01076	0.01082	0.01568	0.01571
	1 subinterval	0.00012	0.00012	0.00005	0.00005

3.3. Comprehensive Overload Capability Assessment Results

The comprehensive overload capability of power transformers is obtained based on the running time duration of the power transformers under overload conditions and the overloading probability calculation results: the running time duration of the power transformer is obtained according to the given ambient temperature and the rated load first, then the overloading probability is obtained from the probability of the current, which is derived from the probability of the corresponding active power. Overload capability measurement of power transformers based on the knowledge of overloading probability provides a more reliable assessment result.

The Weibull distribution can be used to evaluate transformer reliability. The scientific and reasonable assessment of reliability development trends is based on the research and mastery of a large amount of historical materials and accurate methods. On the basis of foregoing research, the reliability assessment of transformers can be performed by using the model of transportation load and test quantity. Therefore, the reliability assessment of transformers can be carried out in these two aspects. The valid assessment means the situation of transportation load and test quantity that can have an influence on the reliability of transformer so that we can obtain the future reliability assessment of the transformer.

The reliability model based on transportation overload is mainly based on the use of the hot-spot temperature of the transformer to evaluate the degree of thermal aging so that the fault probability of transformer can be obtained by analyzing the insulation aging damage. The hot-spot temperature is related to the operation load of the transformer and the environmental temperature; therefore, the key of the assessment is to evaluate the future load level and the environmental temperature. What largely affects the reliability change curve of a transformer is the increase of load level. Without great changes of the network structure, the assessment of future load increases can be conducted by evaluating the local load increases. If the load increase level in the assessment is fast, and the current transformer is burnt-in, one should consider adding new transformers in the future to reduce the load level of the current transformers and decrease the risk of accidents according to specific situations.

4. Conclusions

This paper measures the overload capability of oil-immersed power transformers, which is of particular importance in avoiding their catastrophic failure and guaranteeing the normal operation of power grids. The running time duration of the power transformers under overload conditions is calculated with the help of the hot-spot temperature. Then the overloading probability is fitted by the Weibull distribution, in which the desired parameters are computed according to a new proposed objective function. Compared with the previous two objective functions, the new proposed one acheived much better performance in terms of the convergence speed and the final objective function values. The integration of the running time duration and the overload probability provides a more comprehensive and reliable assessment results to the overload capability of power transformers.

Acknowledgments: Acknowledgments: The work was supported by the National Natural Science Foundation of China (Grant No. 71171102).

Author Contributions: Author Contributions: Wang, C. and Wu, J. conceived and designed the experiments; Wang, C. and Zhao, W.G. performed the experiments; Wang, J.Z. and Zhao, W.G. analyzed the data; Wu, J. wrote the paper and Wang, C. checked the whole paper.

Conflicts of Interest: Conflicts of Interest: The authors declare no conflict of interest.

Appendix A

According to the PDF of the Weibull distribution, the mean ($\bar{a}$) and the standard deviation (σ) of the active power can be obtained by:

$$
\begin{aligned}
\bar{a} &= \int_0^{+\infty} af(a)\,da \\
&= \int_0^{+\infty} a\left(\frac{k}{c}\right)\left(\frac{a}{c}\right)^{k-1}\exp\left[-\left(\frac{a}{c}\right)^k\right]da \\
&= \int_0^{+\infty} a\exp\left[-\left(\frac{a}{c}\right)^k\right]d\left(\frac{a}{c}\right)^k \\
&= \int_0^{+\infty} c\left[\left(\frac{a}{c}\right)^k\right]^{(1+1/k)-1}\exp\left[-\left(\frac{a}{c}\right)^k\right]d\left(\frac{a}{c}\right)^k \\
&= c\int_0^{+\infty} \left[\left(\frac{a}{c}\right)^k\right]^{(1+1/k)-1}\exp\left[-\left(\frac{a}{c}\right)^k\right]d\left(\frac{a}{c}\right)^k \\
&= c\Gamma\left(1+\frac{1}{k}\right)
\end{aligned}
\tag{A1}
$$

$$
\begin{aligned}
\sigma^2 &= E(a-\bar{a})^2 \\
&= Ea^2 - (Ea)^2 \\
&= \int_0^{+\infty} a^2\left(\frac{k}{c}\right)\left(\frac{a}{c}\right)^{k-1}\exp\left[-\left(\frac{a}{c}\right)^k\right]da - c^2\Gamma^2\left(1+\frac{1}{k}\right) \\
&= \int_0^{+\infty} c^2\left[\left(\frac{a}{c}\right)^k\right]^{(1+2/k)-1}\exp\left[-\left(\frac{a}{c}\right)^k\right]d\left(\frac{a}{c}\right)^k - c^2\Gamma^2\left(1+\frac{1}{k}\right) \\
&= c^2\Gamma\left(1+\frac{2}{k}\right) - c^2\Gamma^2\left(1+\frac{1}{k}\right)
\end{aligned}
\tag{A2}
$$

So:

$$
\frac{\sigma^2}{\bar{a}^2} = \frac{\Gamma(1+2/k) - \Gamma^2(1+1/k)}{\Gamma^2(1+1/k)}
\tag{A3}
$$

However, there is always some error between the left side and the right side of the Equation (A3). Thus, the residual value ε defined as below is used as the first objective function in this paper just as Liu *et al.* did in [16]:

$$
\varepsilon = \frac{\sigma^2}{\bar{a}^2} - \frac{\Gamma(1+2/k) - \Gamma^2(1+1/k)}{\Gamma^2(1+1/k)}
\tag{A4}
$$

Appendix B

Given the active power series $\{a_i\}_{i=1}^n$, the joint PDF of the Weibull distribution can be expressed as:

$$
\prod_{i=1}^n f(a_i; k, c) = \left(\frac{k}{c}\right)^n\left(\frac{a_1}{c}\cdot\frac{a_2}{c}\cdots\cdots\frac{a_n}{c}\right)^{k-1}\exp\left[-\left(\frac{a_1}{c}\right)^k - \left(\frac{a_2}{c}\right)^k - \cdots - \left(\frac{a_n}{c}\right)^k\right]
\tag{B1}
$$

Thus, according to the maximum likelihood approach, the parameters k and c can be calculated according to

$$\begin{cases} \dfrac{\partial \prod\limits_{i=1}^{n} f(a_i;k,c)}{\partial k} = 0 \\[4mm] \dfrac{\partial \prod\limits_{i=1}^{n} f(a_i;k,c)}{\partial c} = 0 \end{cases} \tag{B2}$$

That is:

$$c = \left(\frac{1}{n} \sum_{i=1}^{n} a_i^k \right)^{1/k} \tag{B3}$$

and

$$k = \left[\frac{\sum_{i=1}^{n} a_i^k \ln a_i}{\sum_{i=1}^{n} a_i^k} - \frac{\sum_{i=1}^{n} \ln a_i}{n} \right]^{1/k} \tag{B4}$$

Generally, there will be an error between the right and the left side of Equation (B4). Therefore, the following equation has been set as the second objective function in this paper:

$$\varepsilon = k - \left[\frac{\sum_{i=1}^{n} a_i^k \ln a_i}{\sum_{i=1}^{n} a_i^k} - \frac{\sum_{i=1}^{n} \ln a_i}{n} \right]^{1/k} \tag{B5}$$

References

1. Caro, M.A.; Rios, M.A. Super components contingency modeling for security assessment in power systems. *IEEE Lat. Am. Trans.* **2009**, *7*, 552–559. [CrossRef]
2. He, J.; Sun, Y.Z.; Wang, P.; Cheng, L. A hybrid conditions-dependent outage model of a transformer in reliability evaluation. *IEEE Trans. Power Deliv.* **2009**, *24*, 2025–2033. [CrossRef]
3. Zhu, Z.L.; Zhou, J.Y.; Yan, C.H.; Chen, L.J. Power system operation risk assessment based on a novel probability distribution of component repair time and utility theory. In Proceedings of the 2012 Asia-Pacific Power and Energy Engineering Conference (APPEEC), Shanghai, China, 27–29 March 2012.
4. Chen, Q.; Mili, L. Composite power system vulnerability evaluation to cascading failures using importance sampling and antithetic variates. *IEEE Trans. Power Syst.* **2013**, *28*, 2321–2330. [CrossRef]
5. Aubin, J.; Pierce, L.W.; Langhame, Y. Effect of oil viscosity on transformer loading capability at low ambient-temperatures. *IEEE Trans. Power Deliv.* **1992**, *7*, 516–524. [CrossRef]
6. Tenbohlen, S.; Stirl, T.; Stach, M. Assessment of overload capacity of power transformers by on-line monitoring systems. In Proceedings of the IEEE Power Engineering Society Winter Meeting, Columbus, OH, USA, 28 January–1 February 2001.
7. Bosworth, T.; Setford, S.; Heywood, R.; Saini, S. Electrochemical sensor for predicting transformer overload by phenol measurement. *Talanta* **2003**, *59*, 797–807. [CrossRef]
8. Edstrom, F.; Rosenlind, J.; Alvehag, K.; Hilber, P.; Soder, L. Influence of ambient temperature on transformer overloading during cold load pickup. *IEEE Trans. Power Deliv.* **2013**, *28*, 153–161. [CrossRef]
9. Estrada, J.H.; Ramírez, S.V.; Cortés, C.L.; Plata, E.A.C. Magnetic flux entropy as a tool to predict transformer's failures. *IEEE Trans. Magn.* **2013**, *49*, 4729–4732. [CrossRef]
10. Liu, W.J.; Wang, X.; Zheng, Y.H.; Li, L.X.; Xu, Q.S. The assessment of the overload capacity of transformer based on the temperature reverse extrapolation method. *Adv. Mater. Res.* **2014**, *860–863*, 2153–2156. [CrossRef]
11. Galdi, V.; Ippolito, L.; Piccolo, A.; Vaccaro, A. Neural diagnostic system for transformer thermal overload protection. *IEE Proc. Electr. Power Appl.* **2000**, *147*, 415–421. [CrossRef]
12. Galdi, V.; Ippolito, L.; Piccolo, A.; Vaccaro, A. Genetic Algorithm based parameters identification for power transformer thermal overload protection. In *Artificial Neural Nets and Genetic Algorithms*; Springer: Berlin, Germany, 2001; pp. 308–311.

13. Galdi, V.; Ippolito, L.; Piccolo, A.; Vaccaro, A. Application of local memory-based techniques for power transformer thermal overload protection. *IEE Proc. Electr. Power Appl.* **2001**, *148*, 163–170. [CrossRef]

14. Ippolito, L.; Siano, P. A power transformers' predictive overload system based on a Takagi-Sugeno-Kang fuzzy model. In Proceedings of the 12th IEEE Mediterranean Electrotechnical Conference, Dubrovnik, Croatia, 12–15 May 2004; pp. 301–306.

15. Pradhan, M.K.; Ramu, T.S. On-line monitoring of temperature in power transformers using optimal linear combination of ANNs. In Proceedings of the 2004 IEEE International Symposium on Electrical Insulation Conference, Indianapolis, IN, USA, 19–22 September 2004; pp. 70–73.

16. Villacci, D.; Bontempi, G.; Vaccaro, A.; Birattari, M. The role of learning methods in the dynamic assessment of power components loading capability. *IEEE Trans. Ind. Electron.* **2005**, *52*, 280–290. [CrossRef]

17. Jiang, Y.Q.; Lu, Z.H. Research on enhancement of overload capacity for 500 kV transformer. *East China Electr. Power* **2004**, *32*, 13–17.

18. Zhao, D.Y.; Fan, H.; Ren, Z.J. *Reliability Engineering and Applications*; National Defend Industry Press: Beijing, China, 2009.

19. Contin, A.; Montanari, G.C.; Ferraro, C. PD source recognition by weibull processing of pulse height distributions. *IEEE Trans. Dielectr. Electr. Insul.* **2000**, *7*, 48–58. [CrossRef]

20. Mao, S.; Wang, L. *Accelerated Life Testing*; Beijing Science Press: Beijing, China, 2000.

21. Wu, J.; Wang, J.Z.; Chi, D.Z. Wind energy potential assessment for the site of Inner Mongolia in China. *Renew. Sustain. Energy Rev.* **2013**, *21*, 215–228. [CrossRef]

22. Chang, T.P. Estimation of wind energy potential using different probability density functions. *Appl. Energy* **2011**, *88*, 1848–1856. [CrossRef]

23. Fyrippis, I.; Axaopoulos, P.J.; Panayiotou, G. Wind energy potential assessment in Naxos Island, Greece. *Appl. Energy* **2010**, *87*, 577–586. [CrossRef]

energies

MDPI

Article

Study of the Impact of Initial Moisture Content in Oil Impregnated Insulation Paper on Thermal Aging Rate of Condenser Bushing

Youyuan Wang [1], Kun Xiao [1,*], Bijun Chen [1,2] and Yuanlong Li [1]

[1] State Key Laboratory of Power Transmission Equipment & System Security and New Technology,
    Chongqing University, Chongqing 400044, China; y.wang@cqu.edu.cn (Y.W.); 13883957738@163.com (Y.L.)
[2] State Grid Tianjin Electric Power Supply Company, Tianjin 300457, China; bijunch@126.com
* Correspondence: 20104427@cqu.edu.cn; Tel.: +86-133-6836-5907

Academic Editor: Issouf Fofana
Received: 19 October 2015; Accepted: 11 December 2015; Published: 18 December 2015

Abstract: This paper studied the impact of moisture on the correlated characteristics of the condenser bushings oil-paper insulation system. The oil-impregnated paper samples underwent accelerated thermal aging at 130 °C after preparation at different initial moisture contents (1%, 3%, 5% and 7%). All the samples were extracted periodically for the measurement of the moisture content, the degree of polymerization (DP) and frequency domain dielectric spectroscopy (FDS). Next, the measurement results of samples were compared to the related research results of transformer oil-paper insulation, offering a theoretical basis of the parameter analysis. The obtained results show that the moisture fluctuation amplitude can reflect the different initial moisture contents of insulating paper and the mass ratio of oil and paper has little impact on the moisture content fluctuation pattern in oil-paper but has a great impact on moisture fluctuation amplitude; reduction of DP presents an accelerating trend with the increase of initial moisture content, and the aging rate of test samples is higher under low moisture content but lower under high moisture content compared to the insulation paper in transformers. Two obvious "deceleration zones" appeared in the dielectric spectrum with the decrease of frequency, and not only does the integral value of dielectric dissipation factor (tan δ) reflect the aging degree, but it reflects the moisture content in solid insulation. These types of research in this paper can be applied to evaluate the condition of humidified insulation and the aging state of solid insulation for condenser bushings.

Keywords: oil-impregnated paper; initial moisture content; thermal aging; frequency domain dielectric spectroscopy (FDS); degree of polymerization (DP); dielectric dissipation factor (tan δ)

---

1. Introduction

Currently, 30% of the cases of main transformer faults are caused by bushing troubles, which is a key threat to the safety of the power grid [1–5]. Most high voltage bushings are condenser bushings. The main types of insulation of condenser bushings are capacitor cores, which are conductive rods wrapped by multi-layer insulation paper and aluminum foils, and the insulation performance of condenser bushings is vulnerable [1,3]. In the core, the aluminum foils are used to make the electric field uniform; however, the edges of aluminum foil are more likely to have discharge compared to the oil-paper insulation in transformers [1]. In addition, without radiators and cooling devices in bushing, it is easy for heat to accumulate around the conductive rod when the bushing is under operation or even lead to an explosion [1]. The failure rate of the other parts of bushings is far less than that of the capacitor core [6]. Thus, the crucial insulation part of capacitive bushing is the internal capacitive core [7].

Statistical data has shown that the main reasons for oil-paper capacitive bushing failures are the following: moistened insulation, manufacturing defect, oil leakage, insulation aging, and the failures caused by moistened insulation is the most common [2,3]. Studies have shown that thermal degradation, hydrolysis and oxidation degradation are the three main predominant factors causing the deterioration of oil-paper insulation [4]. In addition, the moisture absorption ability of insulation paper is much stronger than that of insulation oil [5]; therefore, studying the influence of moisture on the aging characteristics of oil-paper bushing has engineering significance for evaluating the insulation loss caused by moisture.

At present, dielectric spectroscopy in time or frequency domain offers new opportunities for an off-line, insulation condition assessment of high voltage (HV) electric power equipment and its predictive maintenance nondestructively and reliably in the field [8–11]. Dielectric spectroscopy techniques in time and frequency domain can be applied to monitor the condition of oil-impregnated paper condenser bushings [9]. The results researched by Issouf Fofana *et al.* indicate that capacitance ratio and direct current conductivity deduced from the spectroscopic measurements can be used to accurately monitor insulation condition, and both parameters were found to increase with moisture or aging duration [8]. In addition, the poles computed from frequency domain spectroscopy also can assess oil-paper insulation condition [11]. It is mentioned in [12,13] that the dielectric spectroscopy of oil-paper condenser bushing is different from that of oil-paper in transformers at low frequency interval and the characteristics of dielectric spectroscopy at frequency interval 10^{-2}–10^3 Hz can sensitively reflect the variation of moisture content in condenser bushing. However, the condition of oil-impregnated paper condenser bushings is qualitatively assessed in these research reports. More accurate diagnostic methods are necessary to be researched based on dielectric spectroscopy.

In this article, a 43-day accelerated thermal aging under 130 °C is carried out for samples, referring to the humidified insulation test of transformer oil-paper [14,15]. In addition, the moisture content, degree of polymerization (DP) and dielectric dissipation factor (tan δ) of samples are periodically measured during the aging process. The change rules of these measurements have been analyzed in this article, and the quantitative assessment on the remaining life of oil-paper condenser bushing has also been discussed in this investigation.

2. Preparation for Thermal Aging Test

2.1. Test Sample

The capacitor core of condenser bushing is a conductive rod wound by multi-layer insulation paper and aluminum foils [9]. The construction of capacitor core is shown in Figure 1. It is mentioned in [7] that the main manufacturing steps for a bushing consist of rolling the capacitor core, vacuum drying, assembly and vacuum oil immersion, as shown in Figure 2.

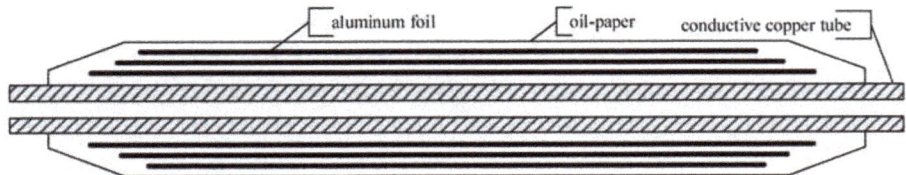

Figure 1. The structure diagram of a condenser core.

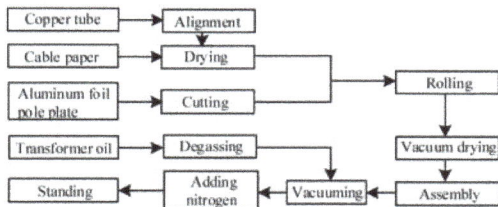

Figure 2. The manufacturing steps of a condenser core [7].

The manufacturing steps are as follows:

(1) Test materials preparation

Insulation paper with 0.12 mm in thickness, aluminum foil with 0.01 mm in thickness, copper tube with 10 mm in outer diameter and 96 mm in length, and #25 Karamay transformer oil ($\rho = 0.8846$ g/cm^3). The insulation paper is shaped into rectangular paper tape with 96 mm in width, 1390 mm in length and each tape weighs 16.62 g.

(2) Identify the layer number of aluminum foil and the thickness of insulation

In accordance with the insulation requirement of a 10 kV bushing, according to reference [7], the number of layers should be three. The common insulation layer thickness is approximately 1.0–1.2 mm, so a nine-layer cable paper (approximately 1.08 mm) is selected as an insulating layer. Because the designed capacitor core model of bushing is far smaller than that of real bushing, the length of the aluminum foil and insulation paper has little effect on the investigation. The length of the aluminum foil and the width of the copper tube and insulation paper are set to the same value for convenience.

(3) Winding capacitor core

Using the modified winding machine to wind the cable paper tightly around the copper tube, one-layer aluminum foil was wound after winding nine-layer paper. The width of aluminum foil is shown in Table 1 and the length is 96 mm, the same as the paper. After winding the three-layer aluminum foils, wind all the remaining insulating paper and then fix with white gauze. The capacitor core model of bushing is shown in Figure 3.

Table 1. The width of aluminum foil.

The Layer Number	1	2	3
The width of aluminum foil/mm	38.33	45.61	53.09

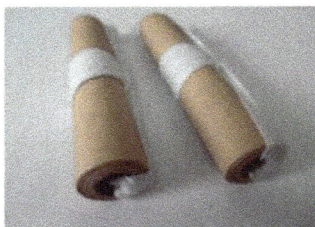

Figure 3. The capacitor core model of condenser bushing.

2.2. Control of the Initial Moisture Content

The capacitor core models of bushing are divided into four groups (respectively named A, B, C, and D) by four kinds of initial moisture content, and each group has seven models. These models are placed into 28 wide mouth flasks, respectively. Each flask contains a capacitor core model and an additional 21 pieces of paper. The size of added paper is 85 mm × 695 mm, and the total mass is 116.77 g. Thus, each flask requires 133.39 g insulating paper and 230 mL of dehydrated and degassed #25 transformer oil to ensure that the mass ratio of oil and paper is roughly equal to 1.5. The details of treating process are as follows:

(1) Place the group A unsealed wide mouth flasks in a vacuum drying oven, set the temperature to 90 °C and the vacuum level to 50 Pa, and let them stand for 24 h. (2) Place the group B unsealed wide mouth flasks in the vacuum drying oven, set the temperature to 30 °C and the vacuum level to 50 Pa, and let them stand for 16 h. (3) Place the group C unsealed wide mouth flasks into the temperature humidity chamber, set the temperature to 40 °C and the relative humidity to 30%, and let them stand for 48 h. (4) Place the group D unsealed wide mouth flasks in the laboratory under normal temperature and pressure and without treatment.

After the above processing, quickly add 230 mL dehydrated and degassed #25 insulating oil into 28 wide mouth flasks, respectively. Next, seal the wide mouth flasks, place them into the vacuum drying oven again, set the temperature to 40 °C and the vacuum level to 50 Pa, and let them stand for 24 h. At the end of this processing, put 24 flasks into six aging tanks. Each tank contains four samples with different moisture contents. The samples in the remaining four flasks are used to measure the initial parameters, which are shown in the Table 2. The six aging tanks are sealed and filled with nitrogen under atmospheric pressure, and placed in the accelerated aging box to undergo thermal aging 43 days at 130 °C.

Table 2. The initial parameters of test samples.

Group	A	B	C	D
Initial average moisture content/%	1.125	3.116	5.093	7.263
DP	1159	1173	1171	1165

2.3. The Measurement of Aging Characteristic Parameters

The Cartesian Coulomb moisture meter KF-831+KF-855 is used to measure the moisture content of the oil paper. The concept 80 testing system manufactured by Novocontrol Company is used to measure broadband dielectric spectroscopy. The testing frequency range of the system is from 10^{-6} Hz to 10^5 Hz. The measurable parameters include the dielectric dissipation factor, the permittivity, the capacitance, the conductivity and so on. The NCY2 automatic viscosity tester manufactured by Shanghai Scientific Instruments Company is used to test the polymerization degree of the insulation paper, according to the relevant national standards referenced by "ASTMD 4243" [5].

3. Effect of Moisture on the Physical and Chemical Properties of the Insulating Paper

3.1. Change Trend of the Moisture Content in Insulating Paper

In the transformer oil paper insulation system, the moisture absorption ability of insulation paper is approximately 10^4 times stronger than that of insulating oil, and the vast majority of moisture exists in the insulation paper when the moisture is in balance in the oil-paper insulation system [16]. For condenser bushing, the thickness of insulation paper is thinner than that of insulation paper in transformers and the moisture absorption ability is stronger, so the moisture is almost completely concentrated in the insulation paper, accelerating the insulation aging.

Figure 4 represents the moisture change rule of the insulation paper with different initial moisture contents during the aging process. The moisture content in the samples is found to show a decline in volatility during the aging process—the higher the initial moisture content, the greater the moisture fluctuation amplitude during the aging process. The moisture contents of group A, B and C reach lower levels after 15 to 20 days of aging—1.9% in group A, 2.3% in group B, and 2.1% in group C, whereas the moisture content of group D reaches 2.5%, a lower level after 30 days of aging. During the whole aging process, the moisture contents of all four groups have different fluctuation amplitude—1.211% in group A, 1.691% in group B, 2.957% in group C, and 4.69% in group D. The moisture change rule of test samples is in accordance with that of oil-paper in transformers—that is, the more initial moisture there is, the greater is the moisture fluctuation amplitude in the paper [17,18].

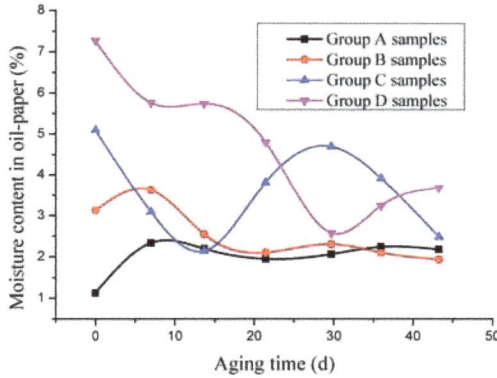

Figure 4. The moisture change rule of test samples.

The moisture contents of groups A and B both slightly increased and then decreased. The explanation for this phenomenon is as follows: the moisture absorbing capacity of insulation paper is very strong and the initial moisture content is at a low level and an unsaturated state, making it inevitable to absorb moisture from the air during the process of operation. Thereby, the moisture content slightly increased during the initial aging period. However, due to the positive feedback of aging byproducts, the consumption rate of moisture will be accelerated. In addition, the moisture may be transferred to oil with an increase of temperature, leading to the decrease of moisture content in insulation paper [19]. Then, the absorption of moisture, the consumption of moisture and the transfer of moisture are in dynamic equilibrium, so large moisture fluctuation amplitude will not appear in the oil-paper insulation system.

The initial moisture contents of group C and D are at a high level after the initial preparations. During the initial aging period, the moisture transfer from insulation paper to insulation oil, and the moisture in oil may be transferred to the air above the oil when the relative humidity of oil is greater than that of air. In addition, the hydrolysis of cellulose will consume moisture, thereby leading to the decrease of moisture content. However, the aging byproduct of insulation paper (acid) will accelerate the aging rate of insulating paper, producing more hydrophilic groups and hydrophilic impurities. The hydrophilic groups and impurities will adsorb more moisture, thereby leading to the increase of moisture content during the later aging period. It is because of the high initial moisture content in insulation paper, which leads to more serious aging and a larger amount of transferred moisture. Therefore, it needs more time to reach dynamic equilibrium, and the moisture fluctuation amplitude is at high level.

Reference [18] researched the moisture change rule of insulation paper in the transformer oil-paper insulation system, undergoing thermal aging at 130 °C. The initial moisture contents of the transformer oil-paper were 1%, 3% and 5%, and the moisture fluctuation amplitude were 0.7%, 2.4% and 4.3%, respectively [20,21]. However, the moisture fluctuation amplitude of test samples were 1.211%, 1.691% and 2.957%, respectively. It is observed that the moisture fluctuation amplitude of test samples is less than that of transformer oil-paper, except the initial moisture content is 1%. The reason is that the ratio of oil and paper is high, the moisture absorbing capacity of insulating paper is much stronger than the insulating oil, and the moisture transfer degree is low. The initial moisture content of group A is the lowest, which is maintained at approximately 2% during the aging process. In addition, the moisture fluctuation amplitude is only 0.389% after 15 days of aging. This phenomenon can be explained as follows: the moisture absorption capacity of tested insulation paper is very strong, which can absorb external moisture easily during the process of operation. The moisture content of test samples is not easily maintained at a low level.

The results show that the mass ratio of oil and paper has little impact on the moisture fluctuation pattern in oil-paper but has great impact on the moisture fluctuation amplitude. The moisture fluctuation amplitude can indirectly reflect the condition of humidified insulation in bushing: the large moisture fluctuation amplitude of insulation paper indicates that insulation failure may occur during actual operation. On the contrary, the moisture content of insulation paper is relatively stable during the aging process, which indicates that the condition of humidified insulation is not serious.

3.2. Polymerization Degree (DP) of the Insulating Paper and Insulation Aging Rate

The degree of polymerization of insulating paper is the most intuitive and reliable indicator that can characterize the insulating paper aging degree [21]. In general, the polymerization degree of new insulating paper is more than 1000, and the paper reaches the end of its life when the polymerization degree decreases to a value of 250 [22]. The relationship between the degree of insulation paper polymerization and the aging time is in accordance with the kinetic model [23]. The work presented here uses a zero-order model to study oil-paper in capacitive bushing formula (1):

$$\frac{1}{d_{DP_t}} - \frac{1}{d_{DP_0}} = kt \tag{1}$$

where t is the aging time, d_{DP_t} is the degree of polymerization of the insulating paper at time t, d_{DP0} is the initial value of the degree of polymerization, and k is the average aging rate, representing the degradation rate of the insulation paper during the aging process.

The DP of the different groups decreases, as shown in Figure 5. Zero order kinetic model fitting is shown in Figure 6. The fitting results of the aging rate and goodness of fit are shown in Table 3. The results show that the higher the initial moisture content, the faster decline in DP of insulating paper in the aging process. This phenomenon can be explained by the hydrolysis of cellulose [24]. In addition, hydrogen bonds between the moisture and the insulation paper can reduce the number of hydrogen bonds between the cellulose chains, thus reducing the stability of the molecular chains and increasing the breaking of cellulose.

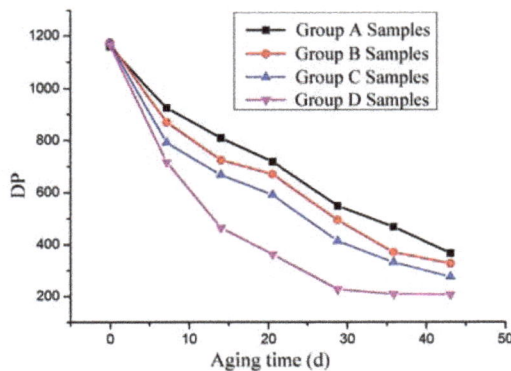

Figure 5. The DP change rule.

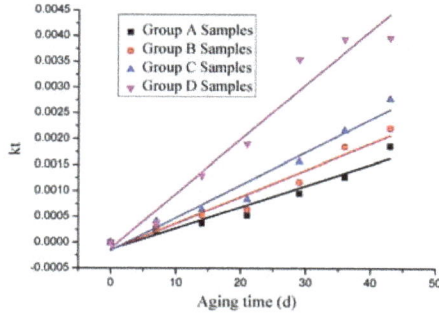

Figure 6. The zero-order dynamics model.

From Table 3, the decrease of insulating paper DP in this test sample is in accordance with the zero-order kinetic model. The aging rate k is between 2×10^{-5}–2.5×10^{-5} in the transformer oil-paper when the initial moisture content is 1% [25]. However, the aging rate of group A is about 4.1×10^{-5}, which is approximately twice as larger as that of paper in transformer when the initial moisture content of paper is 1%. This behavior can be explained as follows: the test paper is much thinner than that used in the transformer, the specific surface area of cellulose is larger, and the moisture absorption ability is stronger. These factors cause the rate of cellulose degradation to increase [25,26]. In addition, the ratio of oil and paper in the bushing model is far less than that in the transformer, and the initial moisture content of insulation paper is the mass ratio of moisture and paper. Thus, for the entire system insulation, the total moisture content in the unit volume sample is far greater than that in the transformer. Thus, small molecule substances such as water, acid, *etc.*, can be easily spread in the cellulose, which can lead to the high degradation rate of the paper.

Table 3. The average aging rate k and goodness of fit R^2.

Sample Group	Sample k	Transformer Oil-Paper k_1	Transformer Oil-Paper k_2	R^2
A	4.132×10^{-5}	2.29×10^{-5}	2.466×10^{-5}	0.9431
B	5.179×10^{-5}	7.42×10^{-5}	8.665×10^{-5}	0.9482
C	6.374×10^{-5}	8.62×10^{-5}	11.75×10^{-5}	0.9611
D	10.59×10^{-5}	—	—	0.9443

Meanwhile, with higher moisture content, the average aging rate of the test sample is lower than that of insulation paper in the transformer. This behavior can be explained as follows: the cellulose molecular chains are easier to fracture among long chains, so the low molecular weight cellulose is harder to fracture compared to the high molecular weight cellulose. Therefore, the decomposition of cellulose is rather intense during the initial aging period. However, the number of long cellulose molecular chains will decrease sharply during the later aging period, leading to the decrease of cellulose decomposition rate. Considering the average decomposition rate during the whole aging process, for the thinner insulation paper with high moisture content in bushing, the number of long cellulose molecular chains is less than that in the transformer, leading to the aging rate being smaller during the later aging period. Thus, the average aging rate of the test sample is lower than that of insulation paper in the transformer during the whole aging process.

From this section, it is clearly observed that bushings are vulnerable to moisture. This vulnerability plays an important role in the accelerated aging of the insulation. However, when applying the observations to onsite assessments, the measurement of DP is a destructive measurement and difficult to realize; as a result, researchers must determine other characteristic quantities that are practicable for bushing insulation onsite monitoring.

4. How Aging and Moisture Content Affect tan δ

4.1. How Aging and Moisture Content Affect tan δ

Dielectric dissipation factor (tan δ) is defined as, dielectric material applied by external voltage, the internal energy loss caused by dielectric conductance and dielectric polarization, which indicates the ratio of active current and reactive current; dielectric dissipation factor does not depend on the geometric structure of the dielectric material [27].

Figure 7 shows the relationships between tan δ and aging time for samples with different initial moisture contents. Analysis of these diagrams indicates the following: first, tan δ tends to increase with decreasing applied frequency; second, the tan δ curve has two "deceleration zone", which appear in the frequency bands of 10^0–10^2 Hz and 10^{-1}–10^{-3} Hz, and in the former middle frequency band, tan δ has a strong relationship with aging time; third, the tan δ curve of high initial moisture content samples has a larger fluctuation range in the "deceleration zone". This phenomenon can be interpreted by Equation (2).

$$\tan\delta = \frac{\varepsilon''}{\varepsilon'} \tag{2}$$

where ε' is the real part of the dielectric coefficient, and ε'' is the imaginary part of the dielectric coefficient. With a reduction in the applied frequency, interfacial polarization is fully developed, leading to increasing polarization loss and an increment of ε''. At the same time, ε' is increasing with the increase of the polarization intensity [28]. The complex correlations between polarization intensity and the speed of polarization result in the "deceleration zone" in a certain frequency band, which is determined by the measuring temperature, oil paper constituents, aging time, and moisture content [24,29].

Because the insulation structure of the capacitance core in the oil-paper bushing is relatively simple, the polarization of the oil-paper is weaker than that of the transformer oil-paper. In addition, the moisture content of the test sample is at a relatively high level, so there are only "deceleration zones" and no minimum point.

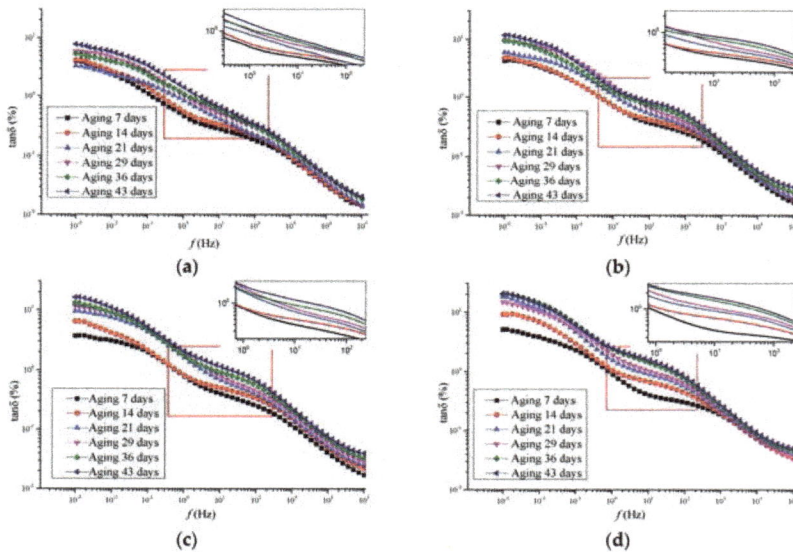

Figure 7. The tan δ curve change with frequency. (**a**) Samples in group A; (**b**) Samples in group B; (**c**) samples In group C; (**d**) samples in Group D.

4.2. Aging and Moisture Characteristics Based on tan δ

This investigation focuses on the integral value of tan δ in the characteristic interval, of which the range is 0.76828 Hz–234.26 Hz, and $I_{\tan\delta}(f)$ of samples with different moisture contents depends linearly on the aging time, as shown in Figure 8, Table 4 and Equation (3).

$$I_{\tan\delta}(f) = \int_{f_1}^{f_2} \tan\delta = A + Bt \qquad (3)$$

where $I_{\tan\delta}(f)$ is equal to the integral value of tan δ in the characteristic interval and the characteristic interval is from f_1 to f_2, $f_1 = 0.76828$ Hz, $f_2 = 234.26$ Hz, t is the aging time, A is intercept and B is slope, which can be received by the fitting straight lines.

In addition, the analysis showed that $\Delta S_{I(\tan\delta)}$ and the initial moisture content in oil-paper apparently follow a linear law. As shown in Figure 9 and Equation (4).

$$\Delta S_{I(\tan\delta)} = P + Q \times (100m) \qquad (4)$$

where $\Delta S_{I(\tan\delta)}$ is equal to the value of $I_{\tan\delta}(f)$ when aging 43 days minus the value of $I_{\tan\delta}(f)$ when aging seven days, m represents the moisture content of oil-paper, P and Q are not a certain values, which can be modified according to the actual situation.

From Table 4, the different initial moisture contents have an obvious influence on slope B, which represents the insulation aging rate characterized by the integral values of tan δ. The k_B represents the aging acceleration factor, the physical meaning of k_B is the increase degree of slope B with the increase of moisture. The value of k_{Bi} is equal to the insulation aging rate $B_{3\%}$, $B_{5\%}$ and $B_{7\%}$ divided by reference insulation aging rate $B_{1\%}$. The results of k_{Bi} are shown in Figure 10, the fitting curve accords with a cubic polynomial, and the goodness of fit is one.

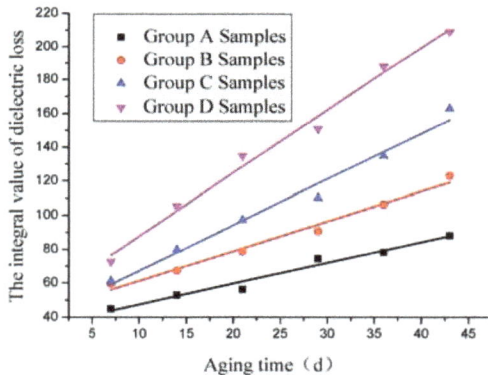

Figure 8. The fitting straight line between $I_{\tan\delta}(f)$ and aging time.

Table 4. The functional fitting parameters.

Parameters	Group A Samples	Group B Samples	Group C Samples	Group D Samples
Intercept A	35.25	43.69	40.20	50.39
Slope B	1.223	1.752	2.697	3.722
Goodness of fit R^2	0.9654	0.9785	0.9765	0.9872

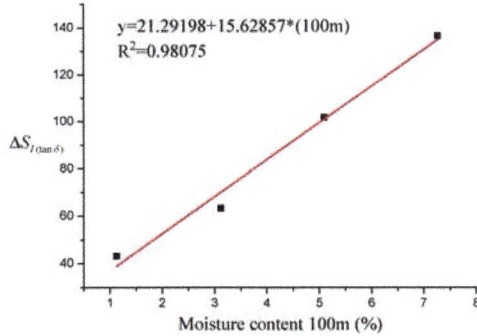

Figure 9. The fitting straight line between $\Delta S_{I(\tan\delta)}$ and moisture content.

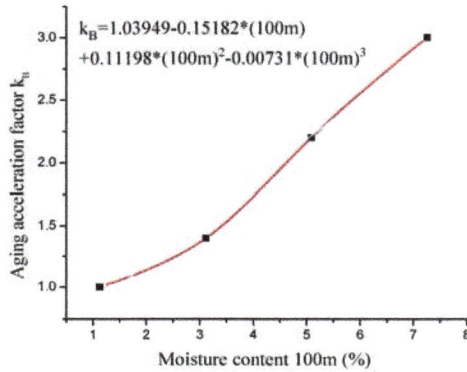

Figure 10. The fitting curve between k_B and moisture.

The life loss of insulation aging caused by damp conditions is calculated by imitating Arrhenius law, which is used to evaluate accelerated aging caused by temperature [28]. First, according to the integral value of the tan δ in the characteristic interval, the equivalent aging stage of the insulation can be calculated by Equation (5) (moisture is not considered for accelerated aging). Second, the damp state of the oil-paper bushing is evaluated by Equation (4), and the accelerated degree of insulation aging caused by the damp state is calculated using Equation (6). Next, the actual insulation aging state is calculated by Equation (7), and the average life of insulation is obtained by statistical data; as a result, the extent of the loss of insulation life can be determined for a device. F_{EQM} in Equation (6) is the equivalent accelerated aging factor calculated according to Figure 10.

$$t_{EQ} = \frac{I_{\tan\delta}(f) - A}{B} \tag{5}$$

$$F_{EQM} = \frac{\sum\limits_{i=1}^{N} k_{Bi}\Delta t_i}{\sum\limits_{i=1}^{N} \Delta t_i} \tag{6}$$

$$t_{loss} = \frac{F_{EQM} \times t_{EQ}}{L_p} \times 100 \tag{7}$$

In Equations (5)–(7), k_{Bi} is the aging acceleration factor caused by moisture at time t_i, Δt_i is the time period of insulation dampness, F_{EQM} is the equivalent accelerated aging factor caused by insulation dampness during the actual time t, t_{loss} is the loss ratio of insulation life (in units of %), t_{EQ} is the equivalent aging stage of insulation, and L_p is the statistics of the normal operating life of oil-paper bushing operating at the condition of normal temperature and dry condition, whose dimension should be consistent with t.

According to the evaluating method provided in this paper, the loss ratio of insulation life t_{loss} of test samples can be evaluated by the test data. The aging time t and DP_T (T is the end point of aging life of insulation paper) are set to 25 days and 250, respectively, and L_p is derived by formula (1), according to test data of samples in group A. The aging state parameters of test samples with different initial moisture contents are shown in Table 5.

Table 5. The state parameters of test samples.

Sample Group	A	B	C	D
k_{B1} (0~7 days)	1.000	1.433	2.205	3.043
k_{B2} (7~14 days)	1.203	1.612	1.423	2.484
k_{B3} (14~21 days)	1.168	1.257	1.155	2.473
k_{B4} (21~25 days)	1.114	1.147	1.683	2.080
F_{EQM}	1.122	1.388	1.609	2.573
L_p/days	76	76	76	76
t_{loss}/%	36.91%	45.66%	52.92%	84.63%

As shown in Table 5, the equivalent accelerated aging factor F_{EQM} and the loss ratio of insulation life t_{loss} have a positive relationship with the initial moisture content, which indicates that the initial moisture content has significant impact on the aging rate of insulation paper and the moisture accelerates the aging of insulation paper. The humidified condition of oil-paper condenser bushing can be quantitatively evaluated by the loss ratio of insulation life based on frequency domain dielectric spectroscopy.

The relationships between $I_{\tan\delta}(f)$ and aging time, $\Delta S_{I(\tan\delta)}$ and moisture content revealed that $I_{\tan\delta}(f)$ not only reflects the aging degree but also the moisture content in solid insulation. From another perspective, the frequency domain dielectric spectroscopy (FDS) results of oil-impregnated paper may be impacted by the moisture content and the aging time, simultaneously. Some separation attempts of moisture content and aging time have been reported recently, but it must be emphasized that moisture and aging separation still constitute a challenging point in this domain [11,30,31].

5. Conclusions

By designing the capacitor core models of condenser bushing with different initial moisture contents, carrying out a 43-day accelerated thermal aging test at 130 °C and studying the variation of the relevant parameters during the aging process, the following conclusions are drawn.

(1) The moisture fluctuation amplitude can reflect the different initial moisture contents of insulating paper; this result is in accordance with the conclusion of transformer oil-paper insulation that the higher the moisture content, the greater the moisture fluctuation amplitude. Furthermore, the moisture fluctuation amplitude of the tested oil-paper was lower than that of the oil-paper in transformer under the same initial moisture content. These results show that the mass ratio of oil and paper has little impact on the moisture content fluctuation pattern in oil-paper but has a great impact on moisture fluctuation amplitude.

(2) The DP of insulation paper in condenser bushing conforms to the zero-order kinetics model. Moreover, the aging rate of test oil-paper is higher than that of oil-paper in transformers under low moisture content but lower than that of oil-paper in transformers under high moisture content. These

results indicate that the initial moisture content has appreciable impact on the decline rate of the degree of polymerization during the initial aging period.

(3) Two obvious "deceleration zones" appeared in the dielectric spectrum with the decrease of frequency: 10^0–10^2 Hz and 10^{-1}–10^{-3} Hz. In addition, tan δ has strong regularity with the aging time in middle-frequency interval. Analysis revealed that $I_{\tan\delta}(f)$ and aging time, $\Delta S_{I(\tan\delta)}$ and moisture content both conform to linear rules. The behavior indicates that $I_{\tan\delta}(f)$ not only reflects the aging degree but also the moisture content in solid insulation. Consequently, the condition of humidified insulation and the aging state of solid insulation can be evaluated by analyzing $I_{\tan\delta}(f)$, and this investigation provides an idea to quantitatively evaluate the insulation condition of busing in the field.

Acknowledgments: The reported study was performed due to the Funds for Innovative Research Groups of China (51321063).

Author Contributions: The article was finished by a team, every author took part in the whole work. The design of the test and the extraction of parameters were provided by Binjun Chen. The analysis method of the impact of initial moisture content on oil impregnated paper was performed by Youyuan Wang. The processing of data was done by Yuanlong Li. Final review was done by Kun Xiao.

Conflicts of Interest: The authors declare no conflict of interest

References

1. Wang, S. Fault situation of transformer bushing and its analysis. *Transformer* **2002**, *39*, 35–40.
2. Li, H.L.; Hao, Y.L.; Zhong, L.; Li, L.; Shen, B.; Wang, M.; Han, L.G. Investigation on AC flashover of a 550 kV oil impregnated paper transformer bushing. *High Volt. Appar.* **2011**, *47*, 68–71.
3. Zhang, J.L.; Yan, J.; Guo, L. The case study of abnormal dielectric loss data of capacitive potential transformer bushings. *Shanxi Electr. Power* **2012**, *1*, 20–22. [CrossRef]
4. Zhang, X.Y.; Jiao, F.; Wang, W.K.; Wei, K.; Zhao, G. Development of oil-oil and Oil-SF6 resin impregnated paper capacitance graded transformer bushing. *Insul. Surg. Arresters* **2004**, *6*, 1–4.
5. Kes, M.; Christensen, B.E. Degradation of cellulosic insulation in power transformers: A SEC–MALLS study of artificially aged transformer papers. *Cellulose* **2013**, *20*, 2003–2011. [CrossRef]
6. Lundgaard, L.; Hansen, W.; Ingebrigtsen, S. Ageing of mineral oil impregnated cellulose by acid catalysis. *IEEE Trans. Dielectr. Electr. Insul.* **2008**, *15*, 540–546. [CrossRef]
7. Ingebrigtsen, S.; Dahlund, M.; Hansen, W.; Linhjell, D.; Lundgaard, L.E. Solubility of carboxylic acids in paper (Kraft)-oil insulation systems. In Proceedings of the 49th IEEE Electrical Insulation and Dielectric Phenomena, Boulder, CO, USA, 17–20 October 2004; pp. 253–257.
8. Setayeshmehr, A.; Fofana, I.; Eichler, C.; Akbari, A.; Borsi, H.; Gockenbach, E. Dielectric spectroscopic measurements on transformer oil-paper insulation under controlled laboratory conditions. *IEEE Trans. Dielectr. Electr. Insul.* **2008**, *15*, 1100–1111. [CrossRef]
9. Bouaicha, A.; Fofana, I.; Farzaneh, M.; Setayeshmehr, A.; Borsi, H.; Gockenbach, E. Dielectric spectroscopy techniques as quality control tool: A feasibility study. *IEEE Electr. Insul. Mag.* **2009**, *25*, 6–14. [CrossRef]
10. Zaengl, W.S. Applications of dielectric spectroscopy in time and frequency domain for HV power equipment. *IEEE Electr. Insul. Mag.* **2003**, *19*, 9–22. [CrossRef]
11. Hadjadj, Y.; Meghnefi, F.; Fofana, I.; Ezzaidi, H. On the feasibility of using poles computed from frequency domain spectroscopy to assess oil impregnated paper insulation conditions. *Energies* **2013**, *6*, 2204–2220. [CrossRef]
12. Fofana, I.; Borsi, H.; Gockenbach, E. Results on aging of cellulose paper under selective conditions. In Proceedings of the IEEE Electrical Insulation and Dielectric Phenomena, Kitchener, ON, Canada, 14–17 October 2001; pp. 205–208.
13. Yang, L.J. Investigation on properties and characteristics of oil-paper insulation in transformer during thermal degradation process. *Trans. China Electrotech. Soc.* **2009**, *24*, 27–33.
14. Emsley, A.; Xiao, X.; Heywood, R.; Ali, M. Degradation of celulosic insulation in power transformers. Part 3: Effects of oxygen and water on ageing in oil. *IEE Proc.-Sci. Meas. Tech.* **2000**, *147*, 115–119. [CrossRef]
15. García, B.; Burgos, J.C.; Alonso, M.; Sanz, J. A moisture-in-oil model for power transformer monitoring-Part II: Experimental verification. *IEEE Trans. Dielectr. Electr. Insul.* **2005**, *20*, 1423–1429.

16. Pradhan, M.K.; Ramu, T. On the estimation of elapsed life of oil-immersed power transformers. *IEEE Trans. Dielectr. Electr. Insul.* **2005**, *20*, 1962–1969. [CrossRef]

17. Liao, R.J.; Wang, K.; Yi, J.G. Influence of Initial moisture on thermal aging characteristics of oil-paper insulation. *High Volt. Eng.* **2012**, *5*, 1172–1178.

18. Saha, T.K. Review of modern diagnostic techniques for assessing insulation condition in aged transformers. *IEEE Trans. Dielectr. Electr. Insul.* **2003**, *10*, 903–917. [CrossRef]

19. Pradhan, M. Assessment of the status of insulation during thermal stress accelerated experiments on transformer prototypes. *IEEE Trans. Dielectr. Electr. Insul.* **2006**, *13*, 227–237. [CrossRef]

20. Bozzo, R.; Gemme, C.; Guastavino, F.; Cacciari, M.; Contin, A.; Montanari, G.C. Aging diagnosis of insulation systems by PD measurements. Extraction of partial discharge features in electrical treeing. *IEEE Trans. Dielectr. Electr. Insul.* **1998**, *5*, 118–124. [CrossRef]

21. Gafvert, U.; Adeen, L.; Tapper, M.; Jonsson, G.B. Dielectric spectroscopy in time and frequency domain applied to diagnostics of power transformers. In Proceedings of the 6th IEEE International Conference on Properties and Applications of Dielectric Materials, Xi'an, China, 21–26 June 2000; pp. 825–830.

22. Saha, T.K.; Purkait, P. Investigation of an expert system for the condition assessment of transformer insulation based on dielectric response measurements. *IEEE Trans. Power Deliv.* **2004**, *19*, 1127–1134. [CrossRef]

23. Linhjell, D.; Lundgaard, L.; Gafvert, U. Dielectric response of mineral oil impregnated cellulose and the impact of aging. *IEEE Trans. Dielectr. Electr. Insul.* **2007**, *14*, 156–169. [CrossRef]

24. Blennow, J.; Ekanayake, C.; Walczak, K.; Garcia, B.; Gubanski, S.M. Field experiences with measurements of dielectric response in frequency domain for power transformer diagnostics. *IEEE Trans. Power Deliv.* **2006**, *21*, 681–688. [CrossRef]

25. Paraskevas, C.D.; Vassiliou, P.; Dervos, C. Temperature dependent dielectric spectroscopy in frequency domain of high-voltage transformer oils compared to physicochemical results. *IEEE Trans. Dielectr. Electr. Insul.* **2006**, *13*, 539–546. [CrossRef]

26. Poovamma, P.; Sudhindra, A.; Mallikarjunappa, K.; Ahamad, T.R.A. Evaluation of transformer insulation by frequency domain technique. In Proceedings of the IEEE International Conference on Solid Dielectrics, Winchester, UK, 8–13 July 2007; pp. 681–684.

27. Saha, T.; Purkait, P. Understanding the impacts of moisture and thermal ageing on transformer's insulation by dielectric response and molecular weight measurements. *IEEE Trans. Dielectr. Electr. Insul.* **2008**, *15*, 568–582. [CrossRef]

28. Koch, M.; Prevost, T. Analysis of dielectric response measurements for condition assessment of oil-paper transformer insulation. *IEEE Trans. Dielectr. Electr. Insul.* **2012**, *19*, 1908–1915. [CrossRef]

29. Lundgaard, L.E.; Hansen, W.; Linhjell, D.; Painter, T.J. Aging of oil-impregnated paper in power transformers. *IEEE Trans. Power Deliv.* **2004**, *19*, 230–239. [CrossRef]

30. Betie, A.; Meghnefi, F.; Fofana, I.; Yeo, Z. Neural network approach to separate aging and moisture from the dielectric response of oil impregnated paper insulation. *IEEE Trans. Dielectr. Electr. Insul.* **2015**, *22*, 2176–2184. [CrossRef]

31. Yao, Z.T.; Saha, T.K. Separation of ageing and moisture impacts on transformer insulation degradation by polarization measurements. In Proceedings of the International Conference on Large High Voltage Electric System, Paris, France, 26–30 August 2002; Volume 15, pp. 1–7.

energies

[MDPI]

Article

Performance of Natural Ester as a Transformer Oil in Moisture-Rich Environments

Kapila Bandara [1], Chandima Ekanayake [2,*], Tapan Saha [1] and Hui Ma [1]

[1] School of Information Technology and Electrical Engineering, The University of Queensland, Brisbane, QLD 4072, Australia; uqkkahaw@uq.edu.au (K.B.); saha@itee.uq.edu.au (T.S.); huima@itee.uq.edu.au (H.M.)
[2] School of Engineering, Griffith University, Gold Coast, QLD 4222, Australia
* Correspondence: c.ekanayake@griffith.edu.au; Tel.: +61-7-5552-7513

Academic Editor: Issouf Fofana
Received: 8 February 2016; Accepted: 14 March 2016; Published: 31 March 2016

Abstract: Interest has risen among utilities in using natural ester (NE) insulating oils in transformers as a substitute for conventional mineral oil. However, present understanding on aging behaviour of NE-paper composite insulation system and knowledge on application of existing condition monitoring tools for NE-based insulation are inadequate. This limits the cost effective and reliable field applications of NE insulating oil. To pave the way the application of NE-based insulation in transformers, a systematic study has been performed to compare the aging behaviour of transformer grade pressboard (PB) impregnated in NE and conventional mineral oil. Applicability of a number of chemical and physical parameters, including acidity value, dielectric dissipation factor (DDF), viscosity, and colour for assessing the quality of NE insulating oil is also discussed in this paper. Comparisons are made based on the limiting values provided in the related IEEE Standard and properties of mineral oil under similar aging conditions.

Keywords: acidity; ageing; colour; dielectric dissipation factor (DDF); hydrolysis; natural ester (NE); mineral oil; oxidation; viscosity

1. Introduction

A transformer is an expensive, indispensable, and strategically-important equipment of any electric power system. Almost all of the large power transformers in power delivery systems around the world are still being insulated with mineral-based insulating oil and cellulosic paper-based solid insulation material [1,2]. Low fire point is a major disadvantage associated with typical mineral insulating oils, which increases the risk of subsequent fire in case of a transformer failure. Moreover, the transformers using mineral oil could cause severe environmental damage during an uncontrolled oil spill due to poor biodegradable characteristics of mineral oil [3,4]. Therefore, in order to improve the environmental sustainability and fire safety, there is an increasing demand for NE-based insulating liquids, which have a higher fire point and excellent biodegradable characteristics [4,5]. However, their application is still limited to sealed-type transformers due to higher oxidation susceptibility of NEs. Moreover, the knowledge and understanding on aging behaviour of NE-paper insulation systems and applicability of existing condition monitoring techniques for NE-paper insulation systems are still inadequate to widely use NEs in power transformers.

NEs possess completely different chemical compositions and physical properties compared to conventional mineral oil. Thus, it is essential to understand the impact of these differences on aging behaviour of NE-paper composite systems and methods utilized for assessing the degree of degradation of NE insulating oil, such as acidity value, DDF, viscosity, and colour. Particularly, investigation of aging behaviour of moderately wet NE-paper insulation system is of paramount significance because even in a well-sealed transformer, moisture in the paper insulation can increase up to 2%–3% over time. In general, pressboards are used as spacers, barriers, and clamping rings in a transformer and they can highly influence the mechanical strength of the transformer's winding structure. Pressboard aging can significantly reduce the withstand capability of winding against mechanical impacts (due to the loss of clamping pressure). In this way, the aging of pressboard insulation has a profound influence on transformer lifetime. This paper was aimed at providing an aging behaviour comparison between moderately wet pressboards impregnated in NE and those impregnated in mineral oil.

In this study, extensive controlled aging experiments of different oil-paper insulation systems are conducted. PB insulation with about 2% of moisture content are put into two different sealed containers, one containing one type of commercially available sunflower oil-based NE, and another containing mineral insulating oil. This arrangement is intended to compare the aging behaviour of moderately wet PB insulation in NE with than in mineral oil. Moreover, impacts of changing physicochemical properties of the NE over aging on PB insulation and its cooling and insulation properties are also investigated by considering mineral oil as the benchmark.

This paper is organized as follows. Sections 2 and 3 explain the experimental setup adopted in this study and kinetic of degradation of paper insulation, respectively. Sections 4 and 5 analyse the experimental results, followed by conclusions in Section 6.

2. Experimental Setup

2.1. Materials

High-density pressboard (PB) insulation (1.2 g·cm⁻³) with a textured surface and thickness of 1.5 mm, Shell Diala mineral oil (MIN), and sunflower oil-based NE insulating oil (NEA) were utilized in this study.

2.2. Sample Preparation and Aging Experiment Setup

A set of disc-shaped PB specimens with diameter of 100 mm were prepared. Firstly, PB specimens were dried in two different sealed chambers under a very high vacuum level (<1 kPa) at 65 °C for 24 h. The temperature was then increased to 95 °C and the drying process was continued for another 24 h. The temperature was then reduced to 40 °C and degassed oil (mineral or NEA) was infused into the chambers while they are kept in vacuum condition (refer to Figure 1a). According to [6], 110 mm thick PB block is fully impregnated with natural ester in a period of 200 h at 60 °C. Therefore, the containers were kept in a temperature-controllable oven for 168 h at 60 °C, which is more than enough for a complete impregnation. Dry oil-impregnated PB samples were then inserted into two different humidity control chambers (refer to Figure 1b).

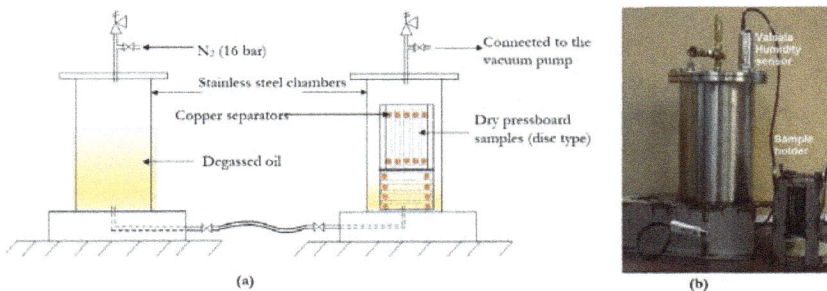

Figure 1. (a) Oil impregnation; (b) Moisture conditioning chamber, and sample holder.

The humidity inside the chambers was controlled at a constant level of 11% using saturated salt solutions prepared using lithium chloride (LiCl). In each of the chambers, a total of 20 pieces of PB specimens were arranged in a horizontal and a vertical stack. PB specimens are separated by small copper bars to allow moisture diffusion through both surfaces. This moisture conditioning process was performed over 28 days at 50 °C. The above moisture conditioning process intended to increase the moisture content of PB to about 2%–2.5% based on the Fessler equation and Jeffries' data [7] and it does not influence the DDF of oil. After completing the moisture condition process, PB specimens, degassed oil (mineral oil/NEA), and copper bars were accommodated in two different stainless steel chambers; in such a way that the mass ratio between oil, PB, and copper was maintained at 10:1:1.

Both chambers were hermetically sealed and headspaces of the chambers were filled with dry nitrogen. Then chambers were placed inside an oven for aging. Aging of PB specimens was carried out at 120 °C. Aging was stopped after 28, 35, 48, 62, 73, and 84 days and oil and PB samples were taken for analysis. Before the sampling, aging chambers were kept at room temperature for seven days. The initial condition of oil-PB insulation system is provided in Table 1. To obtain oil sample from the steel aging chamber, an oil resist plastic tube was connected to the drain valve of the aging chamber. Oil sample was then taken into a 100 mL amber glass bottle. In oil sample collection, we have observed that the ageing chamber's drain valve has been completely blocked after some time of usage due to NE oil oxidation. Therefore, the NE oil sample after 1752 h and 1984 h were collected by opening the top lid of the aging chamber. This can be conducted since the dissolved gases were not collected for analysis in this paper.

Table 1. Initial condition of oil (mineral/NE) impregnated PB insulation.

Impregnated Oil	Moisture Content (%)	DP
Mineral	2.2	1305
NEA	2.4	1307

3. Kinetic Degradation of Cellulose Insulation

Emsley and Stevens [8] have found that most of the published aging data on cellulose paper materials were shown to be in good agreement with the pseudo-zero rate kinetic model developed by Ekenstam in 1936 for linear polymer degradation. As shown in Equation (1) the rate of reaction k of the pseudo-zero model is constant throughout the aging process and it is assumed to be proportional to the number of unbroken polymer chain bonds available in the system.

$$\frac{1}{DP_t} - \frac{1}{DP_0} = kt \tag{1}$$

where DP_0 and DP_t represent the average degree of polymerization at the initial time ($t = 0$) and at any time t, respectively. Emsley [8] has characterized the temperature dependence of reaction rate using the Arrhenius relationship as shown in:

$$k = A \times e^{\left(\frac{-E_a}{RT}\right)} \tag{2}$$

where E_a is the activation energy of degradation reaction in $J \cdot mol^{-1}$, T is temperature in Kelvin, R is the gas constant ($8.314\ J \cdot mol^{-1} \cdot K^{-1}$), and A is a pre-exponential factor in h^{-1}. From their investigations, Lundgaard *et al.* [9] and Emsley [8] claimed that the activation energy for degradation reaction of Kraft paper is about $114\ kJ \cdot mol^{-1}$ and $111\ kJ \cdot mol^{-1}$, respectively, and it does not depend on the condition of the reaction environment. This has been recently confirmed by the activation energy value of $106\ kJ \cdot mol^{-1}$ obtained in an aging study performed under different moisture and oxygen conditions [10]. Factor (A) in Equation (2) shows great dependence on the availability of reactants, such as moisture, low molecular acids in cellulose (paper/pressboard), and dissolved oxygen in oil. Combining the above Equations (1) and (2), the expected lifetime of the cellulose insulation at a given temperature can be calculated as:

$$expected\ life(year) = \frac{\frac{1}{DP_{end}} - \frac{1}{DP_{start}}}{A \times 24 \times 365} \times e^{\frac{E_a}{RT}} \tag{3}$$

4. Comparison of Aging of Pressboard (PB)

4.1. Decrease in Degree of Polymerization (DP) of Pressboard (PB) Insulation

In this study, the average viscometric degree of polymerization of new and aged pressboard insulation is measured according to the test method defined in [11]. After the PB specimen has been cleaned, a considerable portion of PB specimen is stripped off to provide enough sample size for the DP analysis. Samples from two different PB specimens from the same batch are collected and their DP values are measured and the average is reported.

Figure 2a compares the decrease in DP value of PB aged in both mineral and NEA oils. One notable fact that can be seen in Figure 2a is that the measured average DP of PB insulation decreases rapidly at the beginning and then it declines at a relatively lower rate regardless of the types of oils used in the oil-PB insulation system. This is due to typical structural features of cellulose. The long chain cellulose polymers in new PB insulation [12] may contain weak links in the middle, which naturally occurs in every 500 glucose monomer units [8]. These weak links can be sliced easily under thermal stresses, and it would account for fast initial drops in DP [8]. Further, amorphous regions of cellulose degrades more rapidly than the crystalline regions, which would also support the rapid initial aging [8]. This may be because the majority of water and acid produced during aging sits in the amorphous regions [13] due to their greater permeability. On the other hand, greater existence of crystalline regions does not allow water and acid penetration into the inner PB structure [9].

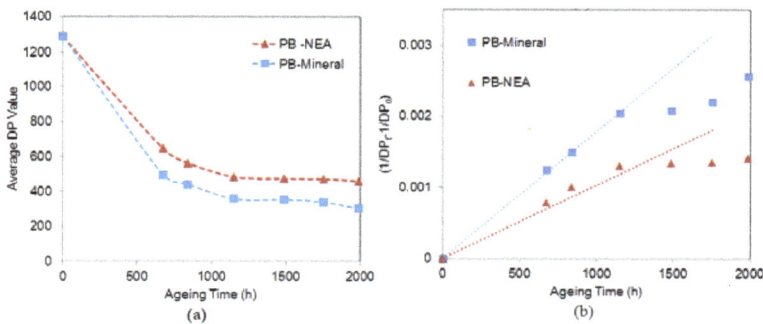

Figure 2. (a) Decrease of DP values of PB impregnated with mineral oil and NE, and (b) $1/DP_{t-1}/DP_0$ *versus* aging time of PB.

Figure 2a clearly indicates that reduction in DP of PB insulation in the NEA is substantially lower than that of mineral oil throughout the aging process in spite of the fact that initial moisture content of PB samples aged in both mineral and NEA oils is nearly same. Moreover, degradation of PB in the NEA (*i.e.*, decrease of DP value) is negligibly small during the last 824 h and its DP is 100 to 150 higher than the DP of PB aged in mineral oil over the whole aging period. This confirms that NE insulating oil shows resistance to ageing of cellulose paper insulation. This behaviour is comparable to aging experimental results presented in [14,15]. As it is proposed in [14], one could assume that pressboard insulation aged in the NEA has reached a levelling-off degree of polymerization (LODP). However, this might not be an appropriate interpretation because LODP of cellulose paper insulation occurs when DP value reaches about 200 mainly due to slower aging rate of the crystalline domains.

In present study, aging of PB mainly occurs via hydrolysis and pyrolysis reactions since the aging experiment has been conducted in minimum oxygen environment. As the aging temperature has been maintained at a constant level throughout the experiment, the observed difference in aging of PB in the mineral and NEA oil is caused by different rate of hydrolysis reaction. Thus, one could conclude that NEA retards the hydrolysis reaction in PB giving higher DP values to PB in NEA over time. This is caused by high moisture solubility [16] and hydrolytic degradation of NE itself. As a result, the interaction between water and PB is reduced and, consequently, the hydrolysis reaction in PB in NE is delayed.

Figure 2b shows that reaction rate of PB degradation in both mineral and NEA decreases after 1152 h. This effect is more substantial for PB aged in NEA. This is mainly caused by the reduction of moisture content in PB insulation, as shown in Figure 3. Moreover, the increase of moisture solubility of oil over aging further reduces the interaction between water and PB. In the case of PB aged in mineral oil, its DP is close to LODP and this may also be a reason for decreasing the aging rate of PB in mineral oil.

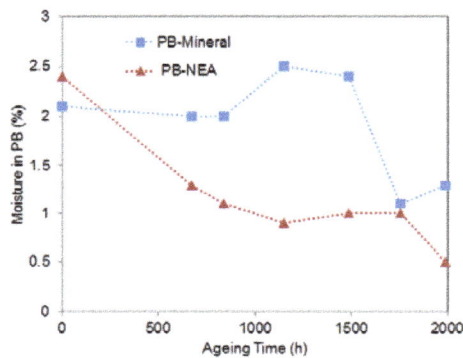

Figure 3. Change of moisture in PB over aging.

As suggested in [9], this study considered the reaction rate of the PB insulation aged in mineral oil and NE in the first 1152 h as the reaction rates correspond to their initial moisture contents. The calculated k values for PB aged in mineral oil and NEA are 18×10^{-7} h^{-1} and 10×10^{-7} h^{-1}, respectively. Since oil does not alter the bond energy of cellulose molecules, this study assumes that E_a for degradation of PB is 111 kJ·mol^{-1} in both types of oils. Using Equations (2) and (3) the life expectancy of PB insulation in the mineral oil and NEA for corresponding initial moisture content have been calculated. The results are compared with the IEEE life expectancy curve [17] for dry paper insulation as illustrated in Figure 4. It is clear that life expectancy of PB in mineral oil at a standard temperature of 110 °C decreases by a factor of 27 due to the increase of moisture to about 2.2%, whilst that of PB with 2.4% moisture in NE is reduced only by a factor of 15.

According to the research works conducted by Coulibaly *et al.* [18], it has been found that pressboard and paper have quite similar aging behaviours under similar condition in mineral and NE oils. Therefore, the results obtained for pressboard insulation in this paper can also be beneficial to understand the aging behaviour of paper insulation under similar conditions.

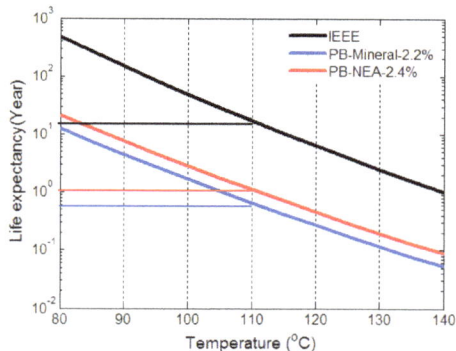

Figure 4. Comparison of life expectancy curve.

4.2. Correlation between Furfural and Pressboard PBAging

Thermal degradation of cellulose paper insulation used in electrical equipment, such as transformers, yields a class of furanic compounds including 2-furfural aldehyde (2-FAL), 2-acetylfuran (2-ACF), 2-furoic acid, 5-methyl-2-furfural (5-MEF), 2-furfurylalcohol (2-FOL), and 5-hydroxymethyl-2-furfural (5-HMF) [19–22]. These furanic compounds are partly dissolved in oil. Thus, this study has analysed the five main types of furanic compounds dissolved in oil in order to identify their correlation with aging conditions of PB insulation. The concentrations of these furanic compounds in oil has been identified and quantified by using high-performance liquid chromatography techniques according to ASTM D5837-99.

As shown in Figure 5, the highest amount of furanic compound detected in both types of oil is 2-FAL, which is a more stable compound at 120 °C than 5-HMF and 2-FOL. Additionally, its amount gradually increases with aging. In all similar aging conditions the 2-FAL concentration detected in mineral oil is much higher than that in NE.

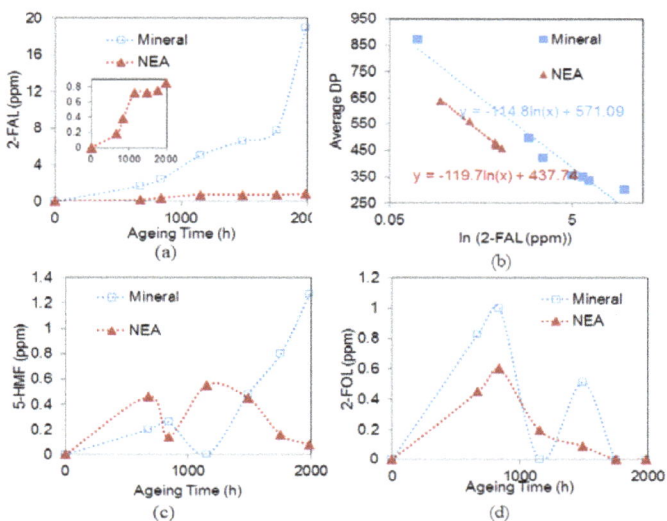

Figure 5. Furanic compounds in oil over aging (**a**) 2-FAL; (**b**) relationship between 2-FAL and DP; (**c**) 5-HMF; and (**d**) 2-FOL.

This observation is consistent with experimental results given in [14,23] where 2-FAL has been detected in very low concentration when the PB is aged in NE. This study hypothesizes that this behaviour is caused by two factors. The first is that DP of PB aged in NE has not reached a level below 400 and, typically, 2-FAL is largely produced when DP value falls below 400. In addition, 2-FAL can be lost due to thermal and hydrolytic decomposition and it is more pronounced in acidic environments [24]. As such, 2-FAL could be less stable in NE due to a comparably high quantity of oxidation inhibitors used in NE insulating oil or due to a significant increase in acidity of NE over thermal aging.

Figure 5b indicates that ln(2-FAL) and DP of PB aged in both types of oils has nearly linear relationship. Relationship corresponds to mineral oil gives DP value of 491, 386, and 347 for 2-FAL concentration of 2, 5, and 7 ppm, respectively. If one uses the relationship obtained by Pablo [25], it gives DP of 551, 386 and 310 for similar concentration of 2-FAL confirming the consistent of our results in this DP region. However, established relationships show dependence on oil type. This means that the existing 2-FAL based interpretation schemes developed for mineral oil-paper insulation systems based on absolute values and the rate of change may not be directly used for NE-based insulation systems.

As seen in Figure 5c,d, one can claim that 5-HMF is the second highest furanic compounds detected in both types of oils in most of the cases. This is mainly because hydrolysis of PB mainly occurs via formation of 5-HMF. Moreover, production of furanic compounds due to degradation of PB insulation in decreasing order is 2-FAL > 5-HMF > 2-FOL [26]. In the case of 677 h and 840 h aged mineral and NEA oil samples, the concentration of 2-FOL is larger than that of 5-HMF and also it is noted that 2-FOL concentration becomes zero at the last stage of aging. This is due to the fact that 2-FOL is less stable compared to 2-FAL and 5-HMF.

5. Aging of Oil

5.1. Viscosity

Oxidation of insulating oils produces large molecular weight compounds leading to the increase of oil viscosity. This study measures the change of viscosity of both mineral and NE insulating oils over thermal aging using method prescribed in ASTM D445.

It can be seen in Figure 6 that viscosity of both types of oils remains almost constant throughout the aging process. It indicates that no severe oxidative degradation has occurred in both types of oils. These results agree with the aging setup (refer to Section 2) because the aging experiment has been conducted in a sealed environment with minimum oxygen. However, NE oil used in this study should essentially hydrolyse because initial moisture content of PB in the aging chamber with NE is 2.4%. Thus, one could hypothesize that hydrolytic degradation of NE insulating oils does not have a significant influence on their viscosity.

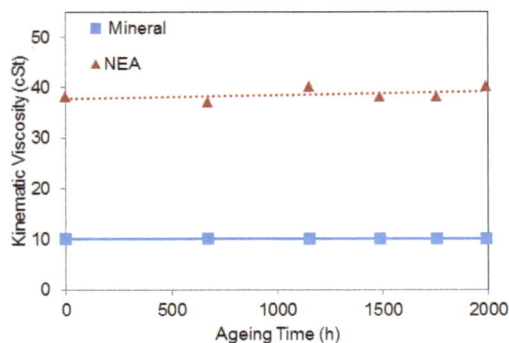

Figure 6. Change of viscosity of oil over aging.

5.2. Acidity

This study investigates the applicability of neutralization number (acidity) for determining the quality of NE insulating oils. The method prescribed in ASTMD 974 has been utilized to determine the acidity level of new and aged oil samples. Figure 7 shows that acidity of both types of oils increases with aging time. This behaviour is more significance in NEA such that acidity of the aged NEA oil samples at 1752 h (4.55 mgKOH/g) and 1984 h (6.2 mgKOH/g) is 76 and 43 times greater than that of mineral oil samples.

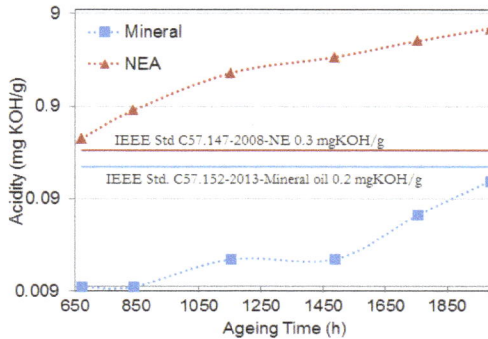

Figure 7. Change of acidity over aging.

It is generally accepted that oxidation of insulating oil and degradation of cellulose insulation in transformers results in increasing the acidity level of oil [27]. However, in this study we cannot expect oxidative degradation of oil because the aging experiment has been conducted under a nitrogen cushion. This is confirmed by the viscosity measurement results presented in Figure 6.

Therefore, this study ascribes the large increase of acidity values of NEA oil to hydrolytic degradation, because the reaction between NE and water mainly yields free fatty acids. Moisture solubility of all types of oil exponentially increases with temperature causing migration of moisture from pressboard to oil at high temperature levels. This behaviour enhances the hydrolysis reaction in NE oil. Moreover, this is an autocatalytic reaction, because free fatty acid molecules themselves accelerate the hydrolysis reaction. Thus, in this study, one could mention that the rapid increase of acidity of NEA oil is solely due to hydrolytic degradation.

It can be observed from Figure 7 that acidity of mineral oil is less than the limiting value (0.2 mgKOH/g) given in [28] throughout the aging process. Thus, one could say that even after 1984 h of ageing mineral insulating oil is in good condition for further use as an insulating liquid. On the other hand, it clearly shows that acidity of NEA has increased beyond acceptable limiting values (0.3 mgKOH/g) after 672 h of ageing and moreover, the acidity of NEA oil after 1752 h and 1984 h aging is 15 and 20 times higher than the acceptable level, respectively. According to the guidelines provided in [29], NE oil used in this experiment at all recorded aging conditions is categorized as unsuitable oil for further use.

However, this study has observed that the aging rate of PB insulation in NEA oil in the last 824 h is negligibly small (refer to Figure 2) in spite of fact that acidity of NEA oil is very high during this period. It confirms that acid produced by hydrolytic degradation of NEs is not detrimental to paper insulation. It could be possibly due to the fact that hydrolysis of NEs mainly yield long-chain fatty acids and they do not dissociate into H+ as low molecular carboxyl acids. Acidic corrosion of copper and steel materials in transformers is also governed by the H+ ions in the system. Therefore, one can hypothesize that acids produced in NEs do not cause extra corrosion in copper conductors and core steel. This hypothesis is confirmed by the fact that copper conductors and the steel sample holder used in this study have not shown any sign of corrosion even after 1984 h of aging with NEA oil. Thus, this study proposes to measure the low molecular acids content, in addition to measuring the total acidity value for diagnostic purposes of in-service aged NE insulating oil.

5.3. Change of Dielectric Dissipation Factor (DDF)

This study analyses the variation of DDF of mineral and NE insulating oils over thermal aging. All measurements have been conducted in a standard three electrodes test cell at 50 Vrms using commercially available equipment (IDA 200). It is worthwhile to mention, at the beginning none of the oil samples considered in this study were saturated with water. Thereby, one could assume that there is no influence of moisture on the measured DDF of oil [30].

Temperature dependence of DDF of insulating oil is solely characterized by its conductivity. Thus, it can also be represented using an Arrhenius-type equation governed by the activation energy. Consequently, activation energy can be calculated by multiplying the gradient of the log (DDF) *vs.* reciprocal of the absolute temperature and Boltzmann constant.

Figure 8 shows that the activation energy of NEA varies within the range of 0.37 eV and 0.45 eV during aging, whilst that of mineral oil is in the range of 0.36 eV and 0.47 eV. The average activation value of both oils is 0.41 eV, which is used to normalize the standard set limit of the DDF to 55 °C.

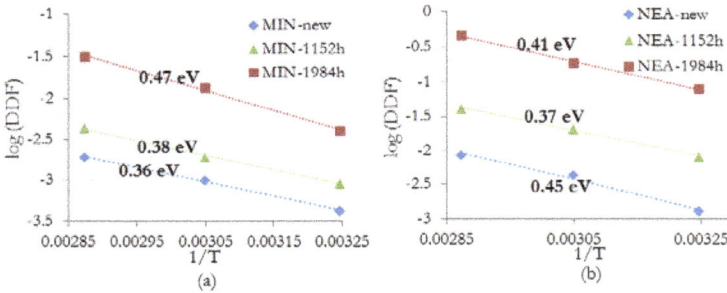

Figure 8. Temperature dependence of (a) DDF mineral oil and (b) NE.

Figure 9 represents the DDF of mineral and NE oil corresponding to oil temperature of 55 °C. It clearly shows that the DDF of both types of oil exponentially increases with aging time. Moreover, this behaviour is paramount significance in NEA oil such that the DDF of NEA oil after 1984 h aging has reached a very high value of 21%, which is almost 15 times greater than that of mineral oil with similar aging conditions.

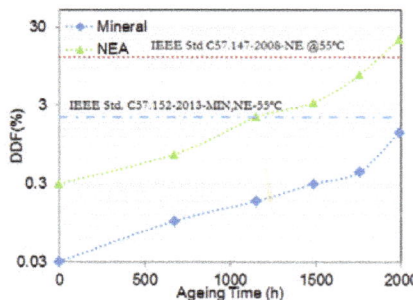

Figure 9. Change of DDF of oil at 55 °C over aging.

It is generally accepted that DDF of oil increases due to the presence of dissociable impurities such as soot, dust, and ageing by-products [18]. Thus, one could claim that aging of NE with cellulosic and metal substances in moisture-rich environments produces more conductive dissociable substances and consequently leads to higher DDF. On the other hand, conductive aging byproducts of paper insulation can largely dissolve in NEs because of their polar nature [31] and this could result in large increases in DDF of NE.

In this paper, the acceptable limiting values provided in [28,29] for DDF of mineral and NE insulating oil at 25 °C have been recalculated to 55 °C using activation energy of 0.41 eV. Figure 9 shows that DDF of any of the mineral oil samples has not reached limiting value indicating their suitability for further use. In case of NE, except the oil sample aged over 1984 h, all other samples are within the acceptable limits. However, reference [28] proposed the same limiting value for both mineral oil and NE oils. If one uses [28], except the sample aged over 674 h, all other NE oil samples would be categorized as being not suitable for further use.

5.4. Colour Change

Colour of oil is a visual parameter, which reflects the degree of degradation and possible contamination of oil during aging. Figure 10 shows that dramatic colour change has occurred in both types of oils over aging. This behaviour is more significant in NEA such that its colour has turned to black after 1488 h of aging whilst colour of mineral oil change to amber after 1752 h. Numeral value based on international colour standards (ASTM D1500) is generally used in expressing colour changes of oil. The colour number of oil at different aging conditions is estimated in this study and presented in Figure 11.

Figure 10. Change of oil colour over aging.

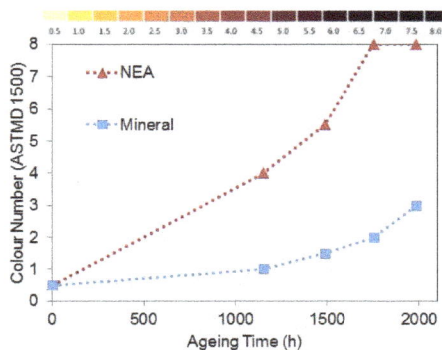

Figure 11. Estimated colour number of oil over aging.

Reference [28] provides guidelines for assessing the condition of mineral oil based on colour. According to that except 1984 h aged mineral oil, other mineral oil samples in this study are categorized as oil with good condition. However, if one applies the same interpretation scheme on NEA, oil samples at 1488 h, 1752 h, and 1984 h aging time can be rated as extremely bad oil whilst oil samples at 1152 h aging time can be characterized as severely aged oil. In the case of mineral oil, severely aged oil (brown in colour) and extremely bad oil (dark brown and/or black in colour) typically contains large amounts of sludge and they possess poor cooling characteristics due to an increase of viscosity [32]. Moreover, such oil contains high concentration of reactive acids. However, it has been observed that no sludge has been formed in the aged NEA oil and its viscosity has remained almost constant over the aging period. Moreover, acids produced in NEA oil are not reactive. Thereby, one can conclude that the overall condition of in-service aged NE oil cannot be determined only with the existing colour-based interpretation schemes.

5.5. Overall Analysis of Oil Condition

Table 2 summarizes the diagnostic results of mineral and NEA oil using their acidity value, DDF, and colour. It clearly shows that acidity and DDF diagnose all mineral oil samples as oil with good condition. However, the sample aged over 1984 h is required to be further investigated because of its higher colour number. In the case of NEA oil, all the oil samples tested in this study are categorized as bad oil by their acidity and colour despite their ability to reduce cellulose degradation. Moreover, viscosity of NEA oil which determines the cooling capability is similar to unaged oil even after 1984 h of aging. In addition, this study has measured the dielectric breakdown strength of 1984 h aged mineral and NEA oil samples using method prescribed in [33]. It has confirmed that the average dielectric breakdown strength of NEA oil is 68 kV and it is 13 kV higher than that of mineral oil. It means that, though aged NEA oil has a higher acidity and colour number, their insulation quality is better than mineral oil which has gone through the same aging process.

Table 2. Summary of diagnostic results.

Aging Time (h)	Mineral Oil			NE		
	Acidity	DDF	Colour	Acidity	DDF	Colour
672	√	√	-	x	√	-
1152	√	√	√	x	√	severe
1488	√	√	√	x	√	extreme
1752	√	√	√	x	√	extreme
1984	√	√	bad	x	x	extreme
	√—acceptable for further use, x—not in good condition to further use					

For an in-service transformer, moisture in its paper insulation can increase to about 2% after 10–15 years of operation. In such a situation, a rapid increase in acidity and colour of NE insulating oil will be expected. Moreover, retrofilling of an in-service transformer with NE oil could also create a similar environment. Thus, in this type of condition, acidity and colour change with an existing set of limits in the standards cannot be utilized to determine the suitability of in-service aged NE insulating oil for further use. As shown in Table 2, one could hypothesize that DDF with limiting values as defined in [29] could be a good indication of the quality of NE insulating oils when subjected to severe hydrolytic degradation. In addition to DDF, this study proposes to measure the viscosity and dielectric breakdown strength. Collectively, these three parameters could reflect the overall condition of NE insulating oils.

6. Conclusions

This study revealed that NE insulating oil possesses resistance to the aging of PB insulation. This behaviour is mainly caused by high moisture solubility and the hydrolysis reaction in NE insulating oil. Experimental results presented in this paper indicate that the furanic compounds may be less stable in NE insulating oils. Thus, it is necessary to further investigate whether 2-FAL can be used as a paper insulation aging indicator for NE-based insulation systems. This study pointed out that acidity and colour of NE ester oils could increase rapidly due to the pronounced hydrolytic degradation in moisture rich environment. This type of behaviour can be expected after retrofilling of an in-service transformer with NE oil. In such a condition, acidity and colour could not reflect the real condition of NE oil. On the other hand, DDF, viscosity, and dielectric breakdown voltage, collectively, can indicate the overall condition of NE insulation oils.

This study revealed that the acids produced by hydrolysis of NE are not detrimental to paper insulation. However, it is necessary to further investigate the effect of high acidity of NE oil on copper and steel materials, particularly its corrosion effects at high temperature.

Acknowledgments: The authors would like to thank the Australian Research Council (ARC) and industry partners AusGrid, Ergon Energy, Powerlink Queensland, TransGrid and Wilson transformer for the financial support.

Author Contributions: Kapila Bandara, Chandima Ekanayake and Tapan Saha conceived and designed the experiments; Kapila Bandara performed the experiments; Kapila Bandara and Chandima Ekanayake analysed the data; Kapila Bandara, Chandima Ekanayake, Tapan Saha and Hui Ma wrote the paper.

Conflicts of Interest: The authors declare no conflict of interest.

References

1. Prevost, T.A.; Oommen, T.V. Cellulose insulation in oil-filled power transformers: Part I—History and development. *IEEE Electr. Insul. Mag.* **2006**, *22*, 28–35. [CrossRef]
2. Rouse, T.O. Mineral insulating oil in transformers. *IEEE Mag. Electr. Insul. Mag.* **1998**, *14*, 6–16. [CrossRef]
3. Oommen, T.V.; Claiborne, C.C.; Mullen, J.T. Biodegradable electrical insulation fluids. In Proceedings of the Electrical Insulation and Electrical Manufacturing & Coil Winding Conference, Rosemont, IL, USA, 22–25 September 1997; pp. 465–468.
4. McShane, C.P.; Corkran, J.; Rapp, K.; Luksich, J. Natural Ester Dielectric Fluid Development. In Proceedings of the IEEE PES Transmission and Distribution Conference and Exhibition, Dallas, TX, USA, 21–24 May 2006; pp. 18–22.
5. Tenbohlen, S.; Koch, M. Aging Performance and Moisture Solubility of Vegetable Oils for Power Transformers. *IEEE Trans. Power Deliv.* **2010**, *25*, 825–830. [CrossRef]
6. Dai, J.; Wang, Z.D. A Comparison of the Impregnation of Cellulose Insulation by Ester and Mineral Oil. *IEEE Trans. Dielectr. Electr. Insul.* **2008**, *15*, 374–381. [CrossRef]
7. Du, Y.; Zahn, M.; Lesieutre, B.C.; Mamishev, A.V.; Lindgren, S.R. Moisture equilibrium in transformer paper-oil systems. *IEEE Electr. Insul. Mag.* **1999**, *15*, 11–20. [CrossRef]
8. Emsley, A.M.; Stevens, G.C. Kinetics and mechanisms of the low-temperature degradation of cellulose. *J. Cellul.* **1994**, *1*, 26–56. [CrossRef]
9. Lundgaard, L.E.; Hansen, W.; Linhjell, D.; Painter, T.J. Aging of oil-impregnated paper in power transformers. *IEEE Trans. Power Deliv.* **2004**, *19*, 230–239. [CrossRef]
10. Lelekakis, N.; Wijaya, J.; Martin, D.; Saha, T.; Susa, D.; Krause, C. Aging rate of grade 3 presspaper insulation used in power transformers. *IEEE Trans. Dielectr. Electr. Insul.* **2014**, *21*, 2355–2362. [CrossRef]
11. Internaltional Electrotechnical Commision (IEC). *Measurement of the Average Viscometric Degree of Polymerization of New and Aged Cellulose Electrically Insualting Materials*; IEC Std. 60450:2004; IEC: Geneva, Switzerland, 2004.
12. Hill, D.J.T.; Le, T.T.; Darveniza, M.; Saha, T. A study of the degradation of cellulosic insulation materials in a power transformer. Part III: Degradation products of cellulose insulation paper. *Polym. Degrad. Stab.* **1996**, *51*, 211–218. [CrossRef]
13. Dissado, L.A.; Hill, R.M. Anomalous low-frequency dispersion. Near direct current conductivity in disordered low-dimensional materials. *J. Chem. Soc. Faraday Trans. 2 Mol. Chem. Phys.* **1984**, *80*, 291–319. [CrossRef]
14. Liao, R.; Liang, S.; Sun, C.; Yang, L.; Sun, H. A comparative study of thermal aging of transformer insulation paper impregnated in natural ester and in mineral oil. *Eur. Trans. Electr. Power* **2010**, *20*, 518–533. [CrossRef]

15. McShane, C.P.; Rapp, K.J.; Corkran, J.L.; Gauger, G.A.; Luksich, J. Aging of Kraft paper in natural ester dielectric fluid. In Proceedings of the 2002 IEEE 14th International Conference on Dielectric Liquids, Graz, Austria, 7–12 July 2002; pp. 173–177.

16. Koch, M.; Tenbohlen, S.; Stirl, T. Diagnostic Application of Moisture Equilibrium for Power Transformers. *IEEE Trans. Power Deliv.* **2010**, *25*, 2574–2581. [CrossRef]

17. IEEE C57.91 Working Group. *IEEE Guide for Loading Mineral-Oil-Immersed Transformers and Step-Voltage Regulators—Redline*; IEEE Std C57.91-2011 (Revision of IEEE Std C57.91-1995)—Redline; IEEE: New York, NY, USA, 2012; pp. 1–172.

18. Coulibaly, M.L.; Perrier, C.; Marugan, M.; Beroual, A. Aging behavior of cellulosic materials in presence of mineral oil and ester liquids under various conditions. *IEEE Trans. Dielectr. Electr. Insul.* **2013**, *20*, 1971–1976. [CrossRef]

19. Cigre Working Group TF D1.01.13. *Furanic Compounds for Diagnosis*; International Council on Large Electric Systems: Paris, France, 2012.

20. Scheirs, J.; Camino, G.; Avidano, M.; Tumiatti, W. Origin of furanic compounds in thermal degradation of cellulosic insulating paper. *J. Appl. Polym. Sci.* **1998**, *69*, 2541–2547. [CrossRef]

21. Emsley, A.M.; Xiao, X.; Heywood, R.J.; Ali, M. Degradation of cellulosic insulation in power transformers. Part 3: Effects of oxygen and water on ageing in oil. *IEE Proc. Sci. Meas. Technol.* **2000**, *147*, 115–119. [CrossRef]

22. Kachler, A.J.; Hohlein, I. Aging of cellulose at transformer service temperatures. Part 1: Influence of type of oil and air on the degree of polymerization of pressboard, dissolved gases, and furanic compounds in oil. *IEEE Electr. Insul. Mag.* **2005**, *21*, 15–21. [CrossRef]

23. Lijun, Y.; Ruijin, L.; Caixin, S.; Huigang, S. Study on the Influence of Natural Ester on Thermal Ageing Characteristics of Oil-paper in Power Transformer. In Proceedings of the International Conference on High Voltage Engineering and Application, Chongqing, China, 9–12 November 2008; pp. 437–440.

24. Emsley, A.M.; Stevens, G.C. Review of chemical indicators of degradation of cellulosic electrical paper insulation in oil-filled transformers. *IEE Proc. Sci. Meas. Technol.* **1994**, *141*, 324–334. [CrossRef]

25. De Pablo, A. Furfural and ageing: How are they related. In Proceedings of the IEE Colloquium on Insulating Liquids, Leatherhead, UK, 27 May 1999; pp. 5/1–5/4.

26. Levchik, S.; Scheirs, J.; Camino, G.; Tumiatti, W.; Avidano, M. Depolymerization processes in the thermal degradation of cellulosic paper insulation in electrical transformers. *Polym. Degrad. Stab.* **1998**, *61*, 507–511. [CrossRef]

27. Jung-Il, J.; Jung-Sik, A.; Chan-Su, H. Accelerated aging effects of mineral and vegetable transformer oils on medium voltage power transformers. *IEEE Trans. Dielectr. Electr. Insul.* **2012**, *19*, 156–161. [CrossRef]

28. IEEE Diagnostic Field Testing Power Transformers and Reactors Working Group. *IEEE Guide for Diagnostic Field Testing of Fluid-Filled Power Transformers, Regulators, and Reactors*; IEEE Std C57.152-2013; IEEE: New York, NY, USA, 2013.

29. IEEE Natural Easter Working Group. *IEEE Guide for Acceptance and Maintenance of Natural Ester Fluids in Transformers*; IEEE Std. C57.147-2008; IEEE: New York, NY, USA, 2008.

30. Duy, C.T.; Denat, A.; Lesaint, O.; Bonifaci, N.; Bertrand, Y. Moisture and temperature effects on conduction and losses in modified rape-seed insulating oil. In Proceedings of the Conference on Electrical Insulation and Dielectric Phenomena, Vancouver, BC, Canada, 14–17 October 2007; pp. 647–650.

31. Fofana, I.; Bouaicha, A.; Farzaneh, M.; Sabau, J.; Bussieres, D.; Robertson, E.B. Decay products in the liquid insulation of power transformers. *IET Electr. Power Appl.* **2010**, *4*, 177–184. [CrossRef]

32. Fofana, I.; Bouaicha, A.; Hadjadj, Y.; N'Cho, J.S.; Aka-Ngnui, T.; Beroual, A. Early stage detection of insulating oil decaying. In Proceedings of the 2010 Annual Report Conference on Electrical Insulation and Dielectric Phenomena (CEIDP), West Lafayette, IN, USA, 17–20 October 2010; pp. 1–4.

33. Internaltional Electrotechnical Commision (IEC). *Insulating liquids -Determination of the Breakdown Voltage at Power Frequency—Test Method*; IEC Std. 60156; IEC: Geneva, Switzerland, 1995.

energies

MDPI

Article

Comparison of Dissolved Gases in Mineral and Vegetable Insulating Oils under Typical Electrical and Thermal Faults

Chenmeng Xiang [1], Quan Zhou [1], Jian Li [1,*], Qingdan Huang [2], Haoyong Song [2] and Zhaotao Zhang [3]

[1] The State Key Laboratory of Power Transmission Equipment and System Security and New Technology, College of Electrical Engineering, Chongqing University, Chongqing 400044, China; xiangchenmeng@cqu.edu.cn (C.X.); zhouquan@cqu.edu.cn (Q.Z.)
[2] Guangzhou Power Supply Company, Guangzhou 510620, China; 13560381038@163.com (Q.H.); songhaoyong1208@163.com (H.S.)
[3] State Grid Chongqing Changshou Power Supply Company, Chongqing 401220, China; zzt7933@163.com
* Correspondence: lijian@cqu.edu.cn; Tel.: +86-23-6510-2437

Academic Editor: Issouf Fofana
Received: 15 February 2016; Accepted: 18 April 2016; Published: 25 April 2016

Abstract: Dissolved gas analysis (DGA) is attracting greater and greater interest from researchers as a fault diagnostic tool for power transformers filled with vegetable insulating oils. This paper presents experimental results of dissolved gases in insulating oils under typical electrical and thermal faults in transformers. The tests covered three types of insulating oils, including two types of vegetable oil, which are camellia insulating oil, Envirotemp FR3, and a type of mineral insulating oil, to simulate thermal faults in oils from 90 °C to 800 °C and electrical faults including breakdown and partial discharges in oils. The experimental results reveal that the content and proportion of dissolved gases in different types of insulating oils under the same fault condition are different, especially under thermal faults due to the obvious differences of their chemical compositions. Four different classic diagnosis methods were applied: ratio method, graphic method, and Duval's triangle and Duval's pentagon method. These confirmed that the diagnosis methods developed for mineral oil were not fully appropriate for diagnosis of electrical and thermal faults in vegetable insulating oils and needs some modification. Therefore, some modification aiming at different types of vegetable oils based on Duval Triangle 3 were proposed in this paper and obtained a good diagnostic result. Furthermore, gas formation mechanisms of different types of vegetable insulating oils under thermal stress are interpreted by means of unimolecular pyrolysis simulation and reaction enthalpies calculation.

Keywords: vegetable insulating oil; electrical fault; thermal fault; dissolved gas analysis (DGA); fault diagnosis; gas formation mechanism

---

1. Introduction

Dissolved gas analysis (DGA) is an important and successful tool to detect incipient faults of oil-filled transformers [1]. Several interpretation methods for DGA, including the ratio methods, the graphic methods, and Duval Triangle or Pentagon methods, are available to identify the different types of faults occurring in operating transformers [2–7].

The vegetable insulating oil in transformers are applied more and more widely [8]. It has already been used in distribution transformers, and the next objective is to extend its use to HV power transformers [9]. It has different compositions between vegetable insulating oil and mineral insulating oil. Vegetable oil consists of hundreds of triglycerides, while mineral oils are mixtures of alkane, cyclones, and aromatic hydrocarbons containing carbon and hydrogen linked together by single and double bonds [10,11]. In addition, different types of vegetable insulating oils are also composed of different kinds and proportions of triglyceride molecules. Thus, there are differences in the variety and proportion of gas production among different types of insulating oils [12].

At present, investigations on comparisons of DGA between vegetable and mineral oils have attracted lots of interests of researchers. Martin *et al.* analyzed dissolved gas levels of a normally-operating power transformers filled with FR3 and indicate that ethane and hydrogen are significantly elevated compared to the same transformers filled with mineral oil [13]. However, since there is a significant lack of fault data of vegetable oil-filled transformers in service, several results of dissolved gases in vegetable oils obtained by laboratory tests. [14–18] concluded that vegetable oil and mineral oil have different dissolved gas characteristics under electrical and thermal faults. Several diagnostic methods, such as the Dornenburg method [15], IEC 60599 method [15], Roger's ratio method [15,16], and classical Duval Triangle method [15–18], which are used for diagnosing the fault type of transformers filled with mineral oil, exist limitations to diagnose the fault of transformers filled with vegetable oils directly. Thus, new versions of the Duval triangle method (Duval Triangle 3) applied to equipment filled with non-mineral oils (silicone, Midel, FR3, and Bio Temp) have been proposed [19]. Furthermore, another modified Duval triangle method (Duval Triangle 6) aiming at the stray gassing diagnosis of FR3 oil-filled transformers has been put forward [20].

According to the aforementioned publications, until now, only a few methods, such as the modified Duval triangle (Duval Triangle 3 and 6), are utilized to identify faults in vegetable oil-filled transformers. The international standard IEEE C57.155-2014 [21] provides the DGA guide application for natural and synthetic ester-immersed transformers. However, previous studies pay more attention on the comparison of dissolved gases between mineral oils and natural or synthetic esters, much less effort is involved in the comparative studies of vegetable insulating oils with different chemical compositions. Due to the fact that different vegetable oils are formed by different kinds and proportions of triglyceride molecules, the dissolved gas characteristics have some differences. Thus, there is a need to verify and improve the DGA diagnostic methods used for FR3 oils to apply it to other vegetable oils. Moreover, it is necessary to study the gas formation mechanism of different vegetable oils and this will help to provide a theoretical basis for designing diagnostic methods of vegetable insulating oils with different chemical compositions.

This work is motivated by problems posed in the present publications for future applications. Experiments simulating typical thermal and electrical faults in transformers are proposed in this paper. Gases dissolved in two types of vegetable insulating oils (FR3 oil and camellia oil) and one mineral oil are analyzed by gas chromatography, the content and proportion of fault gases in three types of insulating oils are compared with each other, the main gas compositions in two types of vegetable insulating oils of different fault types are examined. Three ratio methods, the graph representation method, Duval's Triangle method in the IEC standard [22], and the Duval pentagon method, are used to interpret experiment data, the applicability of these methods to vegetable insulating oil-filled transformers are analyzed. Furthermore, Duval's Triangle 3, which is used for the diagnosis of FR3 oils, is applied to verify the applicability of fault diagnosis in FR3 oils and camellia oils, some modifications of Duval's Triangle 3 aiming at camellia oils are also put forward. Finally, the gas formation mechanism of vegetable insulating oils based on the technique of molecular simulation and reaction enthalpies calculation is proposed in this paper.

2. Experiment

2.1. Preparation and Pretreatment of Samples

A conventional naphthenic-based mineral insulating oil, a kind of commercial soybean-based insulating oil (FR3), and a kind of camellia-based vegetable insulating oil were used in the experiment. The camellia insulating oil was obtained from camellia oil after three refinement procedures, which are alkaline refinement, vacuum distillation, and bleaching. The basic physical, chemical, and electrical properties of the camellia insulation oil are shown in Table 1. The related properties of the FR3 and mineral insulating oil are also presented.

Table 1. Basic physical, chemical, and electrical properties of the three types of insulation oils.

Parameter	Camellia Oil	FR3 Oil [23]	Mineral Oil
Appearance	Light Yellow	Light Green	Transparent
Density (20 °C)/kg· m^{-3}	0.90	0.92	<0.895
Viscosity (40 °C)/mm^2· s^{-1}	39.9	34.1	⩽13.0
Pour point/°C	−28	−21	<−22
Flash point/°C	322	316	⩾135
Acid value/mgKOH· g^{-1}	0.03	0.04	⩽0.03
Interfacial tension/mN· m	25	24	⩾40
AC breakdown voltage/kV	70	56	⩾35
Dissipation factor(90 °C)/%	0.88	0.89	⩽0.1
Volume resistivity/Ω· m	1 × 1010/90 °C	2 × 1011/25 °C	7 × 1011/25 °C
Relative permittivity	2.9/90 °C	3.2/25 °C	2.2/90 °C

The insulating oil and insulating paper were dried under a vacuum of 50 Pa for 72 h at 90 °C. The moisture contents of oil was examined by the Karl Fischer titration method, the moisture contents of mineral, FR3, and camellia oils were 8 ppm, 36 ppm, and 29 ppm, respectively. The insulating paper was impregnated in insulating oils under a vacuum of 50 Pa for 24 h at 40 °C.

2.2. Experimental Setup

2.2.1. Thermal Stress Simulation

According to IEC 60599-2007 [22], thermal faults are classified into three groups (T1 < 300 °C, 300 °C < T2 < 700 °C, and T3 > 700 °C) according the temperature ranges of faults. Since the research was intended to simulate the thermal fault in transformers and analyze proportions of dissolved gases in different types of insulating oils under the same fault condition, thermal tests were carried out with and without insulating paper through setting the oven temperature at 90, 120, 150, 200, 300, 400, 500, 600, 700, or 800 °C.

In this experiment, thermal faults at temperatures below 300 °C (90 °C, 120 °C, 150 °C, 200 °C, and 250 °C) were simulated in sealed glass bottles and heated uniformly in an air circulating oven [14–16]. There was a thermocouple sensor next to the sealed glass to reflect the oil temperature.

For high-temperature thermal faults, due to the high pressure in containers at high temperature, the air circulating oven could not simulate the thermal faults above 300 °C. In addition, currently, some publications applied the method of heating wires in oil to simulate overheating faults [24,25]; however, it was not easy to make fault point temperatures reach above 700 °C (T3 region) because of the limitation of the maximum power source and meltdown of heating wire as presented in these papers. The highest temperature that the heating wire can achieve was 600 °C in [24] and the experimental simulating temperature was 280 °C in [25]. In order to simulate high-temperature thermal faults and obtain fault gas data at high temperature, a specially-designed experiment system containing a pipe heater, a L-shaped stainless steel container, and a temperature controller were designed to simulate thermal faults at temperatures above 300 °C (300 °C, 400 °C, 500 °C, 600 °C, 700 °C, and 800 °C), as shown in Figure 1. There was a thermocouple sensor processed by means of heat insulation and contacting the surface of pipe to reflect the approximate temperature of oil. In practical situations, overheating faults at high temperature will only take place at one point in the transformer, fault gases are generated at the fault point, and then diffuse to the entire oil tank, and this is why samples used in DGA are extracted from the oil drain valve instead of the fault point. In this simulation system, 30 mL oil added to the pipe heater were heated, and fault gases diffused to 0.5 L of oil added to the stainless steel container.

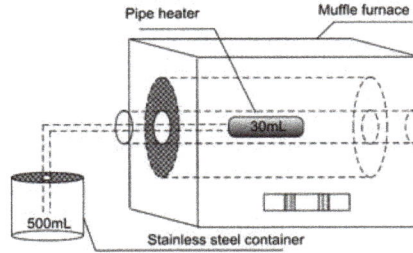

Figure 1. Sketch of thermal faults simulation system.

In order to ensure the 30 mL oil samples achieve the setting temperatures, the oil temperature rising process and rate were simulated before the tests.

The governing equation about the heat conduction is as follows:

$$\begin{cases} \rho c_p \frac{\partial T}{\partial t} + \rho c_p \mathbf{u} \cdot \nabla T + \nabla \cdot \mathbf{q} = Q + Q_p + Q_{vd} \\ \mathbf{q} = -k \nabla T \end{cases} \tag{1}$$

where c_p is the specific heat capacity of material, ρ is the density of material, k is the thermal conductivity of material, Q is the conduction heat, Q_p is the convection heat, and Q_{vd} is the radiation heat.

The boundary condition is as follows:

$$\begin{cases} -n \cdot \mathbf{q} = 0 \\ T = T_0 \end{cases} \tag{2}$$

where T_0 is the temperature of boundary.

Figure 2 shows the temperature distribution of oil samples after heating different times when the oven temperature is 800 °C.

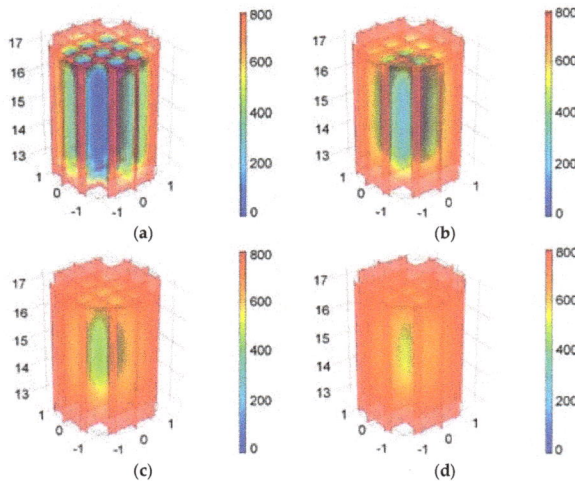

Figure 2. Temperature distribution of oil sample after heating different times when the oven temperature is 800 °C. (**a**) After heating 0.5 min; (**b**) After heating 1 min; (**c**) After heating 1.5 min; and (**d**) After heating 2 min.

Figure 3a,b show the average temperature rising curve of mineral oil and vegetable oil, respectively. It is obvious that the temperature can approximately reach 800 °C during the heating time.

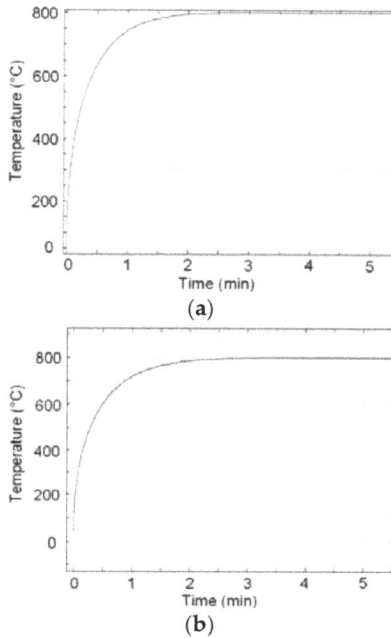

Figure 3. Temperature rising rate curve of mineral and vegetable oil samples: (**a**) Mineral oil; (**b**) Vegetable oil.

Table 2 presents the time of heating duration before the mineral oil and vegetable oil can reach the required temperature from 300 °C to 800 °C. It can be seen that the oil can reach or approach the required temperature before heating of the oil stops.

Table 2. Duration of mineral and vegetable oil samples before reaching required temperatures.

Temperature (°C)		300	400	500	600	700	800
Duration (min)	Mineral oil	2.54	2.36	2.83	2.57	2.84	2.37
	Vegetable oil	3.64	3.34	3.40	3.15	2.82	2.56

In order to simulate thermal faults of operating transformers approximately, the temperature and duration of simulated thermal faults are shown in Table 3.

Table 3. The temperature and duration of simulated thermal tests.

Temperature (°C)	T1					T2					T3
	90	120	150	200	250	300	400	500	600	700	800
Duration (h)	168	168	168	2	1	1/2	1/12	1/12	1/15	1/20	1/24

2.2.2. Electrical Stress Simulation

The experimental setup is shown in Figure 4. The step-up transformer is composed of a self-coupling voltage regulator and a testing transformer. The electrostatic voltmeter V is used to monitor voltage, resistor R is used to limit current. The 2000 pF coupling capacitor capable of withstanding a voltage of 50 kV is used to couple the pulse current generated by a partial discharge.

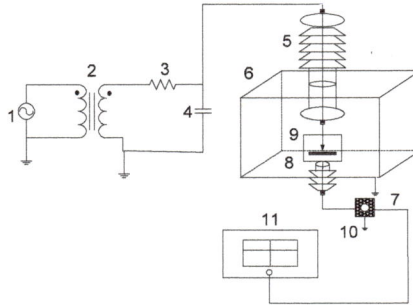

Figure 4. The sketch of electrical faults simulation setup. 1–AC power; 2–transformer; 3–protection resistance; 4–coupling capacitor; 5–high-voltage bushing; 6–tank; 7–ground wire; 8–ground bushing; 9–sample; 10–current sensor; and 11–oscilloscope.

To simulate breakdown in different insulation structures, six breakdown models with and without insulating paper are designed, as shown in Figure 5.

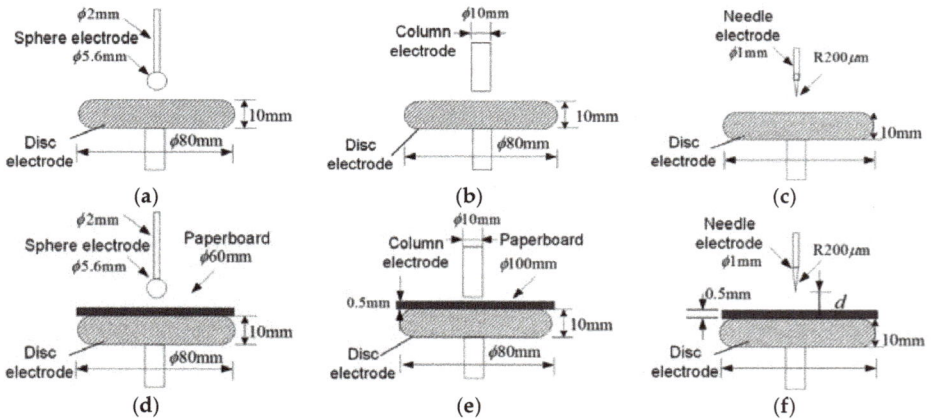

Figure 5. Sketch of breakdown models: **(a)** Sphere-disc electrode; **(b)** Column-disc electrode; **(c)** Needle-disc electrode; **(d)** Sphere-disc electrode (with paper); **(e)** Column-disc electrode (with paper); and **(f)** Needle-disc electrode (with paper).

To simulate a partial discharge in the transformers, four types of typical defect models–air gap discharge model, surface discharge model, floating discharge model, and corona in oil model—are used, as shown in Figure 6.

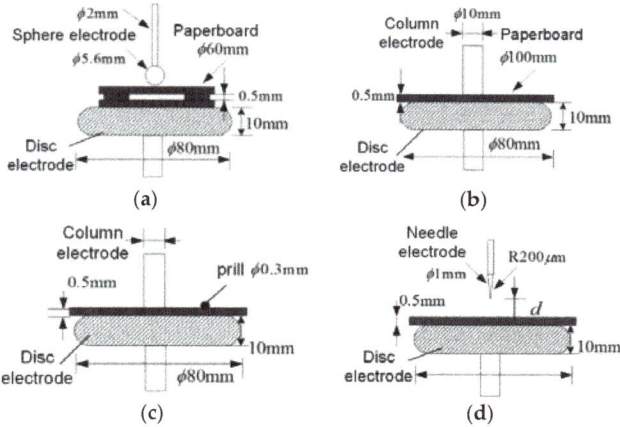

Figure 6. Sketch of typical insulation defect model: (**a**) Air gap discharge; (**b**) Surface discharge; (**c**) Floating discharge; and (**d**) Corona in oil.

3. Dissolved Gas Analysis

3.1. DGA for Thermal Stress Simulation

3.1.1. DGA Results of Thermal Faults below 300 °C

Figure 7 shows the relative percentages of fault gases, except CO and CO_2, in mineral insulating oil, camellia, and FR3 insulating oil, which are overheated in the oven at 90 °C, 120 °C, 150 °C, 200 °C, and 250 °C. C_2H_2 is not obviously observed in all cases. FR3 and camellia oil generate a significant amount of C_2H_6, which does not largely exist in mineral oil. In camellia oil, H_2 is generated in significant quantities. According to the percentage of fault gases, for FR3, the main dissolved gas is C_2H_6; for camellia oil, the main fault gases of are C_2H_6 and H_2. This is different from mineral oil, whose main fault gases are H_2 and CH_4.

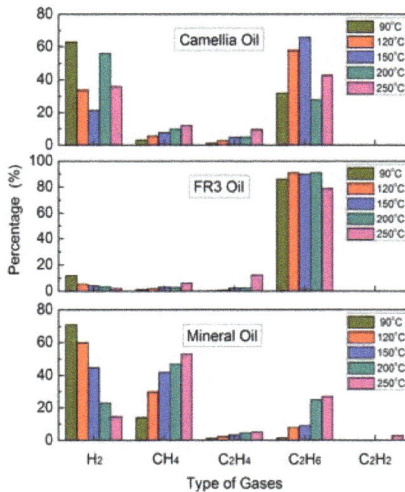

Figure 7. Relative percentages of fault gases in oil as a function of oven temperature (from 90 °C to 250 °C).

As shown in Table 4, compared to the case in oil insulation, the existence of insulating paper increases the amount of gases dissolved in oil. The CO_2 content dissolved in FR3 oil-paper insulation are 2.5 times higher than that in FR3 oil insulation, and the ratio is six times of mineral oil. This is mainly due to the decomposition of cellulose forming hydrocarbons, alcohols, aldehydes, and acids, as well as the further decomposition of these molecules forming gas molecules, like CO and CO_2.

Table 4. CO and CO_2 content in oil under thermal faults below 300 °C.

Insulation Structure	Oil Type	Temperature/°C	CO/ppm	CO_2/ppm
Oil	Camellia oil	90	49.3	1111.2
		200	68.8	1149.6
	FR3 oil	90	24.2	918.9
		200	29.5	542.7
	Mineral oil	90	15.89	800.5
		200	85.4	781.4
Oil-Paper	Camellia oil	90	65.3	1837.0
		200	1157.2	17,883.4
	FR3 oil	90	29.2	1379.3
		200	468.5	11,568.4
	Mineral oil	90	190.3	2638.6
		200	327.9	8192.8

Figure 8 shows the relative percentages of fault gases in oil-paper insulation except CO and CO_2 below 300 °C. In mineral oil, the content of H_2 and CH_4 is the highest. In FR3 oil, the content of C_2H_6 is the highest. In camellia oil, the content of C_2H_6 is slightly higher than other types of gases, except H_2.

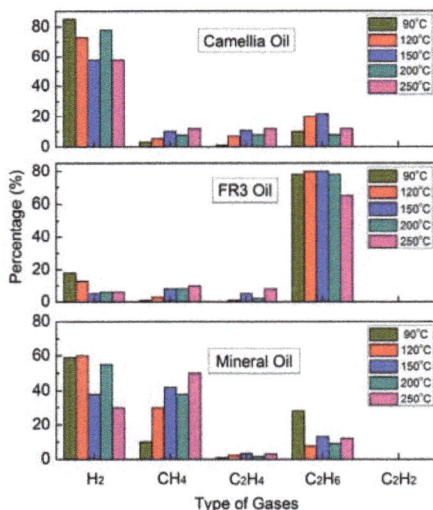

Figure 8. Relative percentages of fault gases in oil-paper insulation as a function of oven temperature (from 90 °C to 250 °C).

3.1.2. DGA Results of Thermal Faults above 300 °C

Figure 9 shows the relative percentages of fault gases, except CO and CO_2, in mineral insulating oil, FR3, and camellia insulating oil which are overheated in the muffle furnace at 300 °C, 400 °C,

500 °C, 600 °C, 700 °C, and 800 °C. C_2H_2 is also not obviously observed in all cases. In mineral oil, CH_4 is a key indicator of overheated oil, and C_2H_4 is a secondary indicator of overheated oil. However, CH_4 and C_2H_4 do not largely exist in FR3 and camellia oil. In contrast, FR3 and camellia oil generate a significant amount of C_2H_6, which does not largely exist in mineral oil. In camellia oil, H_2 is generated in significant quantities. According to the percentage of fault gases, the main dissolved gas for FR3 oil is C_2H_6, and the main dissolved gases in camellia oil are C_2H_6 and H_2, while that for mineral oil is CH_4.

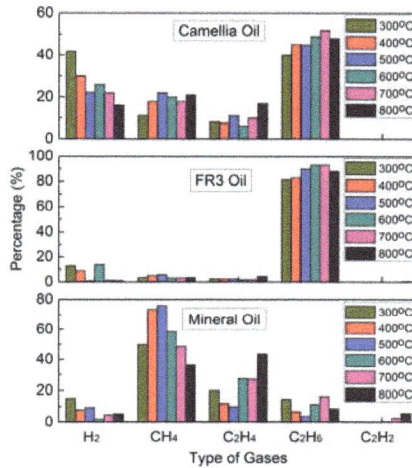

Figure 9. Relative percentages of fault gases in oil as a function of oven temperature (from 300 °C to 800 °C).

As with the result obtained in the case under thermal faults below 300 °C, the existence of insulating paper also increases the amount of CO and CO_2 significantly under thermal faults above 300 °C, as shown in Table 5.

Table 5. CO and CO_2 content in oil under thermal faults above 300 °C.

Insulation Structure	Oil Type	Temperature/°C	CO/ppm	CO_2/ppm
Oil	Camellia oil	400	74.64	2664.4
		700	1854.3	10,517.3
	FR3 oil	400	434.6	2430.7
		700	1553.3	8945.1
	Mineral oil	400	250.8	2038.8
		700	1797.9	9845.1
Oil-Paper	Camellia oil	400	160.2	3628.4
		700	1792.4	12,481.1
	FR3 oil	400	171.5	3536.2
		700	1487.3	21,527.1
	Mineral oil	400	190.3	3160.1
		700	327.9	43,957.3

Figure 10 shows the relative percentages of fault gases in oil-paper insulation, except CO and CO_2, above 300 °C. In mineral oil, the content of CH_4 is highest; in FR3 oil, the content of C_2H_6 is highest; in camellia oil, the content of C_2H_6 is higher than other types of gases, followed by H_2. According to the percentage of fault gases, for FR3, the main dissolved gas is C_2H_6; for camellia oil, the main fault gases are C_2H_6 and H_2. This is different from mineral oil, whose main dissolved gases are CH_4 and C_2H_6.

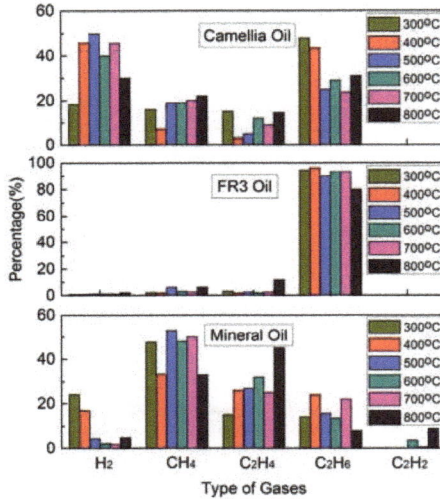

Figure 10. Relative percentages of fault gases in oil-paper insulation as a function of oven temperature (from 300 °C to 800 °C).

3.2. DGA for Electrical Stress Simulation

Figure 11 shows the relative percentages of fault gases, except CO and CO_2, under electrical breakdown. In all cases, a significant amount of H_2 and C_2H_2 are generated, it indicates that for mineral oil, FR3 oil, and camellia oil, the main fault gases of a breakdown fault are the same.

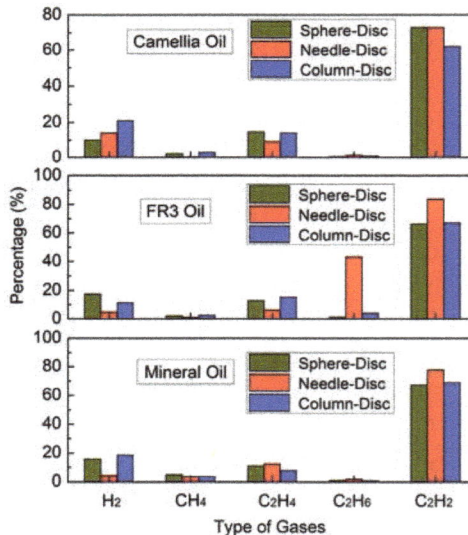

Figure 11. Relative percentages of fault gases in oil under breakdown.

As shown in Table 6, compared to the case in pure oil, the content of CO and CO_2 in oil-paper insulation under breakdown is higher. This is mainly because under electrical stress, the decomposition of C–O bonds in the cellulose forms O_2, the reactions of O_2 and C in cellulose produce CO and CO_2.

Table 6. CO and CO_2 content (in ppm) in oil under needle-disc breakdown.

Insulation Structure	Gas Type	Camellia Oil	FR3 Oil	Mineral Oil
Oil	CO	15.52	9.11	15.52
	CO_2	1259.49	690.16	1295.49
Oil-Paper	CO	442.31	563.85	86.88
	CO_2	1704.2	1012.31	912.74

Figure 12 shows the relative percentages of fault gases except CO and CO_2 under electrical breakdown. As the case in the oil insulation, a significant amount of H_2 and C_2H_2 are dissolved in all samples. It shows that C_2H_2 is the main dissolved gas of electrical breakdown for mineral oil, FR3 oil, and camellia oil.

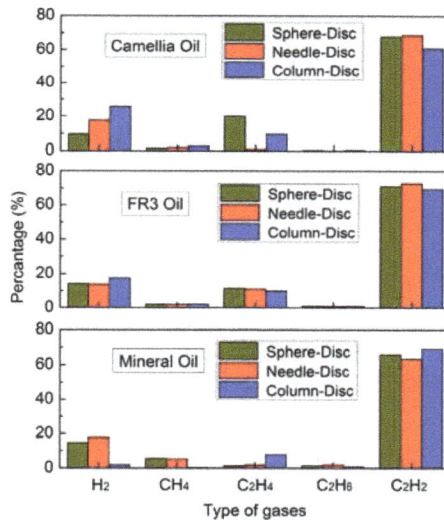

Figure 12. Relative percentages of fault gases in oil-paper under breakdown.

Table 7 shows fault gas contents (in ppm) under partial discharge; the contents are mainly dependent on discharge energy, and it is hard to distinguish a partial discharge pattern through DGA.

Table 7. Fault gas contents (in ppm) in oil under partial discharge.

Model	Gas Type	Camellia Oil	FR3 Oil	Mineral Oil
Air gap	H_2	6.2	25.64	13.54
	THGC *	7.7	23.66	3.39
	CO	37.4	22.47	4.39
	CO_2	357.63	349.63	202.5

* THGC is the total hydrocarbon gas contents.

Figure 13 shows the relative percentages of fault gases, except CO and CO_2, under partial discharge. In mineral oil, the content of H_2 is highest, followed by CH_4; in FR3 oil, the content of H_2 is highest, followed by C_2H_6; in camellia oil, the content of H_2 is highest, and followed by CH_4 and C_2H_6. C_2H_2 does not largely exist in all samples, which shows that C_2H_2 is only the main dissolved gas of high-energy discharge.

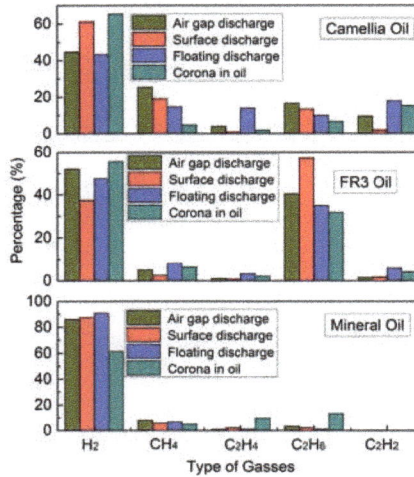

Figure 13. Relative percentages of fault gases in oil under partial discharge.

4. Diagnostic Results Based on DGA

4.1. Three-Ratio Method

The three-ratio method was used to analyze the experiment data, the consistencies of the diagnosis results and actual fault types are shown in Table 8.

Table 8. Consistencies of diagnosis results and simulated fault types.

Temperature/°C	Mineral Oil	FR3	Camellia Oil
90	Conformity	Inconformity	Inconformity
120	Conformity	Inconformity	Inconformity
150	Conformity	Conformity	Inconformity
200	Conformity	Conformity	Inconformity
250	Conformity	Inconformity	Conformity
300	Conformity	Inconformity	Inconformity
400	Conformity	Inconformity	Inconformity
500	Conformity	Inconformity	Inconformity
600	Conformity	Inconformity	Inconformity
700	Conformity	Inconformity	Inconformity
800	Conformity	Inconformity	Inconformity

The three-ratio method can correctly diagnose thermal faults in mineral insulating oil-filled transformers in all simulated situations; however, it makes incorrect conclusions when it is applied to vegetable insulating oils in most cases. This result is attributed to the difference in the molecular chemical structure between mineral insulating oil and vegetable insulating oil. The traditional three-ratio method for mineral insulating oil fill-transformers need to be reconsidered when they are applied to vegetable insulating oil filled-transformer.

When the three-ratio method was applied to analyze the data of simulated electrical faults in mineral oil, the diagnosis results are correct in all cases. However, when it is applied to analyze data in FR3 oil and camellia oil, it only diagnoses breakdown faults correctly; the diagnosis results are not consistent with simulated fault types under partial discharge, as shown in Table 9.

Table 9. Consistencies of diagnosis results and simulated fault types.

Model	Mineral Oil	FR3	Camellia Oil
Sphere-disc (oil)	Conformity	Conformity	Conformity
Needle-disc (oil)	Conformity	Conformity	Conformity
Column-disc (oil)	Conformity	Conformity	Conformity
Sphere-disc (oil-paper)	Conformity	Conformity	Conformity
Needle-disc (oil-paper)	Conformity	Conformity	Conformity
Column-disc (oil-paper)	Conformity	Conformity	Conformity
Air gap	Conformity	Inconformity	Inconformity
Surface discharge	Conformity	Inconformity	Inconformity
Floating discharge	Conformity	Inconformity	Inconformity
Corona in oil	Conformity	Inconformity	Inconformity

4.2. Graph Representaion Method

Figure 14 shows diagnosis results of simulated thermal faults using the graph representation method in IEC 60599. In terms of results of mineral oil, the graph representation method diagnoses the majority of faults correctly. However, for FR3 oil and camellia oil, the majority of thermal faults are identified as the normal state or partial discharge. It shows that the graph representation method is no longer suitable for diagnosis of thermal faults in vegetable insulating oil.

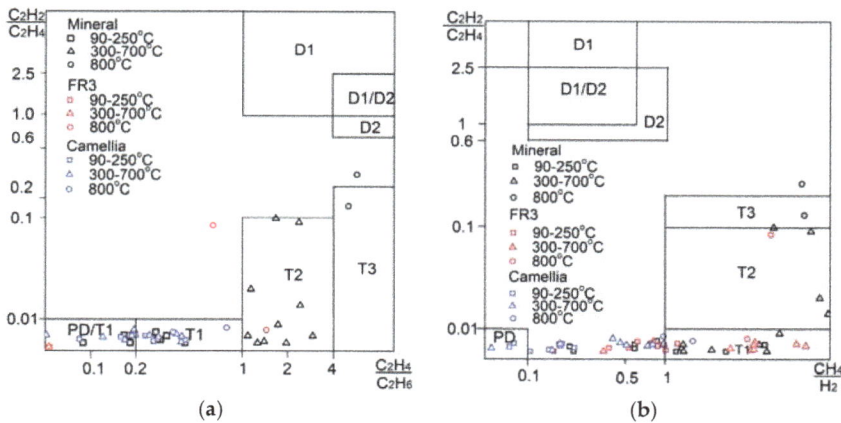

Figure 14. Diagnostic results of simulated thermal faults using graph representation method (data in the figure are expressed as a function of oven temperature): (**a**) According to the ratio of C_2H_2/C_2H_4 and C_2H_4/C_2H_6; (**b**) According to the ratio of C_2H_2/C_2H_4 and CH_4/H_2.

Figure 15 shows diagnosis results of simulated electrical faults using the graph representation method in IEC 60599. For mineral oil, FR3 oil, and camellia oil, the graph representation method correctly diagnoses the majority of breakdown faults. In terms of the diagnosis results of partial discharge faults, most ratio points of mineral oil fall into the correct fault zone; however, for FR3 and camellia oil, the majority of partial discharge faults are not correctly diagnosed.

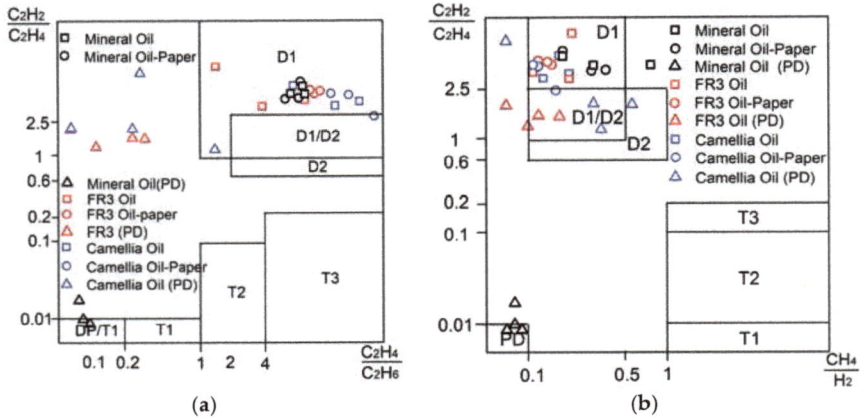

Figure 15. Diagnostic results of simulated electrical faults using graph representation method: (a) According to the ratio of C_2H_2/C_2H_4 and C_2H_4/C_2H_6; (b) According to the ratio of C_2H_2/C_2H_4 and CH_4/H_2.

4.3. Duval Triangle and Pentagon Method

Figure 16 shows the diagnosis results of thermal faults using Duval Triangle 1 in IEC 60599. In terms of mineral oil, Duval Triangle 1 correctly diagnoses all thermal faults. For FR3, part of the simulated faults carried out at 90 °C–250 °C are placed incorrectly into the T2 (300 °C–700 °C) region. For camellia oil, several simulated faults carried out at 90 °C–250 °C are also incorrectly allocated to the T2 region.

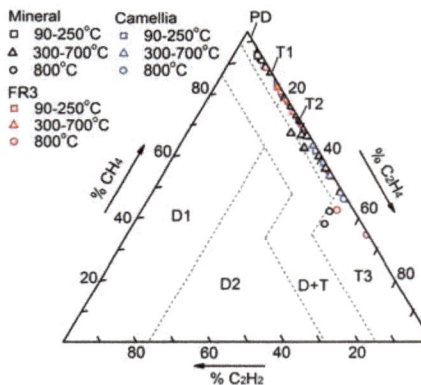

Figure 16. Diagnostic results of simulated thermal faults using Duval Triangle 1 (data in the figure are expressed as a function of oven temperature).

Figure 17 shows the diagnosis results of electrical faults using Duval Triangle 1. Unlike the case in simulated thermal faults, for all oils, the use of the Duval Triangle method diagnose nearly all electrical breakdown cases correctly.

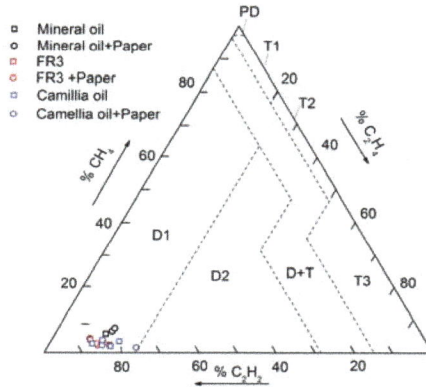

Figure 17. Diagnostic results of simulated electrical faults using Duval Triangle 1.

Figure 18 shows the diagnosis results of thermal faults using the Duval Pentagon proposed by Duval in 2014 [6]. The Duval Pentagon was designed to diagnose the fault of mineral oil. Therefore, for mineral oil, the Duval Pentagon correctly diagnoses almost all thermal faults. However, for FR3 and camellia oil, all of the thermal fault data are placed incorrectly into the stray gassing region. The diagnostic results gathered in one region mainly because percentages of C_2H_6 produced by vegetable oils are much higher than the mineral oil.

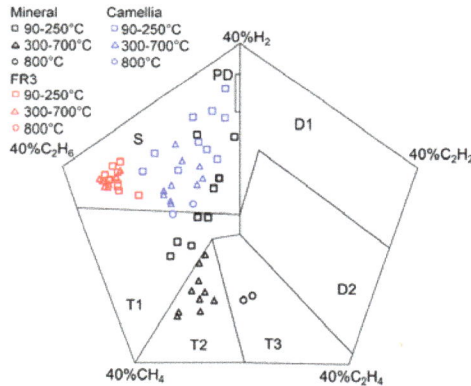

Figure 18. Diagnostic results of simulated thermal faults using the Duval Pentagon (data in the figure are expressed as a function of oven temperature).

Figure 19 shows the diagnosis results of thermal faults using the Duval Pentagon. For all of the three types of oil, the use of the Duval Pentagon method diagnose nearly all electrical breakdown faults correctly.

Furthermore, Duval has proposed Duval Triangle 3, which is applied to diagnose the thermal and electrical faults of four types of natural and synthetic ester, including FR3 [19]. Duval Triangle 3 is obtained by adjusting the zone boundaries of Duval Triangle 1. Figure 20 shows the diagnosis result of electrical and thermal faults of FR3 oil using Duval Triangle 3. For FR3 oil, the modification of the Duval Triangle results in more correct diagnostic results. The fault gases data of electrical faults are all placed in the region D1. The fault data of thermal faults at 300 °C, 300 °C to 700 °C, and above

700 °C are placed more correctly than other diagnostic methods, and only a few of them fall in the wrong region.

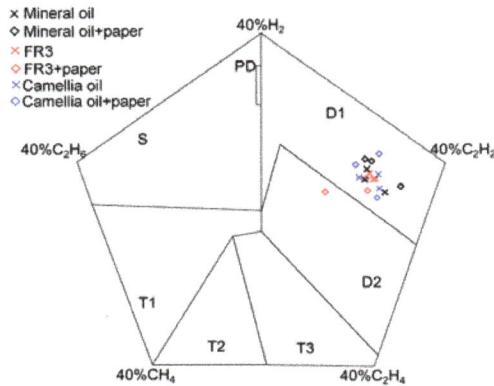

Figure 19. Diagnostic results of simulated electrical faults using the Duval Pentagon.

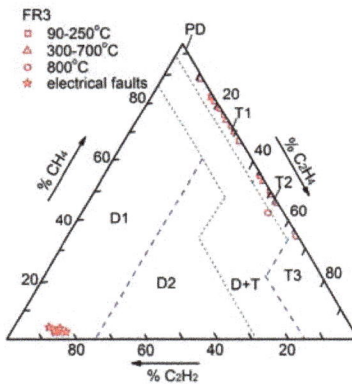

Figure 20. Diagnostic results of thermal and electrical faults of FR3 oil using Duval Triangle 3 (data in the figure are expressed as a function of oven temperature).

As Duval illustrated in [19], non-mineral oil with different chemical structures may result in different gas patterns and zone boundaries. Thus, for camellia oil, since it has different chemical compositions with FR3, the zone boundaries which are suitable for FR3 are not applicable to camellia oil. Figure 21 shows the new boundaries divided according to different types of fault data of camellia oil and the diagnosis results using this modified Duval Triangle 3. As shown in the figure, only two fault data which should be placed in T1 region fall in the region of T2, and also only two data which should be placed in T2 region fall in the T1 region. Other fault data are all placed in the correct regions. It is obvious that the adjustment of zone boundaries of Duval Triangle 3 makes the diagnostic result of thermal and electrical faults of camellia oil more correctly. Of course, this modification needs to be verified by more fault data through further research.

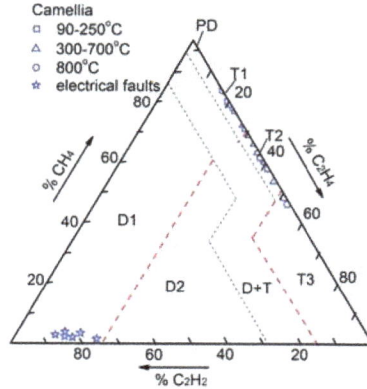

Figure 21. Diagnostic results of thermal and electrical faults of camellia oil based on the modified Duval Triangle 3 (data in the figure are expressed as a function of oven temperature).

4.4. Law of Key Gases Dissolved in Oils

A thermal fault is caused by effective thermal stress with a middle level of energy density. It should be noted that there is some difference between simulation faults and practical operation faults, but the basic mechanisms are the same. According to the experimental results, it could be identified that the main fault gases of overheated oil in mineral oil, FR3, and camellia oil are CH_4 and C_2H_4, C_2H_6, H_2 and C_2H_6, respectively.

The test results demonstrate that the percentage of main fault gases increase regularly with the increase of temperature. In mineral oil, the percentage of CH_4 and C_2H_4 increase with the increasing temperature. This was in good agreement with the results of the practical situation in mineral oil-filled transformer. In the overheating process of FR3, the percentage of C_2H_6 also increases as the temperature increases. In camellia oil, the percentage of H_2 increases while the percentage of C_2H_6 fluctuates with the increase of temperature. The level of thermal faults cannot be determined according to the percentage of C_2H_6 in camellia oil.

Under electrical breakdown, C_2H_2 is the key indicator for mineral insulating oil, FR3 and camellia insulating oil. Due to this consistency, diagnostic methods in IEC 60599 can correctly diagnose electrical breakdown in mineral insulating oil and vegetable insulating oils.

5. Gas Formation Mechanisms under Thermal Stress

A chemical reaction is a process that generates new products through the chain scission mechanism. Vegetable insulating oil mainly consists of triglycerides, which are actually generated from the esterification reaction. The decomposition of vegetable insulating oil, from the microscopic point of view, involves the breaking of chemical bonds, dehydration, and formation of small-molecular gas.

There are hundreds of triglycerides, which are formed by ester groups and various types of fatty acid groups, inside vegetable insulating oil. Therefore, due to the various structures and the multiplicity of possible reactions of mixed triglycerides, mechanisms of the gas generation of vegetable insulating oil are complex. Table 10 shows the composition and the content of various types of fatty acids in soybean oil (the raw material of FR3 oil) and camellia oil. It is obvious that the major differences of the fatty acids content between FR3 oil and camellia oil are the content of mono-unsaturated fatty acids and double-unsaturated fatty acids. In vegetable oil, mono-unsaturated fatty acids are mainly composed of oleic acid while double-unsaturated fatty acids are mainly composed of linoleic acid. Thus, oleic-type triglyceride and linoleic-type triglyceride are chosen to interpret the different characteristics of gas generation between FR3 oil and camellia oil.

Table 10. Fatty acid content of soybean oil and camellia oil (%).

Vegetable Oil	Saturated Fatty Acid	Unsaturated Fatty Acids		
		Mono-Unsaturated	Double-Unsaturated	Poly-Unsaturated
Soybean Oil	14.2	22.5	51.0	12.3
Camellia Oil	10.2	78.3	7.0	4.5

According to several studies of pyrolysis of unsaturated triglyceride [26–29], the principal decomposition reactions of triglyceride are obtained. However there are multichannel reactions; the decomposition pathway of triglycerides and the intermediate product of the reactions could not be explicitly described through current experiments. Thus, unimolecular pyrolysis simulations are studied, and the standard enthalpies of reaction are calculated using M06-2x method with empirical dispersion in conjunction with the 6-31G (d,p) basis sets. As a result, the decomposition pathways of oleic-type triglyceride and linoleic-type triglyceride and the standard reaction enthalpies of each reactions are shown in Figures 22 and 23.

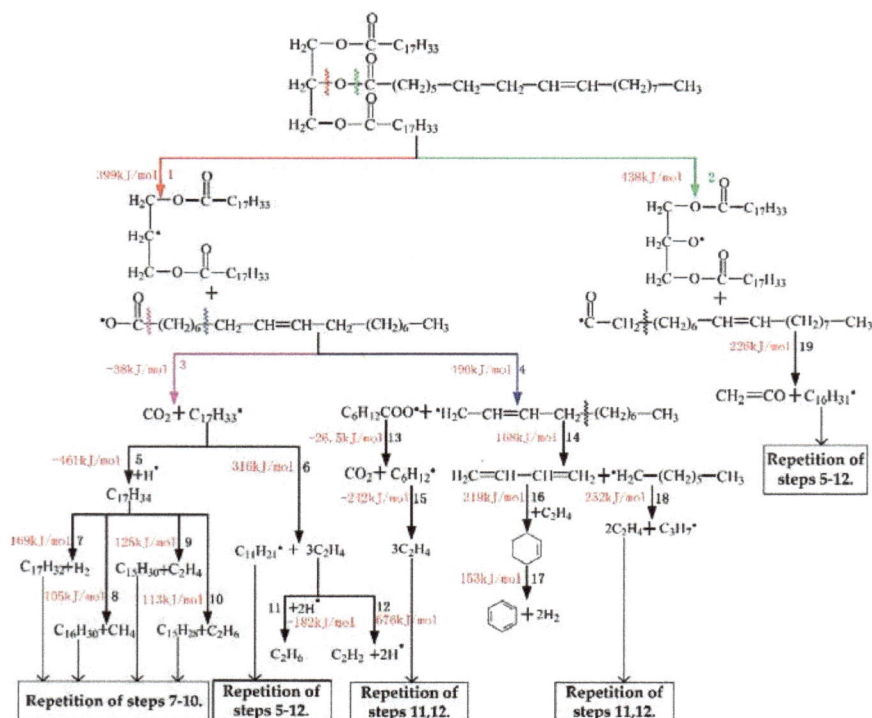

Figure 22. The principal decomposition pathways of oleic-type triglyceride and their standard enthalpies of reactions calculated using M06-2x method.

As it is shown in Figure 22, the $C_{17}H_{33}COO\cdot$ radical and $C_{17}H_{33}CO\cdot$ radical are generated from oleic-type molecule decomposition at first. According to the calculation result of the standard reaction enthalpies (ΔE) of these two reactions, the calculated ΔE value of the cleavage of C–O bond is 399 kJ/mol, while that of the O–C(=O) bond is 438 kJ/mol. This means that it has a higher possibility to break the C–O bond than O–C(=O) bond; therefore, the formation of fatty acid radicals will be the initial decomposition intermediate products. This is consistent with the result obtained in [27] using the GC-MS analysis method.

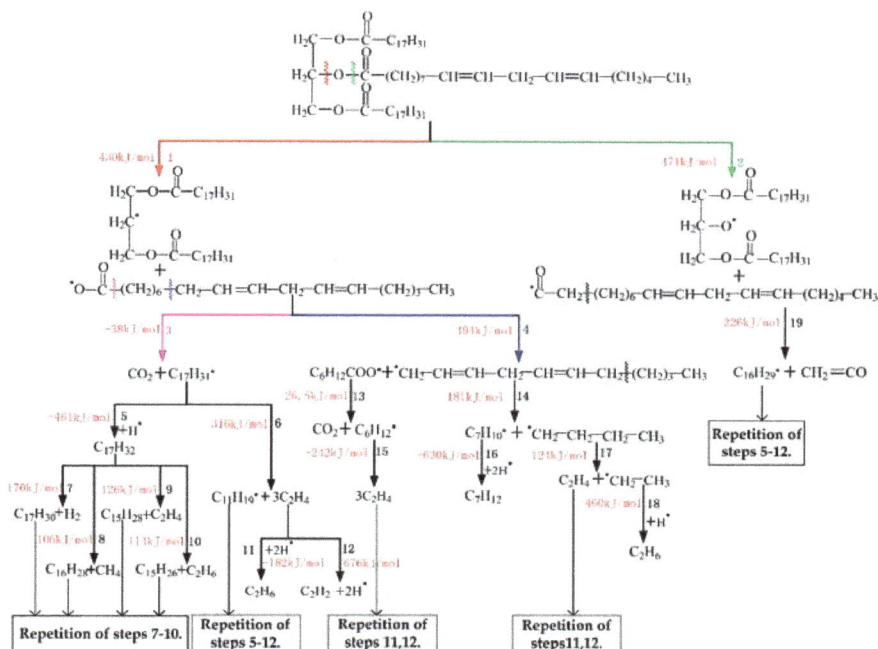

Figure 23. The principal decomposition pathways of linoleic-type triglyceride and their standard enthalpies of reactions calculated using M06-2x method.

Then $C_{17}H_{33}COO\cdot$ radical continues to decompose in several pathways and the two most possible pathways (pathway 3 and 4) are displayed in the figure.

Pathway 3 leads to the formation of $C_{17}H_{33}\cdot$ radicals by decarboxylation, which is the reason why CO_2 in vegetable insulating oil is higher than that in mineral insulating oil. Then, $C_{17}H_{33}\cdot$ radicals combine with H· radicals and generate alkenes $C_{17}H_{34}$ (pathway 5) or decompose directly and generate C_2H_4 (pathway 6). The intermediate product C_2H_4 combines with H· radicals and generates C_2H_6 (pathway 11), which is the main reason that C_2H_6 in vegetable insulating oil is higher than that in mineral insulating oil. The C_2H_4 can also decompose to C_2H_2 through the dehydrogenation reaction (pathway 12), however the calculated ΔE value of the dehydrogenation reaction is very high and it is not easy to reach unless the energy reaches a high level.

Pathway 4 leads to the formation of $C_6H_{12}COO\cdot$ radicals and $C_{11}H_{21}\cdot$ radicals because the unsaturated sites enhance cleavage at the position which is marked in the figure. Then, the $C_6H_{12}COO\cdot$ radical decomposes to CO_2 (pathway 13) and C_2H_4 (pathway 15). The $C_{11}H_{21}\cdot$ radical continues to decompose to $CH_2=CH-CH=CH_2$ and $C_7H_{15}\cdot$ radicals (pathway 14) also because the unsaturated sites enhance of C–C bond cleavage. $CH_2=CH-CH=CH_2$ then combines with C_2H_4 (pathway 16), and generates benzene and H_2 through the dehydrogenation reaction (pathway 17). The $C_7H_{15}\cdot$ radical decomposes through ethylene elimination and then generates C_2H_4 and $C_3H_7\cdot$ radicals (pathway 18).

Comparing Figure 22 with Figure 23, it is obvious that the principal decomposition pathways of oleic-type triglyceride and linoleic-type triglyceride during pyrolysis are basically the same, except pathways 14–18, and the standard reaction enthalpies of the same type of reaction are also consistent. The $C_7H_{10}\cdot$ radical, which is attributed by C–C bond cleavage has a higher degree of unsaturation, so it could not combine with C_2H_4 and then generate benzene and H_2 through the dehydrogenation reaction. This verifies the results that the H_2 concentration in overheated camellia insulating oil is higher than that in FR3.

6. Conclusions

The present work focuses on the dissolved gas analysis of vegetable insulating oil. The experiment and analysis results are summarized as follows:

(1)   The main fault gases of two types of vegetable insulating oils with different chemical compositions under the thermal faults are obtained. In the mineral insulating oil, the main gas composition of overheating is CH_4, while in FR3, it is C_2H_6, and in camellia insulating oil, the main gas compositions are H_2 and C_2H_6. The existence of insulating paper significantly increases the amount of CO and CO_2 dissolved in oil.

(2)   The percentage of main dissolved gases increase regularly with the increase in temperature. In mineral oil, the percentage of CH_4 and C_2H_4 increase as the temperature increases. In FR3 oil, the percentage of C_2H_6 also increases as the temperature increases. In camellia oil, the percentage of H_2 increases while the percentage of C_2H_6 fluctuates with the increase of temperature.

(3)   A large amount of C_2H_2 is generated under high energy electrical breakdown both in vegetable insulating oil and mineral insulating oil, which shows that the main dissolved gas under electrical breakdown in vegetable insulating oil and mineral insulating oil are the same.

(4)   The three-ratio method, graph representation method, Duval Triangle 1, and Duval Pentagon method are not applicable to diagnose thermal faults in vegetable insulating oils. When these interpretation methods are applied to interpret data of simulated electrical faults in vegetable insulating oils, the graph representation method, Duval Triangle, and Duval Pentagon methods can correctly diagnose electrical breakdown. Moreover, the modified Duval Triangle method based on Duval Triangle 3 is used to diagnose the thermal and electrical fault of FR3 oil and camellia oil through redefining zone boundaries of Duval Triangle 1 and obtains more accurate diagnostic results.

(5)   The gas formation mechanisms of FR3 oil and camellia oil under thermal stress are studied in this paper. The principle decomposition pathways of these two type of oils have been analyzed, and the different generation mechanisms of gases in FR3 oil, camellia oil, and mineral oil have been interpreted by means of unimolecular pyrolysis simulation and reaction enthalpies calculation.

Acknowledgments: The authors acknowledge National Science Foundation of China (No. 51425702 and No. 51321063) and the National "111" Project (B08036). We also appreciate National Supercomputing Center in Shenzhen for providing the computational resources and Gaussian (Gaussian 09 D01: Gaussian, TCP-Linda, GaussView).

Author Contributions: The article was finished by a team, every author took part in the whole work. Quan Zhou and Jian Li designed and organized the experiment. Chenmeng Xiang carried out the experiments with Zhaotao Zhang, analyze the test results with Danqing Huang and Haoyong Song, make unimolecular simulation and write this paper.

Conflicts of Interest: The authors declare no conflict of interest.

References

1.   Zheng, Y.B.; Sun, C.X.; Li, J.; Yang, Q.; Chen, W.G. Entropy-based bagging for fault prediction of transformers using oil-dissolved gas data. *Energies* **2011**, *4*, 1138–1147. [CrossRef]
2.   Bakar, N.A.; Abu-Siada, A.; Islam, S. A review of dissolved gas analysis measurement and interpretation techniques. *IEEE Electr. Insul. Mag.* **2014**, *30*, 39–49. [CrossRef]
3.   Sun, H.C.; Huang, Y.C.; Huang, C.M. A review of dissolved gas analysis in power transformers. *Energy Procedia* **2012**, *14*, 1220–1225. [CrossRef]

4. Kim, S.-W.; Kim, S.-J.; Seo, H.-D.; Jung, J.-R.; Yang, H.-J.; Duval, M. New methods of DGA diagnosis using IEC TC 10 and related databases Part 1: Application of gas-ratio combinations, IEEE Dielectrics and Electrical Insulation. *IEEE Trans. Dielectr. Electr. Insul.* **2013**, *20*, 685–690.
5. Duval, M.; dePabla, A. Interpretation of gas-in-oil analysis using new IEC publication 60599 and IEC TC 10 databases. *IEEE Electr. Insul. Mag.* **2001**, *17*, 31–41. [CrossRef]
6. Duval, M.; Lamarre, L. The Duval pentagon—A new complementary tool for the interpretation of dissolved gas analysis in transformers. *IEEE Electr. Insul. Mag.* **2014**, *30*, 9–12.
7. Chen, W.G.; Chen, X.; Peng, S.Y.; Li, J. Canonical correlation between partial discharges and gas formation in transformer oil paper insulation. *Energies* **2012**, *5*, 1081–1097. [CrossRef]
8. Fofana, I. 50 years in the development of insulating liquids. *IEEE Electr. Insul. Mag.* **2013**, *29*, 13–25. [CrossRef]
9. Li, J.; Yao, S.H.; Du, B.; Yao, W. Analysis to principle problems and future prospect of research on vegetable insulating oils and their applications. *High Volt. Eng.* **2015**, *2*, 353–363.
10. Li, J.; Zhang, Z.T.; Grzybowski, S.; Zahn, M. A new mathematical model of moisture equilibrium in mineral and vegetable oil-paper insulation. *IEEE Electr. Insul. Mag.* **2012**, *19*, 1615–1622. [CrossRef]
11. Martin, D.; Lelekakis, N.; Wenyu, G.; Odarenko, Y. Further studies of a vegetable-oil-filled power transformer. *IEEE Electr. Insul. Mag.* **2011**, *27*, 6–13. [CrossRef]
12. IEEE Natural Ester Working Group. *IEEE Guide for Acceptance and Maintenance of Natural Ester Fluids in Transformers*; IEEE Std. C57.147-2008; Institute of Electrical and Electronics Engineers (IEEE): New York, NY, USA, 2008.
13. Martin, D.; Lelekakis, N.; Davydov, V.; Orarenko, Y. Preliminary results for dissolved gas levels in a vegetable oil-filled power transformer. *IEEE Electr. Insul. Mag.* **2010**, *26*, 41–48. [CrossRef]
14. Imad, U.K.; Zhongdong, W.; Cotton, I.; Northcote, S. Dissolved gas analysis of alternative fluids for power transformers. *IEEE Electr. Insul. Mag.* **2007**, *23*, 5–14. [CrossRef]
15. Wilhelm, H.M.; Santos, C.C.; Stocco, G.B. Dissolved gas analysis (DGA) of natural ester insulating fluids with different chemical compositions. *IEEE Trans. Dielectr. Electr. Insul.* **2013**, *21*, 1071–1078.
16. Muhamad, N.A.; Phung, B.T.; Blackburn, T.R. Dissolved gas analysis for common transformer faults in soy seed-based oil. *IET Electr. Power Appl.* **2011**, *5*, 133–142. [CrossRef]
17. Perrier, C.; Marugan, M.; Beroual, A. DGA comparison between ester and mineral oils. *IEEE Trans. Dielectr. Electr. Insul.* **2012**, *19*, 1609–1614. [CrossRef]
18. Iovalekic, M.; Vukovic, D.; Tenbohlen, S. Dissolved gas analysis of alternative dielectric fluids under thermal and electric stress. In Proceedings of the IEEE International Conference on Dielectric Liquids, Trondheim, Norway, 26–30 June 2011; pp. 1–4.
19. Duval, M. The duval triangle for load tap changers, non-mineral oils and low temperature faults in transformers. *IEEE Electr. Insul. Mag.* **2008**, *24*, 22–29. [CrossRef]
20. Duval, M.; Baldyga, R. Stray gassing of FR3 oils in transformers in service. In Proceedings of the 76th Annual International Doble Client Conference, Boston, MA, USA, 29 March–3 April 2009.
21. IEEE Interpretation of Gases Generated in Natural Ester and Synthetic Ester-Immersed Transformers Working Group. *IEEE Guide for Interpretation of Gases Generated in Natural Ester and Synthetic Ester-Immersed Transformers*; IEEE Std. C57.155-2014; Institute of Electrical and Electronics Engineers (IEEE): New York, NY, USA, 2014.
22. International Electrotechnical Commission (IEC). *Mineral Oil-Impregnated Electrical Equipment in Service—Guide to the Interpretation of Dissolved and Free Gases Analysis*; IEC Std. 60599; International Electrotechnical Commission (IEC): Geneva, Switzerland, 2007.
23. Cargill. Envirotemp FR3 Fluid. Available online: http://www.cargill.com/products/industrial/dielectric-ester-fluids/envirotemp-fr3/index.jsp (accessed on 1 February 2015).
24. Jovalekic, M.; Vukovic, D.; Tenbohlen, S. Gassing behavior of various alternative insulating liquids under thermal and electrical stress. In Proceedings of the IEEE International Symposium on Electrical Insulation, San Juan, Puerto Rico, 10–13 June 2012; pp. 490–493.
25. Kassi, K.S.; Fofana, I.; Meghnefi, F.; Yeo, Z. Impact of local overheating on conventional and hybrid insulations for power transformers. *IEEE Trans. Dielectr. Electr. Insul.* **2015**, *22*, 2543–2553.
26. Alencar, J.; Alves, P.; Craveiro, A. Pyrolysis of tropical vegetable oils. *J. Agric. Food Chem.* **1983**, *31*, 1268–1270. [CrossRef]

27. Schwab, A.; Dykstra, G.; Selke, E.; Sorenson, S.; Pryde, E. Diesel fuel from thermal decomposition of soybean oil. *J. Am. Oil Chem. Soc.* **1988**, *65*, 1781–1786. [CrossRef]

28. Wang, Z.; Yi, X.; Huang, J.; Hinshaw, J.V.; Noakhes, J. Fault gas generation in natural-ester fluid under localized thermal faults. *IEEE Electr. Insul. Mag.* **2012**, *28*, 45–56. [CrossRef]

29. Fofana, I.; Sabau, J.; Bussieres, D.; Robertson, E. The mechanism of gassing in power transformers. In Proceedings of the IEEE International Conference on Dielectric Liquids, Poitiers, France, 30 June–3 July 2008; pp. 1–4.

MDPI

St. Alban-Anlage 66

4052 Basel

Switzerland

Tel. +41 61 683 77 34

Fax +41 61 302 89 18

www.mdpi.com

Energies Editorial Office

E-mail: energies@mdpi.com

www.mdpi.com/journal/energies

www.ingramcontent.com/pod-product-compliance
Lightning Source LLC
Chambersburg PA
CBHW051727210326
41597CB00032B/5636